PASTOR DAN BATES
MILLICAN BAPTIST CHURCH, S.B.C.
MILLICAN, TEXAS 77866

Footprints

One night a man had a dream. He dreamed he was walking along the beach with the Lord. Across the sky flashed scenes from his life. For each scene, he noticed two sets of footprints in the sand: one belonging to him, and the other to the Lord.

When the last scene of his life flashed before him, he looked back at the footprints in the sand. He noticed that many times along the path of his life there was only one set of footprints. He also noticed that it happened at the very lowest and saddest times in his life.

This really bothered him and he questioned the Lord about it.

"Lord, you said that once I decided to follow you, you'd walk with me all the way. But I have noticed that during the most troublesome times in my life, there is only one set of footprints. I don't understand why when I needed you the most you would leave me."

The Lord replied, "My son, My precious child, I love you and would never leave you. During your times of trial and suffering, when you see only one set of footprints, it was then that I carried you."

Author unknown

THIS BOOK BELONGS TO

BIBLICAL SOLUTIONS TO CONTEMPORARY PROBLEMS

BIBLICAL SOLUTIONS TO CONTEMPORARY PROBLEMS

A HANDBOOK

Rus Walton

Wolgemuth & Hyatt, Publishers, Inc.
Brentwood, Tennessee

Most Scripture quotations are from the New King James
Version of the Bible, © 1984 by Thomas Nelson, Inc.,
Nashville, Tennessee and are used by permission. Some
Scripture quotations are from the King James Version
of the Bible.

The author gratefully acknowledges the research assistance
of Dugan Flanakin and Glenn Hall, CBN University,
in the preparation of the manuscript.

Wolgemuth & Hyatt, Publishers, Inc.
P.O. Box 1941, Brentwood, Tennessee 37027.

Printed in the United States of America.

Library of Congress Cataloging-in-Publication Data

Walton, Rus, —
    Biblical solutions to contemporary problems: a handbook /
    Russell Walton. — 1st ed.   p.   cm.

Bibliography: p. 371
ISBN 0-943497-15-9 : $9.95

    1. Church and social problems — United States.
    2. United States — Moral conditions.
    3. Bible — United States — Criticism, interpretation, etc. I. Title.

HN65.W34   1988   261.8'3 — dc19   88-14207

CONTENTS

INTRODUCTION

"How does one decide what is true or false, what is right or wrong, what is good or bad?"

With that question, George Marston began his splendid book, *The Voice of Authority.*

"Every man," he answered, "has a standard in matters of truth and conduct. That is his *voice of authority.* That voice is found in either God, or man."

This, then, is the question every Christian must ask in his or her life: Who shall be my *voice of authority*? God? Or government? Or self?

Is that not in essence the challenge which Joshua put before the people of Israel? "Choose you this day whom you will serve!" (Joshua 24:15).

Perhaps we could paraphrase Joshua's challenge in this manner: "Choose you this day your *voice of authority*!" Is that not valid? After all, whatever we choose as our *voice of authority* is what we will ultimately seek to serve and obey.

> The people said unto Joshua, the Lord our God will we serve, and His voice will we obey (Joshua 24:16).

Can our response be any different?

Jesus said, "If you love Me, keep My commandments" (John 14:15).

It is essential that we joyfully acknowledge the Lord God to be the Authority in all things, in all of life, in all issues of life. In love and adoration we must embrace His Word as our *voice of authority*; on it and by it we must frame our deliberations, make our decisions, pledge our fidelity, control our deportment, and take our stand on the issues of our day. His Word is the authority by which we draw the line between that which is right and that which is wrong, between good and evil, and between truth and error.

> Cast down imaginations and every high thing that exalts itself against the knowledge of God, and bring into captivity every thought to the obedience of Christ (2 Corinthians 10:5).

Blessed are those who delight in the Law of the Lord, and in His truth, and in His authority. They shall bring forth fruit to the glory of the Living God!

Sadly, the ungodly are not so.

Their *voice of authority* is the desire of the flesh, the way of the world, the call of the majority. For them, the dictates of the carnal and the decrees of the Caesars take precedence over the Word of God.

> The carnal mind is enmity against God: For it is not subject to the Law of God, neither indeed can be. So then, they that are in the flesh cannot please God (Romans 8:7, 8).

The world may count such men wise, and accept their errors as profundities, but God counts them as fools. They are doomed "to flounder in the morass of subjectivism, skepticism, agnosticism, and atheism." The Authority they reject, rejects them (Psalm 1:4-6).

Of course, most men are neither hot nor cold. They neither pursue the things of God nor purposefully pursue ungodliness. They fall in between; they are those who are stuck in the crack between the Word of the Lord and the voice of the world. Their inner voice is schizoid, split, torn. They "moderate" between two opinions. For them, God's authority is not total, not all-encompassing; to them, His Word is a collection of electives from which they pick and choose. But according to Jesus, their "moderation" is not a virtue, but a vice.

> So then, because you are lukewarm, and neither hot nor cold, I will spew you out of My mouth (Revelation 3:16).

No man can serve two masters. The double-minded individual is "unstable in all his ways" (James 1:8). He becomes flotsam and jetsam on the tides of human passion and uncivil appetite. He seeks the lowest popular denominator — to get along by going along.

As it is with individuals, so it is with nations.

The God-fearing nation, like the God-fearing person, acknowledges the Lord as its *voice of authority.* It not only stamps that affirmation on its coins, it impresses it into its laws. It prays for God's guidance, relies on God's providence, and walks according to His Word. Blessed is that nation!

The ungodly nation rejects God. It trusts in itself — in its wealth, its munitions, its trappings of power, its corporate intellect. Its *voice of authority* is the voice of humanism: *Vox populi, Vox dei.* Thus, God is made over in the image of man.

And what of those nations in which there is a split authority — those which profess faith in God and stamp His Word in the marble of their halls, but follow other gods? Such nations are unsure and insecure. They weasel. They waffle. They are tossed on the tides of uncertainty. They are blown by inconsistent winds. They sound an uncertain trumpet. There are few who follow their call (1 Corinthians 14:8).

Consider those early days in America — those days when the seeds of this republic were being planted in the hearts and minds of godly men and women. In the appointed time, as the people moved to install their civil institutions, God was their *voice of authority.* They grafted His Word into their covenants. From the pulpit, from the hearth, and in the heart, they affirmed the sovereignty of God over every area of life.

"All law," asserted Wycliffe, "ought to order itself according to the Law of God." Those early Americans believed that. Thus, the Holy Bible became the Book "for the government of the people, by the people, and for the people."

Consider the *Fundamental Orders of Connecticut,* the first constitution written in the New World, adopted in 1638:

> It is ordered, sentenced and decreed, that there shall be yearly two General Assemblies of Courts . . . that shall have the power to administer justice according to the laws here established, and for want thereof according to the rule of the Word of God.

Consider, also, the *Massachusetts Body of Liberties,* adopted in 1641:

> No man's life shall be taken away, no man's honor or good name shall be stayned, no man's person shall be arrested . . . no man's goods or estaite shall be taken . . . unless it be by vertue or equities of some expresse law of the Country warranting the same . . . or in case of the defect of a law in any particular case by the Word of God . . . and if there be any defect of the law . . . then it shall be administered according to the Word of God.

Can we imagine such a bill being introduced—much less being passed—in either house of the Congress today?

Small wonder then that so many today long for, and pray for, a Christian rebirth of our great republic. Small wonder then that we cry out, "Revive us, O Lord. Revive us again!"

Of course, the rebuilding does not start under the capitol dome or at political rallies or even with candidates and bumper stickers. It starts in our hearts. It starts with His Word in our hearts. It starts when we seek to make sure that He is our *voice of authority* (Psalm 139:23, 24).

First, the heart, the mind, and the individual deportment must be restored and reformed. Then—and only then—the home, the church, the school, the community, and the nation must be restored and reformed.

Revival, reformation, rebuilding—it all starts with this: "Your word have I hid in my heart that I might not sin against you" (Psalm 119:11).

This book was written with the conviction that if Christians are to make Jesus Christ our King as well as our Redeemer, we must acknowledge Him as Sovereign of all our affairs—our public and civic affairs as well as our private lives. We must seek to "obey God rather than man" in all things as Christ's early disciples and followers did.

Thus, this book was written with the assured belief that God's Word does indeed speak to the issues of this day and all days, that Scripture is our *voice of authority.*

As we go forth to honor Him in all things, as we seek to fulfill His Great Commission, we would do well to follow the lead of our forebears: to make His Word our comprehensive guide for life and living. It is my prayer that this book will help in that regard.

It should be clear, however, that this book does not purport to be any kind of "final authority" or "last word" on the issues it examines. Only God's Word is *the* Word. What is written here is designed to serve as a "direction finder" for today's Pilgrims as they study His written Word, pray for His guidance, listen to His voice, and go forth to serve and obey Him in all things — to "occupy" until He returns (Luke 19:13).

Man shall not live by bread alone, but by every word that proceeds out of the mouth of God (Matthew 4:4).

RUS WALTON
Windchime,
Marlborough, New Hampshire
March, 1988

ONE

ABORTION

Since 1973 when the United States Supreme Court ruled that a preborn baby is not a person, there have been more than twenty million "legal" abortions. Now, the fetuses are being cannibalized for parts and tissue.

Background Briefing

Somewhere on a flight between Kansas City and Miami, Julie Killen went into the plane's lavatory and gave birth to a child. When she arrived at the Miami International Airport, she dropped the baby into a trash can. Two days later the dead child was found. Julie Killen pleaded guilty to manslaughter.[1]

In Racine, Wisconsin, a woman was charged with murder for dumping her newborn child in a highway rest area toilet.[2]

If those two women had had abortions a week or two before delivery, they would not have been in trouble with the law. It would still have been murder, but it would have been (pardon the misuse of the term) "legal." Federal and state courts have held that abortions are permitted virtually to the full term of the unborn child.

Abortion, the murder of a preborn child, is the number one killer in the United States (cardio-vascular diseases are second). "In the United States it is statistically confirmed that the most dangerous place for anyone to be, with regard to the preservation of one's life, is in the mother's womb."[3] The greatest threat to the child in gestation is not from measles, smallpox, PCBs in the mother's diet or acid rain. The greatest threat is the "would-not-be" mother who opts for abortion.

Abortion is a major business in the United States: there are about 5,500 aborturies in the nation; *Fortune* magazine esti-

7

mated that their take is more than half a billion dollars a year. That does not include revenue from the sale of aborted babies' bodies.[4] Planned Parenthood receives about $30 million a year from Title X appropriations, a program originally intended to provide "preventative family planning services," and it receives millions more from Title V, Title XIX, Title XX, and dozens of other tax-supported programs.[5] Its 50 chapters, 200 affiliates, and 800 clinics perform more than 80,000 abortions annually.[6]

There were some 1.5 million babies aborted in 1986. That's more than 4,000 abortions each day, 3 murders each minute, or 1 abortion every twenty-one seconds. (That does not include an estimated 260,000 that are not reported.) About 25 percent of the women having abortions are "repeats"—they have had one or more prior abortions. Abortuary centers report that women who have abortions are generally young, unmarried, and are not likely to have ever given birth to a live infant.[7]

Kansas was the first state to legalize abortion-on-demand to time of birth. The national floodgates for abortion were opened on January 22, 1973, when the United States Supreme Court in *Roe v. Wade*, held that a woman has the right to do as she chooses with her body. The seven-to-two majority concluded that a pre-born child is not "legally" a person; thus, it has no legal rights until it's delivered.

On that same day, in *Doe v. Bolton*, the Supreme Court held that babies may be aborted (killed) until the day they are to leave the womb. These decisions made it constitutionally impossible for any state to prohibit abortion at any time during pregnancy.[8] Since then, more than 20 million preborn babies have been slaughtered by currette or syringe—an average of 4,100 every day from 1973 through 1986 with only a slight decline in 1987. That is the American holocaust and that is America's shame!

Human sacrifice on the altar of nihilistic humanism continues. There are about three abortions to every live birth in the District of Columbia. The ratio of birth to abortions in New York City is about one-to-one. Michael R. Gilstrap, in *The Phineas Report,* suggests that "abortion is an act of religious faith . . . [for the woman who undergoes an abortion] it affirms a belief in man as ultimate rather than as created in the image of

God. It is a commitment to an alien faith that rivals Christianity at the most fundamental levels."⁹

The advocates of the right to abortion-on-demand insist it is a woman's right to terminate an unwanted pregnancy; it is part of her freedom of choice, part of her freedom to control her own body. They assert that abortion is just one method of contraception (a position being taught in many high school and even elementary sex education classes).

Supporters of abortion (murder) include several religious denominations: American Baptists, United Methodists, United Presbyterian Church, Episcopal Church, and Evangelical Lutheran Church. Spokesmen for those and other churches have made public statements that "continuance of pregnancy is not a moral necessity." (See Matthew 7:15; Luke 11:23; Revelation 3:15, 16.) Federal Judge John F. Dooling, Jr. cited their statements when arguing that the Court's pro-abortion decision was "in the mainstream of the nation's religious tradition." (See Matthew 6:24.)

Consider the case of Joan Andrews. On March 26, 1986, she disconnected the plug on the suction machine in the procedure room at the Ladies Center abortuary in Pensacola, Florida. She did not break into the abortion clinic; the door was open. When she was pulled away from the machine by police, she went limp, was handcuffed and dragged out. She did not resist the officers; there was no assault involved.

The charge against her was resisting arrest and burglary, although she stole nothing and destroyed nothing. When she was removed from the center, the machine was hooked up again.

At her sentencing she told the judge, "My intentions were to save lives by trying to nonviolently prevent the abortion of pre-born children." The prosecution asked for a one-year sentence. The judge sentenced her to five years in maximum security at a Florida state prison. Why? Because he was annoyed that Joan Andrews would not promise to stay away from abortion clinics. That, she said, "would be an agreement to let human beings be killed."

Joan Andrews began serving the five years in maximum security in September 1986. She is currently incarcerated in Broward Correctional Institute in a cell in which the window has been painted over so that she cannot see outside. Her imprisonment extends until April 1991. The Florida Court of Appeals denied her appeal without comment. The only avenue left open to her is a pardon from Florida Governor Robert Martinez.

In a separate case, on the same day and in the same courtroom, the same Judge Anderson who sentenced Joan Andrews sentenced an accomplice to murder to four years in prison with time off for good behavior. The felon could be out of prison in two and a half years.

Biblical Christians and other pro-life advocates do not agree with the Court's decisions and must work to overturn them. They assert that the willful termination of pregnancy and wanton aborting of a preborn child is against a higher law—God's Law. Abortion, they insist, is murder. They note that in no other area of society is homicide condoned. In 1986 the Washington State Supreme Court restricted an anti-abortion group's use of the words "murder" and "kill" in describing abortion. The court held that a restriction on the group's right of free speech was necessary to protect children from the harmful effects of such language. The court did not rule on the harmful effects of abortion on children.[10]

The anti-abortion forces insist, further, that a woman should control her body by controlling herself (and her emotions); that such control should come before, not after the act; that women have no moral or legal right to murder a preborn baby to avoid the fruit of sin. (Less than 3 percent of all abortions are performed for medical reasons or following rape or incest; 97 percent are strictly a matter of convenience. Many abortions in the United States are performed to cover up pre- or extra-marital sex.)

Some pro-abortionists argue that it is cheaper to do away with unwanted babies than to let them be born and go on welfare or end up in prison. In 1984, vice-presidential nominee, Geraldine Ferraro (Zacarro), agreed: "The cost of putting an unwanted child through the [welfare] system far outweighs the cost [the federal funding] of these [abortion] procedures." As for the costs of "justice," former Representative Ferraro said during a House debate on federal funding of abortions: "It is a simple matter of economics. Unwanted children so often end up in the criminal justice systems. . . . it's very expensive to take care of them."[11]

Pro-death advocates urge the termination of pregnancies as a way to ease economic dislocation (poverty), remedy sexual promiscuity, and build a "planned" and "perfect" society. The journal of the *American Academy of Pediatrics* carried an article arguing that handicapped children may have less (social) value than dogs or pigs with "superior capacities." (So much for the Hippocratic Oath physicians once subscribed to: "I will not give a woman a pessary to produce abortion.")

In the journal article, Peter Singer asserted: "Once the religious mumbo-jumbo surrounding the term 'human' has been stripped away . . . we will not regard as sacrosanct the life of each and every member of our species."[12]

Thus, anti-life groups would have physicians be "social executioners" according to a state blueprint. The pro-life forces say that (1) putting a value on human life on the basis of such crass economic determinism, if accepted, would enforce a "Hitlerian concept" — a continuing holocaust to eliminate those individuals considered "non-productive" (the deformed and handicapped, the elderly, and the unwanted preborns who fail to meet predetermined genetic standards); (2) committing abortion to escape the fruits of promiscuity simply adds one sin on top of another; (3) the issue of public funding of abortion should be resolved by prohibiting abortion-on-demand; and (4) the suggestions of either pre- or post-partum murder reveal a total disregard for the sanctity of life.

In Communist China, the government's birth control policy permits one child per couple, with a maximum of two in rural areas. Women whose pregnancy would exceed the birth quota must abort.[13] The *New York Times* hailed Red China's policy as "most effective in implementing birth control and population planning."[14]

In the Soviet Union, about 10 million abortions are performed each year; that is 2 to 3 abortions for every live birth. In Romania, 60 percent of pregnancies end in abortion. In Greece, 56 percent of the pregnant women have abortions after their first child; thereafter, it's 2 abortions for every birth. In Communist-dominated Poland, while 700,000 children are born, 800,000 are aborted.[15]

Dr. Bernard Nathanson, a founder of the National Abortion Rights League, performed about 5,000 abortions following the

1973 *Roe v. Wade* court decision. Dr. Nathanson once vehemently subscribed to and promoted pro-abortion arguments. He has changed his mind; he now fights against abortions and abortionists. As to a woman's right to control her own body, Nathanson retorts: "I think everyone should control their own body . . . BUT we have very sound data which have demonstrated that the fetus is not part of a woman's body. It is an uneasy tenant . . . immunologically distinct, biologically distinct . . . it is not in fact a part of a woman's body."[16]

Pro-abortionists claim that the preborn baby is simply "fetal tissue" and not a living entity until delivery (or, at the earliest, third trimester). Thus, they argue, having an abortion is no different from having a tooth pulled, or getting a haircut. They do not object to the fetal tissues of an aborted baby being used for face creams or other cosmetics.

Pro-life advocates counter: the preborn baby is in reality a living human being who dies a painful death when aborted. By the seventh week, the child has its own (measurable) brain waves. And, they point out, the presence of brain waves is one of the legal criteria determining whether an individual is alive or dead! The pro-choice/pro-death groups also argue "viability": as long as the preborn baby depends upon its mother's life-support system, it is not a viable life. But, argue the anti-abortion spokesmen, consider kidney dialysis, respirators, life-support systems: many adults depend on such life-support systems to exist. If a doctor or nurse were to turn off the life-support system under such circumstances, the charge would be murder.

In a letter to President Reagan, twenty-six doctors emphasized that scientific methods make it clear that preborn babies feel pain during abortion. "Nerves are in place by six to eight weeks after conception. . . . chemicals to transmit sensations from nerves through the spinal cord to the brain exist by twelve weeks. . . . the fetus reacts the same way a full-grown individual would when exposed to something painful, by squirming, thrashing . . . accelerated heartbeat and higher blood pressure."[17] (Note: At six weeks, the kidneys, stomach, and liver begin to function; at seven weeks, the tiny baby has all its outer and inner organs; at ten weeks, the preborn child has everything found in a newborn baby; at twelve weeks, the fingerprints are completely formed, the baby weighs about one ounce — all that is left is to grow.)

Dr. Nathanson made public an ultrasonic filming of abortion (*The Silent Scream*) which shows the preborn baby in the womb, thrashing about, trying to avoid the suction device which is tearing off its head. Viewers of the film saw the child dismembered, its head crushed, as it was sucked out of the womb. The physician who performed the abortion that was filmed has never performed another.[18] (Dr. and Mrs. Nathanson have produced an award-winning pro-life film and videocassette, *Eclipse of Reason* featuring Charlton Heston.)

So much for the key premises of the United States Supreme Court's 1973 pro-abortion decision. Dr. Nathanson argues, "Some of the key premises [of that decision] are now so outdated, now so anachronistic that the decision itself has been rendered an anachronism. . . . the times, the new data, the new perceptions, and the new science, cry out for a change in that decision."[19] Supreme Court Justice Sandra Day O'Connor warned: "The *Roe* framework . . . is clearly on a collision course with itself. . . . it has no justification in law or logic."

On December 27, 1987, Dr. Nathanson wrote the McDonald's Corporation criticizing the Ray Kroc and Roberta L. Kroc Leadership and Visiting Scholars Endowment for funding research in the use of human fetal tissues in the treatment of diabetes. (The Krocs were founders of McDonald's.) Dr. Nathanson wrote, "Laudable though its aim — the cure of diabetes — surely more humane methods than the wholesale destruction of viable unborn babies should have been pursued." McDonald's responded that it is not connected with the Kroc foundation. However, several members of the Kroc foundation are also members of the McDonald's corporate board.[20]

In January, 1987, President Reagan submitted the President's Pro-Life Bill of 1987 to the Congress. The bill was carried in the United States Senate by Senator Gordon Humphrey (New Hampshire) and in the House by Representative Henry Hyde (Illinois). That bill would have put Congress on record as being opposed to the *Roe v. Wade* decision and would have permanently prohibited federal funding of abortion and denied Title X family planning funds to organizations (such as Planned Parenthood) which perform or refer for abortions. Senator Humphrey also introduced a bill to rescind tax breaks for abortion clinics. The Abortion Rights Mobilization (a pro-abortion coalition) brought suit against the Internal Revenue Service for not revoking the tax-exempt status of the Catholic Church. The group charged that the church used tax-exempt funds for political action (fighting abortion) and that put the pro-abortion groups at a disadvantage.[21]

Representative Robert Dornan (California) placed bills before the House proposing a pro-life amendment, restrictions on interstate transport of fetal tissue, and a ban on federal aid to any educational institution that performs abortions except to prevent the death of the mother. Representative Philip Crane (Illinois) introduced a bill which would have eliminated Supreme Court and Federal District Court jurisdiction to hear or review cases arising out of state laws relating to abortion.

The so-called Civil Rights Restoration Act of 1987 included "abortion neutral" amendments which held that (1) nothing in the bill was meant to force any hospital or school receiving federal funds to perform or pay for abortions and (2) laws barring sex discrimination could not be construed to require or prohibit any person or public or private entity to provide for or pay for any benefit or service related to abortion. (For more details see chapter 23 on "Religious Liberty.")

101 Uses For A Dead (or Alive) Baby[22]

What's new in earrings? Australia's *People* magazine published an article featuring ten-week-old aborted babies, freeze-dried with an eye-hook in their tiny heads, and made into dangle earrings. The product was labelled, "Jewels for Ghouls" (Action News, Christian Action Council, June/July 1986, based on Chicago station WMBI talk show, June 2, 1986). Pro-Life News reports that a Chicago biological supply firm sold plastic paperweights in which were encased the bodies and organs of aborted babies (a human brain went for $90, a foot for $70). And, Right to Life of Huntsville, Texas, reports that a French magazine promoted pendants featuring a tiny fetus encased in plastic and strung on a gold necklace.

A workman in Wichita, Kansas, who was tossing bags of "pathological waste" into an incinerator from Wesley Medical Center (owned and operated by the United Methodist Church) discovered that the bags contained bodies of dead babies.

In Milwaukee, Wisconsin, police found four children in a parking lot behind Mill Medical Center playing with plastic jars containing aborted fetuses. "They told the officers they were throwing little people."

Not all bodies are "trashed." Babies' bodies are sold by the bag, $25 a batch—up to $5,500 a pound. Sales of aborted preborns brought Washington D.C. General Hospital $68,000 between 1966 and 1976. Money was used to buy TV sets and cookies for visiting professors.

In Richmond, Virginia, an abortion center used a trash compactor to mash one hundred babies' bodies which were tied up in plastic bags and tossed in a trash bin. Dogs dragged the bags away and fought over the contents.

In Cincinnati, Ohio, an abortuary allowed dense smoke to pour from its chimney. When firemen arrived on the scene, they were told, "We're burning babies."

In Jacksonville, Florida, the Women's Center for Reproductive Health, run by the Clergy Consultation Service, boasted "a decade of service."

The Massachusetts Supreme Court ruled that goldfish could not be awarded as prizes because that would violate the state's anti-cruelty laws. The same court upheld the mandatory state funding of abortions.

In California, babies still alive after having been aborted at six months were submerged in jars of liquid to see if they could breathe through their skin. (They couldn't.)

An Ohio medical research company tested brains and hearts of one hundred fetuses as part of a $300,000 pesticide contract.

Forty-seven United States senators voted to protect dogs from experimentation with poisonous gas. They then voted against an amendment by Senator Jesse Helms to prohibit federal funding of abortions.

Baby placentas are sold to drug companies for 50 cents a piece (for products like Placenta Plus Shampoo).

Human collagen from preborns (the gelatinous substance found in connective tissue, bone, and cartilage) is sold to cosmetic firms for use in beauty products.

Dr. Jeronimo Dominguez writes, "On any Monday you can see about thirty garbage bags with fetal material in them along the sidewalks of abortion clinics in New York."

In Houston, Texas, a funeral home which has abortion clinic contracts to dispose of fetuses ran afoul of the law when formaldehyde began seeping from a mass grave where some one hundred aborted babies were buried.

It is illegal to ship pregnant lobsters to market. In Maryland a $5,000 reward was offered for the arrest of the person responsible for the death of an American eagle. If preborn babies were animals instead of humans, they might fare better in courts and legislatures.

Now the latest development is using tissue from aborted babies to treat patients with diabetes, Parkinson's, Huntington's, and Alzheimer's disease.[23] Business analysts envision a $6 billion market in the United States for this type of industry.[24] Dr. Abraham Lieberman, of New York University Medical Center, states that fetal brain transplants are "to medicine what superconductivity is to physics."[25] The *New York Times* enthusiastically concurred: "Some of the prospects are enticing."[26] Dr. Robert Gale, University of California at Los Angeles, implanted liver cells from aborted fetuses into three victims of the Chernobyl nuclear plant disaster hoping the cells would multiply and replace bone marrow that had been destroyed by radiation. The patients died from burns before results of the therapy could be determined.[27]

The argument in favor of such an abomination goes like this: "Since abortions are legal, why waste the fetuses? Let's use them for social benefits." As Patrick Buchanan warns, such logic is frighteningly similar to the rationale of Hitler's Third Reich doctors who argued that since euthanasia was public policy, why waste the vital organs of the murdered?[28] A holocaust is a holocaust, whether it's gas ovens or saline solutions.

Pro-lifers see grave ethical threats involved in such fetal transplants. First, there could be pressure to perform an even greater number of abortions to fuel the new "business." They raise the specter of white-suited entrepreneurs recruiting indigent Third World women to become pregnant so that their fetuses can be sold to the highest bidder. Dr. John Wilke, president of the National Right to Life Committee, said "We are now destroying tiny lives and using their tissues."

Some one hundred years ago an Italian attorney, Raffaello Balestrini, warned: "Whenever abortion becomes a social custom, it is the external manifestation of a people's decadence."

Consider the Biblical Principles

God's Word makes it clear: Abortion is murder, the wanton taking of an innocent human life. And, murder is prohibited: "Thou shalt not commit murder" (Exodus 20:13; see also Genesis 9:5-7; Proverbs 6:16, 17).

"Know you that the Lord He is God: It is He that has made us, and not we ourselves; we are His people, and the sheep of His pasture" (Psalm 100:3). All life is created by the Lord God, "and by Him all things consist" (Colossians 1:17b). All life is under God's Law. God, not the state, not the individual, not the parent, is the Lord of life. God's will governs. Men and nations may deny that fact but neither man nor nation can escape it — or the consequences for violating it.

Man is to preserve and protect life. Physicians and surgeons once took an oath to do that (Christian physicians still do). Once the courts were a sanctuary for the sanctity of life; now, they are more often partners of death.

"If men strive and hurt a woman with child [one who is pregnant] so that her fruit [child] depart from her . . . and if any harm follow [if the child dies], then you shall give life for life" (Exodus 21:22-24). If God requires capital punishment when a fatal miscarriage is caused, surely His judgment for premeditated abortion can be no less severe toward those who are party to such murder.

Pro-abortionists claim that terminating a pregnancy is not murder because the fetus is not a human life (they refuse to acknowledge it is a preborn child). Thus, the question: When does life begin? The Bible has always given the answer, and the more science learns through study and research, the more science affirms the Scriptures. Life begins at the moment of conception. When a zygote ("genesis" cell) is formed by the fusion of the sperm and the egg, life commences.

"Marvelous are Your works, and that my soul knows right well! My substance was not hidden from You when I was made in secret and intricately wrought. . . . Your eyes did see my substance, yet being unformed; and in Your book all my members were written, which in continuance were fashioned, when as yet there was none of them" (Psalm 139:14-16).

Consider Matthew Henry's commentary:

> Each individual is God's work, according to His divine model; His eternal wisdom formed the plan and mold. As a great mercy, all our members in continuance were fashioned as they were written in the book of God's wise counsel when as yet there was none of them. Thus, who dares to destroy His handiwork and purpose? And, at what stage of life's span shall it be destroyed? Six days? Six weeks? Six months, or sixty years?[29]

"Before I formed you in the womb, I knew you; and before you came forth from the womb, I sanctified you, and I ordained you" (Jeremiah 1:5). God did not sanctify a glob of protoplasm; He sanctified unto His work a living human being of great potential and inestimable worth. (See Ephesians 1:4-5.)

Isaiah testified to the beginning of life: "Thus says the Lord, your Redeemer, and He Who formed you from the womb: I am the Lord Who makes all things" (Isaiah 44:24). (For further insight into the life of the preborn child, read Luke 1:41, 44.) When Mary, the mother of Jesus, visited Elizabeth, pregnant with John, the babe "leaped in [her] womb for joy"! Thus does the Bible tell what medical doctors now know: preborn babies do feel, they do experience, and they do react!

And consider the words of Job (measure them against what we now know about the development of the child—about gestation—in the womb): "Have You not poured me out as milk, and curdled me like cheese? You have clothed me with skin and flesh, and have fenced me with bones and sinews. You have granted me life and favor, and Your visitation has preserved my spirit" (Job 10:10-12; see also Genesis 25:21-23; Exodus 23:7; Deuteronomy 27:25; Psalm 57:5; Matthew 1:18; 2:18; 18:10, 14; and John 9:2, 3).

It is the Lord God, not the "planners" and social engineers, who writes the span and sets the stretch of life for each of His creations. We are instruments of His power and providence through His gift of procreation, evidence of His incredible love (Genesis 1:27, 28; John 3:16). The soul that animates the body is His gift (Genesis 2:7). The astounding structure of the body — that which the abortionist slashes apart with a scalpel, or rips apart with a suction pump, or burns to death with saline solution — that body is the product of His omniscience and omnipotence and grace. Into it the Lord God breathes the soul of life that through His grace it may become a temple of the Holy Ghost — "and you are not your own" (1 Corinthians 6:19).

Mark this well, abortionist, you who are pro-death: Give heed to what you destroy in your gravest act of blasphemy! Even in your unbelief, hear the words of the King: "Lo, children are an heritage of the Lord; and the fruit of the womb is His reward" (Psalm 127:3).

And, this, civil magistrates: You are to be servants (ministers) of God to the people for good (Romans 13:1-4). How, then, can magistrates (justices, legislators, executives) serve God or His people by decreeing abortion (murder) to be "legal"? That which is in direct violation of God's unchanging Law is not moral and can never be legal.

Citizens and nations: In a representative form of government, in a nation wherein the people make the final public decisions, the majority that approve (condone) abortion will be held accountable unto the Lord. They and the nation are, in God's sight, culpable; accomplices to murder (Numbers 35:30, 33; Psalm 14:3, 4; Hosea 4; Isaiah 59:1-9)!

Consider the words of Francis Schaeffer and C. Everett Koop:

> Churches and other groups opposed to abortion must be prepared to extend practical help to . . . the unmarried woman who is pregnant. . . . Merely to say "you must not have an abortion" without being ready to involve ourselves in the problem is another way of being inhuman.[30]

T W O

AIDS (Acquired Immune Deficiency Syndrome)

The spread of AIDS is a national crisis. By 1990 there may be 271,000 infected with the disease. Yet few public officials seem willing to tackle the major cause head-on.

Background Briefing

"With each passing week I become more and more convinced that the most important story of the last half of the 1980s is not going to be world terrorism; not nuclear proliferation, not street crime. . . . the most important story is going to be AIDS."[1]

"No doubt taxes will be at issue in campaign '88. But the big issue will be death—AIDS—and how the parties confront it."[2]

What is AIDS? Drs. Fauci and Love, of the National Institute of Allergy and Infectious Diseases, write that AIDS is characterized by a profound defect in cell-mediated immunity leading to opportunistic infections and unusual malignancies. AIDS is caused by a retrovirus of the human T-cell leukemia virus family (termed HTLV-III/LAV). The virus selectively infects a particular subset of lymphocytes (white blood cells) accounting for profound defects in immunity.[3]

The mortality rate of the full-blown syndrome approaches 100 percent (80 percent of AIDS victims die within two years of diagnosis).[4] It has been estimated that 1 million to 1.5 million persons in United States are now exposed to the AIDS virus and that between 5 percent and 30 percent (between 50,000 and 450,000) will die from AIDS within the next five to seven years.[5]

AIDS—Acquired Immune Deficiency Syndrome—was first called GRID—Gay Related Immune Deficiency. AIDS is fatal; it slowly destroys the body's immune system leaving a person vulnerable to a host of infectious diseases including one form of cancer (Kaposi's Sarcoma).

Although the AIDS virus has been isolated from saliva, tears, mother's milk, and urine, the evidence seems to indicate that AIDS is transmitted primarily by exposure to a direct dose of the virus through blood or semen.

However, Dr. John R. Seale, a British venereologist, told the House of Commons that the public is being misled by those who tell the populace that people are okay as long as "we practice safe sex, don't shoot drugs intravenously with unsterilized needles and make sure we don't get transfusions of blood containing the AIDS virus." Seale believes that AIDS can be transmitted by casual contact and by insects, and that this will become more evident as the number of virus carriers reaches critical mass. Seale described AIDS as "the molecular biological equivalent of nuclear war against man."[6]

"The AIDS epidemic is a plague. AIDS is an absolute catastrophe. There is no other word for it." Rosalyn Yomtovian, M.D., urges education and avoidance of high-risk behavior which she defines as "promiscuous sex," she says, "Basically, promiscuity is what spreads this disease."[7]

Some health officials say fear of AIDS is unwarranted. But, psychologist Joyce Brothers argues, "AIDS is a death sentence for which there is no appeal. The fear of AIDS is not irrational. If you are anything but celibate, whether you are involved in a heterosexual, homosexual or bisexual relationship, it is not irrational to be afraid."[8] Three years ago Life's July 1985 cover, "Now, No One Is Safe From Aids," was criticized as being blatant overkill.

But consider these stark realities:

The World Health Organization (WHO) reports that, as of January 21, 1988, there are 75,392 confirmed AIDS cases in 130 countries.[9] Here's WHO's breakdown:

The Americas, 56,958; Africa, 8,693; Europe, 8,775; Australia-New Zealand, 742.

In addition, WHO estimates that there are from 5 million to 10 million AIDS virus carriers worldwide and that it may take from five to seven years for the disease to manifest itself fully.[10]

The United States leads the world with 51,361 cases. At least 30,355 have died since 1981.[11] AIDS cases by category were: homosexuals and bisexuals, 34,687; intravenous drug users, 9,473; homosexual IV drug users, 4,016; recipients of blood transfusions, 2,015; heterosexuals, 2,169; children of AIDS parents, 683; and undetermined, 1,700.[12]

AIDS in the United States is spreading most rapidly among blacks and other minorities. The United States Centers for Disease Control reported the following data in August 1987: the number of cases per million people among whites, 168.3; among Hispanics, 454.5; and among blacks, 520.7.[13]

In 1987 there were 20,620 new cases of AIDS reported, an average of 400 each week. An additional 30,000 cases are projected for the year 1988, and a total of 271,000 by 1991.[14] The Centers for Disease Control projects that by the year 2000 there could be 7 to 10 million persons infected with AIDS, 1 million to 1.5 million reported cases of AIDS, and 600,000 to 900,000 deaths.[15]

"The [AIDS] virus . . . is mutating much faster than previously thought. It may be transforming itself as much as five times faster than the influenza virus."[16] Gerald Myers, a molecular geneticist at Los Alamos National Laboratory, reports that because the virus mutates rapidly, a single vaccine might not work for all forms.[17] If nothing else, the Myers report underscores the prediction of federal officials that a useful vaccine will not be available for at least five years, if then.[18] Further, researchers at the Third International Conference on AIDS reported that "carriers of the AIDS virus become more infectious with time and increase their ability to pass on the infection."[19]

What are the costs of AIDS—in addition to the suffering and death of its victims and relatives?

Medical care costs average $100,000 per AIDS patient. In 1988 some $600 million in Medicaid funds will go to AIDS patients, not including costs at the state and local levels. Estimates are that by 1991, the total annual cost for AIDS health care will come to $8.5 billion, with over $2 billion coming from Medicaid.

In the interim, it is estimated that the loss of productivity due to AIDS will total $65 billion.[20]

In a paper presented at an AIDS conference, the New York University Medical Center estimated that by 1991, AIDS patients will take at least five million bed-days a year at a cost of $3.5 billion, and AIDS patients will occupy fourteen thousand hospital beds on any given day. At present, one day's hospitalization for AIDS costs about $800. "That is 60 to 70 percent higher than the average daily cost of hospitalization for all other patients," according to Dr. Jo Ivy Boufford of New York City Health and Hospitals Corporation.[21] Already cities such as Los Angeles, San Francisco, and New York are struggling with the mounting costs of AIDS care which are taking more and more of their budgets.[22] They and other major cities are demanding that the federal government help them meet those costs.

The economic costs of AIDS are already rising sharply. In 1985 it was nearly $5 billion annually. In 1987 it was more than $10 billion. By the year 1991, it will top $65 billion a year, according to health economists Anne Scitovsky and Dorothy Rice.[23] "What is now becoming clear to an array of leaders—in medicine, business, government and academia—is that AIDS not only threatens untold death and suffering but could bankrupt America's health-care system as well."[24] And this at a time when the rising life-expectancy will increase costs for the care of the elderly who are under federal health care systems.

Fern Schumer Chapman warns, "Don't rob other medical research." She expressed a concern that because of federal deficits and tax rates, AIDS funds will come from other sources in the budget. That, she warns, may cause the "government to rob Peter to pay Paul—in these cases Peter is likely to be the research kitties for other diseases that account for a much greater number of deaths in the United States."[25] For instance, heart diseases kill about one million persons a year and cancer takes a toll of about five hundred thousand.

The President's Commission on AIDS reported to Mr. Reagan that AIDS is the "most significant serious infectious disease" the nation has ever faced.[26] The commission has recommended that the federal government spend $2 billion a year for ten years to combat AIDS: Of that, $1.5 billion would be spent on treatment and counselling for IV drug addicts, creating thirty-three hundred new treatment centers and thirty-two thousand drug counselling jobs. In 1987 the Reagan administration allocated $1.25 billion for AIDS treatment and education.[27]

Legislatures in all fifty states are under intense pressure to enact laws to combat the spread of AIDS, including laws mandating AIDS testing (for marriage license applicants, etc.) and laws to force insurance companies to provide health and life insurance policies to AIDS victims (California and the District of Columbia have already enacted such laws). Insurance companies say, "forcing insurance carriers to write such policies would be like forcing them to write fire insurance on a house already ablaze, or to insure a client against cancer when he already has cancer." The costs for such policies would have to be transferred to the other policy holders.[28]

Now, there is a new concern: experts are putting teenagers on the "high-risk" list for AIDS. "If there is such a thing as a high-risk group . . . the highest-risk group most certainly is American teenagers," said David Brunbach, director of the Montgomery and Prince George's chapters of HERO, the Maryland Health Education Resource Organization.[29] His concerns are shared by Dr. Harold Jaffe, chief epidemiologist in the AIDS program at the federal Centers for Disease Control. Dr. Jaffe said, in addition to young male homosexuals, "there's also concern about possible heterosexual transmission of the HIV (AIDS) virus by teens, because adolescence is not only an age where people are apt to experiment sexually, but also to experiment with drugs."[30]

"The problem is," wrote Dr. Gary North, "the AIDS plague is now being used to push sex education programs in public schools. The problem isn't education; it's morals. Sex education courses have multiplied over the past generation, and sexual promiscuity has multiplied alongside it."[31]

What is being done about AIDS, in addition to "crash" research to find a vaccine to halt or cure the disease?

For the most part, it's an ostrich approach comprised of "safe sex" education and a campaign to either slow down or halt rampant IV drug abuse (including programs to hand out condoms to teenagers and new needles to drug abusers). Little, if anything, is said about the evils of homosexuality.

Government officials, left-wing politicians, and educators are loathe to meet the most important problem head-on: homosexuality and the gay community. The fear of the over-rated political clout of homosexuals has sent many politicians running for cover.

"The public senses a very deep problem, one where their safety and welfare are threatened, but the politicians have been scared because the homosexual lobby, like the civil rights lobby, has exaggerated its importance in Washington" and many state capitols.[32] Civil authorities have chosen to legalize and protect homosexual activity at the expense of the public's health and life.[33]

The Public Health Service has an official policy to avoid blaming homosexuals for AIDS. Dr. Paul Cameron, of the Institute for Scientific Investigation of Sexuality, claims such "emphasis on protecting gays' feelings has led the Centers for Disease Control to suspend normal tracking systems for individuals infected with communicable disease. . . . our lives are being endangered to placate gay feelings."[34]

The official guidelines of the American Broadcasting Corporation (ABC) specifically instruct its personnel "not to blame gays for AIDS in television programming."[35] And, the American College Health Association endorses the view that homosexual behavior is not wrong.[36]

Dr. William Haseltine, a renowned AIDS researcher at Harvard University, urges authorities to consider past experience in dealing with venereal diseases. In the sixteenth century, the rampant spread of syphilis was largely contained by quarantine. Today, such measures are rejected as a violation of the civil rights of homosexuals.[37] But, Dr. Richard Retak, a neurologist who has been studying AIDS-related brain disorders, has noted: "What some are describing as 'discrimination' and 'segregation' has a long and not inglorious history in medicine. . . . by protecting the well from the ill we follow a long-established sensible and ultimately compassionate course."[38] However, with as many as three to five million infected with the AIDS virus, quarantine could be an administrative nightmare and a tremendous expense.

Notification and contact tracing has been effective in similar public health crises in the past. The name of the infected person is reported to local public health officials who then determine all the patient's sexual contacts since infection. Those persons are then asked to report their sexual contacts, etc. This routine proved very effective in halting the spread of syphilis in the 1930s and 1940s. That, too, has been rejected. Even though AIDS cases have been reported in all fifty states, only Colorado, Minnesota, and Idaho require all cases of AIDS infection to be reported.[39]

Representative William Dannemeyer (California) insists that the "choice of protecting the public must take precedence over the sensitivities of the group in our culture that has contributed the largest percentage of these AIDS cases — namely, male homosexuals."[40]

Dannemeyer has reported that it is impossible to get legislation through Congress to prompt the action necessary to combat AIDS because of homosexual influence on the Health and Environment Subcommittee of the House Commerce Committee. The chairman of that subcommittee, Representative Henry Waxman (California), represents a district where homosexuals are a potent force.[41] None of the 1988 presidential candidates has approached the issue of AIDS and its control.

What is the "origin" of AIDS? The Soviet Union claimed the virus leaked from a United States Army laboratory conducting experiments in biological warfare; that disinformation was easily exploded but only after the Soviets had spread it through the Third World countries.[42]

Dr. Seale, of Great Britain, thinks AIDS may have been accidentally "created" by a scientist doing cancer research without realizing what he had done. Some believe the AIDS virus, which infects wild colonies of green monkeys in Central Africa, was transmitted from monkeys to humans, thence to the Caribbean, especially to Haiti, and from there to the United States. Dr. William Haseltine of Harvard Medical School reports that 10 percent of the population in the Central Africa "AIDS belt" is infected with the disease.[43] That's more than ten million persons. Whatever the origin, it seems evident that AIDS is transmitted in more ways than just sexual contact, IV needles, and blood transfusions.[44]

AIDS in the United States started in the New York male homosexual population in 1979 (there were few cases reported prior to that). The Centers for Disease Control (CDC) indicate that the first AIDS cases in women were reported in 1982. These were mostly among prostitutes who are often IV drug abusers and partners for hire with men infected with the AIDS virus.

Danger of contacting AIDS from blood transfusion—that's another matter. "Early-on, health and blood bank officials were assuring us there was minimal danger of AIDS transmission through the blood supply. When people started dying of transfusion AIDS, that assurance was forgotten."[45] Today it is estimated that at least 460 persons a year will contract AIDS through transfusion with tainted blood.[46] Testing for the AIDS virus at blood banks is now routine and authorities insist the blood supply is safe. But, some researchers say the ELISA test (used to screen donated blood for AIDS) is not reliable. Thus, there is an increased demand by patients and doctors to have designated donors or direct blood donors (family members, close friends, etc.).

At Washington's National Cathedral, the Holy Communion ritual was changed in response to concern about AIDS; 40 percent of the communicants chose the option of a wafer dipped in wine rather than drinking from a common chalice. The rector of New York Trinity Episcopal Church assured his parishioners that there was no evidence that AIDS was spread by the common cup but asserted that "full and valid" Communion was made by consuming only the bread.

A Harris poll in early 1988 found that two out of three parents would send their children to schools which admitted students with AIDS; but, 50 percent want the AIDS-infected child identified.[47] Dr. Don Boys wrote, "I would not permit my children to go to school where mumps, measles, or meningitis are present, so I sure wouldn't permit them to attend where AIDS is present."[48]

In summary, the United States is threatened by a plague which is sweeping through the sodomite and drug addict communities. It is expanding with geometric progression. There is no known cure or viable treatment now available. The "straight" world is threatened to a lesser degree through exposure to blood and blood products (hemophiliacs), the birth canal of AIDS-carrying mothers (babies), accidental needle sticks (medical personnel) — and even legitimate sexual relations (spouses of infected persons). Some authorities in the field of medical science believe other means of transmission (close contacts, insects) are possible. The rapid spread of the disease and increasing social pressure are forcing a reevaluation of sexual "freedom" spawned by the anti-culture revolution of the 1960s and 1970s. But public officials and most elected representatives have been severely irresponsible in not taking rational and reasonable action to contain and halt the spread of AIDS. Thus, they leave the nation at risk.

"At one time, societies had the common sense to try to protect themselves from those with lethal, contagious and incurable diseases. That was before the homosexual lobby became politically powerful."[49]

Consider the Biblical Principles

In the beginning God created them male and female (Adam and Eve, not Adam and Steve). And, He pronounced His creation good (Genesis 1:27, 31).

God commanded heterosexual marital fidelity at Sinai in the Seventh Commandment (Exodus 20:14). In Leviticus, God warned:

> You shall not lie with mankind as with womankind: It is abomination [sin]. Neither shall you lie with any beast to defile yourself therewith: Neither shall any woman stand before a beast to lie down thereto: it is confusion [perversion]. Defile not yourself in any of these things: for in all these the nations are defiled which I cast out before you: And the land is defiled: therefore I do visit the iniquity thereof upon it and the land itself vomited out her inhabitants. You shall therefore keep [obey] My statutes, and My judgments, and shall not commit any of these abominations [sins] (Leviticus 18:22ff).

The Old Testament penalty for homosexual activity was death (Leviticus 20:13). God's Word indicates that certain diseases are the result of sin (indicating the seriousness in which the aberration was held).

If you will diligently hearken to the voice of the Lord your God, and will do that which is right in His sight, and give ear to His commandments and keep all His Statutes, I will put none of the diseases before you, which I have brought upon the Egyptians, for I am the Lord that healeth you (Exodus 15:26).

If you will not observe to do all the words of this law that are written in this book, that you may fear [respect] this glorious and fearful name, the Lord Thy God; Then the Lord will make your plagues [troubles] wonderful [tremendous] and the plagues of your seed, even great plagues, and of long continuance, and sore sicknesses, and of long continuance. Moreover He will bring unto you all the diseases of Egypt, which you were afraid of; and they shall cleave unto you. Also every sickness, and every plague, which is not written in the book of this law, them will the Lord bring unto you, until you be destroyed (Deuteronomy 28:58-62).

Rebellion against God's command may result in a plague seven times as severe as the sin (Leviticus 26:21). He clearly warned Israel that sin brought judgment not only to sinners but also to succeeding generations through their great-great-grandchildren (Exodus 34:6, 7). Anti-Biblical human wisdom (1 Corinthians 3:19ff) has decreed that sodomy is a normal alternative lifestyle, but God's Spirit observes, "There is a way which seems right to a man, but its end is the way of death" (Proverbs 16:25). "Every man is tempted, when he is drawn away of his own lust. . . . Then when lust hath conceived, it bringeth forth sin; and sin, when it is finished, bringeth forth death" (James 1:14-15).

In the second half of Romans, chapter 1, the Apostle Paul gives a penetrating picture of the step-by-step plunge of the man who refuses to honor God or give Him thanks, and who rejects His truth, resulting in the wrath of God: (1) suppression of the truth, (2) futile thinking and a darkened mind, (3) worship of the creature rather than the Creator (the essence of humanism), (4) adultery, (5) homosexuality, and (6) a base mind and improper conduct filled with all manner of wickedness. Depraved sinners not only commit sin themselves but encourage others to do likewise (Romans 1:18-32). Note verse 26: "for even their women did change the natural use into that which is against nature: And likewise also the men, leaving the natural use of the woman, burned in their lust one toward another; men with men working that which is unseemly, and receiving in themselves that recompense [reward] of their error which was meet [due]."

"Be not deceived, God is not mocked: for whatsoever a man soweth, that shall he also reap. For he that soweth to his flesh shall of the flesh reap corruption. But he that soweth to the Spirit shall of the Spirit reap life everlasting" (Galatians 6:7, 8). "But the fearful, and unbelieving, and the abominable, and murderers, and whoremongers, and sorcerers, and idolaters, and all liars, shall have their part in the lake which burneth with fire and brimstone, which is the second death" (Revelation 21:8). "Know you not that the unrighteous shall not inherit the kingdom of God? Be not deceived: neither fornicators, nor idolaters, nor adulterers, nor effeminate [sodomites], nor abusers of themselves . . . shall inherit the kingdom of God" (1 Corinthians 6:9, 10).

And then Paul gives *the solution* to the problem:

> And such were some of you: but you are washed, but you are sanctified, but you are justified in the name of the Lord Jesus, and by the Spirit of our God (1 Corinthians 6:11).

> Know you not that you are the temple of God, and that the Spirit of God dwells in you? If any man defile [destroy] the temple of God, him shall God destroy; for the temple of God is holy, which temple you are (1 Corinthians 3:16, 17).

Premarital sexual continence, followed by faithful heterosexual monogamy — this is the Creator's design for joyful and truly safe sex. Any other system is outside His revealed will and protection.

Is AIDS a plague from God? His holy Word would indicate that it is, as are syphilis, gonorrhea, genital herpes, and a host of other diseases that are basically transmitted by sinful acts which are so rampant throughout the world in these days. Some Biblical scholars think that Numbers 25:1-9 possibly refers to AIDS or a similar plague caused by sexual misconduct. God's laws for sex cannot be broken any more than His law of gravity. (One breaks himself or herself on the Law rather than breaking the Law itself—Psalm 119:89.) Do the innocent suffer with the guilty? In some cases, yes. Even to the third and fourth generations. Is our nation—indeed the whole world—in danger? Yes.

For the Lord God does indeed hold a society responsible for allowing such immoralities to take hold and to proliferate.

The medical profession must explore ways and means to control this devastating disease (which may well prove not to have a medical cure). And, we as God's people have the responsibility to declare the truth (Ezekiel 33): homosexuality and adultery are sins, devastating to society as well as to the individual sinner. The time is past to preach only "the positive Gospel"; the time is now to preach and teach in Christian love the whole counsel of God—of salvation, yes, but also of all His commandments: of obedience, of accountability, and of compassion. The hope, the one true hope, for the homosexual is this: a new birth in Christ Jesus—repentance and regeneration—which is available regardless of the depth of one's sin (Mark 1:15; Acts 3:19; 2 Corinthians 5:17).

In that same love, we must work for those laws and procedures which will protect the innocent and the unsuspecting: (1) states should once again hold sodomy to be illegal; (2) educational establishments must cease presenting sodomy as a normal alternative lifestyle; (3) bath houses and porn shops should be closed for being what they are, health hazards; (4) all infected homosexuals should be required to register (with limited immunity from prosecution) and to provide health officials a list of their sex partners; and (5) sodomites who infect others with AIDS should be liable for prosecution for manslaughter.

We who are His must not use the AIDS crisis as an excuse to engage in un-Christian actions. While we shun and speak out against the sin of sodomy, we must also be compassionate toward those who are suffering the terrible consequences of AIDS. In their darkness, God gives us the opportunity—the requirement—to be light, to bring comfort, to tell of His love and explain His truth, to minister to the body and to the soul of those who suffer. To introduce them to Him who is the Way, the Truth, and the Light. The Redeemer, the Giver of Eternal Life. The Great Physician.[50]

"The issue is one of life and death (physical and spiritual). It is not a matter of civil rights. It is a matter of civil wrongs—wrongs committed by those whose behavior is responsible for the epidemic confronting us." And those who have been vested with the authority and the responsibility to protect the public well-being—and are found wanting.

THREE

CAPITAL PUNISHMENT

How much is life worth? Seven years. That's the median time convicted murderers serve behind bars. One of every seven inmates sentenced to "life" for murder serves three years or less.

Background Briefing

Capital punishment is as old as human civilization. The Romans crucified criminals. Death was the mandatory sentence for murder under English common law. The Pilgrims and the Puritans brought capital punishment to this land, restricting its enforcement to the most serious crimes such as murder, rape, and blasphemy.

Capital punishment was accepted as law when the framers of the Constitution wrote the Fifth Amendment: "No person shall be held to answer for a capital crime" without indictment; no person "shall be put twice into jeopardy of life and limb" and no person shall be "deprived of life" without due process.

Some states abolished the death penalty in the mid-1800s: Michigan in 1846, Rhode Island in 1852, Wisconsin in 1853, Iowa in 1872, and Maine in 1876. Many then reenacted the death penalty with the advent of more sophisticated methods of execution (the electric chair, lethal injection, etc.). Enforcement of the death penalty reached its peak in the 1930s; in 1935, 195 convicts were executed. By the 1960s, executions had dropped off rapidly. In 1962 there were 47 executions, and in 1966, only 1.[1]

In 1967 the United States Supreme Court announced it was taking the question of capital punishment under advisement. Lower courts then put the death penalty "on hold," awaiting the high court's decision. In 1972 the Supreme Court held that the death penalty laws of forty-one states were unconstitutional on the grounds that they were applied arbitrarily and in a discriminatory manner. In 1976, in *Gregg v. Georgia*, the Supreme Court ruled that capital punishment was constitutional if imposed within strict procedural safeguards. Thirty-seven states then enacted capital punishment laws within those guidelines. Incidentally, Troy Gregg, whose suit brought about the hiatus, was not executed. In 1980 he and three others on death row escaped from the Georgia state prison. The three conspirators were recaptured; but Gregg had been stomped to death by his fellow escapees.[2]

During the ten years (1977-1987) following the reinstitution of the death penalty, some one hundred criminals were executed.

Thirty-two states have some 2,000 inmates on death row and about 250 are added each year.[3] Ernest van den Haag, of the Fordham University Law School and an authority on capital punishment, has predicted that there will be some fifty executions in 1988.[4]

"Out of the approximately twenty thousand homicides committed annually in the United States, fewer than three hundred lead to a death sentence."[5] Only 1 out of every 42 death row inmates was executed from 1977 through 1986. Bureau of Justice statistics from that period report that of the 2,839 convicts sentenced to death, only 68 were executed.[6]

Three rounds of appeal are provided for every convict before the death sentence is executed. Pursuit of those appeals can stretch out for years. Robert Sullivan, convicted of the 1973 shooting of a restaurant manager, had his case reviewed twenty times by appellate courts including five trips to the United States Supreme Court. Sullivan was finally electrocuted in December 1983. In another notorious case, Jimmy Lee Gray was sentenced to death for the 1976 sex slaying of three-year-old Deressa Jean Scales. At the time Gray murdered Deressa Jean, he was on parole after serving seven years of a twenty-year sentence for the murder of his sixteen-year-old girlfriend. Gray was put to death seven years after his conviction. Chief Justice Warren Burger wrote in the prevailing decision, "Over the past seven years, judicial action reviewing this case has been taken eighty-two times by twenty-six different state and Federal judges."[7]

Opponents of capital punishment continue the campaign to prevent additional executions and seek to outlaw the death penalty. They contend that the death penalty violates the Eighth Amendment which prohibits "cruel and unusual punishment." The United States Supreme Court disagreed. Justice Potter Stewart, joined by Justices Stevens and Powell, held that the death penalty was not "cruel and unusual" and stated his belief that the state can properly seek vengeance. "Expression of society's moral outrage is essential in an ordered society that asks its citizens to rely on legal processes rather than self-help to vindicate their wrongs." He added that "retribution is neither a forbidden objective nor one inconsistent with the dignity of man."[8]

Opinion polls show the public agrees: it strongly favors capital punishment for crimes such as premeditated murder and kidnapping. Recent opinion polls found that seventy-five percent of the public approves of the death penalty for capital crimes.[9]

The advocates of the death penalty contend that capital punishment is necessary to protect the public because it serves as a deterrent to capital crimes. Opponents disagree; they say the death penalty is no deterrent. But statistics would seem to support the assertion of deterrence: during the ten years the death penalty was outlawed, the number of murders per year in the United States almost doubled—from 10,000 in 1967 to more than 19,000 in 1977. As executions declined, murders increased: In 1965 there were 76 executions and 7,000 murders. In 1960 there were 56 executions and 8,000 murders. In 1972 there were no executions and 18,000 murders. In 1978 there were no executions and 19,555 murders. Since 1980 the capital crime rate has increased phenomenally.[10] Law enforcement authorities chalk that up to the epidemic of drug abuse in the United States.

After making a study of crime and punishment, Gordon Tullock, of the Virginia Polytechnic Institute, concluded: "Eighty percent of the people who seriously think about crime think of punishment as a deterrent—except for the sociologists and they wrote all the books." A study made by an inmate-published newspaper in the Texas prison system concluded that a majority of inmates believed the death penalty for prison murders might reduce violence within the prisons. Two-thirds of the inmates favored the death penalty for murder, child abuse, and sex crimes.[11]

Professor Isaac Ehrlich, a University of Chicago sociologist and himself an opponent of capital punishment, nevertheless reported that his studies indicated that if the death penalty were really enforced, eight murders would be prevented for every one execution. Others who had researched the subject contended that Ehrlich's estimate is off by a factor of at least five — that for each execution at least fifty murderers were deterred.[12]

Professor Stephen K. Lawson, of the University of North Carolina at Greensboro, recently published his study of the effect of executions on the murder rate. He reported that "every execution of a murderer deters, on the average, eighteen murders that would have occurred without it."[13] Professor van den Haag wrote, "Obviously people fear death more than life imprisonment. . . . Actual murderers feel that way: 99.9 percent prefer life imprisonment to death . . . what is feared most deters most."[14]

Professor Charles E. Rice, of the Notre Dame University School of Law, comments: "Statistics show the number of murders that were committed in spite of capital punishment, but they cannot show the number of murders that were deterred, and therefore never committed." Dr. Rice added, "The best evidence that the death penalty has a uniquely deterrent impact with respect to such crimes [as premeditated and deliberate homicide] is not based on statistics but is rather based on common sense and experience."[15]

Dr. Rice concluded: "A more basic justification for the death penalty is retribution, which is often wrongly equated with vengeance. To exact retribution is to fit the punishment to the crime in accord with the requirements of justice."[16]

Opponents of the death penalty claim it is a "cruel and unusual" punishment and thus prohibited by the Constitution. But the courts have held to the contrary. No court has ever deviated from the position taken by the United States Supreme Court in 1890:

> Punishments are cruel when they involve torture or lingering death; but the punishment of death is not cruel within the meaning of that word as used in the Constitution. It implies something inhuman and barbarous.

The opponents also insist that capital punishment is "racist," that it is applied most often against members of minorities. A study of capital punishment indicates that about 42 percent of those sentenced to die are black. But, the FBI Uniform Crime code disclosed that 57 percent of those arrested for willful homicide were black.[17] Further, statistics show 50 percent of all murder victims are black. Thus, it is argued, failure to apply the death penalty for first degree murder is in fact "racist" since it deprives the black community of a demonstrable deterrent to homicide.

Responding to the assertion that the chances of being executed for a capital crime are three to ten times greater for killing a white person than a black person, Lawrence W. Johnson wrote that such arguments disregard "the fact that most murders are committed within one's own race, . . . 93 percent of black victims were killed by blacks while 88 percent of the whites murdered were slain by whites. Not only are inter-racial murders uncommon, but such as do occur are far more likely to entail blacks killing whites than the reverse."[18]

The latest controversy concerning capital punishment is whether to permit execution of those who committed a capital crime before age eighteen. Paula Cooper was fifteen when she and her companions murdered Bible teacher, Ruth Pelke, seventy-eight. Wayne Thompson, now twenty-one, was fifteen when he helped kill his brother-in-law in Amber, Oklahoma.[19] Since then, several other cases in which juveniles murdered their parents and other members of their families have occurred.

Those opposed to the execution of teenage murderers insist it is inhumane to execute someone who was too young to fully comprehend the meaning of the crime. One of Wayne Thompson's lawyers, Victor Streib, argues that juveniles "don't know what death really means. They are quite honestly surprised the victim is dead forever" because of what they see on television. Streib says that while 75 percent of the public favor the death penalty, only 25 to 30 percent support the death penalty for juveniles.[20]

Law enforcement officers reject such arguments. They say no one should escape the death penalty simply because of age. "We're not talking about juvenile delinquents or the Brady bunch. They are hardened criminals, and they know . . . well what they were doing." Oklahoma's Assistant Attorney General, Bob Nance, said that Thompson's murder of Charles Keene was "just about as cold as you can get." Keene was shot twice, stabbed, his body weighted down, and dropped in a river.[21]

Of the thirty-seven states which have death penalty laws, twenty-seven have minimum ages for capital punishment ranging from ten- to eighteen-years-old. Nine of the states have not set minimums.[22]

Consider the Biblical Principles

For those who would obey the Lord God, capital punishment is not a matter of choice or opinion poll, or even court decree. It is God's requirement; it stands as a Biblical principle.

God established the death penalty for willful murder: "Whosoever sheddeth man's blood, by man shall his blood be shed: for in the image of God made He man" (Genesis 9:6). Thus, capital punishment was ordained — not just for Noah or Noah's time, but "for perpetual generations" (Genesis 9:12).

Capital punishment and the manner in which it was to be applied is detailed and reaffirmed many times in the Scriptures (Exodus 21:12-15; Leviticus 25:17-23; Numbers 35:9-34; Deuteronomy 21:1-9, etc.). Some of these sentences may seem harsh, yet it is clear that if they had been continued many of the ills that plague society today would never have arisen. In His perfect justice, the Lord God provided for protection of the lawful from the lawless. In Acts 25:10-12, the Apostle Paul makes it clear that he recognizes the continuing validity of the death penalty: "For if I be an offender, or have committed anything worthy of death, I refuse not to die."

Importantly, in its application of justice, the Bible carefully and clearly delineates between the crime of willful homicide (premeditated murder) and accidental death (manslaughter). God's Word also declares that causing the death of an unborn child (miscarriage or abortion) is murder (Exodus 21:22, 23).

Capital punishment is not to be used for personal revenge; it is a matter of retribution to be exercised as a requirement from the Lord God. God instructs us that (1) the person who willfully takes another's life must pay for that act by forfeiting his own; (2) the death penalty is not to be exercised by an individual or group but by the properly constituted civil authorities; and

(3) this must be done to uphold the sacredness (sanctity) of human life ("in the image of God created He man").

When the Lord God established capital punishment, He also ordained the institution to enforce it (to bear the sword). That institution is civil government — the corporate body politic (Genesis 9:5). The Apostle Paul refers to this power to protect the innocent and to punish the lawbreaker in Romans 13:4, "[the magistrate] beareth not the sword in vain; for he is the minister of God, a revenger to execute wrath upon him who does evil."

The foundation (basis) of civil government is power (implied or applied) bestowed upon it by the citizenry. When that power is abused or not used, government is weakened and eventually overturned. When that occurs, the individual, the family, the home, and most if not all lawful aspects of society are imperiled. Capital punishment is essential for the protection of the innocent and the maintenance of a safe and peaceful society. It is part of God's grace, one of His provisions for the protection of His creation, man.

Some Christians insist that capital punishment violates God's Sixth Commandment: "Thou shalt not kill" (Exodus 20:13). In fact, that admonition is directly tied to the penalty for murder. As Rev. David E. Goodrum points out, the word translated "kill" — when considered in its original meaning and in its usage throughout the Bible — clearly means "murder." Properly translated, it reads "Thou shalt not murder." Further, as Goodrum emphasizes, God Himself gives instructions that violators are to be killed for certain crimes and under certain conditions (Exodus 21:12; Leviticus 24:17, etc.).[23]

In the early days of this republic, our judicial laws were based upon the Word of God. In *A Course of Legal Study* — a popular law textbook published in 1836 — this sentiment is expressed: "The purity and sublimity of the morals of the Bible have at no time been questioned; it is the foundation of the common law of every Christian nation. The Christian religion is part of the law of the land, and, as such, should certainly receive no inconsiderable portion of the lawyer's attention. In vain do we look among the writings of ancient philosophers for a system of moral law comparable with that of the Old and New Testament."[24]

In a brilliant thesis on capital punishment, Dr. Francis Nigel Lee explains that it is the duty of civil authorities ("ministers of God to the people for good") to see to it that all murderers receive the death penalty. "For, the lips of a ruler are to speak the Word of God; and his mouth should not betray justice" (Proverbs 16:10). Judges are rulers who are to "detest wrongdoing"; for a government is "strengthened through righteousness" (Proverbs 16:12-15). "When a ruler executes judgment, he scatters away all evil" (Proverbs 20:8).

Dr. Lee emphasizes, "It is the same after Calvary!" For "governors . . . are sent . . . to punish those who do wrong" (1 Peter 2:14). Accordingly, "anyone who kills with the sword, must himself be killed by the sword" (Revelation 13:10).[25]

Corrupt government, unrighteous judges, justice denied and not enforced — these incur the wrath of God and should incur the censure of godly Christians. "Why do you show Me iniquity, and cause Me to behold grievance? For spoiling and violence are before Me: and those there are that raise up strife and contention. Therefore the Law is slacked, and judgment does never go forth: for the wicked do compass about the righteous; therefore wrong judgment proceeds" (Habakkuk 1:3, 4).

It is a small wonder our nation's justice system has deteriorated! When God's Word is put on the back shelf, the laws of man ignore the Laws of the Lord God — and the people suffer.

The Bible tells us that murder pollutes the land, and that the only way to cleanse the land is capital punishment (Numbers 35:33-34). The Bible also instructs us that those nations that fail to enforce capital punishment will be harshly judged (Jeremiah 2:34-37; Hosea 1:4; 4:1-5). By obeying the Lord God and enforcing the death penalty for capital crimes, the nation cleanses itself of the guilt of innocent blood; conversely, the nation that refuses to obey God and avenge the taking of innocent human life must share the guilt of the murderer (Deuteronomy 21:7-8).

God's Word sets forth certain definite rules so that this ultimate exercise of civil power — the death penalty — will not be abused: (1) capital punishment is to be enforced judiciously, impartially, and only after full and proper (and swift) legal proceedings; (2) testimony in such cases must be corroborated by at least two witnesses and should a witness give false testimony (perjury), thus to jeopardize the accused improperly, that witness shall be subject to the penalty attached to the crime under consideration; and (3) capital punishment is not to be enforced in a spirit of maliciousness or revenge (that is forbidden — Matthew 5:38-44), but used only as God directed.

Thus, we may keep His commandments and statutes so that "it may go well with thee" (Deuteronomy 19:13; Numbers 35:31-34; see also: Proverbs 18:5; 19:19; 21:11, 15; 28:17; 29:4).

F O U R

CHILD ABUSE

The rising incidence of child abuse is a mark of this "modern" age. Some experts see it as a product of forsaking America's historic Christian culture.

Background Briefing

Every sixty seconds in the United States a child is abused. That's an average of one victim every minute, more than one million cases a year. And, the actual total may be much higher than that due to underreporting. Thousands of children die each year as a result of abusive treatment. More than seven hundred are killed by their own parents. Child abuse is the fifth most common cause of child death in the United States. The average age of an abused child is less than three years. The average age of the abusive mother is twenty-six; of the abusive father, thirty.

The idea that child abuse is nothing new, that it has always been prevalent and is simply receiving increased exposure and attention now, is wrong. Dr. John Demos, professor of history at Yale University, found almost no evidence of child abuse in his studies of prior cultures. His surveys of colonial New England turned up very few reports of child abuse.[1] Professor Demos suggests that "child abuse is a uniquely modern phenomenon caused by urbanization, industrial development, and on-the-job alienation." Also, he attributes it to the collapse of "the providential world view of our forebears — their belief that all things, no matter how surprising and inscrutable, must be attributed to God's overarching will."[2]

Physical violence is not the only form of child abuse. In addition there are two other major forms: emotional abuse and sexual abuse.

43

Physical abuse is the intentional use of physical force or a purposeful omission of caution or protection on the part of the abuser aimed at hurting, injuring, or destroying the child.[3]

Emotional abuse is perhaps even more insidious in that it is more difficult to detect. It takes two forms: neglect and assault. Abusive parents may care for a child's physical needs but deprive the child of emotional nourishment (love, attention, caring, etc.). "To develop a sense of self-worth, humans need to feel wanted and to have a sense of belonging—certainly a parental responsibility."[4] Emotional assault is usually verbal though: critical, demeaning, and destructive criticism.

The third type of child abuse is sexual abuse. Sexually aggressive behavior cuts across all social, economic and racial boundaries. Although young females are the highest at-risk population, about one-fifth of the estimated one million sexually abused children in 1984 were males. Child abuse researchers and law officials say only 15 to 20 percent of the perpetrators were strangers to the sexually abused victims. The sexual abuser usually is someone the child knows.[5]

It is estimated that in the United States a child is sexually abused every two minutes. Some experts admit that the number could range higher than one million a year. National studies report that one out of every five victims of sexual abuse is less than seven years old.

Experience indicates that only about 2 percent of sexual molestations against pre-school children are ever reported. In many cases the child is warned not to tell under threat of harm to the child or a loved one; in other cases, children won't tell because the abuse was committed by someone they love (incest accounts for a large number of child abuse cases). And, when children do tell, many adults refuse to believe, thinking that the child is fantasizing.

One of the most shocking cases is that of alleged sexual abuse involving more than 400 four- and five-year-old children (committed over a period of ten years) at a highly respected (and quite exclusive) day care center in Manhattan Beach, California. The preliminary hearings in that case dragged on for more than eighteen months at a public cost of more than $4 million.

Parents of the children involved were angered when sex-abuse charges were dropped against five of the seven defendants.[6]

One of the major factors in child sexual abuse is pornography, according to reports presented to the United States Attorney General's Commission on Pornography.[7]

An increasing emphasis and levels of extremes regarding children in sexual contact with adults in magazines such as *Playboy, Hustler,* and *Penthouse* have been documented by Dr. Judith Reisman of American University. Dr. Reisman told the commission that such depiction has appeared particularly in cartoon format — "a format historically used to challenge social taboos."[8] Dr. Reisman reported, "We found 520 with a child in some kind of a sexual encounter with an adult, and sixty with an older child. Nearly half of the principal children [depicted] were between the ages of three and eleven years old. The age most often depicted was six to eleven, the most common years of child sexual abuse.[9] We have found children as young as four or five months old with venereal disease from sexual abuse."[10]

Two child development specialists were asked to analyze the samples from the three magazines. In their analysis they included these opinions: "One possible dangerous effect of these pictures is that they disinhibit the prohibition, making less secure people more aware of inappropriate sexual feelings and more confused about what to do about them." And, "There is also an inherent permission given to indulge in this kind of sexual behavior when viewed in the media. . . . To have media present scenes of child seduction may make it more difficult for men to consciously suppress their feelings."[11]

Alcohol plays a role in more than 50 percent of child abuse cases. Many cases occur due to ignorance of even the most basic postnatal care. Frustrated parents (many in their teens) have severely beaten infants whose only offense was the crying and fussing that accompanies colic or teething. Usually, incidents of abuse follow a pattern. First, the parent ignores the child and withdraws affection. Second, the parent may verbally berate the child, complaining that the child is clumsy, dumb, always under foot, a nuisance, etc. That may lead to physical neglect. The child may not be properly or regularly fed; he may be dressed inappropriately for weather conditions or may lack clean clothing. Finally comes the actual physical abuse.

Nearly half of abuse incidents could have been prevented by other adults who realized that abuse was probable but chose not to get involved. Because of the fear of the weaker spouse or the apathy of relatives, friends, or neighbors, little or nothing is done to protect the child. Then, government agencies intervene. The child may be taken from his parents—but, state-operated orphanages and foster homes can be as bad or worse than the child's own home.

Many cases have been reported in which government social workers took, or tried to take, children from their parents under the guise or charge of abuse because the agency did not approve of the children's religious training, Christian schooling, or discipline. (For more details on that aspect of the problem, see chapter 19 on "Parental Abuse.")

Child abuse is often the bitter fruit of humanism. Those who do not respect the Lord God usually have little or no respect for those made in His image. Humanism does not glorify man as God's handiwork; it dehumanizes man, making it easier to excuse violating the individual either mentally or physically. And, young children are very vulnerable. God requires nurturing of children (loving care, training, education). False gods, however, call for their exploitation, abuse, and destruction (Leviticus 18:21).

Not all child abuse occurs in the home or involves physical or sexual violence. Much child abuse occurs in classrooms of state-controlled schools. Testimony by some thirteen hundred parents in seven different cities during March 1984 spelled out "eye-witness accounts of psychological abuse of children in public schools." The testimony was given at the United States Department of Education Hearings on proposed regulations for the Protection of Pupil Rights Amendment (Hatch Amendment; Section 439 of General Education Code P1232h).[12]

Parents "related how classroom courses have confused school children about life, about standards of behavior, about moral choices, about religious loyalties, and about relationships with parents and with peers."

In her foreword to *Child Abuse in the Classroom* (excerpts from the official transcripts of the hearings), Phyllis Schlafly observed that the hearings substantiated the predictions of former United States Senator S. I. Hayakawa. The Senator from California had warned that schools have become vehicles for a "heresy that rejects the idea of education as the acquisition of knowledge and skills" and instead "regards the fundamental task in education as therapy." It is, said Senator Hayakawa, a therapy that seeks to replace cognitive education with effective (or manipulative) education. That, Hayakawa told the Senate in 1978, is a "serious invasion of privacy."[13]

Mrs. Schlafly commented:

> These hearings explain how schools have alienated children from their parents, from traditional morality such as the Ten Commandments, and from our American heritage. . . . These hearings explain why we have twenty-three million adult illiterates who graduated from public schools, and why young people are experiencing high rates of teenage suicide, loneliness, premarital sex and pregnancies.[14]

It is clear that such heresy in the classrooms of the state-controlled schools can only be classified as "child abuse" — leaving a long trail of wrecked lives and broken families.

Sex education, in many if not most state schools, is little more than values manipulation that encourages a lessening of self-control (abstinence). Such "education" sets the stage for the subsequent "child abuse" of abortion. After the United States Supreme Court's *Roe v. Wade* decision legalized abortion, the number of abortions doubled in just four years. And, in that same period (1972-76), the number of incidents of child abuse soared more than 800 percent.

Christian theologian and philosopher Francis Schaeffer commented at the time, "There has been a dramatic rise of crimes against children since abortion-on-demand became legal in the United States. We are convinced that this increase is caused in part by the liberalization of abortion laws and the resultant drastic lowering of the value placed on human life and children's lives in particular."[15]

Professor, author, and pro-life crusader Dr. Harold O. J. Brown suggested that legalized abortion may well have caused some parents to reason, "I didn't have to have him; I could have killed him before he was born. So, if I want to throw him around . . . isn't that my right?"

Consider the Biblical Principles

Jacob said of his offspring that they were "children which God has graciously given Thy servant" (Genesis 33:5). Children belong to God and are placed in the care of earthly parents as a trust, a stewardship (Genesis 4:1). The Scriptures direct parents to nurture, strengthen, discipline, and teach their child—not abuse him (Deuteronomy 6:7; 18-21).

In many pagan religions, parents have a life-and-death power over their offspring; in Christianity, the command to honor parents (Exodus 20:12) is followed by the prohibition of murder (Exodus 20:13). Parents are to be respected, but the authority of the parent is not without limits: parents are under God and must obey His Law.

Jesus was indignant with His disciples when they attempted to prevent children from coming to Him (Mark 10:14). Children were to be allowed to come and were not to be despised (Matthew 18:10). Those who harm God's little ones will suffer His wrath (Matthew 18:6; see also Isaiah 40:11). Unknowingly, faithful disciples render service to Christ by ministering to the needs of these little ones (Matthew 25:35-40). To combat child abuse, preventive measures must be taken, and they must begin in the most important unit of society, the family. If there is a possibility of abuse in a home, the involvement of nearby relatives may be crucial. The relatives must not close their eyes or ears to reality, or hope that the problem will simply "go away." They should counsel with the family member, pray with and for him or her, offer to temporarily care for the children if that will help, and encourage the parent to seek a Biblical change of heart and lifestyle through the power of the Holy Spirit. The fruits of the Spirit include patience (forbearance) and temperance (self-control, right self-governance) (Galatians 5:23).

Several decades ago, neighborhoods and communities were strong deterrents to child abuse; disapproval was clear and swift. Also, employers would take action against an employee guilty of child abuse. Now, in our crowded, techno-industrial society with its mega-cities, such "closeness" is largely gone and Caesar moves in to fill the void. Christians should claim that territory for Christ — not as meddlers or vigilantes, but in Christian love and service; it should be part of their witness and their walk with Jesus.

The Church should demonstrate its "saltiness" and manifest its good works in the areas of child abuse. Every congregation should determine that one of its central functions is to build strong, Christ-centered families — places of love, learning, godliness, and stability. They should help families build a "fortress" of protection against the storms of life.

Paul commands the mature women of the Church to teach the younger women how to love their children (Titus 2:3, 4). The mature man should help teach young fathers how to avoid provoking their children to wrath (Colossians 3:21) and how to raise them in the nurture and admonition of the Lord (Ephesians 6:4). God deals mercifully with us because He loves us and He remembers that we are dust (Psalm 103:14). Parents should know the capacities of their children and not expect more from them than is proper. Discipline is an expression of love and caring (Proverbs 12; 13:24; Hebrews 12:6, 7), and it must never be exercised in wrath or meanness.

God shows special concern for the fatherless (Psalm 27:10). The Hebrew word for *fatherless* indicates that the child may not necessarily be deprived of biological parents but may be destitute, lonely, helpless, and exposed to injury. As God is Father to the fatherless in their affliction (Psalm 68:5), so too must Christ's Church reach out to the fatherless in their afflictions (James 1:27). If civil magistrates remove children from their homes, the Church should be ready to place the children in Christian foster homes in which these little ones may be nurtured and brought up in the love and care of God's stewards. Tithes are to go, in part, to the relief of the fatherless (Isaiah 1:17).

"Lo," sang the sweet Psalmist, "children are an heritage of the Lord and the fruit of the womb" (Psalm 127:3). "Suffer the little children to come unto Me," called Jesus, "for of such is the kingdom of heaven" (Matthew 10:14). "And whoso shall receive one such little child in My name receiveth Me. But whoso offend one of these little ones which believe in Me, it were better for him that a millstone were hanged about his neck and that he were drowned in the depth of the sea" (Matthew 18:5, 6).

FIVE

THE COST OF
GOVERNMENT

*The cost of civil government is increasing faster than the growth in popu-
lation and personal earnings. The American eagle seems to be turning into
a wild turkey — or a voracious porker.*

Background Briefing

Civil government is one of the three basic institutions ordained by God (family, church, and state). Government is necessary and need not be evil (it is the excesses and extremes which
are evil, not the institution itself).

What is the purpose of civil government? Consider the Pre-
amble to the Constitution of these United States: "We the people
. . . in order to form a more perfect union, establish justice, insure domestic tranquility, provide for the common defense, promote the general welfare, and secure the blessings of liberty . . ."
The Apostle Paul said much the same thing, in fewer words, and
added that for that cause "we pay tribute [taxes] to whom taxes
are due" (Romans 13:1-6).

American taxpayers have reason to ask, How much is right-
fully due Caesar? How much is too much? The Conference Board
announced a few years ago that "government is the biggest
growth industry."

Government (all levels and branches of civil government —
federal, state, and local) now consumes almost one-half of the
total United States personal income. Each year the governmental machines gobble up 35 percent of the gross national product (GNP); that's all the goods and services produced in the nation

each year. And, that does not even include the deficits; we pay for that later.

Consider that it took 174 years (from 1787 to 1962) for federal spending to reach $100 billion a year. It took only the next two years to hit $200 billion, four more years to reach $300 billion, two more to top $400 billion, and only nine more years to zoom past $1 trillion. In 1987 the federal government all by itself cost over $1 trillion. Add the cost of state and local governments and the total cost of government in 1987 came to nearly $2 trillion.[1] It was higher in 1988 and it will be higher still in fiscal 1989. By then, the FICA taxes (Social Security, etc.) will be taking an additional $14 billion out of the workers' pockets.[2]

Congress blames the President, the President blames the Congress, and the taxpayer is caught in the middle. Both branches of government are to blame. In his first seven budgets (1982-1988), Reagan's requests totaled just under $6 trillion while Congress added another $150 billion.[3]

Congressional Democratic leaders have proposed a trillion dollar federal budget for 1989 with built-in tax increases of $23 billion in 1988 and a total of about $65 billion more over a three-year period. United States Senator Steve Symms (Idaho) points out that Congress has raised taxes 194 times in the past fifty-six years but spending continues to outpace income: "We have had deficits in all but eight of those fifty-six years." The record is clear: "Increased taxes do not result in decreased spending or deficits." A case in point: the largest single tax increase in history was enacted in 1982; deficits have increased since then.[4]

A trillion is a million millions. That's a thousand billions. It's a one with twelve zeros attached. (And those zeros don't stand for "nothing"; they represent a reaping of your money.) As the late United States Senator Everett Dirksen would say, "That's real money!" Look at it this way: a million seconds add up to 11.5 days; a billion seconds come to 31.7 years. But, a trillion seconds would run to 31,700 years. Suppose someone handed you a one hundred dollar bill once every second—and kept on handing you one hundred dollars every second of every day—night and day—until you had a trillion dollars. It would take 317 years. Caesar will spend that much, and more, in just one year. Washington will spend it at a rate of $136,702 every second of every working day in 1988. Just the interest on the federal debt comes to $500 million a day. Or, say you packed one trillion dollars, in one dollar bills, in fifty-foot-long railroad boxcars. It would take a string of 15,753 boxcars — 167 miles long — to hold the trillion bucks. Or, look at it end-to-end. One million dollar bills laid end-to-end would reach 96.7 miles. One billion would stretch for 96,700 miles. But a trillion? A trillion dollar bills would go on and on and on — for 96.7 million miles; far enough to reach from the earth to the sun — and then some. Finally, there's this: if you had started spending at the rate of one million dollars a day on the day Jesus was born, you'd be spending a million dollars a day, every day, year after year, until November 2704. That's $4,149 for every man, woman, and child in America. That's a trillion![5]

From 1940 to 1980 (forty years), the cost of government increased twice as fast as personal income (per capita personal income increased 1,000 percent; the per capita cost of government rose 2,000 percent). That does not include the hidden tax of inflation (loss of purchasing power). During the past ten years, the cost of government has risen three times faster than the cost of living. Until recently, inflation took almost as much as all federal personal income taxes, even more when computed on an over-the-years, compounded basis. (Inflation is now running at an annual rate of almost 4.5 percent.) The Federal Reserve is pumping funny money into the system at a rate of about 10 percent a year.[6]

When asked which level of government gives most for the tax dollar, only 24 percent of those surveyed picked the federal government. Local governments ranked best (35 percent); state governments came next (27 percent). In 1930, 34 percent of all tax revenues went to Washington; 66 percent went to state and local governments. In 1988, though, 67 percent of the total take went to Washington; only 33 percent went to the state and local governments. Thus, most tax dollars go to the least efficient level. One reason cited for the jump in federal and state spending is the aid provided to local governments (revenue sharing, grants, etc.). But, in the ten years from 1976 through 1986, while federal expenditures more than tripled (from $340 billion to $1.07 trillion) and state expenditures more than doubled (from $122.1 billion to $341.9 billion), local (own source) spending almost tripled (from ($97.4 billion to $263.5 billion). Property taxes, about 53 percent of all local government revenues, more than doubled.[7]

In 1982 President Reagan formed the Private Sector Survey on Cost Control (the Grace Commission). The commission concluded that 2,478 major cuts could be made in federal spending. In twenty-three thousand pages, it detailed how cuts could save taxpayers $424 billion over a three-year period just by implementing common-sense, good-business practices. Chairman J. Peter Grace observed: "Federal government is the worst-run enterprise in America." Mr. Grace worried that annual deficits will continue to bloat and reach $1.9 trillion by fiscal year 2000. If that were to happen, federal income taxes would have to be more than doubled.[8] "A stickler would complain that Mr. Grace overlooked a few minor details such as: To find the true deficit, one has to add in the annual amounts needed to cover Social Security and government pension obligations. If that is done, the true deficit . . . reaches an elephantine $3.8 trillion by the year 2000."[9]

About one in every five non-agricultural jobs in the United States is in government. The Grace Commission estimated that the federal government could save about $48 billion a year if it provided its employees with pay and benefits comparable to those in the private sector (sick leave, pensions, vacation, and health benefits, etc.). Speaking of pensions, United States Senator Edward Kennedy's pension fund from the federal government now totals in excess of $1.5 million. Others whose pension trusts total more than $1 million include: Senators Robert Dole and Lowell Weicker; Representatives John Dingell, Daniel Rostenkowski, and twenty-five others; and former Senators John Tower and Howard Baker.

On Christmas Eve, 1987, President Reagan signed into law the massive $604 billion omnibus appropriations bill. Congress had sent the twenty-one-hundred-page bill to his desk twenty-four hours earlier. Buried in that indefensible legislation was a little item of $250,000 "for preventing wild pigs from attacking exotic plants in Hawaii." Columnist Patrick J. Buchanan was moved to comment, "It's not the 'wild pigs' of Oaha who are America's problem; it's the wild pigs on Capitol Hill."[10] Talk about a pork barrel; the latest money-spending bill is the biggest barrel ever. Your tax money is being squandered on "fresh pork."

Here are a few more little doozies included in those appropriations: $25 million for an airport in House Speaker Jim Wright's home district (which the Federal Aviation Administration says is not needed); a guarantee that the government will buy up to $10 million worth of sunflower oil; $8 million for a School for North African Jewish (Sephardic) settlers in France (that little item—"It's only $8 million!"—caused such a storm that the sponsor, Senator Daniel Inouye (Hawaii), withdrew the request); $13 million for a privately owned dam in South Carolina for Senator Fritz Hollings; another $280,000 for Speaker Wright for a civic award achievement program for fifth to eighth graders (which the Speaker will administer); $14 million to improve the Baltimore-Washington Parkway; and $103 million to widen the Red River in Louisiana. Some of that "pork" had been rejected in previous committee hearings; they were sneaked through in the "emergency" spending bill.[11]

In 1970 $340 million was enough to fund the House and Senate for a year. Now, it costs about $2 billion a year to operate the growing bureaucracy attached to the two houses of Congress.

And, how about this: in the midst of all the talk about cutting the budget, in 1987 Congress approved hefty increases in their travel expenses, mailing funds, committee budgets, and furniture allowance—and backed into a 15.6 percent pay raise (up from $77,400 to $89,500). They also approved generous pay raises for ten thousand other top government officials including federal judges, cabinet officers, and regulatory commission members. At the same time, congressmen who took office prior to January 1980 were given the green light to transfer surplus cash from election campaign accounts to their personal accounts. "For some lawmakers, that means a seven-figure payoff."[12]

Finally, this little item: 146 dairy owners will receive $1 million each, and another 9,000 will receive in excess of $50,000 each to slaughter their cows and curb milk production. It's a five-year program under the Department of Agriculture.[13] The cost? $1.8 billion. It's your money.

Despite the talk about "cut and trim and save," it's still pretty much "tax and spend and elect." Taxpayers continue to have their pockets picked for such dubious programs as the National Endowment for the Arts, National Endowment for the Humanities, and

Institute for Museum Services. Are such expenditures essential to building a stronger republic? Are they legitimate functions of federal government? "No way!" concluded the Heritage Foundation after studying programs of the three agencies. Said Heritage, the National Endowment for the Arts might well be tagged the "National Endowment for Pornography"—it has funded "gross vulgarity, obscenity, viciousness, fierce anti-religious sentiments, contempt for democracy, and just sheer perversity."

Consider the Biblical Principles

A nation's system of paying for the costs of civil government depends largely upon its form and system of government—whether the people worship the Lord God or the state; whether they put their trust and their obedience in God and His Law-Word or Caesar's.

We may fault the politicians and bureaucrats for the nation's fiscal woes and weighty tax burdens. But, such conditions would not have developed and could not continue if alert, self-governing Christians had resisted the arrogance of officialdom and the tyranny of irresponsibility and sought to obey God's cultural mandate. A people do, in fact, reap the kind of government they resemble.

Centuries ago Sir Alex Fraser Tyler (1714-1778), professor at the University of Edinburgh, raised the warning flag:

> A democracy cannot exist as a permanent form of government. It can only exist until the voters discover they can vote themselves largesse from the public treasury. From that moment on, the majority always votes for the candidates promising the most benefits from the public treasury, with the result that a democracy always collapses over loose fiscal policies. The average age of the world's great civilizations has been two hundred years.
>
> These nations have progressed through this sequence: From bondage to spiritual faith, from spiritual faith to great courage, from courage to liberty to abundance to selfishness, from selfishness to complacency, from complacency to apathy to dependency, from dependency back again to bondage.

Is that not true? Where, do you think, this nation is on that cycle?

The only two 1988 presidential candidates who bluntly and specifically spoke out on the urgent need for fiscal integrity and a hard look at reality were voted out of the race after the first primary. People didn't want to hear the message; they got rid of the messengers. Are we truly that far gone?

Consider the following Biblical principles. They require a nation of self-reliant, compassionate people.

1. Each person is to carry his or her fair share of the cost of government (both ecclesiastical and civil). In the Old Testament, there were established two basic forms of taxation: the head tax and the tithe (the tithe was both a religious and a secular tax).

Every man over the age of twenty paid the head tax (Exodus 30:11-16). The tax was the same for all (one half shekel of silver a year). This tax was used for state affairs (courts, military needs, etc.). In addition to this head tax was the income tax (the tithe).

The tithe was not (and is not) a free-will gift; it was (and it is) a tax required by the Lord God; all are to pay it. There were two types of tithe: the "first" or regular tithe, 10 percent of a family's income, no more no less; and the "poor" tithe, to be paid every other year to help those in need. Together, the tithes came to about 15 percent of the family's income. Failure to pay the tithe was (and is) to rob God of what is His (Malachi 3:8-12).

The head tax was paid to the civil authority (the state). The tithe was paid to the local priests (Levites) and used locally. Thus, there was local authority and representation regarding the collection and expenditure of the tithe for such functions as education, welfare, and other civic functions. (This principle was adhered to in the early days of this republic; the county was the basic unit of government; taxes were paid at that level.)

2. Discriminatory taxation is prohibited (Exodus 30:15). There is to be equality of taxation. Progressive taxation (progressive tax rates, taxation based on politics) is anti-Biblical. Each individual (head of household) was to pay the same percentage of income to support the government.

3. Excessive taxation is theft (legalized plunder) and violates both the Sixth and Eighth Commandments. Excessive taxation destroys capital (the economic "seed"). If this "seed" is confiscated and spent by Caesar, it cannot be invested and employed by God's stewards to "multiply, subdue, and have dominion" for the Lord.

The purpose of taxation is to raise only those revenues needed to support the proper functions of government (justice); it is not to be used for social reform. Social reform is a part of the work of the Church and is to be based on the principles and precepts set forth in God's Word.

4. Ideally, there should be no land or property tax and no estate or inheritance tax. The earth (land) belongs to the Lord God; to tax the earth is to tax that which belongs to Him (Exodus 9:29; Psalm 24:1; 1 Corinthians 10:26). Through the tithe, God makes provision to tax income (i.e., that which the land produces) rather than the land itself. Property taxes, inheritance taxes, and estate taxes threaten the continuity of the family (God's basic social unit), the home, and the local community. Note how exorbitant property taxes today are depriving the elderly of their homes and preventing young married couples from being able to afford real estate. These taxes attack the perpetuation of the family structure. They open the door to confiscation, centralization, and control and promote speculation rather than productivity and true wealth.

5. It is anti-Biblical to tax the receipts (fruits) of crime (the sins of gambling, prostitution, sodomy, drug abuse, traffic in liquor, etc.) (Deuteronomy 23:18). Revenues from such ill-gotten gains are ill-gotten themselves and unacceptable in the eyes of God. By taxing crime, the state legitimizes the immoral, condones the sin, and encourages the sinner.

By failing to follow God's plan and purpose for society and His system of taxation, we pay the penalty of having to live under an ungodly and oppressive system of taxation. In so doing, we are forced to render in excess to Caesar. Samuel warned of these consequences when the Israelites rejected God and demanded an earthly king (1 Samuel 8:1-18).

Dr. R. J. Rushdoony once wrote: "Without the tithe, a totalitarian State progressively develops to play god over society. With the tithe, the rule of society is restored to God through His ordained law."

SIX

CRIMES AGAINST PROPERTY
(Retribution or Restitution?)

In cases of crimes against a person's property, the Bible calls for restitution. The criminal is to work and pay back the value of that which was stolen or destroyed. As our prisons become overcrowded time bombs and schools for crime, more and more civil authorities are beginning to understand that Biblical wisdom.

Background Briefing

Every three seconds in the United States, the clock ticks off one more crime against someone's property (theft, robbery, burglary, fraud, embezzlement, etc.). That's about twenty-nine thousand each and every day of the year. And, that does not include capital and other violent crimes such as murder, rape, aggravated assault, kidnapping; approximately every thirty-five seconds a crime of that type occurs. (We're dealing here only with crimes against property. For background and Biblical principles concerning capital crimes, see chapter 3 on "Capital Punishment.")

The number of crimes against property in the United States has increased dramatically during recent years. The number of inmates in state and federal prisons is now the highest in history— more than five hundred thousand. That's more than double the number incarcerated in 1974.[1] (During the twenty years, 1960 to 1980, the number of serious crimes committed in the United States increased by 322 percent and arrests rose 271 percent. However, during that period prison population grew by only 61 percent and prison capacity increased only 27 percent.)[2]

In 1985 taxpayers shelled out $13 billion for jails and prisons — an average of over $16,000 per inmate. The total cost of law enforcement was more than $40 billion.[3] There are more than 1.5 million persons employed in the various governmental justice systems (federal, state, and local); about $400,000 of those are employed in the penal (corrections) operations.[4] It is estimated that 1 out of every 250 persons is in jail or prison — the world's highest per capita ratio.[5] In 1984, 1 out of every 65 United States adults was either in jail or prison, or on parole or probation.

There is serious overcrowding in virtually all prison facilities; the federal prisons are 49 percent over capacity with 41,289 inmates.[6] All told, the prison system in the nation (all levels of government) is 114 percent of capacity.[7] "Overcrowding raises the level of tension, which people express in different ways. Some with sexual assaults, others with suicide." There were 126 suicides in United States jails in 1984.[8]

The prison population is increasing fifteen times faster than the general population.[9] States are spending or planning to spend more than $7 billion on new prisons and jails.[10] In New York State the prison population is more than forty-five hundred inmates over capacity; that state is now spending about $700 million for an additional eighty-six hundred beds. New York City is housing some of its convicts in out-of-date ferry boats which were drydocked. In Illinois the number of inmates has more than doubled in the past ten years. In California some thirty-seven thousand inmates arc crowded into facilities meant for twenty-six thousand. California is spending more than a billion dollars on new prison facilities and the commissioner of corrections figures that when those are completed, the system will still have a ten-thousand-cell shortage.[11] Charles Colson has said that "prisons are like parking lots — once built they get filled up."[12] Construction costs now run about $50,000 per cell and operating costs can exceed $50 per day per inmate. That comes to $18,000 a year, higher than the costs at many colleges.[13]

"Four out of five of the USA's twelve-year-olds will become victims of violent crimes in their lifetimes," according to a Justice Department study. "Figures like that show that crime is really a national crisis."[14] Thus, an increasing prison population is being forecast.

Most jails and prisons operate on the basis of retribution rather than restitution. In the main, prisons are time bombs (prison riots are more frequent). Thus, there is a growing demand for prison reform, for an overhauling of the system while protecting the law-abiding citizens, their families, and property.

Prisons are often termed *correctional institutions*. More and more they are becoming centers of violence — filled with racial tensions, homosexual and ethnic gangs, assaults (even murders), and drug trafficking. Human dignity goes by the boards; savagery is often widespread, indeed, commonplace. In 1983 attacks on prisoners in Texas totaled 541, compared with 171 for 1979. The latest threat in prisons is the rampant spread of AIDS due to homosexual practices and assaults. New York hands out condoms to its inmates.

Few prisons are truly "correctional." More often they are "schools for crime." Repeat offenders learn to sharpen their "skills" from older inmates; first-time inmates, many of them young (25 percent of prisoners are between the ages of eighteen and twenty-four), are thrown in with hardened criminals, emerging hardened themselves. Thus, they exit determined not to avoid crime but to avoid getting caught again. United States Senator Mark Hatfield (Oregon) calls it the "boomerang effect." "We throw the book at the criminals, they do their time in overcrowded prisons, come out, and then throw the book back at us."[15]

Taxpayers are forced to pay for convicts' housing, clothing, food, and educational and medical benefits. (In Chicago, the city spends an average of $20,000 a year to lock up an offender.) Inmates are often paid for work done in prison. Some, such as New York's infamous Son of Samuel (convicted of multiple murders), received disability benefits via the Social Security program.

Approximately 90 percent of those in jail and/or prison were found guilty of crimes against property — i.e., not violent crimes against other persons. The average sentence for such crimes ranges from three to five years. "The average criminal released from prison in 1984 served less than half his court-ordered sentence (45 percent) and an average of one year and five months behind bars, according to a United States Justice Department study.

The study said the prison terms served . . . ranged from an average of six and a half years for murder and manslaughter, to one year and four months for drug trafficking. The median time served for rape was three years and eight months; for robbery, two and a half years and burglary, one year and five months."[16]

Dependent upon prison behavior, parole is granted after about 50 percent of the sentence is served (for one reason, to relieve strain on overcrowded facilities). More than a million Americans are on probation — they are outside of prison as long as they stay out of trouble. And, in many cases, judges are refusing to sentence convicts to prison or jail because of the vile conditions there. (An individual convicted and sentenced does not lose his basic civil rights, such as personal safety and security.)

What about victims of property (non-violent) crimes? The criminal code is based on retribution (vengeance); the victim is seldom granted restitution. Generally, the victims are forced to seek restitution (if any) through civil suits which can be costly in court costs, legal fees, and time. On occasion, the victim is treated more like a criminal than the aggrieved.

Movements are now afoot to compensate victims of personal assault and, in case of homicide, the victim's survivors. Some twenty states have victim "compensation" programs; the total budgets are about $50 million in taxpayer funds. Thus, society, including the victim and his dependents, not the criminal, makes the reparations. Other programs include partial restitution from fines collected from federal offenses, forfeited bail monies, and all revenues raised by federal offenders from media presentations (books, TV program rights, etc.).[17]

More states are now emphasizing work programs, either in prison or through released time. The inmate learns a skill and at the same time helps reduce taxpayer cost of the prison system. Congress approved the interstate sale of goods made by inmates. In Kansas inmates working for a steel company paid the state $241,000 in room and board over a four-year period. In Texas convicts earned some $42.5 million in 1983. Most of those funds go to reduce the cost of operating the prison system (some inmates are allowed to keep a small amount of pocket money for personal extras — toiletries, tobacco, etc.). But, none of that money goes to make restitution to the victim of property crimes who actually helps pay the cost of imprisoning his violator.

The estimated loss suffered by victims of property crimes is almost $11 billion annually.[18] There are very few plans in process that require the felon to make restitution to victims for crimes against the individual's property. It is a part of prison reform that cries out for justice—for the victim. Many within the justice and prison systems feel that inmates convicted of crimes against property should be closely screened and permitted to work on parole with most of the earnings going to reimburse the victim or his estate.

There is a light at the end of the cell block. The omnibus crime law enacted in 1984 created the United States Sentencing Commission to draw up guidelines for uniform sentencing in federal courts. That legislation also included a resolution by United States Senators William Armstrong (Colorado) and Samuel Nunn (Georgia) calling on the commission to prescribe prison sentences for violent and serious offenders to protect the public, but to sentence non-violent and non-serious offenders to pay restitution to victims and to perform free community service.[19]

Consider the Biblical Principles

1. Civil prisons (institutions in which persons are held for a lengthy period of time) are anti-Biblical except as they apply to Satan and his demons (see I Peter 3:19; Revelation 20:2, 3). Satan has succeeded in pawning off on man the punishment God has established for him and his rebellious spirits.

There are no provisions for prisons in God's civil code. The closest thing to a prison in God's order is a temporary holding place ("ward") where bona fide suspects (indicted) are to be held pending speedy trial and swift punishment if found to be guilty (Leviticus 24:12; Numbers 15:34).

2. God's laws for punishment of crimes against property are clear. The punishment is to fit the crime; the more grievous the crime, the more severe the punishment (the law of just returns).

The guilty person is to make restitution to the victim; that is part of the penalty-payment God demands of those who break His laws (in this case, the Sixth and Eighth Commandments).

And, mark this: it is the offender, not society, who is to make restitution. God's perfect justice is thus employed: (a) the guilty person is held accountable and must really "pay" for his crime, rather than languish in prison, he is to work and earn in money or kind that which is required for reparation of what he stole; (b) the victim receives the restitution (the payment goes not to the state but to the offended); (c) would-be lawbreakers get the message in a very positive manner (Deuteronomy 19:20); and (d) the citizenry is not compelled to subsidize crime or support the criminal.

Surely the purpose and the workings of God's perfect plan in this is far more humane and equitable (and constructive) than the bankrupt and chaotic system of a humanistic state!

The Biblical laws of restitution (reparations, payment of damages) are set forth in the Scriptures. Restitution is required (a) of the thief (Exodus 22:3); (b) of one who wrongfully appropriates and/or violates another's property (Exodus 22:5); (c) of one who destroys another's property by arson (Exodus 22:6); (d) of one who loses or damages or destroys another's property while it is in his care (Leviticus 24:21); and (e) of one who assaults another individual, thus committing a crime against a person's "self"—the most basic property of all (Exodus 21:19). Generally, restitution is to be required in an amount not only equal to that which was stolen or lost or destroyed but in a larger amount sufficient to compensate for loss of time, loss of income, inconvenience, etc. The punishment of restitution may range from 100 to 400 percent of that which was stolen or destroyed.

At its root, crime against property is a crime against God as well as against the person victimized. The retribution for such a crime belongs to God ("vengeance is Mine"); the restitution (part of God's plan of redemption) is to go to both God and the victim (Leviticus 20:4-6; Numbers 5:6-8). That is God's Law. Under the laws of humanism, retribution belongs to the state, restitution is largely ignored, and God and the victim are denied.

God's perfect plan and Law provides the proper solution to man's errors and fall. In the case of property crimes, faithful adherence to His institutes would (a) resolve the problems and ease the burden of an ungodly prison system, since 90 percent of the inmates were found guilty of crimes against property and many of those could be rehabilitated through working to make restitution; (b) invoke true and complete justice by requiring the guilty to work and earn that which is required for restitution to the victim; and (c) establish a clear and consistent and compelling deterrent for those who might otherwise be tempted to engage in similar criminal acts (is that not the finest rehabilitation program — to cause the individual to repent at the thought — before the act — rather than after the crime?).

Under God's plan and Law, there would be fewer criminals and fewer victims and less burden on the taxpayer.

SEVEN

DEBTS AND DEFICITS

During recent decades, Americans and their governments have been living beyond their means and paying exorbitant interest rates. Now the nation's total debt comes to about $10 trillion — that's about $35,000 per person!

Background Briefing

In 1791, just three years after the ratification of the Constitution, the federal debt totaled $75 million. That averaged less than $19 per person — which was a goodly sum of money in those days. The debt was in essence a fiscal hangover from the War for Independence. By 1836 the debt was virtually eliminated; it was down to $38,000.

The United States began the twentieth century with a federal debt of more than $1 billion which came to almost $17 per capita. At the start of World War I, the debt had climbed to $3 billion. In 1940 the debt was $51 billion. Just the interest on that debt was $1 billion annually, equal to the total debt in 1916. By the end of World War II, the debt stood at about $256 billion; and it has been growing ever since.

Today, the federal debt is listed at about $2.5 trillion; that comes to more than $10,000 per capita.[1] That's twice as much as it was in 1980, just eight years ago. And, right now, the debt burden is increasing faster than economic growth.[2]

In 1974 the interest on the federal debt was $20 billion (about $100 per capita). By 1984 it had jumped to $125 billion, and in fiscal 1988 the interest will be about $154 billion.

Just the interest on the federal debt costs the United States taxpayers $500 million a day; that's $21 million an hour, $35,000 a minute. Say "just a second," and there goes another $5,700!

As of 1987 foreign investors held about $270 billion of the federal debt and received interest payments totaling $24 billion.[3] In 1986 the federal government's borrowing from foreign nations more than doubled to a total of $265 billion making it the world's biggest debtor nation. Only four years before that, in 1982, the United States was the world's largest creditor nation.[4] And, in 1988, foreign firms had $300 billion more invested in the United States than this nation's corporations had in investments abroad.[5] Japan has been on a buying binge in recent years. They have already gobbled up about $50 billion in United States stocks and bonds. By 1988 Japanese firms had $13 billion invested in United States real estate and brokers expect them to spend another $69 billion on land and property by 1990.[6]

The federal debt has been rising and gaining momentum since 1960. That year it totaled $290 billion. In 1970 it stood at $382 billion, and by 1980 it had reached over a trillion dollars. From then on it only picked up speed.

The deficits are the consequence of excessive spending rather than any reduction in federal revenues. "Federal revenues today are approximately 19 percent of the gross national product, slightly higher than they were in the 1960s. Federal spending, which remained less than 20 percent of the GNP in the 1960s, has grown to nearly 24 percent of the GNP in the 1980s. Given soaring spending and stable revenues, the deficit has ballooned to over 5 percent of the GNP."[7]

In fact, while revenues increased from $517 billion in 1980 to $769 billion in 1986, spending increased from $591 billion in 1960 to $990 billion by 1986. During those years, federal spending increased by 67 percent while revenues rose only 50 percent — the difference was made up by borrowing (increasing the federal debt).[8]

There was some hope that the Gramm-Rudman deficit reduction bill would put a rein on the deficits. It has had some impact (the deficit in 1986 hit $221 billion; it has been cut $50 billion since then, partly due to tax increases). But, the Reagan administration has issued budget projections for fiscal 1989 which exceed by anywhere from $36 billion to $76 billion the Gramm-Rudman goal of $100 billion. The Office of Management and Budget's projections for 1990 and beyond also exceed the deficit targets set by the Gramm-Rudman law ($64 billion by 1991 and $28 billion by 1992). The Congressional Budget Office predicts that the deficits will stay around $160 billion a year for several years.[9]

Some economists insist that the actual federal debt is closer to $9 trillion when unfunded liabilities are counted, such as Social Security payments, civil service pensions, military retirement pensions, etc.[10]

The federal debt is just a tip of the United States debt iceberg. All told, when the debts of the various governments (federal, state, and local), and corporate and personal debt are added up, it comes to more than $7 trillion — and that figures out to $35,000 for every man, woman, and child in the United States. Look at it this way: the total combined debt is more than twice the total annual gross national product. In other words, it would take all the proceeds from all the products produced and all the services performed for two years to equal all the debts in the nation.

In 1947 consumer loans equaled about 2 percent of the total personal income; in 1987 those loans had increased to about 20 percent of the total national personal income. Home mortgages are now thirty times greater than they were in 1950.[11]

At the same time that consumer debt is up, personal savings are down: savings dropped from 4.5 percent in 1986 to 3 percent of disposable personal income in 1987 and were lower for 1988.[12] Former Secretary of the Treasury William Simon warned that the government debt itself is "soaking up" about 80 percent of the net savings in the nation. Several years ago Simon expressed the belief that given the gargantuan deficits, any talk of continued rapid growth, moderate inflation, and declining interest rates was ridiculous.[13]

The National Taxpayers Union figures that if present trends continue, the total of all debt in the United States will be $13 trillion by the year 2000. Citicorp, the giant financial institution, thinks that if things go on as they are now, by the year 2000 the national debt will total $12 trillion, with interest costing about $1 trillion a year. (The Holt Advisory investment newsletter reports that American debtors are already paying creditors more than $1 trillion a year.)

Economist Sanford Kahn sees the United States, fiscal and economic future through dark glasses: "If we follow the same economic path we have for the past fifteen years, then by the year 2012, it will take the entire gross national product to service the interest only on the federal debt."[14]

John Seigenthaler, in an editorial in *USA Today*, warns, "Eventually, either we the people get our financial house in order, or we the people go to the poorhouse. That could come through hyperinflation like Brazil's 200 percent a year, or a crippling inflation like we had in the 1930s." He wrote that back in 1987; so far little has been done to set the house in order.[15]

Suppose that a husband and wife obtain a $50,000 mortgage (home loan) at 14 percent for a thirty-year term. If the mortgage should go to its full thirty years, payments on that mortgage will add up to about $200,000, principal and interest. That is more than four times the amount originally borrowed. Mortgages seldom run the full term. According to *Financial Publishing*, the average life of a mortgage is eight years. So, suppose our young family ($50,000 at 14 percent for thirty years) sold the house at the end of seven years. What was the cost of their loan? Over those eighty-four months they would have paid $49,728 on the mortgage. How much did that reduce their loan? $3,760! The rest of their seven years of payments ($45,968) went to pay the interest/usury. After seven years of paying $592 a month, they still owed $46,240 on that $50,000 mortgage. That is economic slavery.

Truth in lending: recently someone in the computer department of Wells Fargo Bank, San Francisco, typed the following note at the bottom of the bank's seven thousand monthly home-equity loan statements: "You owe your soul to the company store. Why not owe your home to Wells Fargo?" The bank executives were not amused (*USA Today*, February 18, 1988).

Can we get "our federal house" in order? Can we bring a halt — or, at least a real slowdown — to the "debilitating disease" of debt and deficits with its massive borrowing which stunts our present and mortgages the future?

The Heritage Foundation, a conservative Washington think-tank, has one agenda for cutting the Fed's spending binge. Its seventy-five recommendations for spending cuts and privatization would save $122 billion. Here are a few: (1) cut our United Nations contributions and save almost $500 million a year; (2) require employable welfare and food stamp recipients (except mothers with children under seven) to participate in work programs, and save $300 million; (3) cut civil service pay and make it more comparable with private sector schedules and save $2.5 billion; (4) expand contracting out those government services which can be done better and cheaper by the private sector and save $3 billion; (5) cut subsidized housing, convert subsidies into a voucher system and a "right to buy" program so that tenants could purchase their homes and save $2.5 billion.[16]

Others suggest closing obsolete military bases, freezing cost-of-living adjustments on entitlement programs and pensions which would save $20 billion, or slashing direct payments to farmers which cost $23 billion in 1987 while providing only seventeen cents per dollar to poor farmers. There are other cuts that could be relatively painless in the $250 billion of discretionary spending lumped in that $604 billion omnibus appropriations bill (passed and signed all within a space of twenty-four hours).[17]

There are two other important items:

(1) The line-item veto would empower the President to "blue pencil" budget items which are patently ridiculous and wasteful. Every President since Woodrow Wilson has called for the line-item veto and many states now employ it. But, Congress obstinately refuses to take that prudent step. There are those who believe that a President already has such power. They insist that Article I, Section 7, Clause 3 of the Constitution already gives it to the Chief Executive: It provides that "every Order, Resolution or Vote" must be presented for the President's signature or veto. As the *Wall Street Journal* urged, "It is time for some leader to lead, for some President to act like a President."[18]

(2) A constitutional amendment requiring that Congress and the Executive Office adopt a balanced budget each year would also help. A *New York Times*/CBS News poll taken in 1987 found that 85 percent of Americans favor such an amendment.[19] If there is a risk in calling a constitutional convention on such a measure, then the voters should demand that their congressmen bring such an amendment before the states for ratification. (Thirty-two of the required thirty-four states have passed resolutions calling on Congress to do just that.)

The swelling tides of a fiscal red sea are threatening to engulf the economic and fiscal survival of the republic. But, will the

Congress act? That does not seem likely. The Grace Commission's recommendations are mute testimony to that: so far most of its twenty-four hundred-plus ways to cut the fat out of federal spending lie gathering dust in Washington. And, when United States Senator Phil Gramm (Texas) found ways to cut $285 million out of the budget (for such "emergencies" as studying weeds and eliminating the ceiling on loans to beekeepers and sending taxpayers' money to countries in southern Africa), his bill was voted down by the Senate 61-to-33.[20]

Alfred L. Malabre, Jr., in *Beyond Our Means,* is afraid that little or nothing will be done to stem the deadly flow of the nation's economic lifeblood. Among the scenarios he sees coming is one he fears is the most likely: "I believe that there's a 50 percent chance that our economy will avoid both hyperinflation and . . . severe, prolonged deflation . . . and instead will enter a new era of intensifying governmental regulation over the economy."[21]

In other words, fascism.

Consider the Biblical Principles

God's Word calls debt a form of slavery: "The borrower is servant to the lender" (Proverbs 22:7). If we are truly His, we cannot be slaves to any man or men or institution (public or private). Debt permits the past to govern the present and to dictate the future. We cannot (should not) be enslaved to debt because the present and the future belong to Christ—and we are called to be free men and women in Him (John 8:36).

The Bible recognizes that debt may be necessary in times of acute distress and emergency, but not for luxuries or pleasures. The Scriptures set definite time limits on such debt: six years. By the seventh year debts are to be paid off, or forgiven. This in no way relieves the debtor of his debt. "The wicked borrow and pay not again" (Psalm 37:21a). Through such a sabbatical rule, the Lord has established a system to keep individuals from debt and slavery.

God's Word prohibits both perpetual debt and multiple indebtedness. We are not to make borrowing a habit; we are not to go into debt beyond our ability to pay the debt within the prescribed time. And, we are not to pledge as collateral that which has already been pledged. Thus does God seek to protect both the debtor and the creditor.

The present (Babylonian) credit economy (a calculated debt system) is built on the ungodly, anti-Biblical concept that the individual, and the nation, need not worry about perpetual debt or multiple indebtedness: we should live for today and not lay aside that which will see us through tomorrow. Thus is laid the foundation for Caesar's growing power and control. The system, in fact, encourages debt and caters to the "live now, buy now" appetite (interest is deductible; it's not what you owe but how it fits into your monthly budget—meaning, pay the interest and don't worry about the principal). Thus, the debtor is seduced into the world of perpetual economic servitude.

Writing in *Economics, Money and Banking,* Dr. E. L. Hebden Taylor described the Babylonian system of economics based on debt and high rates of interest (20 percent). The entire Babylonian concept of social control and imperialism rested on usury (as it does in today's debt-usury system). Dr. Taylor reminded his readers that "it is not surprising that Babylon the Great, the harlot, is the type in the Book of Revelation of the one-world order which shall seduce all nations." Revelation 18:4 calls upon God's people to come out from such a world system and not be partakers of its sin.

In Deuteronomy 28:44, Moses warned of the consequences of debt. "He shall lend to you and you shall not lend to him: he shall be the head, and you shall be the tail." Holding an individual in debt holds him down; that is a form of economic bondage. The fetters of inflation are one device of such bondage; usury is another. Part of the material cost of debt is the usury exacted. In many cases, the compounded interest exceeds the principal which was borrowed.

The Bible tells us that we are not to take usury (interest) when we loan to a brother in need. It also makes clear that when the collateral is a necessity of life, it must be returned to the debtor should he need it to sustain life or earn a living (Exodus 22:25-27). A reasonable charge may be made for the use of money in the normal course of business transactions; the individual is entitled to a fair return on his property (Luke 19:23; Matthew 25:27).

The evil of taking monetary advantage of a person in distress is clearly prohibited (Deuteronomy 15 and Leviticus 25). The evil of those who take advantage of a community or a nation (its citizens) in distress or peril by charging usury on the loan-money needed to protect or rebuild a nation is also prohibited (Nehemiah 5:1-13).

When God gave His chosen people a land "to possess it," He also drove the rebellious out of it because they disobeyed His laws. Among the reasons for their expulsion was "You have taken usury and increase and you have greedily gained of your neighbors by extortion and have forgotten Me, said the Lord God" (Ezekiel 22:12-15).

And what did our Savior, our Lord and Master, say about usury? "And if you lend to them of whom you hope to receive, what thanks have you? For sinners also lend to sinners, to receive as much again. But, love your enemies and do good, and lend, hoping for nothing again and your reward shall be great, and you shall be children of the Highest" (Luke 6:34, 35).

In summary, debt should be resisted by Christians. We must reject the debt economy and shun debt and usury, putting our trust in God. When an emergency or unforeseen and dire circumstance makes debt a necessity, it should be on the shortest term possible and paid in full in the appointed term. Perpetual debt is prohibited. All that we have is His; we are His servants, His stewards. What we have is to be used for Him. We are not free to serve the Lord when we mortgage ourselves, our labors, and our property to others. We must not become slaves to others because we are slaves to Jesus Christ.

The Apostle Paul reminds us of the one approved debt: "Owe no man anything but to love one another" (Romans 13:8). Such a debt is always due — and payable. As is the greatest debt of all — our forever debt to Him who died on Calvary that we might have life eternal.

EIGHT

DEALING WITH GOD'S ENEMIES

While the United States taxpayers carry the burden of some $300 billion a year, mostly to meet the threat of Soviet domination, businessmen and politicians make covenants with the "Evil Empire."

Background Briefing

According to United States Senator William Armstrong (Colorado), "The great irony for Americans, who will be asked to tighten their belts in order to pay for our defense needs, is that much of the additional money . . . is required to offset Soviet weapons that probably could not have been built without our assistance."

Richard Lessner, an editorial writer for *The Arizona Republic,* agreed. He set out to learn just what United States business companies held export licenses to the Soviet Union and what they were selling. Lessner learned that the United States Commerce Department keeps secret the identity of those firms. He and his newspaper sought the information under the Freedom of Information Act.

The government brought in eight federal attorneys to stop Lessner's search for the facts. Two federal courts upheld the Commerce Department's argument that the information regarding export licenses and shipper's permits to the USSR is exempt from Freedom of Information requests. It was a two-year battle which cost the *Republic* some $20,000. In the end, Lessner and the newspaper lost. "As taxpayers you and I are expected to ante up about $300 billion annually for defense, primarily to indemnify our national security against the Soviet Union, but our government will not reveal who among us is trading with the enemy."[1] Finally Patrick Murphy, editor of *The Arizona Republic,* wrote, "We therefore don't know what these United States businesses are selling to the Soviet Union, and can't judge whether Americans are figuratively selling the Soviets the rope they may use to hang us someday."[2]

Consider for a moment the US-USSR Trade and Economic Council (USTEC). Its specific aim is not only to give United States aid and trade to the Soviets but also to work to shape our national policies toward that objective. USTEC has a Soviet co-chairman and a United States co-chairman, and sixty directors split evenly between the United States and USSR members. "Fully one-third of its [USTEC's] members have been identified as known or suspected KGB agents."[3] "Some of the chamber's trade promotion activities involve exploiting or misleading Western business and government leaders by (1) systematically using international trade exhibitions and seminars for economic collection and (2) falsifying end-user documentation during inspection of Western equipment coming into the USSR."[4]

Now, think about this: William C. Verity, Jr., President Reagan's personal choice to be Secretary of Commerce, was a founder and longtime co-chairman of USTEC. (Secretary of State George Shultz is also a founding member of USTEC.) The organization is so secret that its list of directors and members is not available (even though it is a Section 501(c)(6) tax-exempt organization which, by law, must make its IRS tax forms available to the public, including a list of officers and directors).[5]

USTEC is pushing for most-favored-nation status for the USSR which makes it eligible for Export-Import Bank and International Monetary Fund loans, membership in GATT (General Agreement on Trade and Tariffs), and repeal of the Jackson-Vanik Amendment which ties relations with the USSR to a relaxation of its restrictions on Jewish emigrants.

These are virtually the same concessions General Secretary Mikhail Gorbachev sought during his recent Washington summit visit. (See chapter 16 on the "INF Treaty.")

Anthony Sutton has claimed that 95 percent of the technology used by the Soviet military-industrial complex came from the West—especially the United States. The basis for his assertion is detailed documentation based on extensive research (presented in his three-volume *Western Technology and Soviet Economic Development*).

Writing in the Heritage Foundation study, "The Economics of Détente," Miles M. Costick concluded that "it seems certain that a transfer of American technology to the USSR has primarily benefited the Soviet military-industrial complex and as a consequence enhanced Soviet military power."[6] Author Steven V. Cole asks, "When the history of this century is written, will the United States be seen as a nation that sold its enemies the means with which to destroy it?"[7]

Commenting on the strict export controls to the USSR and Soviet-bloc nations, a senior White House aide said, "We've only succeeded in losing markets to our allies who do not operate by the same rules."[7] Thus, under then-National Security Council Adviser and now Secretary of Defense Frank C. Carlucci, the Reagan administration began to determine which controls could be eliminated. Representative Don Bonker (Washington) warned that if the White House failed to act, Congress would take the lead in revising the policy. Congressman Bonker's district included the giant Boeing Airplane Corporation.[8]

At the White House, after the attack on Korean Airlines Flight 007, in which 269 innocent victims, including United States Representative Larry McDonald, were murdered, top aides decided not to cancel the sale of pipeline equipment to the Soviets. They feared to do so might lose votes in Peoria, the home of Caterpillar, the maker of that equipment.[9]

And Don Bell reported that even while United States Marines were being killed in Beirut by Soviet and Syrian-backed Druze, then-Secretary of Agriculture John Block and a delegation of American agri-businessmen and farm equipment manufacturers were in Moscow selling combines, reapers, and other farm machinery—and making plans to finance and construct factories in the USSR for the manufacture of other farm equipment.[10]

President Reagan at one time assailed the Soviet Union as the "focus of evil"—"an evil empire"—in the modern world. He insisted that he had "significantly slowed the transfer of valuable free world technology to the Soviet Union." But, the United States Commerce Department data reveal an increase in all types of trade with the USSR—plus continued bailouts on loan defaults, etc. Columnist William Safire reported that the Reagan administration had actually opened the "flood-gates" of trade. Wrote Safire: "It's not merely 'business as usual' [with the USSR] but more business than ever."[11]

That "more business than ever" took a big leap as a result of Gorbachev's December 1987 visit to Washington. "More than a dozen major United States firms signed large contracts for joint ventures with the Soviets."[12] And a Commerce official confirmed that there had been "a gush of applications for export licenses, roughly double or triple the same period in 1986. For every firm that has already signed with Gorbachev Incorporated, there are now several companies in line hoping for their spot on the gravy train."[13]

Can we, as a nation, see the Soviets as a real and present danger and then rationalize selling them four million metric tons of subsidized wheat and expect the free world to find any kind of credibility in our foreign policy? Is it any wonder that the Western world is confused? And what must the tax-burdened families in this country think when their government makes "it possible for a Soviet housewife to buy American-produced food at lower prices than an American housewife"?[14]

Recent events, particularly over the control of nuclear weapons, have shaken the confidence of many thoughtful friends of America. . . . the truth is that the allies are . . . exasperated with the United States.[15]

The president's new message (of friendly competition with the USSR) does not fit the old role or the old Reagan. It involves too much contradiction with too many past positions. . . . He spoke too often about the Soviet expansionist tendencies and the necessity for strength. . . . The old message not only criticized specific arms agreements, it criticized the "arms control" approach to American and Western security. . . . Our allies are dismayed by Reagan's new enthusiasm.[16]

How do you explain to the Afghanis this new-found willingness to jump in bed with the Soviets? To those who witnessed Soviet troops trapping 105 Afghani women and children in an underground irrigation channel and then flooding the ditch with kerosene and setting it on fire?[17] To those who have seen their children's hands blown off by the insidious Soviet butterfly mines which look like toys and are dropped from planes and helicopters? Are the children of Afghanistan really such a threat to the USSR?

What must the "freedom fighters" in Central America think when the United States rails against the "evil empire" establishing bases on this continent while cutting off military aid to the Contras and at the same time increasing trade and aid to the Soviets?

In 1981 United States exports to Communist-bloc nations totaled $6.5 billion. Under Carter they fell to $2.2 billion a year; under Ford, to $1.9 billion a year; and under Nixon, to $442 million a year. Under the Reagan administration, the exports zoomed and have averaged more than $2.5 billion a year.

In 1986 the Soviet bloc received about $2 billion a month in loans from the West. According to the Organization for Economic Cooperation and Development, "the Soviet bloc now has an estimated indebtedness of $127 billion to the Western banks," including many banks in the United States.[18] "Our own banks, on the one hand, make loans to the Soviets, while our taxpayers have to support growing budget deficits to upgrade the military posture of the United States to counter the adventurism which is funded by those Western banks."[19]

On February 19, 1987, President Reagan restored most-favored-nation trade status to Communist Poland which in effect bolsters a regime that tramples on the rights of the Polish citizenry. This made the Communist regime eligible for United States government credits despite the fact that Poland already owes the United States $2 billion which it is unwilling to repay.[20]

The Soviets had to rely on Western loans to support their commitments to Nicaragua, Vietnam, Cambodia, Syria and South Africa Communists, among others. Consider the absurdity of the United States policy in Central America: while President Reagan insists on getting additional tens of millions of dollars

for the Contra fighters, the Soviet Communists are able to borrow tens of billions of dollars from Western banks which help
finance the Sandinistas.[21]

And what of the terms of those loans? Most of them are
made at about 7.5 percent. Let the American taxpayer try to
match that when he goes to borrow money.

James Giffin is a long-time friend of newly-appointed Commerce Secretary William Verity and a fellow-traveler on East-
West trade. When asked, on the "Today Show," whether the
United States really wanted to make the Soviet Union an economic superpower, he responded, "I think we do."[22]

Gorbachev knows he cannot be successful in rescuing a failing Soviet economy without further and continued massive
amounts of Western aid. And once again, the United States and
the Western bankers, who have breathed life into a dying empire
since 1917, seem ready to come to the aid and comfort of the "evil
empire."[23] Apparently, to them, business and profits are more
important than the lives of those who may someday be called
upon to save the world from total Communist domination.

When Congress voted $8.4 billion more for the International
Monetary Fund (IMF), the majority defeated a move to restrict
the allocation of those funds to non-Communist governments.
(In November 1983 Congress approved a $25 billion foreign aid
bill — after deleting language to prevent any funds from going to
Communists nations.)

Leonid Brezhnev once explained détente to the Warsaw Pact
nations: "We need their [United States and the Western world]
credits, their technology and their agriculture." Why? Because,
said Brezhnev, "we are going to continue massive military programs and by the middle '80s we will be in a position to return to
a much more aggressive foreign policy designed to gain the upper hand."

Richard Nixon, in his book, *Real Peace,* reminded his readers
that, following the Russian Revolution, Western corporations
rushed to do business with the USSR. Nixon wrote: "That first
round of economic cooperation in the 1920s did not bring the
West and the Soviets closer together. It did help turn the Soviet
Union into a much stronger adversary. . . . by trading with an

aggressive, expansionist power you are fueling a fire that could eventually consume you." Yet, it was the Brezhnev-Nixon grain deals which helped prevent a severe Soviet crisis from 1971 to 1976 while the USSR was "swallowing up countries from Nicaragua to Angola to Afghanistan."[24]

Consider the Smoot-Hawley Tariff Act of 1930. It prohibits importation of products from any country if the products are manufactured by slave labor. United States Customs Commissioner William von Raab tagged at least thirty-six different Soviet imports made by forced labor. Von Raab asked Secretary George Shultz to ban importation. Shultz failed to act on von Raab's recommendation. (The Committee for Defense of Human Rights in the Soviet Union claims tens of thousands of prisoners are serving long terms in USSR slave labor camps.)[25]

Proponents of trade with the USSR say it's a key part of promoting détente. " 'Rubble-happy' businessmen engage in a propaganda campaign to legitimize US-USSR trade," reported the Washington weekly, *Human Events.*

In 1981 Brezhnev boasted: "We are achieving with détente what our predecessors have been unable to achieve using the mailed fist." V. I. Lenin put the matter in (Soviet) focus:

> The capitalists of the world and their governments, in pursuit of . . . the Soviet market, will close their eyes to the higher reality and thus will turn into deaf-mute blind men. They will extend credits, which will strengthen . . . the Communist party . . . and, giving us the materials and technology we lack, they will restore our military industry, indispensable for our future victorious attack on our suppliers. In other words, they will labor for the preparations for their own suicide.

Major American firms which over the years have sold or helped sell vital technological equipment or have had science and technology transfer contracts with the Soviet Union or its Warsaw Pact nations and satellites include: Allen-Bradley (machine tools); Armco Steel; Bechtel (construction); Boeing; Borg-Warner (machine tools); Chase Manhattan Bank (loans and financial arrangements); Clark Equipment (machine tools); Control Data (advanced computers); Dow Chemical; El Paso Natural Gas (gas technology); Exxon; General Dynamics (aeronautical technology); General Electric; Gulf Oil (James E. Lee, Chairman of the Board of Gulf, claims a personal relationship with God: "I turn to His Word every day for guidance and inner strength." Gulf, along with Texaco, Mobil, and Cities Service is a major proponent of United States trade with Marxist Angola, a "Communist surrogate"); Hewlett Packard; Honeywell (computers); IBM; ITT; Kaiser Aluminum & Chemicals; Litton Industries; Lockheed; McDonnell Douglas (aircraft); Monsanto (chemicals); Occidental Petroleum; Pepsi-Cola; Reynolds Metals; Sikorsky Aircraft; Sperry Rand (machine tools); Stanford Research Institute; Swindler-Dressler (trucks built at its Kama River plant were used in both Vietnam and Afghanistan); Tenneco (chemicals); Textron; Union Carbide; and Xerox (electronics).

Those pushing trade with the Soviets argue, "If we don't sell it to them, someone else will." What are the fruits of such pragmatism, according to Lenin? "The bourgeoisie [citizens of free societies] will sell us rope; and then we will let the bourgeoisie hang itself."

The sale of sensitive hi-tech equipment is especially treacherous. United States firms are often the only source; thus, to sell such unique and advanced equipment or know-how to the Soviets is, as Joel Skoussen has said, "technological treason." The nation was indignant when it learned that Toshiba, of Japan, had sold the Soviets technology which makes it possible for their submarines to be virtually undetectable. Several congressmen held a Toshiba smashing rally in which equipment made by that company was smashed with sledge hammers. Yet, Congress has done little about American firms which have engaged in deals with the Soviets which are even more damaging to the defense of the nation.

Consider sales to the Soviets of just four types of hi-tech items. These enabled the USSR to develop both first-strike capabilities and advanced nuclear defense management systems:

- The Soviet defense management system was designed by and utilizes American-made computers (IBM 370 and Control Data Corp.'s Cyber 73/76).

- Generations of Soviet ICBM missiles could not operate without their US-designed micro-chips and integrated systems which insure reliability and pinpoint accuracy.

- Centalign-B micro-precision ball-bearings from the United States enabled the USSR to perfect inertial guidance and separation systems for its multi-warheaded ICBM/MIRVs (Bryant Chucking Grinding Co).

- State of the art anti-submarine equipment gave the Soviets capabilities which exceeded those of the United States (Geospace Corp.)

Advocates of trade with Moscow cry, "free trade." Joel Skousen, of the Conservative National Committee, retorts: "The right to defend oneself against an enemy of our freedom is a higher principle than the right of free trade."

Recently the Soviets boasted that their latest-generation ICBMs are so accurate that one traveled thousands of miles and hit its target—a small wooden peg. How did they do it? Experts say they purloined United States technology. And what about proliferation of chemical and biological terror weapons by the USSR? The United States continues to export vital chemical and biological agents and gene-splicing data to Soviet-bloc nations.

Consider the Biblical Principles

Clearly, a nation which seeks to honor and serve the Lord can have no business with an ungodly regime. Does this apply? "What fellowship has righteousness with unrighteousness, and what communion has light with darkness?" (2 Corinthians 6:14). Or is it that as a nation we can no longer be counted righteous, that our light has dimmed almost to darkness? Is that one reason that we find the "enemies are [also] men within our own house" (Micah 7:6b)?

God's Word tells us that he who is joined (has relations) with a harlot becomes one with the harlot (1 Corinthians 6:15). What becomes of a nation which does business with God's avowed enemies?

Those who would trade with the Soviets say it's for the money. Paul told us that it is the love of money that is the root of all the evil (1 Timothy 6:10). Remember the parable of the rich man whose barns were full to overflowing? He would build bigger barns to store his goods; he would take his ease and eat, drink, and be merry. "You fool," said the Lord. "This night your soul shall be required of you" (Luke 12:16-20). The soul of a nation is its integrity (or lack of integrity), its moral (or amoral) standards, its obedience (or disobedience) to God. When? When will the soul be required of this nation?

The followers of Jesus Christ are in this world to be His servants and His vice-regents in the here and now. We are to be effective in His work, thus we must be aware of and seek to exert a godly influence on social, economic, and (geo)political affairs and policies. Is this not a reason God gave our forefathers a free nation and representative government? Does that not make us accountable as to what we do and how we exercise those blessings? Because we are His and because He is our King, we must give preeminence to Him and to His Word in all things and above all powers and must seek to influence our elected officials to do the same.

What does God demand of His people in regard to those nations that are His enemies? What does He command regarding those that have set themselves against the Living God as a matter of their national policy? This:

> Should you help the ungodly, and love them that hate the Lord? Therefore is wrath upon you from before the Lord (2 Chronicles 19:2).

> Surely Thou wilt slay the wicked, O God: depart from me therefore, ye bloody men. For they speak against Thee wickedly, and Thine enemies take Thy name in vain. Do I not hate them, O Lord, that hate Thee? And am I not grieved with those that rise up against Thee? I hate them with a perfect hatred: I count them mine enemies (Psalm 139:19-22).

Those who are His are not to do business with or make covenants with God's enemies. Further, God's people in a nation must not make or condone covenants with His enemies. If we do, if we turn from Him, will His wrath not be upon us? To be yoked with the forces of evil in any manner is to disobey God. Such alliances and/or agreements deny His Supreme Sovereignty, place trust in the pacts and treaties of fallen men, and place such alliances ahead of covenants with the King of Kings and His assured fruits of faith and obedience (trust and obey!). Do not those who make agreements with the Soviet Union in essence put the Communist Manifesto on a par with, or even above, the Christian Manifesto? (Psalm 2; Acts 4:24-31).

God's Word would seem to make it very clear: His people are not to be yoked with or trust in those who compromise with God's enemies (Exodus 23:32; Deuteronomy 7:2; 2 Corinthians 6:14). To do so is to make "a covenant with death and with hell" (Isaiah 28:15).

> I have hated them that regard lying vanities; but I trust in the Lord (Psalm 31:6).

> It is better to trust in the Lord than to put confidence in man. It is better to trust in the Lord than to put confidence in princes [ungodly rulers/leaders] (Psalm 118:8, 9).

> So are the paths of all that forget God; and the hypocrite's hope shall perish: whose hope shall be cut off, and whose trust shall be a spider's web (Job 8:13, 14).

Our nation and its leaders would do well to take note: For disobeying God, and for making a covenant with God's enemy, Ahab was eventually killed in battle and the Israelites were taken into captivity (1 Kings 20:42).

Who, today, is numbered among God's enemies? What political system denies God and persecutes His people? Surely the USSR — the Soviet Union, Marxism, the Communist Party (as distinguished from the Russian people) — must be considered one of God's arch enemies.

"The struggle against the Gospel and Christian legend must be conducted ruthlessly and with all the means at the disposal of Communism."[26]

Heed the words of V. I. Lenin: "Atheism is a natural and inseparable part of Marxism, of the theory and practice of socialism." And these words of Josef Stalin: "We have deposed the czars of the earth; we shall now dethrone the Lord of heaven."

Is not the official Communist position plain? The state is god. The One True God must bow to the Kremlin-god. Communism is anti-Christ. "We hate Christians and Christianity. Even the best of them must be considered our worst enemies.

Christian love is an obstacle to the development of the revolution. Down with love of one's neighbor! What we want is hate. . . . Only then can we conquer the universe."[27]

Communism is one of the most virulent, most militant anti-Christian systems in the world today. It denies God; it mocks God; it persecutes His people.

In the USSR, from 1918 to 1977, some 250,000 clergy were liquidated, 88,000 religious buildings were destroyed, $4 billion in church funds confiscated. As early as 1975, *Time* magazine reported that:

> Though the plight of Soviet Jews and intellectuals is far better publicized in the West, Baptists have suffered every bit as much. At least seven hundred have been jailed and one civil rights leader reports that Baptists have comprised more than one third of the known political prisoners during the past two decades.

"And another, a red horse, went out; and to him who sat on it, it was granted to take peace from the earth, and that men should slay one another: and a great sword was given him" (Revelation 6:4). Consider the cost of Communism's red ride across the world: Between 21 million and 32 million people were slaughtered as Communism was established in the USSR. Fifteen thousand Poles were exterminated in the Warsaw uprising of 1944. In the 1956 Hungarian Revolt, more than 15,000 were killed. In the three years following the Communist takeover of Czechoslovakia, 152,000 Czechs were executed or sent to slave-labor camps and many died there. In Lithuania, 1.2 million were liquidated or deported during the first fifteen years of Communist rule. In China, more than 64 million have lost their lives under Communism. In Vietnam, Communists killed 700,000 persons from 1953 to 1959. In Cambodia, between 1 million and 2 million persons were murdered in just two years of Communist-mandated genocide. All told, between 150 and 200 million persons have been liquidated since that red horseman started its sweep across the earth—"and a great sword was given him."

Since Marxists/Communists are avowed enemies of God, are they not also the enemies of God's people? How, then, can a nation whose President and Congress proclaim The Year of The Bible and acknowledge The Bible as 'the rock on which our republic rests'—how can such a nation permit its Chief Executives, its public officials, its business elite, and its mega-bankers to make covenants that yoke the United States with its avowed enemy?

May we not see a parallel between those who do business with the Soviets today and the money-changers and usurers in the time of Nehemiah? Are they not similar to those who sought to profit from the citizens of Jerusalem who worked and sacrificed to rebuild the city's walls/defenses (Nehemiah 5)? And did not Nehemiah find it necessary to "set a great assembly against" such men? Did he not realize, then—and should we not realize, now—that (as Micah wrote) "a man's enemies are the men of his own house" (Micah 7:6)?

> Woe unto them that call evil good . . . that put darkness for light . . . Which justify the wicked for reward. . . . Therefore as the fire devoureth the stubble, and the flame consumeth the chaff, so their root shall be as rottenness, and their blossom shall go up as dust; because they have cast away the Law of the Lord of Hosts, and despised the Word of the Holy One of Israel (Isaiah 5:20-24).

How then should God's people—those who would obey Him and serve Him—seek true security? With whom shall we make a covenant for godly peace and safety?

Well, how about following the example of Joshua? "But, as for me and my house, we will serve the Lord" (Joshua 24:15). "And Joshua said unto the people, You are witnesses against yourselves that you have chosen you the Lord, to serve Him" (Joshua 24:22). "And the people said unto Joshua, the Lord our God will we serve, and His voice will we obey" (Joshua 24:24).

"Blessed is the nation whose God is the Lord!"

NINE

EVOLUTION VS. CREATION

Even though Darwin's "Devil's Gospel" is flawed with gaps and missing links, its adherents demand exclusive rights to our public schools.

Background Briefing

The state of Louisiana enacted a "balanced treatment" law in 1981 requiring its public schools to teach scientific evidences for both creation and evolution. In a poll of its members, the American Bar Association (ABA) found that 63 percent of its members "believe there is no First Amendment obstacle to teaching creationism in the public schools."[1] But the law was challenged by the American Civil Liberties Union (ACLU) and struck down as unconstitutional by the United States Court of Appeals for the Fifth Circuit. When the case (*Aguillard v. Edwards*) reached the United States Supreme Court, it was again struck down.

In 1981 Arkansas also enacted a law requiring both creation and evolution be taught in public schools. A federal district judge ruled that the law was unconstitutional. Also in 1981 a California Superior Court ruled that the state must advise school districts that evolution is to be presented as theory, not fact. Judge Irving Perluss ruled that religious beliefs must be respected. In recent years some twenty states have had bills before their legislatures requiring that state schools give equal time and emphasis to creation science.

Who are the major and most persistent opponents of teaching creationism in public schools? The ACLU and the American Humanist Association, an atheistic organization. The National

Academy of Sciences distributed a twenty-eight-page book urging science teachers not to teach creationism; it rejected the idea of "balanced" teaching.

By contrast, Cuyahoga Valley Christian Academy, Cuyahoga Falls, Ohio, adopted the equal-time policy for teaching creationism. Academy President, Alex Ward, explained: "We examine man's theories through the lens of Scripture. If we find they are not in harmony, we reject man's theory and accept God's version." Ward adds, "We do believe there are absolutes from the Word of God" and "one of those absolutes is a creation that took place in seven twenty-four-hour days."[2]

Dr. Jerry Bergman, who lost his teaching position at Bowling Green [Ohio] State University because he wrote a paper defending a Scriptural view of creation, found that evolutionist-humanists exercise almost total censorship in regard to books and teaching materials on creationism. His research led him to conclude: "Creationist literature has been self-censored from nearly every major secular university in America. Creationist theories are censored in the schools, in the media, and in textbooks published by major publishers. Libraries, even if they want to, find it difficult to stock creationist books.[3] Yet," reported Bergman, ". . . hundreds of books and monographs on creationism are in print, actually more exist in support of creationism than evolution."[4]

Responding to such obvious censorship, Dr. Richard Bliss of the Institute for Creation Research charged: "What the anti-creationists are doing to the minds of Americans today is reprehensible in that they are moving to have our children believe what science has proven to be a fantasy."[5]

Evolution was a part of the official dogma of the Third Reich. Anthropologist Arthur Keith observed, "The German Führer . . . has consciously sought to make the practice of Germany conform to the theory of evolution." In Germany the leaders of the eugenics movement (which was totally interwoven into the Nazi system), using evolution as their justification, caused sterilization laws and immigration restriction laws to be enacted.[6] Ed Garret wrote, in an article in *Creation Ex Nihilo*, "Hitler's case teaches us the danger of denying the existence of a sovereign Creator."[7]

Karl Marx was so impressed with Charles Darwin's *Origin of the Species* and other works that he offered to dedicate the English version of his *Das Kapital* to Darwin. Marx believed Darwin had provided "scientific proof" of his own theories.[8] Many see in this fact the master link which binds socialists to evolution.

Advocates of creation science say they take the scientific approach rather than a Biblical stance because the courts have ruled that the Bible is not admissible in public classrooms. Thus, they argue that if creation were presented as a Biblical truth, their case would take on an additional and difficult legal burden. In their arguments before the United States Supreme Court, creationist attorneys assured the court that creationism did not imply a Creator; creation science is simply the insistence that the world came into being through one, immediate creative act rather than through an evolutionary process.

Others, who espouse the Biblical truths of creation, question whether that approach to creation science is an expediency which ultimately denies God before men. God's Word warns against seeking to do God's work through deceitful means (Jeremiah 48:10) and enjoins God's people to seek to please Him rather than men.

The controversy over evolution vs. creation centers basically in three areas: constitutional, academic, and scientific. Here's how the battle shapes up:

Constitutional: Evolutionists contend that teaching creation in state schools violates the First Amendment. They argue that it would be tantamount to "teaching religion." The ABA survey indicated that only 28 percent of the lawyers in the United States agree with them.[9] Creationists respond that the Constitution demands "neutrality" in regard to religion. They contend that neutrality is violated by the exclusive teaching of the theory of evolution because it is a basic tenet of the religion of humanism.

Indeed, evolution is a system of faith. Those who have embraced it have built their own religion, a religion which requires an incredible amount of faith. "Evolutionists reject the inclusion of a Creator or Christianity. . . . but isn't that hypocritical? Isn't evolution a religion by definition as well?"[10]

In addition, from the beginning the founders of evolution were anti-Christian. Darwin once called evolution his "Devil's

Gospel." He rejected God and saw his writings as a sacred text for the secular religions of atheism, agnosticism, and humanism.[11] T. H. Huxley, Darwin's early huckster, constantly belittled Christ and Christianity. Sir Julian Huxley boasted that "evolutionary man can no longer take refuge . . . [in] the arms of a divinized father-figure whom he has himself created."[12] The vast majority of those who propound evolution today continue to be anti-Christian.

Conversely, some of the historically great scientists have been devout Christians: Francis Bacon, father of the scientific method of study ("there are two books laid before us to study, to prevent our falling into error; first, the volume of the Scriptures, which reveal the will of God; then the volume of the Creatures, which express His power"); John Ray, the great botanist ("the physical universe is the work created by God at the first . . ."); Robert Boyle, the renowned chemist ("God, indeed, gave motion to matter"); Louis Pasteur; and Lord Kelvin, to name a few.[13]

Today, more and more scientists are concluding that "the evolutionary record leaks like a sieve. . . . There are so many flaws in Darwinism that one can wonder why it . . . is still endemic today."[14] "I believe God's thought controls our three-dimensional world from outside of the three-dimensions."[15] Dr. Colin Patterson, a world-renowned evolutionist at the London Museum of Natural History, now has labeled evolution "anti-science."[16] Dr. Pierre P. Grasse, one of the world's greatest living biologists has said of evolution, "Through use and abuse of hidden postulates, of bold, often ill-founded extrapolations, a pseudo-science has been created."[17]

Creationists also argue that the exclusive teaching of evolution violates the free exercise of rights of students who believe in creation, that it violates the "establishment" clause of the First Amendment (no state religion), and also that it violates the Fourteenth Amendment (discrimination on the basis of religion). Further, excluding creationism from the classroom violates the parental right to direct the child's moral and spiritual beliefs (puts undue burden on both parents and child) and deprives the student of the "right to hear" all relevant educational material (the latter point has been held to be a constitutional right).

Academic: Evolutionists insist that the requirement to teach creationism violates academic freedom. They contend that the teacher must be "free" to teach as he or she chooses. Creationists retort that academic freedom means the freedom, in fact, the necessity to teach all aspects of a subject; it means freedom to educate, not freedom to indoctrinate. They argue that prohibiting or failing to examine creationism is a violation of true academic freedom, which is not confined to the teacher's right to teach but must include the student's right to be taught comparative subjects (freedom to hear, consider, conclude). Thus, a balanced presentation in which creationism and evolution are taught is the only way to uphold, practice, and preserve academic freedom.

The ACLU presents itself as the protector of free speech and academic freedom. But when William Z. Baumgartner, Christian environmental engineer and member of the Plymouth Rock Foundation, formed a speakers bureau to explain creationism to public school students in Tennessee, ACLU director Hedy Weinberg objected. Weinberg said, "It's a blatant violation of the First Amendment."[18]

Scientific: The evolution establishment argues that creation is a religious myth; that science has proven that man is a product of bio-chemistry, and that life has progressed from nothing to one-celled origins to its present state of development through a series of biological changes over a period of billions of years.

Creationists insist that science proves man was created, and assert that the creation dogma is supported by far more evidentiary fact than is evolution. Evolution, they assert, is the myth; it is based on assumptions, conjectures, shifting suppositions, and a chain of missing links. They point out that Charles Darwin in his *The Origin of Species* warned about the unanswered questions and speculations he included in his theory. In his books Darwin used such subjective phrases as "let us assume" eight hundred times.

Further, say creationists, evolution flies in the face of some basic, hard cold facts and laws:

(1) The theory of evolution contradicts the second law of thermodynamics (without outside interference, all things tend toward the state of greatest disorder). Indeed, the Scriptures validate the second law of thermodynamics: "In the beginning, O Lord, you laid the foundations of the earth, and the heavens are the works of Your

hand. They will perish, but You remain; They will wear out like a garment" (Hebrews 1:10-11);

(2) Apollo astronauts found only one-eighth of an inch of dust on the moon's surface. If the moon and earth had been in existence for billions of years (as evolutionists claim) there should be at least one hundred feet of dust lying on the moon;

(3) The magnetic field of the earth is decaying at a measurable rate. By reverse projection based on existing data, it is clear that the earth could not have existed in its present state for more than ten thousand years;

(4) The earth's population has been increasing through history at a determinable rate. If man evolved ages ago as claimed, the population of the earth would be many times what it is today;

(5) Fossil records do not support evolution. Not only is there a missing link, there are thousands of missing links between supposedly related species;

(6) Evidence of "fossil men" is shaky at best and largely discredited. Many of them were proven to be "fakes"—Peking man, Pilt-down man, etc.; and

(7) Evolution flies in the face of the law of biogenesis (living matter comes only from previously living matter).

Here are some additional points creationists raise against evolution: There is an absence of transitional forms to fill gaps. All the major theses of evolution have been discredited or discarded (acquired characteristics, natural selection, large mutation, small mutation, accidental alteration, etc.). Countless experiments dating back to 1780 prove that life does not come from non-life; inanimate does not beget the animate. Advanced studies in molecular biology show that man's DNA code is totally distinctive from animals; the study of amino acid components attests that the flesh of each species is (as the Bible says) distinct from that of others.

As for the age of the earth, creationists say that it has been proven that the earth is "young" by extensive research in such fields as earth spin, comet decay and dust, ocean concentration and sediment, decay of the earth's magnetic field, sun shrink, etc. As for the Great Flood, they assert that fossil finds and stratigraphic records over the face of the globe substantiate the Genesis account.

Writing on the "big bang" theory of the earth's origin, and how that might be proof of Genesis 1:1, astronomer Robert Jastrow concluded:

> For the scientist who has lived by his faith in the power of reason, the story ends like a bad dream. He has scaled the mountains of ignorance, he is about to conquer the highest peak; as he pulls himself over the biggest rock, he is greeted by a band of theologians who have been sitting there for centuries.

Consider the Biblical Principles

Creation is mentioned seventy-five times in passages throughout the Old and New Testaments. In addition to Genesis, twenty-three books of the Bible allude to God's creative acts. Creation is not some "minor doctrine"; it is the starting point of all Divine revelation. All other Scriptures build upon creation.

"In the beginning, God created (Hebrew word *bara* means "created out of nothing") the heavens and the earth" (Genesis 1:1; John 1:1, 2). God created all things and by Him all things exist and consist (Colossians 1:16, 17). That which is seen was made from that which is not seen (atoms, neutrons, molecules, electrons, etc.) (Hebrews 11:3). God created plant life, the seed of which is in itself each after its own kind — God's law of reproduction. God created animal life, each to reproduce after its own kind (Genesis 1:11-25). And God created man after His own image, in His own likeness (His attributes) out of the dust of the earth, wherein are found all the basic elements, and He breathed into him the breath of life and man became a living soul (Genesis 1:26, 27; 2:7). All flesh is not the same flesh; the flesh of man is distinct from that of animal life (1 Corinthians 15:39). And God told man to be fruitful and to multiply (reproduce his own kind; man cannot procreate with animals). For greater detail of God's creative acts, read Job, chapters 38-39.

"And of every living thing of all flesh, two of every sort, shall you bring into the ark, to keep them alive with you; they shall be male and female" so that after the Great Flood had subsided they might continue to reproduce and multiply — not by evolution but by procreation (Genesis 6:19).

In no word, no verse, no book in the Bible is there any evidence of a gradual development of life of any kind. Certain passages show clearly that creation occurred in a short time and that the act of creation involved a miracle (Exodus 20:11; Psalm 33:6; see also Deuteronomy 32:6; Isaiah 43:1; 45:12, 15, 17; Ezra 5:11; Nehemiah 9:6).

These are but a few of the Biblical facts concerning the origin of man and his continuance after the Great Flood. "Yes, let God be true, but every man a liar; as it is written, that you might be justified in the sayings and might overcome when you are judged" (Romans 3:4).

Those who attack creationism and fight to keep it out of the public classrooms are most often those same individuals and groups who fight against the Bible. Why the attack on God's written Word at the same time that unregenerate man attacks the truth of creation? Because there is power in God's Word; thus, man must try to deny the truth of God's Word before he can make any headway in attacking or discrediting the facts of creation. But God assures us that all things may pass away but His Word, the Truth, will never pass away.

EXECUTIVE ORDERS AND THE CONSTITUTION

Few Americans realize that the nation has been divided into ten regions and that the regional governments are empowered to take over in a national emergency.

Background Briefing

In an article which appeared in the *Miami Herald,* reporter Alfonso Chardy stated that "Lt. Col. Oliver North . . . helped draw up a controversial plan to suspend the Constitution in the event of a national crisis. . . . In a secret assessment of the activities [of a so-called 'shadow government'] the lead counsel for the Senate Iran-Contra Committee called it a 'secret government within a government.'"[1] The Associated Press, Miami, also charged that North drafted plans to place the control of the United States in the hands of the Federal Emergency Management Agency (FEMA), plans for the declaration of martial law, and plans for the appointment of military commanders to run state and local governments.[2]

During the Iran-Contra hearings, Representative Jack Brooks (Texas) asked, "Colonel North, in your work at the NSC [National Security Council], were you not assigned at one time to work on plans for the continuity of government in the event of a major disaster?"

Senator Daniel Inouye (Hawaii) replied: "I believe that question touches upon a highly sensitive and classified area, so may I request that you do not touch upon that."

Representative Brooks responded, "I was particularly concerned, Mr. Chairman, because I read in the Miami papers, and several others, that there had been a plan developed by that same agency, a contingency plan in the event of emergency that would suspend the American Constitution. And I was deeply concerned about it and wondered if that was the area in which he had worked. I believe it was and I wanted to get his confirmation."

Senator Inouye said, "May I most respectfully request that that matter not be touched upon, at this stage. If we wish to get into this, I'm certain arrangements can be made for an executive session."[3]

Archibald E. Roberts asked the Committee to Restore the Constitution:

> "Whose fingerprints are on the plan to suspend the Constitution?" Why did Iran/Contra Committee chairman Daniel Inouye censor Representative Jack Brooks when Brooks attempted to question Colonel North on the Associated Press allegations of "suspension of the Constitution"?
>
> Was it because Brooks was treading in an area of classified information vital to national security, as Inouye claimed? Or, was it because Senator Inouye did not want the American people to learn the truth about the "secret contingency plan"?[4]

Perhaps now is a good time to review the genesis and evolution of that "secret contingency plan." Mr. Chardy and Mr. Brooks are some eighteen years late and quite a few facts short. The move to override the Constitution had its seeds not with Colonel North or the NSC, but with President Richard M. Nixon—back in 1969.

On March 27, 1969, Mr. Nixon announced that the United States was to be divided (restructured) into ten federal regions, each with its own "capitol." Calling for a restructuring of government service systems to "stream-line" their operations, he established "uniform boundaries and regional office locations" for Federal Departments of Labor, Health, Education, & Welfare; Housing and Urban Development; Office of Economic Opportunity; and Small Business Administration. Boundaries of the ten new federal regions closely paralleled the Federal Reserve System districts.

On May 28, 1969, Representative Reuss introduced HR 11764, providing federal grants to those states meeting "regional" requirements (including combining counties into sub-regions within the federal regions). The bill also proposed that the control of $22.5 billion in tax revenues for funding the regional operations be assigned to the President.

On October 30, 1969, Mr. Nixon issued Executive Order Number 11490 "Assigning Emergency Preparedness Functions to Federal Departments." The order authorized Regional Councils, in the event of an emergency, to control all food supplies, money and credit, transportation, communications, and public utilities. The term and scope of a "national emergency" was not defined.

Richard C. Weaver, then-Secretary of Housing and Urban Development, said "Regional government means absolute federal control over all property and its development regardless of location, anywhere in the United States, to be administered on the federal official's determination. [Regional government] would supersede state and local laws. . . . Through this authority we seek to recapture control of the use of the land, most of which the government has already given to the people."[5]

> Regionalism: The Quiet Revolution. Local government is changing itself in an effort to better meet the needs of the people. Across the nation, cities, counties, towns and school districts that serve a common area are joining together in a regional effort to solve mutual problems. In a quiet way, regionalism is a revolution in the structure of our federal system.[6]

On August 15, 1971, Mr. Nixon issued Executive Order Number 11615. It designated the Chairman of the Board of Governors of the Federal Reserve System to be director of Cost of Living Council. Under the order's provisions, the director is authorized to request the Department of Justice to take action (issue injunction) "whenever it appears to the [Cost of Living] Council that any person has engaged, is engaged, or is about to engage in any acts or practices constituting a violation of any regulation or order." In effect, this gave the Federal Reserve chairman control over prices, rents, wages, salaries, etc.

On February 12, 1972, Mr. Nixon issued Executive Order Number 11647, establishing a Federal Regional Council for each of the ten regions. It authorized Council staffs and Council chairmen (to be appointed by the President). The Council comprises the regional directors of the federal grant-making agencies: the United States Departments of Labor, Health, Education, and Welfare, Housing and Urban Development, Transportation, Office of Economic Opportunity, Environmental Protection Agency, and the Law Enforcement Assistance Administration.

The advocates of "regional government" asserted that such consolidation was essential to efficiency, and would enable greater cost-effectiveness. They suggested that the original federal structure was no longer sufficient to match modern needs and meet national emergencies. Further, they insisted regionalism was necessary to make sure that state and local governments comply with the Fourteenth Amendment (due process and equal protection under the law).

Opponents warned that a multitude of sins can be committed under the guise of "efficiency." Further, they protested that regionalism violated Article IV, Section 4 of the Constitution ("the United States shall guarantee to every state in this union a republican form of government"), and Section 3-1 ("no new state shall be formed or erected within the Jurisdiction of any other state; nor any state be formed by the Junction of two or more states, or parts of states, without the consent of the Legislatures of the states concerned as well as of the Congress"). In addition, the opponents of the plan warned, such regionalization would (1) make the several states into creatures of the federal government and subvert home rule (city, county, state, and school districts); (2) arbitrarily reduce the number and authority of county governments; (3) eliminate local governments "too small" to be efficient; (4) replace popular elections of some offices with appointed bureaucratic "policy makers"; and (5) liberalize municipal annexation of unincorporated areas.

Ten Federal Regions

In March 1969 President Nixon announced that the United States was to be divided into ten federal (metro) regions. In 1982 the United States Supreme Court outlawed the regional "capitols": and yet, the regions remain. Following are the areas comprising each of the ten regions and the location of the central office:

- REGION I—Maine, Massachusetts, New Hampshire, Rhode Island, Vermont (Boston).

- REGION II—New Jersey, New York, Puerto Rico, Virgin Islands (New York).

- REGION III—Delaware, Maryland, Pennsylvania, Virginia, West Virginia, Washington, D.C. (Philadelphia).

- REGION IV—Alabama, Florida, Georgia, Kentucky, Mississippi, North Carolina, South Carolina, Tennessee (Atlanta).

- REGION V—Illinois, Michigan, Minnesota, Ohio, Wisconsin (Chicago).

- REGION VI—Arkansas, Louisiana, New Mexico, Oklahoma, Texas (Dallas-Ft. Worth).

- REGION VII—Iowa, Kansas, Missouri, Nebraska (Kansas City).

- REGION VIII—Colorado, Montana, North Dakota, South Dakota, Utah, Wyoming (Denver).

- REGION IX—Arizona, California, Hawaii, Nevada (San Francisco).

- REGION X—Alaska, Oregon, Washington, Idaho (Seattle).

On July 24, 1979, President Jimmy Carter issued Executive Order Number 12148 naming the Federal Emergency Management Agency (FEMA) to be the "general manager" of the United States in the event a national emergency is declared.

On January 13, 1982, the United States Supreme Court outlawed the ten regional capitols.

On February 22, 1982, President Reagan issued Executive Order Number 12407 dismantling the ten regional capitols. Opponents of regionalism called the order "cosmetic." They pointed out that the regional grant-making agencies still remained in place.[7]

In 1965 the federal government created the Office of Law Enforcement Assistance (OLEA). In 1968 Congress passed the Omnibus Crime Control Act; OLEA became part of the Law Enforcement Assistance Administration (LEAA) in the Department of Justice. Associate LEAA Administrator, Clarence Coster, told the nation's police chiefs that the nation's law enforcement "must be regionalized." Coster said the United States had 40,235 law enforcement agencies and "this many units form a completely ungovernable body." In 1973 the LEAA agency recommended that police departments be regionalized and that all departments with fewer than ten members be eliminated (that would include about 80 percent of all local police forces in the United States).[8]

On November 14, 1979, President Carter issued Executive Order Number 12170, declaring a state of national emergency "constituted by the situation in Iran." On November 10, 1986, President Reagan announced that "in accordance with Section 202[d] of the National Emergency Act," he was "continuing the national emergency with respect to Iran."[9]

What level of local government is most vulnerable to regionalism? County government. Consolidations and controls under the regional plan would vitiate it. In the beginning of the American republic, the county was the basic unit of government. It held jurisdiction in important areas of civil governance: property tax was levied and controlled there so that citizens could hold officials accountable; criminal law was enforced at that level; civil law was mostly enacted and enforced by local officials. Now, much of that is in jeopardy through abridgement and preemption.

> The solution to regional chaos is lawful enforcement of the law. It demands local enforcement. There is no other way. If you can make your county government function, you will have thrown back the crazed mobs of regional revolutionaries. Effective law enforcement by county government will shatter the federal regionalism concept under which we are now existing so shamefully. Here are the battlements of Christian liberty in the United States: county governments administering justice as they are empowered and commanded to do.[10]

Consider the Biblical Principles

Centralism, or collectivism and unrepresentative government, is in direct conflict with the Christian idea of man and Christian methodology of self-government with union. The Founding Fathers of the United States were well-read in such Christian philosophers and statesmen as Sidney, Montesquieu,

Blackstone, and Locke. For the majority of the early Americans, the Bible was the "great political textbook."

Further, they had a burning recollection of the grievances listed in the Declaration of Independence. "The history of the present king of Great Britain is a history of repeated injuries and usurpations, all having in direct object the establishment of an absolute tyranny over these states."

Thus, they established a republic with (1) clear separation of powers at the federal level; (2) definite barriers between federal, state, and local governments; and (3) hefty chains of law to bind those who might seek to usurp or centralize the flow of power.

The United States Constitution grants 80 powers to the federal government; it places 115 restrictions upon it. It sets 20 points of federal legislative power, but implants 70 definite restraints. The original states demanded Articles IX and X which reserve to the states and to the people all power not specifically delegated to the federal government. In recent years the tides of federal government have eroded state and local sovereignty. What was once a spread-eagle republic is being preempted by federal centralism and unilateral, arbitrary control.

View these as among central tenets of the Christian idea and methodology of government:

(1) God is sovereign (Deuteronomy 6:4, 5); power flows from Him to the individual. The individual citizens, in concert (the corporate body politic), assign certain definite authorities to civil government (Genesis 9:5, 6; Romans 13:1-6);

(2) The individual is of prime importance (John 3:16); God is the Author of the individual's liberty (Leviticus 26:13; John 8:36). As man is in the eyes of God, so he should be in the eyes of the state;

(3) Local government (home rule) is to be the basic seat of ecclesiastical (church) government and civil government (2 Corinthians 1:24);

(4) We are to be one nation under God with voluntary association and unity of purpose (versus enforced uniformity) or with one hope and one faith through obedience to God and love for our neighbors (Matthew 22:37-40; 1 Corinthians 1:10; Ephesians 3:3-6; Galatians 3:15);

(5) The affairs of government are to be administered by elected representatives (Deuteronomy 1:13, 14; Joshua 18:4; Judges 11:11; 2 Samuel 3, 4, 5, 12);

(6) Elected officers are answerable (accountable) to the people and are to be "ministers" of God unto the people for good (Deuteronomy 1:9-18; Romans 13:4); and

(7) Separation of church and state is designed as a "division of labor" for God: the church is charged with the ministry of grace (God's love); the state is charged with the ministry of justice (God's laws).

An example of Christian methodology of civil government can be seen in the governance of the early Christian churches.

Each was independent; each was accountable to Christ, the Master upon whose shoulders all government rests. Even the Apostle Paul, used of God to found many early churches, had no dominion over them, but was a teacher and a counselor.

Each local church was a "little republic or commonwealth" and, with regard to its internal concerns, "was wholly regulated by a code of laws, that, if they did not originate with, had at least the sanction of, the people constituting such church." Though miles apart, churches were united in common faith. It was that "republican" concept of self-government with union which was applied to American civil government in a balanced federal union of the sovereign states, as set forth in the federal Constitution.

Consider these additional attributes of a Christian republic: individual liberty under God was protected (Leviticus 26:13); the sanctity of human life was protected (Exodus 21:12, 14; 21-23); all persons were considered equal under the law (Deuteronomy 1:16, 17); the power to elect civil officials and enact civil laws was reserved for the people (Deuteronomy 1:13, 14); elected officials were to be accountable to the people (1 Samuel 10:25; 1 Kings 12); there was to be an established system of impartial, inexpensive, and accessible and speedy justice for all (Deuteronomy 1:16-18; 6:18; Exodus 18:21); the sanctity of family and the right of private property (including conscience) was upheld and protected; universal education in civil and self-government for all was based on God's written Word (Deuteronomy 6:6-9).

Consider, also, these basic attributes of the Hebrew republic. Each of the twelve tribes was sovereign, each was independent, and each was co-equal with each of the other tribes in terms of political stature and authority in the national councils.

Each had its own government, each administered its own municipal, district, and tribal affairs (Joshua 7:15; 1 Chronicles 5:18-23). When matters of national concern or emergency arose (defense, inter-tribal conflicts, etc.), the leaders of the twelve tribes met in council to determine the action to be taken.

ELEVEN

FARMS AND FAMILIES

Although the United States is now an industrial/technological society, the American farm and farm family is a vital essential to the nation's moral and cultural stability. Government policies, conglomerates, and foreign incursions are a threat to its survival.

Background Briefing

Farmers and small landowners have always been vital to a stable culture. They have been a bulwark of self-government, reliance, and independence against the reckless, often purposeful, growth of tyranny. Those who produce raw materials (farmers, foresters, fishermen, miners) are originators and producers of new real wealth. Agriculture is the basic industry, the major economic entity, vital to the well-being and stability of any nation.

"Farming has been more than an economic enterprise, producing for a free market. Historically, it has also been an important social institution, producing good people. . . . the disappearance of the farm community is little short of a national disaster."[1]

American agriculture and its related industries are the world's largest commercial enterprise. Total assets for just the farm sector in 1986 were $866.6 billion. Direct from-the-farm products accounted for about 5 percent of the nation's total gross national product (GNP) in 1986. There is no measurement of the percentage of GNP from farm-related industries, but it is sizable. Agriculture employed more than three million persons in 1986. But millions more are directly dependent upon farmers for jobs (processing, packaging, transportation, sales, etc.). Every farm job lost means another three jobs lost somewhere down the food and fiber system.[2]

Some 2.3 million farms occupy about half of the total United States land mass — 1 billion acres (400 million for farming with the balance for cattle and livestock grazing, etc.). The Carter administration, as part of its "Global 2000" analysis, claimed the United States was losing agricultural land to urban sprawl at a rate of 3 million acres a year. Actually, as the United States Department of Agriculture's Economic Research Service has shown, the United States has been gaining — not losing — cropland. In recent years cropland acreage has increased from 413 million acres to about 420 million acres. (But, in the winter of 1983-84, wind erosion did peel off about 3.5 million acres of top soil in 519 counties in the ten Great Plains states.)

The average farm size is 429 acres. In 1947, one farmer produced enough food/fiber for forty-seven persons; today, one farmer produces enough for seventy-eight persons. Farm output per man-hour has increased twice as fast as industrial production. The total value of farm commodities in 1986 was $106 billion ($75.5 billion in crops and about $30 billion in cattle and livestock).

The gross income from farming increased from about $100 billion in 1975 to about $166 billion in 1985. But, the costs rose more rapidly: from $75 billion in 1975 to more than $136 billion in 1985. In the past ten years, while farm revenues rose 132 percent the costs of production rose 153 percent (wages went up 123 percent; tractors and equipment went up 178 percent; taxes went up 68 percent, etc.). Net farm income in 1983 was about $20 billion, down from $30 billion in 1979, and the lowest since 1941. When adjusted for inflation, farmers' income in 1986 was less than at any time since 1934. Profit margins on most crops are now about half what they were in 1974. Net farm income per capita was down from $11 in 1950 to $6 in 1985.

Only thirty-six cents of the retail food dollar goes to the farmer/rancher. Eighty-seven percent of those thirty-six cents goes to the cost of production.

There have been some ominous developments in American agriculture! Since 1950 an average of two thousand farms a week have gone out of business. The number of farms in the United States has declined by 54 percent since 1945; farm population as a percentage of the total United States population was down from 14 percent in 1950 to just over 2 percent in 1985. In 1959 the farm population was 16.5 million persons; in 1985 it was down to about 5.5 million. (There has been a slight upturn in the mid-1980s as more families moved to small farms to escape the perils of urban/suburban life.)

The United States Department of Agriculture warns that the United States is on the verge of having "a few large firms controlling food production." The department fears the unique and productive American system of individual/family ownership and operation of farmland is about extinct. It worries that in less than twenty years about one million farm families will lose or leave their farms. Then, predicts the USDA, just 1 percent of the remaining farm operators (multinational corporations and conglomerates) could possess half of the nation's farmlands and control the production of at least one-half of the nation's food and fiber supply.

In 1969 only one in every thousand farms rang up $500,000 sales or more a year. Today, the $500,000 farms number about one in every hundred. Is this rise caused by inflation? Only in small part. The large farms, encompassing only 8 percent of all United States farmland, turn out more than one-fourth of the total value of farm production and reap 60 percent of the net farm income.

At the same time, purchases of United States farmland by foreign entities is increasing. As of 1982 some 13 million acres were foreign-owned, an increase of 5 million acres in one year. Foreign purchases for farm land have increased since then.

Does that tell the whole story? Some say no. They warn that it is impossible to uncover most foreign ownership because of numbered trust accounts, holdings through United States affiliates, and false fronts. Foreign firms are also buying other links in the United States food and fiber chain (processing, marketing, etc.).

Are such predictions of farm consolidations and takeovers far-fetched? Are the worries unfounded? Observers warn, "not necessarily." Already 7 percent of the largest farmholders control 54 percent of the farmland and about one-half of all the agricultural sales. Many major corporations are into farming in a big way (Southern Pacific, Tenneco, Standard Oil of California, etc.). Tenneco, the Houston-based oil corporation, owns 1 million acres in California. The United States General Accounting Office (GAO) estimates that 50 percent of the United States farmland is owned by non-farm operators—conglomerates, banks, holding companies, etc. Four firms control 83 percent of all the farm equipment manufactured and sold in the United States. Five multinationals control the grain trade. Multinationals have also cornered the United States seed business.

Is bigger better? Not necessarily. Bigger can be dangerous. Studies show that increased efficiency and productivity comes from improved farm practices, not increased size. Research over a period of years indicates that the highest efficiency can be reached on a 400-acre farm. There is no real evidence to support the argument that megafarms are in the public's best interest; cartels and monopolies seldom are. Such control and size simply creates "superior ability to control the market," and to stack the deck in commodities—which may explain the megaboast that "the heart of America's food belt is no longer the Midwest but the trading centers of Chicago and New York."

What is the outlook for American agriculture? For a time it was "catastrophic." The cry was that the "farm sector of the United States . . . is teetering on the brink of a depression reminiscent of the '30s." Debt load and bankruptcies were at a level unseen since the depression. In 1907 farm debt was about $54 billion; by 1985 it had soared to more than $200 billion. The Farmers Home Mortgage debt rose from $2.4 billion in 1970 to $10.4 billion in 1988. The average debt delinquency rate jumped from about 4 percent in 1982 to over 5 percent in 1985. (The USDA estimates that 43 percent of all farmland is mortgaged.) As for all the FMHA borrowers in 1984, 41 percent were behind in payments. Now, many farmers are getting back on their feet due to the "Reagan Recovery." But how long will that last?

What was the cause of this crisis? It was a combination of factors including poor business practices by some farmers, greater and more complex demands for business management techniques, and prolonged dependence on government subsidies, which benefit mostly larger operators. Three percent of farm operators received 46 percent of government benefits (the Southern Pacific conglomerate gets about $3 million a year in farm subsidies).

Excessive debt load is a problem; most of it is taken for buying land and equipment (farming is now a capital intensive industry). Increased debt combined with soaring interest rates (usury) has been disastrous for many farmers (the interest rates on debt jumped 24 percent during recent years, up a total of 200 percent since 1977). Each 1 percent hike in interest causes a 5 percent loss in net farm income. Such is the toll of debt capitalism.

The profit margin has also decreased dramatically. Margins on most crops have dropped 50 percent since 1974. Grain corn sold for $3.25 a bushel in 1983 and was down to $2.41 in 1985. Soybeans dropped from $7.81 to $5.16; wheat from $3.53 to $3.16; cotton down from 66.4 cents to 54.8 cents. During that period, cost of equipment, feed, and fertilizer, went up due to inflation, higher taxes, etc.

Also, government farm policies must share some of the blame for the farm crisis. Farmers were encouraged to increase debt to grow (under President Eisenhower, Secretary of Agriculture Ezra Benson told farmers that they should "get big or get out"). Such policies have virtually killed the free market in agriculture. "The federal government has been bribing an industry to commit economic suicide."[3] Incidentally, despite their vital importance to the national well-being, farmers are only about 3 percent of the national vote; that means little clout against militant interest groups (check the past ten federal budgets; almost all categories were up except farm support—that went down).

Next, overproduction and excessive surpluses depressed prices. Good weather and highly competitive markets boosted outputs.

Finally, the "macro-economic" world economy has seen a dramatic loss of markets due to worldwide depression. The strength (increased value) of the United States dollar, which has meant higher prices to foreign purchasers, has also hurt. But with a falling dollar on world markets, that pressure is somewhat relieved. Other factors have included rising East-West tensions, the loss of credit/purchasing powers of underdeveloped and Third World countries, and "unfair" trade practices by some European nations. Also, United States agriculture no longer "feeds the world" but, due to increased production in other nations, must compete for world markets.

As more and more family farms go under, the question is this, What is the government doing to halt the tide of bankruptcies and foreclosures? The United States paid $322 million to banks on loans owed by Poland's (Communist) government and deferred the 1982 debt payment for eight years. Recently it okayed making another $2 billion in low-interest bank loans to Poland.

The government gave $35 million to Brazil in 1983, $82 million in 1984, and $366 million in 1985. It has now extended more credit to Brazil even though that nation is far behind on its paybacks. And a new "zero-based" credit arrangement was "jury-rigged" for Mexico to help support that nation's economy. The United States pours more billions into the International Monetary Fund (IMF) and World Bank, arranges loans and credits for Communist-bloc nations, and bails out floundering mega-banks—and the taxpayers stand to pick up that tab in case of default.

What about the American farmer? The federal government wants to curtail the emergency loan program, reduce the Farmers Home Administration's lending, and pay price supports in surplus grain credits. The United States Controller General has charged that FMHA "illegally denies farmers access to emergency disaster loan[s]." These same farmers in some five hundred counties have been improperly denied opportunities for emergency loans to save their farms. Thus, more and more farmers ask, How come the United States bails out foreign nations and international bankers but won't help save the United States farmer?

The most urgent task for farmers and politicians is to develop new policies which get the government off the farmer's back and the farmer back into a free market economy.

Consider the Biblical Principles

In the beginning God created . . . the earth, the seas, the grass, the herbs, the fruit trees (each with its seed within itself), and the fish of the sea and the fowl of the air and the beasts of the earth (each with its seed within itself to reproduce after its own kind) . . . and God created man to be fruitful and to multiply and to replenish and subdue the earth and to have dominion over it (Genesis 1:1-31).

Thus, the earth and the fullness thereof belongs to the Lord God, Creator and Sovereign. And man is to care for it, to cultivate it, to conserve it, and to keep it for the Lord (Genesis 2:15). Man, then, is to be the caretaker, the husbandman, of God's good earth — not simply to serve his own self-interests (i.e., survival, comfort, etc.) but, first and foremost, as a steward to serve the Living God. All that he does, man is to do in a manner and with a purpose that will glorify and honor God (Colossians 3:23).

Man is to be fruitful; he is not to waste, misuse, or abuse the land or let it stand idle and unproductive. He is to till the soil, farm the land, husband the stock so as to multiply the fruit (crops/ stock) it produces. He is not to deplete or ravage the land or deplete the stock. And he is to replenish it, meaning that he is to care for it through those practices and methods that build the soil, that do not cause it to be eroded or sterile. The farmer or farm-company failing to care for the land disobeys and dishonors the Creator.

The family is God's basic social and economic unit. God has established His Law to protect the rights, safety, and well-being of the individual and his family. Thus, in the apportionment and preservation of the land, Moses was instructed to make sure that each family was given the right and responsibility of caring for a definite portion of land. Further, through Moses, God set forth certain basic laws to insure that the land would stay with the family (laws of private property, laws of inheritance), and that the land would be conserved and cared for so as to provide continuity of sustenance for the family (laws concerning tilling the soil, letting it lay fallow, keeping it unpolluted; laws of stewardship).

Consider some of God's laws regarding His land, its care and use — laws that govern man's stewardship. And, if they seem "far out," perhaps that is a measure of just how far from obedience to God man has strayed.

The farmer is to let his land rest every seventh year. ("six years you shall sow the field, and six years you shall prune your vineyard and gather in the fruit thereof; but in the seventh year shall be a sabbath of rest unto the land, a sabbath of rest for the Lord." (Leviticus 25:2-7; Exodus 23:10, 11). And to those who asked of the Lord how they would exist during the fallow year, God gave the answer: "[If you obey Me] I will command My blessing upon you in the sixth year and it [the land] shall bring forth fruit for three years" (Leviticus 25:20-22; see also Exodus 16:25-30).

And what if man disobeys God, as so many do now?

> If you will not hearken unto Me . . . and if you shall despise My statutes . . . so that you will not do all My commandments . . . your land shall be desolate and your cities waste. Then shall the land enjoy her sabbath . . . even then shall the land rest and enjoy her sabbaths. As long as it lieth desolate it shall rest; because it did not rest in your sabbaths, when you dwelt upon it (Leviticus 26:14-35; see also 2 Chronicles 36:21).

Farm land is to remain with the family. It is not to be sold. "City" land may be sold. If family farmland must be mortgaged, it is to be released in the Jubilee year (the fiftieth year after the week of weeks, or forty-ninth year) (Leviticus 25:8-23).

> Proclaim liberty throughout the land unto all the inhabitants thereof (Leviticus 25:10).

There is a deeper meaning to those words inscribed on the Liberty Bell than most people — even most Christians — realize: our Founding Fathers were determined not to be tenants or bond-servants on indentured land. If the land is leased or sold, the price is to be based on its productivity for that period of years between the date of the lease or sale and the time it must be released or redeemed (returned) to the family heirs.

God's laws concerning land prohibit land speculation (Numbers 36:7-9). Giant land holdings and megafarms are not in keeping with God's plan or purpose for His property.

> Woe unto them that join house to house, that lay field to field, till there be no place, that they may be placed alone in the midst of the earth (Isaiah 5:8; see also Jeremiah 22:17).

Great proprietorships are the scourge of a nation and the en-slavers of men.

"And they covet fields, and take them by violence; and houses and take them away: so they oppress a man and his house, even a man and his heritage" (Micah 2:2). When the land is held by individual families, worked by the family, and kept as an inheritance from the Lord God, then men will be free and can direct the affairs of civil government. Government policies that cause families to lose their land or force them to leave the land are ungodly.

Usury is an abomination before the Lord (Exodus 22:25; Leviticus 25:36, 37; Deuteronomy 23:19, 20; Ezekiel 22:12-15). Many of today's farmers are in a position similar to that of the inhabitants of Jerusalem in the days of Nehemiah:

> "We have mortgaged our land, vineyards, and houses that we might buy corn.". . . There were also those that said, "We have borrowed money for the king's tribute [tax], and that upon our lands and vineyards . . . neither is it in our power to redeem them; for other men have our lands and vineyards" (Nehemiah 5:3-5).

Man says God's laws are no longer relevant or binding. Who is it that puts its desire and its tactics above the Law of God? Not some communist cell or front group; instead it is the Committee on Economic Development (CED) in its *Adaptive Program for Agriculture*. "Where there are religious obstacles to modern economic progress, the religion may have to be taken less seriously or its character altered."

But, God says, "If you turn away and forsake My commandments . . . and shall go and serve other gods and worship them . . . this house, which is high, shall be an astonishment to every one that passeth by; so that he shall say, Why hath the Lord done thus unto this land, and unto this house?" (2 Chronicles 7:19-22).

In summary, the earth is the Lord's and the fullness thereof (Psalm 24:1). Agriculture is a Biblical institution ordained by God to care for His earth (Genesis 2:15; 3:19, 23). Man is to be God's husbandman, tending the earth to His honor and glory (Genesis 1:28; Proverbs 27:23-27). God is to be acknowledged and honored through the proper care of His land (Jeremiah 5:24). The fruits of the land will be diminished if sin prevails (Isaiah 5:10; 7:23; Jeremiah 12:13; Joel 1:10, 11). The first fruits of the land belong to the Lord—whether that be animal, vegetable, or mineral (Proverbs 3:9, 10). The land is to rest, to lie fallow or dormant, every seventh year (Leviticus 25:2). If God is obeyed in this way, He will bless the land and its product (Leviticus 25:20-21). If He is not obeyed, He will blight the land (Leviticus

26:32-35). The land is to remain with the family. The products of the land are to be a benefit to all (Ecclesiastes 5:9). There is a definite law of charity connected to stewardship of the land (Deuteronomy 24:19-21; Leviticus 19:9, 10; 2 Chronicles 9:6).

GAMBLING
(And State Lotteries)

The quest is for easy money — tax avoidance by the state and "hitting it big" by the gambler. But too often the reality is human misery, and social and economic woes.

Background Briefing

America's first lottery dates back to 1612 and Jamestown, Virginia. The Virginia Company was having trouble staying in business. It was granted permission from the king of England to hold a lottery to raise money.

By the 1770s most of the American colonial governments had begun to hold lotteries. "Lotteries were used to raise money for churches, schools, public buildings, roads, and bridges."[1] The Continental Congress turned to the lottery to help raise money for the War for Independence. In 1798 Alexandria, Virginia held a lottery to help pay for the paving of its streets.[2]

As the number and size of the lotteries increased, so did the fraud. In 1830 a lottery reform movement took shape and by 1840 twelve states, mostly in New England, had outlawed lotteries. By 1878 only one state lottery remained — the Louisiana Lottery. "It controlled legislatures, newspapers, banks and governors . . . suppressed opposition through bribery . . . and made profits of as high as $13 million a year."[3]

Finally, in 1895 the United States Congress prohibited interstate commerce in lottery tickets and outlawed the import of lottery material. That was the end of state lotteries — until 1963.[4]

New Hampshire, suffering from a lack of funds and refusing to enact either a state income or sales tax, approved a New Hampshire Sweepstakes in 1964. It brought in almost $3 million in its first year, far short of the rosy promises the lottery backers had promised. New York was the second state to hold a state lottery (1965). Its lottery also fell far short of expected receipts.[5]

Today twenty-seven states and the District of Columbia hold "official" lotteries (thirty-six states permit pari-mutuel betting on horse and/or dog racing). Now a "super-super" multi-state lottery is underway. Six states have joined in a "Lotto-America" game with anticipated minimum prizes of $2 million.[6]

Only in the south with its vestige of Bible Belt morality are a few states still holding out against state lotteries: Alabama, Arkansas, Georgia, Kentucky, Louisiana, Mississippi, and North and South Carolina. Lottery legislation is pending in Texas, and Florida started its state lottery in 1988; ticket sales totaled about $25 million the first week.

"We're definitely heading for fifty states having lotteries, maybe in a decade," believes Teri Lafluer, an editor of *Gaming and Wagering Business* magazine. "Lotteries are the success story of the decade." Lefluer admits the possible exception of "Mormon-dominated Utah."[7] She adds, "The hardest states to get into will be in the Bible Belt. But with the price of oil dropping and the threat of Gramm-Rudman [which mandates a balanced budget by 1992], more and more states are going to be forced to start lotteries because, simply, it's easier than raising taxes."[8]

Lawrence Torrance, a Houston, Texas pollster, believes that "lotteries are not seen as a moral disgrace any more." Yet, he discounts the likelihood of a federal lottery: "There's an antipathy of giving more money to the federal government when people think the Feds should save what they've already got."[9]

Lottery promoter Joe Rees says, "[A federal lottery] is a threat to state revenues and about half the congressional delegation comes from states that have lotteries."[10] For several years there have been bills introduced calling for a federal lottery; 40 percent of the revenues would go to the Social Security fund. To date those bills have died in congressional committees.

In 1987 the total annual yearly take by state lotteries was almost $15 billion. About 40 percent of the gross take goes to prize money, 40 percent is the state's skim (which goes for such programs as education and public projects), and the balance goes for operating expenses (equipment, administration, agents' commissions).

The "big winners" ($15 million, $20 million, and $40 million jackpots) grab the headlines and continue to promote the sale of lottery tickets. But the odds are against the players: for picking four numbers out of six, it's ten thousand-to-one; and for picking all six numbers, the odds are 3.5 million-to-one. The estimated odds on winning Illinois' super Lotto is 7 million-to-one. J. Quinn, director of the New York State Lottery, estimates that the chances of winning are less than the chances of getting hit by lightning—which is about one in two million.[11]

It is estimated that there are at least ten million compulsive gamblers in the United States (some are as young as fourteen). Some experts on pathological gambling figure that at least 2 percent of American adults suffer from an uncontrollable urge to gamble, "an urge that can drive them to lose it all—their jobs, their homes, their friends and families."[12]

Holiday Quality Food stores announced in a California newspaper advertisement that "since the California state lottery program started . . . we have sold in excess of $1 million worth of lottery tickets. Our food business during this same period has declined [by] the same amount. Morally, we feel that it is wrong to offer our customers the opportunity to gamble with their food dollars and therefore we will no longer be selling lottery tickets."[13]

Gamblers Anonymous struggles to help the compulsive gambler (96 percent of those interviewed said they began gambling before they were fourteen). Psychiatrist Robert Custer of Maryland says "gambling, like alcohol, is a narcotic."

Backers of legalized gambling (including state lotteries) promote it as an easy source of public funds—a "painless" tax. They picture gambling as an industry which provides a source of extra money for the public treasury. But critics dispute the value of lotteries as a revenue-raising device. On an average, the revenues from lotteries come to about 5 percent of a state's general revenues. Attendant socioeconomic ills and civic problems generally result in increased public expenditures that exceed the so-called revenue bonanza. Sociologist H. Roy Kaplan described lotteries as "stopgap measures that lull the populace into a state of complacency while social and fiscal problems multiply."[14]

Even after New Jersey legalized gaming and early annual revenues were $430 million, the state increased sales taxes and instituted an income tax. In Nevada, the "gaming empire" of the nation, state authorities needed an increase in property taxes plus a new tax on hotel and motel rooms to help offset an $80 million deficit.

Opponents of legalized gambling counter that the introduction of gambling breeds a decay and corruption that permeates all levels of society. They warn that gambling feeds on greed and misery of the weak and seeks to hook the young (one seventeen-year-old boy piled up $34,000 in gambling debts). Austin McGuigan, chief law enforcement officer in Connecticut, has prosecuted more than one thousand cases involving gambling since it was legalized in that state. In a cassette tape, "What You Need to Know About the Gambling Menace," McGuigan offers "irrefutable evidence" that legalized gambling begets increased illegal gambling.[15]

The Organized Crime Section of the Department of Justice reports that "the rate of illegal gambling in those states which have some legalized form of gambling was three times as high as in those states where there was no legalized gambling."[16]

Durand F. Jacobs, chief of psychology services at the Veterans Administration Hospital in Loma Linda, California, states, "We have firm evidence to show that once a state promotes or endorses any kind of gambling, both legal and illegal forms of gambling accelerate."[17]

According to Dr. Robert Custer, who directs treatment programs for gambling addicts, lottery playing is one of the least addictive types of gambling but it attracts new gamblers who may later become addicted.[18] And, S. Irving, the national secretary of Gamblers Anonymous, says that although state lotteries seem harmless, they creep up on players. Irving reported that when columnist Ann Landers runs her semi-annual piece on Gamblers Anonymous, "the mail floods in. That week we get eight hundred letters, of which two hundred are from women with this problem. It's just a national epidemic."[19]

Anti-gambling forces insist that it is immoral for the state to encourage or condone or profit from immorality. They cite statistics that show gambling brings with it crime (organized and unorganized) and vice (prostitution, assault, robbery, drugs). Rev. Timothy Kehl, chairman of the Wisconsin Conference of Churches' Gambling Issue Task Force, which opposed that state's lottery, said the issue is whether "it's right or wrong for the government to be involved in a multi-million dollar numbers racket" that exploits its citizens by luring them into gambling. "We believe the role of government . . . is to promote the general welfare, not to devise schemes to swindle people out of their hard-earned money."[20]

Norman Cousins, former editor of *Saturday Review*, expressed his concern about state-promoted lotteries: "No force on earth can prevent people from throwing their money away, but government should not entice them or cheer them on."[21]

A survey by the accounting firm of Laventhol & Horwath found that Massachusetts had the highest per capita lottery sales in 1985, $212.[22] The District of Columbia ranked second with an average of $180 per resident; Maryland was third ($172), and Connecticut was fourth ($149).[23]

And gambling preys on those who can least afford it.

A University of Michigan study indicated that the poor spend a greater proportion of income on gambling; thus, says the study, "government receipts from gambling become a regressive tax." A study of the Chicago lottery indicated that a larger proportion of tickets were sold in poor areas than affluent ones. "Of the revenue from tickets, 15 percent came from low-income areas where only 9 percent of the people live. The study also showed that 22 percent of the revenues came from black communities where 12 percent of the people live."[24] Many of the lottery losers are on Social Security or unemployment compensation; their dream is to "hit it big."

"Lotteries are a regressive form of taxation because they are not based on ability to pay."[25] New York's busiest lottery agent reported, "Seventy percent of those who buy my tickets are poor, black, or Hispanic." And, recounts Charles Colson, one study concluded that the lotteries in Connecticut and Massachusetts were the equivalent of a state sales tax of 60 to 90 percent on lower-income poor.[26] A poll taken in California indicated that "poor families don't contribute as much, but what they do contribute is a bigger percentage of their income than the wealthier people."[27]

As for higher employment and more business, records indicate that employment and revenues may increase for businesses feeding off gambling but dry up for other enterprises. And as for economic impact, opponents suggest many of the dollars gambled away would have been spent on tangible items and productive pursuits that could have turned money over and over in the market place, thus generating jobs and taxes, etc.

Supporters of legalized gambling argue that some people will always gamble. Why not legalize it and let the state in on the take? Opponents counter that availability increases participation and spreads the disease. Further, they argue such a rationale would suggest that the state should also legalize and profit from the sale of drugs, prostitution, and other illicit pursuits. Sociologist Edward Devereaux (Cornell University) says compulsive gambling has the makings of a major socioeconomic problem, that it could equal the magnitude of drugs and alcohol "as wagering opportunities become more and more available."

Atlantic City, New Jersey, is an example of what gambling can do to a city and county. Gaming casinos there are legal. The city has become "Las Vegas of the East." It draws people from as far south as Washington and as far north as Boston. Atlantic City has one of the highest welfare rates in the United States. Jobs were scarce in that seaside resort before advent of gambling. With the influx of casino workers, how has the job market fared? Unemployment is the same as it was before the casinos were opened.

Local authorities have reported a high incidence of drug use among casino employees and worry that the drug culture will infect the youth. The city has had a "phenomenal" increase in crime. Downtown churches in Atlantic City have reported a fall-off in attendance (especially at evening services) because many would-be churchgoers are afraid to walk down the streets or through parking lots.

Land values have soared as speculators have looked for quick and sky-rocketing profits. But the resultant tax assessments are driving middle- and low-income residents out of the city.

Except for areas around casinos, the city has deteriorated, and social problems have increased.

After assessing the impact of gambling on the people of Atlantic City and the surrounding areas, Ovid DeMaris reported: "Gambling is a parasitic enterprise that thrives on the weaknesses of people. It leaves in its wake corruption, debasement, despair, and the subversion of moral authority. That is the bottom line that states should assess before plunging into the maelstrom created by the gambling craze."[28]

Consider the Biblical Principles

Gambling is both a fruit and a root of sin; it springs from sin, it generates (germinates) sin. Consider first the result (fruit) of sin. Gambling is a vice that is spawned by the violation of God's Tenth Commandment, "Thou shalt not covet" (Exodus 20:17).

Dr. G. Campbell Morgan, renowned Bible scholar, points out that the urge to gamble goes far beyond the desire for amusement or entertainment; it involves an inordinate (and often uncontrolled) appetite that is covetousness. The Apostle Paul used the terms "lust" and "concupiscence" to describe covetousness (1 Thessalonians 4:5) and urged Christians to "mortify" such evil in themselves. Covetousness, he wrote, is a form of "idolatry" (Colossians 3:4, 5); that which a person covets can (will) become his or her "god."

"Covetousness," Matthew Henry commented, is "the very root of evil before the act, the thought — before the commission of sin, the desire."

"Incline my heart unto Thy testimonies, and not to covetousness," prayed the Psalmist (Psalm 119:36). He warned of the fate of those who covet: "So are the ways of everyone that is greedy of gain; which taketh away the life of the owners thereof" (Psalm 1:19). In Proverbs we read, "The desire of the slothful killeth him; for his hands refuse to labor. He coveteth greedily all the day long " (Proverbs 21:25, 26). In his letter to the church at Ephesus, Paul cautioned, "For this you know, that no . . . covetous man, who is an idolator, hath any inheritance in the kingdom of Christ and of God" (Ephesians 5:5).

God's first nine commandments (Exodus 20:3-16) forbid certain overt sinful acts; the Tenth Commandment forbids (warns against) internal sin (sinful thought). As our Savior and King emphasized, the thought is as sinful as the act itself (Matthew 5:27, 28). That which invites the sinful act is the basic sin. In a very real sense, then, breaking the Tenth Commandment often results in breaking several more or most of the first nine.

Consider this also: all men, because of their sinful nature, are susceptible to sin (Romans 3:23), and the wages of sin is death (Romans 6:23). For this reason a loving God sent His only Son to pay the penalty for sin so that whosoever believes on Christ should not die but have eternal life. Thus, sin abounds but grace abounds more abundantly (Romans 5:20); our gracious Heavenly Father has provided the escape from death and the way to life eternal.

Conversely, it is Satan, the tempter, who suggests the sin and tempts the sinner (God tempts no man [James 1:13]). Therefore, may we not conclude, with validity, that the person or agency that condones, promotes, or profits from sin is an instrument of the prince of darkness? What, then, does that say of the state that "legalizes" and promotes gaming (licenses casinos, slot machines, various games and sports of chance, etc.) and the state that sponsors its own lotteries?

God warned the priests of old not to accept the "hire of a whore, or the price of a dog [homosexual], into the house of the Lord thy God" (Deuteronomy 23:18)—meaning the tithes or offerings from those who engage in such abominations. Are not the tax receipts on the gains from the sin of gambling (sin-taxes) also an abomination in the sight of God? For, is not the state (the civil authority) to be a minister (servant) of God to the people for good (Romans 13:1-4)? And when civil authorities encourage gambling, is not the state taking unto itself the role of pimp— promoting lust and covetousness by encouraging the weak and susceptible to engage in sin for the state's profit?

There is also the matter of acknowledging (honoring) God's total sovereignty. The individual who gambles deliberately creates uncertainties that would otherwise not exist and are not a part of God's perfect plan and purpose. As Gary North suggests, the person who gambles embraces a chance-dominated universe, a cosmos of luck, rather than the universe of order created by the Omniscient and Omnipotent Creator. Such an individual makes his god the god of fortune; he chooses to follow the laws of chance rather than obey the laws of God. Thus, in a very real sense, he puts other gods before God and thereby violates God's First Commandment: "Thou shalt have no other God's before me" (Exodus 20:3). The gambler-idolator also rejects and disobeys that which Christ, our Savior and our King, emphasized as the First and Great Commandment: "Thou shalt love the Lord thy God with all thy heart and with all thy soul and with all thy mind" (Matthew 22:37, 38).

Jesus warned, "You cannot serve God and mammon" (Matthew 6:24). That which one puts first in his life is that which he will serve. Beware, warned Moses; forget not the Lord and His commandments (Deuteronomy 8:11).

The person who gambles is a disobedient steward. He or she not only fails to use what God has provided to serve Him, but also risks losing those God-given assets through selfish (ungodly) pursuits. Thus, such an individual fails to meet the most basic requirements of stewardship (Matthew 6:24; 1 Corinthians 4:1, 2; Titus 1:7).

Now, consider gambling (gaming) as the root sin of additional sins:

Gambling is a major cause of neglect of the family and the break-up of the family. Monies that should be spent on food, clothing, and housing go for gambling. God's Word tells us that the husband is to "cleave to his wife" (Genesis 2:24; Matthew 19:5), to provide for her, and to love her as he loves himself (Ephesians 5:33). The man who refuses to care for his family is worse than an infidel (1 Timothy 5:8). The father is to provide for his children until they can care for themselves (2 Corinthians 12:14).

Gambling is often a cause of neglecting and dishonoring parents. This is a violation of the Fifth Commandment (Exodus 20:12) and a dereliction of filial duty as set forth in the Scriptures (Matthew 7:11; 15:4; 19:19; Ephesians 6:2, 3).

Gambling has caused many a man to steal, thus leading him to break God's Seventh Commandment (Exodus 20:15). It has driven some to murder, thus to violate God's Sixth Commandment (Exodus 20:13).

Finally, gambling often engenders slothfulness and double-mindedness, leading the individual to neglect his labors and to be caught up in dreams of a "free ride" and the "big win."

God's rule of labor is this: "In the sweat of thy brow shalt thou eat bread" (Genesis 3:19). To God's servant, work is no longer a curse but a blessing; it is a way to express love and gratitude to the Lord for all His many blessings. Each person is to "bear his own burden" (Galatians 6:5) and to "eat his own bread" (2 Thessalonians 3:12)—meaning, in the modern idiom, "there is no such thing as a free lunch." Each individual is to "work with [his] own hands" (1 Thessalonians 4:11, 12) at whatever calling God has ordained.

Clearly, it is not God's will that man live by the ill-gotten gains of gambling or engage in the sin of covetousness that is the seedbed for additional sins. "Take heed," warned the Master, "and beware of covetousness: for a man's life consists not in the abundance of the things he possesses" (Luke 12:15). "For what is a man profited," our Savior asked, "if he shall gain the whole world . . . and lose his own soul?" (Matthew 16:26).

THIRTEEN

HOME SCHOOLS AND CHRISTIAN EDUCATION

Christian home schooling is the fastest growing segment of education as parents seek to obey God and escape the ravages of state-controlled teachings.

Background Briefing

What's the fastest growing segment of education in the United States today? Christian schools. And what's the fastest growing segment of Christian education? Home schooling.

In Los Angeles, it's not unusual for more than 1,000 home-schoolers to convene at workshops and seminars. In Nebraska, a state notoriously anti-Christian in regard to education, 350 or more gather for various Christian home school seminars. So it goes throughout the nation. It's estimated that about 1 million children are being taught (tutored) at home and the greatest percentage of those are in Christian home schools.[1]

Why the exodus from public (state) schools? Why the swing to Christian education? It's a basic part of the "parental revolution" in which parents seek to regain control of their children and strengthen the family unit. State-controlled schools, with their values manipulation and situational ethics, are a major cause of alienation between (Christian) parents and children and the breakdown of the family. Also, many parents complain that state schools fail in teaching solid academics, are often plagued by drugs, including alcohol, and are rife with vandalism, teenage pregnancy, venereal disease, pornography, and promiscuity (lack of discipline). "Having cast out the Ten Commandments, the public schools now bid the students to behave. It is an impossibility. . . . teacher and student alike reflect the lawlessness that ever appears in the absence of God's Law."[2]

Christian parents are concerned about all that—and more. They see an anti-Christian state school system that excludes (in fact, often denies and belittles) God, contradicts Bible truths, promotes atheism (the religion of secular humanism), challenges (works to curtail) the authority of godly parents and promotes evolution and rubberized moral values. "Students aware of a teacher's opinion in a classroom, even if obviously wrong, will limit the range of their views and conform their beliefs more to that opinion."[3]

As the number of Christian church and home schools accelerates, the opposition from government education agencies and teachers' union mounts. Why? There are several reasons. Opponents of Christian education, and those who seek to license/control it, insist they must protect the child from "incompetent, neglectful" parents. They argue that it's their responsibility because of compulsory education laws. But some state supreme courts have recognized that the responsibility for bringing up children is in other hands: " The responsibility of parents [is] not to leave their children in ignorance and in some way make them capable of functioning in society."[4] Further, the Kentucky Supreme Court said this in 1979: "The state should never use its power to require attendance at tax-supported public schools. Private schools, both church-related and secular, have a right to exist, so long as they rely on private support and meet the basic standards of health, safety, and educational effectiveness. . . . Their presence, not their absence, is an evidence of a free society."[5] (Note: many states consider home schools to be private schools.)

The issue is not mandatory education. The issue is who shall control education? The parent? The state? The National Education Association (NEA)? Or the American Federation of Teachers (AFT)?

The opponents of Christian education, whether in home or church, insist that they "simply want to ensure a quality education for all citizens." But, retort Christian parents and educators, Christian schools are where the quality education is. There are no reports of rape or robbery coming from Christian schools, no problems with drugs or vandalism, no assaults on teachers. Further, standard achievement test results demonstrate that Christian school students, in home and in church, rank several grade levels above their peers in the state schools. Christian parents and educators conclude the issue of "quality education" advanced by the state and education establishment affords no real grounds for opposition to Christian education. "If the state were truly interested in ensuring a 'quality education for its citizens,' it would be working to adopt the superior standards and match the achievements of Christian education."[6]

Why is there such strident, persistent opposition? Two reasons: (1) finances—for the school district, the more students there are in Christian schools the lower the average daily attendance (ADA) and that means a loss of state and federal aid (about three thousand dollars per student). And for teachers and teachers' unions, fewer students in state schools can mean a loss of jobs and political power; (2) control—the increase in Christian education threatens the state's monopoly.

Dr. Anthony Sutton suggests that the basic purpose of government schools "is not to teach subject matter but to condition children to live as socially integrated citizen units in an organic society . . . (the) absolute state. In this state the individual finds freedom only in obedience to the state."[7]

Those who would outlaw Christian home education assert that parents are not competent to teach. However, test results show that parents are in reality the best teachers of their young. Elaine Rapp contends, "It is not credentials, but the parents' intimate knowledge of the children and their own initiative in accepting and pursuing the sound education of their own children which are important. These provide the real basis for a creative and effective educational program."[8] Meg Johnson, formerly of the Home Education Resource Center, reports "We often find that certification or a degree in teaching can be a hindrance in some ways. . . . It is a fallacy to imagine that a teacher's certificate would magically make a parent tutor more qualified to educate her own children. The techniques of group management and group discipline, as well as the outlines which provide varying forms of 'busy-work' to keep things under control in a classroom simply don't apply at home."[9]

Further, the average teacher in a state classroom has little control over curriculum or texts or methodology; often she simply follows a structured teacher's manual. Parents, by contrast, can select texts, determine curriculum, and use personalized methods to train their children.

State authorities (and social workers) criticize home education for "lack of socialization" — meaning a loss of "benefits" from being a member of group, not learning how to "function" in society and get along with peers. Parents respond that socialization in today's world can be negative; indeed, harmful. And many studies show that group learning is not really beneficial; it often stunts individual ingenuity and motivation, and can reduce achievement by lowering it to a common denominator. Further, parents ask, what about peer group pressure? A peer is not simply a member or members of a herd; it is one who is equal in excellence, a companion, an associate who shares common values and views. Thus, a proper peer for a Christian young person as he or she is developing in the Lord is another Christian and other Christian young people. (More and more Christian home schoolers are getting together on a regular basis for field trips, outings, and tours.)

Some Christian parents suggest that putting their children in public schools provides an opportunity for them to witness for Christ. Witnessing for Christ is important; all believers are commissioned to do so. However, the purpose of school is not to evangelize but to educate, to train students to grow in that mind which was in Christ Jesus. Further, placing immature young Christians in harm's way (negative environments and ungodly pressures) may force them to take a stand that even an adult Christian might find difficult. To do that to a child would be contrary to Christ's teachings (Matthew 18:6, 7).

Finally, Christian education challenges (meets head-on) the religion of humanism that has gained control of most if not all the state education systems. Secular humanists cannot allow that. For humanists, education is the key to victory in the battle for the minds of young people — and, thus, an important key to their design of the future.

Dr. W. David Gamble of the American Reformation Movement emphasizes: "Mr. Dunphy is correct when he states that the classroom has become an arena of conflict between Christianity and secular humanism. Both religions place a premium on education. . . . Any Christian school which does not challenge and rebuke humanistic education is not truly Christian."[10]

Cornelius Van Til wrote, "If you say you are involved in the struggle between Christ and Satan in the area of family and in the church, but not in the school, you are deceiving yourself. . . . You cannot expect to train intelligent, well-informed soldiers of the Cross of Christ unless Christ is held up before men as the Lord of culture as well as the Lord of religion. It is the nature of the conflict between Christ and Satan to be all-comprehensive."[11]

The Battle for the Future

The humanists understand only too well how important education is. John Dunphy, a renowned educator and a leader in the secular humanist movement, recently asserted that:

> The battle for humankind's future must be waged and won in the public school classroom by teachers who correctly perceive their roles as the proselytizers of a new faith: a religion of humanity that recognizes and respects the spark of what the theologians call divinity in every human being. These teachers must embody the same selfless dedication as the most rabid fundamentalist preachers, for they will be ministers of another sort, utilizing a classroom instead of a pulpit to convey humanist values in whatever subject they teach, regardless of the educational level — preschool, day care or large state university. The classroom must and will become an arena of conflict between the old and the new — the rotting corpse of Christianity . . . and the new faith of humanism, resplendent in its promise of a world in which the never-realized Christian ideal of "love thy neighbor" will finally be achieved.[12]

Consider the Biblical Principles

Children do not belong to the state. They belong to God and by Him are entrusted to parents for care and training in His Word and way. "Lo, children are an heritage of the Lord: the fruit of the womb is His reward" (Psalm 127:3). "And he lifted up his eyes, and saw the women and the children; and said, Who are those with you? And he said, the children which God has graciously given me" (Genesis 33:5; see also Deuteronomy 7:13; 28:4; Psalm 24:1; Ezekiel 16:20, 21; Isaiah 8:18).

God gives the parents, not Caesar, the responsibility for educating their children (wisdom and training). "And, you fathers, provoke not your children to wrath: but bring them up in the nurture and admonition of the Lord" (Ephesians 6:4). "Train up a child in the way he should go: and when he is old, he will not depart from it" (Proverbs 22:6). "And these words which I command you this day, shall be in your heart: And you shall teach them diligently unto your children, and shall talk of them when you sit in your house and when you walk by the way, and when you lie down, and when you rise up" (Deuteronomy 6:6-9). "Now I say, that the heir as long as he is a child, differeth nothing from a servant, though he be lord of all; but is under tutors and governors until the time appointed of the father" (Galatians 4:1,2; see also Deuteronomy 11:18-21; Proverbs 4:1-27; 23:12, 13; Titus 1:6; Hebrews 12:9-11).

God has set the home, not the school, as the basic center of learning; the church and the school are but extensions of the home and parents.

> Therefore shall you lay up these words in your heart and in your soul, and bind them for a sign upon your hand, that they may be frontlets between your eyes. And you shall teach them to your children, speaking of them when you sit in your house . . . and you shalt write them upon the door posts of your house and upon your gates (Deuteronomy 11:18-21; see also Genesis 18:19; Exodus 10:2; Deuteronomy 4:9; Proverbs 31:26-28; Isaiah 38:19; Joel 1:3; 1 Timothy 3:5).

True knowledge (wisdom) comes from God through His Word and not from the ways or wiles of the world. "The fear of the Lord is the beginning of wisdom: a good understanding have all they that do His commandments" (Psalm 111:10). "Casting down imaginations, and every high thing that exalts itself against the knowledge of God, and bringing into captivity every thought to the obedience of Christ" (2 Corinthians 10:5). "If any of you lack wisdom, let him ask of God, that gives to all men liberally and upbraids not; and it shall be given unto him" (James 1:5). "In Whom are hid all the treasures of wisdom and knowledge" (Colossians 2:3; see also Deuteronomy 7:12-16; Psalm 90:12; Proverbs 21:30; Isaiah 55:8-9).

God's Word is the measure of all things, the scale on which His people are to weigh all issues of life; He is the foundation of true education. "To the Law and to the Testimony: if they speak not according to this Word, it is because there is no light in them" (Isaiah 8:20). "Man shall not live by bread alone, but by every Word that proceeds out of the mouth of God" (Deuteronomy 8:3; Matthew 4:4). "Yea, let God be true, but every man a liar; as it is written, 'That you might be justified in your sayings, and might overcome when you are judged'" (Romans 3:4). "Beware, lest any man spoil you through philosophy and vain deceit, after the tradition of men, after the rudiments of the world and not after Christ" (Colossians 2:8; see also Deuteronomy 11:1; Philippians 4:8).

The purpose of education is to train the child to be a faithful servant of God, to seek to be holy even as He is holy, and to be equipped (competent) to fulfill God's cultural mandate and Great Commission (Genesis 1:26-28; Matthew 28:18-20). The goal of education is not simply to gain degrees or fame but to promulgate the faith. "And herein do I exercise myself, to have always a conscience void of offense toward God, and toward men" (Acts 24:16). "Let this mind be in you, which was also in Christ Jesus" (Philippians 2:5). "They are not of the world, even as I am not of the world. Sanctify them through Thy Truth, Thy Word is Truth" (John 17:16, 17).

"And they that shall be of Thee shall build the old waste places: Thou shalt raise up the foundations of many generations" (Isaiah 58:12; see also Psalm 1:1-3; 78:1-7; Titus 2:11-15).

Academic freedom is not a license to study evil or the ways of evil. "Cease, my son, to hear the instruction that causes you to err from the Words of Knowledge" (Proverbs 19:27). "Yet I would have you wise unto that which is good and simple [innocent] concerning [as to what is] evil" (Romans 16:19).

"Beloved, believe [trust] not every spirit, but try [prove] the spirits whether they are of God: because many false prophets are gone out into the world" (1 John 4:1).

Christians are not to have the ungodly as peers; parents must protect their children from the pressures of worldly peers. No parent may render unto the world or Caesar that which belongs to Christ! "Be you not unequally yoked together with unbelievers: for what fellowship has righteousness with unrighteousness? and what communion has light with darkness?" (2 Corinthians 6:14-18). "My son, if sinners entice you, consent you not" (Proverbs 1:10-19). "He that walketh with wise men shall be wise: but a companion of fools shall be destroyed" (Proverbs 13:20). "And be not conformed to this world: but be you transformed by the renewing of your mind, that you may prove what is that good and acceptable, and perfect will of God" (Romans 12:2).

> Let no man despise [look down upon] your youth; but be you
> an example of the believers, in word, in conversation [lifestyle],
> in charity, in spirit, in faith, in purity (1 Timothy 4:12).

FOURTEEN

HUMANISM

"Humanism is a polite term for atheism," admitted a former president of the American Humanist Association. Quite simply, humanism is man seeking to be God. The courts have labeled it a religion and as such it pervades our public schools.

Background Briefing

"By the year 2000 we will—I hope—raise our children to believe in human potential, not God." So said Gloria Steinem, militant feminist and editor of *Ms.* magazine.[1]

"Any child who believes in God is mentally ill," said social psychologist Paul Baldwin. Baldwin followed that up by boasting that national "mental health programs" are being developed to help children who believe in God to have "healthier, more balanced" attitudes.[2]

"The Bible is not merely another book, an outmoded and archaic book. . . . it has been and remains an incredibly dangerous book," asserts educator John Dunphy.[3]

Gary Griswold, a twenty-five-year-old student who plans to seek a college-level teaching position upon graduation, writes, "I am concerned that a belief in God, particularly in the traditional Christian sense, is a subtle but very real obstacle to the survival of the human species." He goes on to say that "the minds of young people in our schools and colleges today" should be "challenged and developed—not indoctrinated and molded."[4]

The divorce from the more repressive moral strictures of traditional Christianity can never be complete as long as the Bible is regarded as the ultimate reference text.[5]

What is all this? Humanism. It is both the root and fruit of humanism. And what is humanism?

James Curry, a former president of the American Humanist Association, is reported to have said, "Humanism is a polite term for atheism. . . . Humanism . . . relieves mankind from the necessity either to believe in God or to look to Him as the fundamental source of all good."

Mr. Curry was echoing, in essence, the words of another humanist and signer of the first *Humanist Manifesto* (1933), John Dewey:

> There is no God, and there is no soul. Hence, there are no needs for the props of traditional religion. With dogma and creed excluded then immutable truth is also dead and buried. There is no room for fixed natural law or permanent moral absolutes (*Living Philosophies,* 1930).

Humanism, wrote John Dunphy in *The Humanist,* is "a new faith: a religion of humanity." He argued that traditional theism is "an unproven and outmoded faith" and that "salvationism, based on mere affirmation, still appears as harmful, diverting people with false hopes of heaven hereafter."[6]

Is humanism a religion? Yes, it is, according to the United States Supreme Court in 1961 (*Torcaso v. Watkins*) and again in 1964 (*U.S. v. Seeger*). ("Among religions in this country which do not teach what would generally be considered a belief in God are Buddhism, Taoism, Ethical Cultural, secular humanism, and others." [Footnote 11, *Torcaso v. Watkins*], see also United States Supreme Court's findings in the Schmepp case [1963]: "We agree of course, that the state may not establish 'a religion of secularism' in the sense of affirmatively opposing or showing hostility to religion, thus preferring those who believe in no religion over those who do believe.")

Some, including many Christians, discount the existence of humanism. They insist it is simply a fantasy concocted by religious zealots and at most a "philosophical" point of view. But humanism is real, indeed. It has a specific dogma and definite goals.

Pastor Steve Hallman, a graduate of Asbury Seminary and Vice President of the National Federation for Decency, issues this warning:

The Church, the body of Christ, must begin to understand the nature of humanism, a system which has no place for a supernatural God or a Savior who died for sinners.[7]

"At the present time," warns Laurain Mills, "Christians face a peril which could subvert the truth of their beliefs. This danger stems from the subtle, pervasive influence of humanism."[8]

Consider its basic tenets. They are set forth in *Humanist Manifesto I* (1933) and *Humanist Manifesto II* (1973). Weigh humanists by their own words. "For by your words you shall be justified, and by your words you shall be condemned" (Matthew 12:37).

1. Humanism denies the existence of God. "As non-theists, we begin with humans not God, nature not deity. . . . we can discover no divine purpose or providence for the human species. . . . No deity will save us; we must save ourselves" (*Humanist Manifesto II*).

2. Humanism holds that man creates his own god; gods, insist the humanists, are products of man's imagination. "The cultivation of moral devotion and creative imagination is an expression of genuine 'spiritual' experience and aspiration. We believe, however, that traditional dogmatic or authoritarian religions that place revelation, God, ritual or creed above human needs and experience do a disservice to the human species. Any account of nature should pass the tests of scientific evidence; in our judgment, the dogmas and myths of traditional religion do not do so" (*Humanist Manifesto II*).

3. Humanism denies the Creator, and His creation. "Religious humanists regard the universe as self-existing and not created. . . . Humanism believes that man is a part of nature and that he has emerged as the result of a continuous process" (*Humanist Manifesto I*). "Rather, science affirms that the human species is an emergence from natural evolutionary forces" (*Humanist Manifesto II*).

4. Humanism denies the existence of man's soul. "Modern science discredits such historic concepts as . . . the 'separable soul'. . . . As far as we know, the total personality is a function of the biological organism transacting in a social and cultural context. . . . There is no credible evidence that life survives the death of the body" (*Humanist Manifesto II*).

5. Humanism denies the hope of salvation and ridicules the fear of judgment. "Promises of immortal Salvation or fear of eternal damnation are both illusory and harmful" (*Humanist Manifesto II*).

6. Humanism holds there are no absolutes, no set right or wrong. "We affirm that moral values derive their source from human experience. Ethics is autonomous and situational, needing no theological or ideological sanction. Ethics stems from human needs and interest" (*Humanist Manifesto II*).

In an interview with the *Boston Herald* in 1982, humanist Charles F. Potter commented that "education is thus a most powerful ally of humanism and every American public school is a school of humanism."[9]

That, of course, is exactly what troubled a group of six hundred Christian parents in Mobile County, Alabama. They found that the religion of humanism was rampant in the textbooks used in the public schools and that the religion of humanism was being systematically taught in the schools of Mobile.[10] They took their case against the Board of School Commissioners to court. After a lengthy trial, and an examination of forty-nine textbooks, Judge William Brevard Hand, United States District Court in Mobile, Alabama, handed down his 111-page decision. He decreed that humanism is, indeed, a religion:

> The most important belief of this religion is its denial of the transcendent and/or supernatural: there is no God, no creator, no divinity. Such a belief rests upon faith.

Judge Hand concluded that therefore, for First Amendment purposes, humanism is "a religious statement." Further, determined Judge Hand, the textbooks he examined were so loaded with the doctrines of humanism that they violated the "establishment clause" of the First Amendment.

The Judge said he found the textbooks taught a "highly relativistic and individualistic approach which constitutes the promotion of a fundamental faith claim opposed to other religious faiths. . . . [it] strikes at the heart of many theistic religions' belief." He ordered the books removed.

The American Civil Liberties Union and the People for the American Way rose to new heights of indignation. The two groups charged that the religious "far right" was intent on forcing fundamentalist Christian ideas into the public schools. As far as they are concerned, the public schools are the private preserve of the humanists. As columnist James J. Kilpatrick wrote, "It is a curious thing. The ACLU and People for the American Way, in defending the humanists [right to promote their faith], make precisely the same arguments when they are attacking the Baptists [for seeking to defend their faith]. It does make a difference, as the Proverb tells us, to see whose ox is gored."[11] The ACLU and PAW appealed Judge Hand's decision to a higher court, and it was overturned by the Appeals Court.

How deeply do the roots penetrate into the state-controlled, taxpayer-funded school system? What is being propagated in those classrooms? Inspect a few of its evil fruits:

1. God is denied in the classroom, separated from state, from state schools, and (during school hours) from the state's students. God's written Word is also barred except as a "quaint historical manuscript" or a reference to an outmoded set of ethics.

2. The increasingly discredited theory of evolution is found in most state school textbooks and is taught in the classrooms of most state schools. Efforts to obtain "equal time" for creationism have been consistently denied. Humanists protest consideration of creation, say it is religious myth. Yet, assert Christians, evolution is a humanistic theory and humanism has been decreed a religion. Why then the double standard?

3. The Ten Commandments are removed from public school and barred from classrooms. "We reject those features of traditional religious morality that deny humans a full appreciation of their own potentialities" (*Humanist Manifesto II*). The new-world words are situational ethics and flexible moral values. Within that framework is a pluralism that decrees all viewpoints equal and all modes of expression acceptable — the profane as well as the noble, the perverted as well as the pure.

4. Self-authority and the autonomy of man (apart from God) are expounded. "Reason and intelligence are the most effective instruments that humankind possesses. There is no substitute: neither faith nor passion suffices in itself." Thus, we beget the "ME" generation — juvenile anarchy, self-centeredness, self-indulgence, self-gratification. "Nothing that is part of contemporary life is taboo" (*The Humanist*, 1976).

5. *Sexual permissiveness is not only tolerated but promoted.* "In the area of sexuality, we believe that intolerant attitudes, often cultivated by orthodox religions and puritanical cultures, unduly repress sexual conduct. . . . The many varieties of sexual exploration should not in themselves be considered 'evil' " (*Humanist Manifesto II*).

6. *Free individual enterprise is opposed and collectivism (socialism-communism) is promoted.* "The humanists are firmly convinced that existing acquisitive and profit-motivated society has shown itself to be inadequate and that a radical change in methods, controls and motives must be instituted. . . . The goal of humanism is a free and universal society in which people voluntarily and intelligently cooperate. . . . Humanists demand a shared life in a shared world" (*Humanist Manifesto I*).

7. *One-world government and "global citizenship" is promoted instead of patriotism and national sovereignty.* "We deplore the division of humankind on nationalistic grounds. We have reached a turning point in human history where the best option is to transcend the limits of national sovereignty and move toward the building of a world community in which all sectors of the human family can participate. Thus, we look to the development of a system of world law and a world order based upon transnational federal government" (*Humanist Manifesto II*).

Of such is the gospel of humanism. But it gets even worse:

- It is pro-abortion ("the right to abortion . . . should be recognized").

- It is pro-gay rights ("we do not wish to prohibit by law or social sanction sexual behavior between consenting adults. . . . a civilized society should be a tolerant one").

- It is pro-ERA ("equal rights for both women and men to fulfill their unique careers and potentialities as they see fit, free of invidious discrimination").

- It supports a guaranteed annual minimum wage for all.

Thus, the battle rages: God's Word versus the "reasonings" of man. The humanists know, if Christians do not, that "the battle for humankind's future must be waged and won in the public school classroom by teachers who correctly perceive their roles as the proselytizers of a new faith: a religion of humanity. . . . These teachers must embody the same selfless dedication as the most rabid fundamentalist preachers . . . for they will be ministers of another sort, utilizing a classroom instead of a pulpit to convey humanist values in whatever subject they teach."[12]

Consider the Biblical Principles

The Lord God — not man — is Sovereign. God, alone, is the Creator — not man, not biochemistry. God is the source of all power. "And He is before all things, and by Him all things consist" (Colossians 1:17).

The earth, the heavens, the seas — and man — did not evolve; they were created — by the Lord God. "In the beginning, God created the heaven and the earth" (Genesis 1:1). "And God said, Let the earth bring forth the living creature after his kind. . . . And God said, Let Us make man in Our image, after Our likeness" (Genesis 1:24, 26). "All things were made by Him; and without Him was not any thing made that was made" (John 1:3).

Humanism is not new to this world. It made its entrance in the Garden of Eden. It slithered in, subtle and beautiful to behold — and evil.

> And the serpent said to the woman, "You shall surely not die: For God knows that in the day you eat thereof [of the tree of the knowledge of good and evil], then your eyes shall be opened, and you shall be as gods, knowing good and evil" (Genesis 3:4, 5).

"You shall be as gods!" And Eve fell, and Adam — and man has been falling for that snare and delusion ever since.

Humanism calls for the worship of the creature rather than the Creator. God's Word makes it clear: those who do so are liars. "Who changed the truth of God into a lie, and worshipped and served the creature more than the Creator, who is blessed forever" (Romans 1:25).

Humanists reject God's Word and deny God's Truth. They are corrupt, doers of abominable works. "Behold, you walk every one after the imagination of his evil heart, that they may not hearken unto Me" (Jeremiah 16:12). "The fool has said in his heart, There is no God. They are corrupt, they have done abominable works" (Psalm 14:1). "The hand of our God is upon all them for good that seek Him; but His power and His wrath is against all them that forsake Him" (Ezra 8:22). "There is none that understands, there is none that seek after God. They are all gone out of the way, they are together become unprofitable; there is none that does good, no, not one" (Romans 3:11-12).

The humanists put their gods before God; they create a false religion. "You shall have no other gods before Me" (Exodus 20:3). "But there were false prophets also among the people, even as there shall be false teachers among you, who privily shall bring in damnable heresies, even denying the Lord" (2 Peter 2:1).

The humanist holds that man is autonomous, that man is the means and measure of all things. He puts himself, and human reason and intelligence above God; he relies on man's intellect and reasoning rather than God's Word; God warns us to turn away from such ungodly individuals. "For men shall be lovers of their own selves, covetous, boasters, proud, blasphemers, disobedient to parents, unthankful, unholy, without natural affection, trucebreakers, false accusers, incontinent, fierce, despisers of those that are good, traitors, heady, high-minded, lovers of pleasure more than lovers of God; Having a form of godliness, but denying the power thereof: from such turn away" (2 Timothy 3:2-5).

Humanism seeks to please man (self and society) rather than God. Thus, it cannot please God. "For do I now persuade men, or God? Or do I seek to please men? For if I yet pleased men, I should not be the servant of Christ" (Galatians 1:10).

Thus, there lies the heart and the heat of the battle for the minds and souls of our children — and the fate of our nation. Dr. Robert Simonds has marked some of the battle zones: the right to life (for the preborn and the elderly) versus abortion-on-demand and euthanasia; heterosexuality (husband and wife and family) versus sodomy; morality, chastity, and fidelity versus sexual license and promiscuity; Christian virtues and health versus licentiousness and VD, AIDS, and herpes; Christian faith and creation versus religious atheism and evolution; and parental rights and responsibilities as ordained by the Lord God versus state's rights and child's rights above the parent's.

For the Christian, the follower of Christ, there is no alternative: "The Word of God has been revealed in Personal and in written form — in Christ, that is, and in Scripture. As Christ is the Complete Personal Word of God, valid in all times and places, Scripture is the absolute written Word of God, applicable in all times and places."[13]

"But as for me, and my house, we will serve the Lord" (Joshua 24:15b).

INFLATION

The Bible warns against false weights and deceitful measures. Inflation is all that — and more. It is a thief that steals the working man's wages.

Background Briefing

Inflation is the artful plundering of the people through the continual, apparently never-ending debauchery and manipulation of the value of our money. It is one of the greatest dangers to our nation and to our civilization.

What are the ravages of inflation? Figure it this way. Get yourself one hundred pennies. Take thirty-one of them and chuck them in the trash. That's what inflation has done to the purchasing power of your dollar since 1980. That's right! Since the year 1980, the value of your hard-earned buck has lost more that one-third of its purchasing power.

In 1987 the rate of inflation was 4.4 percent.[1] Economists figure it will be slightly higher in 1988 and really speed up in 1989 and beyond. Politicians tell us we should be happy because the present rate of inflation has "cooled" down to just over 4 percent a year. They say that's "mild," a "bite-size" after years of tearing off big chunks of our purchasing power. But, at 4 percent a year, by the year 2000 the 1988 "dollar" would be worth about forty-three cents.[2] And, if inflation were to go even higher, which is quite likely, by the turn of the century, that one-dollar bill in your pocket would shrink to the point where it would buy only about a dime's worth of what it purchases today.[3] Call it "the passing of the buck!" It's like Will Rogers said, "What this country needs is a good five-cent nickel."

Sure, wages and salaries rose at a slightly higher rate in 1987 than they did in 1986, but inflation rose even more rapidly. Thus, 1987 was the first year since 1979 that wages failed to keep up with rising prices.[4] Some "bite"!

The United States Commerce Department says our 1987 disposable income — what's left in our pockets after taxes and inflation — rose about 1 percent over 1986, the weakest rise since 1982. It predicts we won't see much of an increase in 1988, either.[5]

You say you "play" the stock market? Before that October crash, things looked pretty rosy, right? The stock exchange indices were way up there, right. But, consider this: the New York Stock Exchange (NYSE) index would have to hit 175 (about three times where it was in 1965) just to make up for all those years of inflation.[6]

In the beginning, the Lord God created the heavens and the earth *ex nihilo* — out of nothing (the Hebrew word is *bara*). As the Apostle Paul wrote, that which is seen was brought forth from the unseen (Hebrews 11:3). Those who handle our money system do the same: they create "money" *ex nihilo*. Every time they do, our currency loses that much more purchasing power. Thus do men play God! In 808 B.C. the prophet Amos took the higher powers to task for "making the ephah small and the shekel great and falsifying the balance by deceit" (Amos 8:5).

Economist Milton Friedman has said, "I have demonstrated on the basis of a twelve-year analysis spanning five centuries that inflation has always only one single cause: the creation of money by the state. Governments today are thus solely responsible for inflation."[7]

> Lenin is said to have declared that the best way to destroy the Capitalist System was to debauch the currency. . . . Lenin was certainly right. There is no subtler, no surer, means of overturning the existing basis of society than to debauch the currency. The process engages all the hidden forces of economic law on the side of destruction, and does it in a manner which not one man in a million is able to diagnose.[8]

The ancient Roman Caesars, when they had reached an explosive level of taxation, and knew they faced a revolt of the people, resorted to inflation (a form of hidden taxation) by adding baser metals to the coins—and also by shaving gold coins and using the shavings to make more coins.

In 1690, to meet the payroll for soldiers, the Massachusetts legislature issued paper money (hoping there would be revenues coming in from higher taxes). The soldiers lost out: they had to accept discounts on their paper money before the merchants would accept it. But the government got off the hook; it was relieved of its just debts and avoided a revolt. Getting away with it prompted the Bay Colony government to issue a sea of paper money to cover all of its debts and expenses. That paper money drove the gold and silver out of circulation. Finally, the purchasing power of the fiat (paper) money dropped to one-eighth of its face value. It was only after Spanish coins were imported to serve as money that the economy recovered.[9]

The Continental Congress issued paper money to help pay for the American War for Independence. Without backing, the currency became worthless (thus, the expression "Not worth a Continental"). France went through a reign—a downpour—of paper money during the period from 1789 to 1796. Even church property was confiscated as "backing" for accelerated issues of the fake money. Before financial ruin and spiritual depravity took over, the cost of a barrel of flour had soared from forty-five cents to forty-five dollars. Finally, there was no bread at any price—to which Marie Antoinette reacted, "Let them eat cake!" (Today, there is talk that the government should start taxing all church property to raise more revenue to try and curb the growing deficit and malignant inflation.)

In Germany, in the 1920s, the printing presses went wild; they ran night and day turning out "money." There were some three hundred paper mills and two thousand printing houses churning out the fake bills. A one million mark bank note was worth thirty-three cents. At the end, that big red balloon exploded: a loaf of bread cost 1.25 trillion marks. The workers were paid several times a day; their wives waited at the factory gates for their pay checks and then rushed to the markets to try to get a jump on the hour-by-hour decline of purchasing power (some women used wheelbarrows to carry their husband's paper wages). The uncontrolled inflation was one of the major factors in the rise of Hitler's Third Reich. Inflation breeds anarchy; anarchy begets tyranny.

Way back in 1947, President Harry Truman warned the Congress: "We have an alarming degree of inflation and, even more alarming, it is getting worse." When Truman uttered those words, the one hundred cents of purchasing power of the 1940 dollar had already shrunk to sixty-three cents. The gangrene of inflation had set in.

But that past was only a prologue: as Neil McCaffrey said a few years ago, "With inflation alone, people must earn about ten times what their fathers earned in 1965. And, with inflation plus taxes, they have to earn about thirteen times more to keep up."

In August 1984 the American Institute of Economic Research calculated that, during the twelve-year period 1971-1983, inflation embezzled more than $3 trillion in lost purchasing power from savings accounts, insurance policies, pensions, etc. That was about equal to all the federal income taxes paid during those same twelve years, which means that the American taxpayer paid twice as much for government than the politicians let on: once in direct taxation and again in indirect taxation.

We're told that the purchasing power of the dollar today is about thirty cents. But that is not entirely true. The thirty-three cents figure is based on an arbitrary price index set at one hundred back in 1967. But, in 1967, the one hundred cents of purchasing power of the 1939 dollar had already shriveled to less than fifty cents. So, figure it this way: Compared to that 1939 dollar, the buck in your pocket is worth about one thin dime!

What is this sliding scale and rubber yardstick of the Consumer Price Index? How can they keep changing the rules as the game goes along? Well, when the purchasing power of the monetary unit drops to an "indefensible" level and the natives get restless, the base year for the index is changed to make it appear that the dollar is worth more than it is. It's the old "smoke and mirrors" game. It's easier to "falsify the balance by deceit" than it is to engage in the discipline necessary to halt inflation and work to restore a measure of integrity and value to the currency.

"And I heard a voice in the midst of the four beasts say, A measure of wheat for a penny" (Revelation 6:6). In today's bizarre bazaar, that figures out to a dry quart of wheat for a day's wages.

Today, growing numbers of people hunger to learn why social evils exist; this is especially true of godly Christians. We search for truth and strive to learn what we can do to bring about needed change. In the basic institutional ways of each nation — including its monetary system — we discern that there are right actions under God, and there are wrong ones. We see that His basic Moral Law is involved. And we know that God has told us that He rewards the dutiful nation and punishes the unrighteous one.

To really get a handle on inflation, to understand what it is and what it does, one must first understand money — what it is (and isn't) and how it is created (and how its value can be destroyed).

What is money?

Money is a medium of exchange — period.

To be effective, money must be recognized and accepted as a measure (standard) of value. Money should serve as a store of value, a commodity which would be saved for future use and would maintain its value in the interim.

When men first went beyond direct barter, they searched for a stable monetary commodity to serve as a medium of exchange and store of value. In their search it was revealed to them that gold, a precious metal, was the most nearly ideal monetary commodity. Silver and a few other valuable metals also emerged as partially acceptable money for coinage.

Throughout Scripture it is clear that money commodities are always gold and silver (see "Consider The Biblical Principles" below).

"Money substitutes" such as bills, notes, and bank credit papers are only representations of the real money which is the money commodity. All history tells us that whoever holds civil authority in a nation will be tempted strongly to manipulate or to alter the value of the money commodity. That temptation must be eliminated as far as human resourcefulness can accomplish it — thus, the necessity of the discipline of a gold standard. Keep firmly in mind that gold serves as a disciplinary agent; it is not to be an idol!

Politicians and economist-apologists go as far as they can to convince people that money substitutes are real money. Sleight-of-hand artists want printed paper in the form of bills, notes or bank credit thought of as money; that makes it easier for them to manipulate the monetary system and dilute the value of money substitutes.

The dilution of the value of money by government and banks occurs in this manner: suppose that the total United States money stock in a given year is $600 billion, and suppose that it is increased during the year by $195 billion. If total goods and services available for purchase during that period increased only $15 billion, the net increase in the money stock (to buy those goods and services) would be $180 billion. What happens? The purchasing power (value) of the dollar in your pocket is cut by 30 percent. Why? Because the value of the original $600 million money stock was diluted by that net increase of the $180 billion (30 percent) created by fiat (ex nihilo!).

Consider the "beneficent cycle," the dynamic which occurred in the United States in years gone by as a result of obeying God's Word. See how obedience to God and successful economic policies go hand-in-hand!

Outstanding economic growth occurred in America during the nineteenth century because of two primary factors: (1) a favorable economic climate generated by a society whose Scripturally-directed people were hardworking, frugal, and charitable, and (2) a Scripturally-constituted civil government which followed non-inflationary monetary policies while it protected the right of citizens to own, use, and develop private property.

In recent decades government has almost constantly pursued inflationary policies; incentives to save and invest have been (and are now being) systematically undermined. Such periods of persistent inflationary practices produce distressing consequences. Leap-frogging wages and interest rates — which some believe to be causes of inflation — are but dire results of more and more make-believe money being created by monetary authorities who either reject or are ignorant of God's laws of economics.

How can we, the people — and more specifically we, God's people — turn away from the present inflation-prone system of money-by-government-fiat? How can we move toward a sound 100 percent gold-based banking system? If there comes to be sufficient recognition of these truths so that they can be acted upon, how can decades of inflation be undone?

With so much of the structure of society erected on this false foundation, and with countless millions of innocent participants held captive in the process, can there be hope for a successful return to honest money? That is a real problem. While man may be inclined to resist undue governmental intervention, his flawed and imperfectible nature all too often succumbs to calculated political promises of a free lunch and cradle-to-the-grave security.

Since money pervades every aspect of society, any corrective steps must be taken carefully and judiciously to ease the transition and avoid unnecessary economic shocks. But it can be done provided it is done gradually and persistently. Some drastic actions will be necessary.

Returning to Honest Money

1. Stop all lending by financial institutions of any funds not placed with them for savings purposes. An exception: loans made for the movement of goods in the production or marketing process should be phased out over a five-year period and then prohibited.

2. Two years following the implementation of the first goal, we should cancel the charter of the central bank (the "engine of inflation," the Federal Reserve Bank.) Where a sound banking system exists there is no need for a central bank. Contrary to popular thinking, the Federal Reserve is not a government entity any more than Federal Express is a government agency. The "Fed" is a private corporation to which Congress gave the monopoly of issuing paper money.

3. Mandate that the federal budget be balanced within a period of three fiscal years. The proper and comparatively small expenditures of a constitutionally limited government (which we once had and to which we must return) can be funded by modest and equitable taxation.

4. By a constitutional amendment define the monetary unit in terms of gold by weight (one ounce of gold equals X dollars). This should become effective at the end of a five-year period at which time the value of gold should be determined and fixed by free market price.

5. Remove the civil government from all money issuance, coinage, and handling activities. Limit its function in this realm to its legitimate role, rendering justice. In monetary affairs, the government would then supervise private banks as they carry out their proper and moral operations. (The history of banking has repeatedly

shown a periodic lack of public safety and a capacity and temptation for improper manipulation of the money supply; careful
supervision by governmental authorities is required.)

6. *After the five-year period, and when the value of the dollar is defined
in terms of gold, prohibit the creation of any make-believe money by any
party — bank, government, or otherwise — unless that substitute (certificate, note or bank credit) is 100 percent backed by gold on deposit
with the issuer.* An exception would be small-change coins made
of lesser metals (silver and copper) with their metal content
substantially in proportion to gold's defined value for that coin
(half dollar, quarter, dime, etc.).

Since the actions necessary to establish a sound and moral
monetary system are so far-reaching compared to what we now
have, we must surely undergo some form of crisis to bring them
about. But, disobedience to God's laws and our departure from
sound and right ways generally are moving us steadily toward
such a climax.[10]

Consider the Biblical Principles

Inflation violates God's principles and precepts. It breaks the
laws He established to protect His people. There is, indeed, a
Biblical system of economics: the way of the Lord versus the
ways of man; the right way (stewardship) versus the wrong way
(humanism).

The Scriptural principle throughout the Bible is this: money
is to be something of stable value, an always honestly-weighed
commodity for exchange purposes. In 808 B.C., Amos took the
higher powers (civil authorities) to task for "making the ephah
small and the shekel great and falsifying the balance by deceit"
(Amos 8:5).

Inflation disobeys God's laws against thievery, covetousness,
and deceit. It takes advantage of the elderly, encumbers the young,
and threatens the stability of the home; it robs laborers of a fair
wage and investors of fair return. It discourages thrift, weakens
the tithe, and violates God's mandated purpose for civil authorities
(to be ministers of justice protecting citizens and their property).

"You shall not steal," says the Lord (Exodus 20:15). Inflation
steals. It is a thief. By reducing the value of the established

medium of exchange, it robs the people of their wealth. It plunders property which is to be used to serve the Lord (it takes the "first fruits" which belong to Him). It confiscates that which is to be handed down from generation to generation (thus subverting God's basic social unit — the family).

"You shall not steal, neither deal falsely, neither lie to one another" (Leviticus 19:11). Inflation is a deceit, a hidden tax. Through it government and financial institutions deal falsely with the people. Thus, it breaks God's Ninth Commandment, "You shall not bear false witness" (Exodus 20:16). Isaiah condemned the adulteration (dilution) of silver with dross (Isaiah 1:22). Ezekiel prophesied to the Israelites concerning the consequences of debasing money (Ezekiel 22:18-22); so did Isaiah (Isaiah 1:25). Jesus drove money-changers from the temple, not only because they were desecrating the Lord's house but also because they were cheating the people ("You have made it a den of thieves" [Matthew 21:13].)

"You shall not covet," said the Lord (Exodus 20:17; Luke 12:15). Inflation is the seed and fruit of covetousness. It proceeds from a "carnal mind" (Romans 8:7).

"The laborer is worthy of his hire" (Luke 10:7; 1 Timothy 5:18). Inflation robs workers and producers of the fruit of their labor and investment (Matthew 25:14-23). It "muzzles the ox that treads out the corn." It is difficult for the employer to pay the employee "that which is just and equal" (Colossians 4:1) when the value of money is manipulated.

The greatest sin (and cost) of inflation is not economic, but spiritual: it is the sin of the wicked heart that denies God, refuses to obey His laws, and puts other gods before Him. When those in higher power violate the integrity of the medium of exchange, or when they enable or assist others in such deceit, they destroy the property of the people. Thus, they are not ministers of God to the people for good but do, in fact, serve other gods and worship graven images.

It is the responsibility of those who would serve and obey God to set things straight. If we do not, God will: "I will turn My hand against you, and thoroughly purge away your dross, and take away all your alloy" (Isaiah 1:25). As we witness the degradation of our currency, the plundering of the fruits of our labor, the ravages of the rampant anti-Scriptural Babylonian economic system, and the decline of the American republic economically and spiritually, can it be that the Lord is dealing with us now? (See also Genesis 23:15,16; 1 Chronicles 21:25; Proverbs 20:10; and references to gold and silver as noted in concordances.)

THE INF TREATY
(Strategic Arms Talks)

President Reagan and General Secretary Gorbachev have signed a treaty to remove intermediate-range missiles from Europe. Some worry that this weakens our NATO allies and makes them vulnerable to the Soviet's conventional forces.

Background Briefing

On December 7, 1987, Soviet General Secretary Mikhail Gorbachev arrived in Washington, D.C. The head of what President Reagan once called an "evil empire" received full military honors; the gold and red Hammer and Sickle flew from lamp posts in front of the White House. The media termed Mr. Gorbachev "charismatic" — a "great communicator."

On Tuesday, December 8, on the Lincoln table beneath the crystal chandeliers in the East Room of the White House, President Reagan and Secretary Gorbachev signed the INF treaty. Mr. Reagan presented "Mikhail" with a set of gold cuff links engraved with the words of Isaiah 2:4, "They shall beat their swords into plowshares." Others were moved to quote Jeremiah 2:33, "For My people have committed two evils: they have forsaken Me, the fountain of living waters, And hewn themselves cisterns — broken cisterns that can hold no water."

As the roar of the greasepaint and smell of the crowd died away, *USA Today* commented: The TV lights are off. The speechifying is over. The stars of the most heartening spectacle to grace the world stage this year have returned to their dressing rooms. The question now is, have Ronald Reagan and Mikhail Gorbachev found . . . the elusive key to a new, safer superpower relationship? Or will we, in the end, be bitten by the iron teeth that Soviet President Andrei Gromyko said wait behind Gorbachev's charming smile?[1]

The White House calls the treaty a step toward peace. Furious, opponents of the treaty call it "the second 'day of infamy.'" Gus Hall, General Secretary of the Communist Party of the United States, writes in the *People's Daily World,* "1988 will be a turning point year." Sir James Goldsmith, international financier and chairman of the editorial board of the leading French weekly, *L'Express,* suggests "perhaps we live in tragic times. Perhaps this is one of those great turning points of history . . . a historic seismic shift" when the leadership of the world changes hands.[2]

L'Express said it this way: "Ronald Reagan will have, perhaps—will have, without doubt—the Nobel Peace Prize to which he aspires. Those who will come after him will pay dearly, very dearly, for his final illusions."[3]

The INF treaty (its full title is "The Treaty Between the United States and the USSR on the Elimination of Their Intermediate-Range and Shorter-Range Missiles") runs 169 single-spaced pages of legalistic text. It has seventeen articles and three annexes ("protocols") detailing implementation of treaty provisions. Here are the basic terms:

1. The treaty obligates the United States and the USSR to eliminate all intermediate- and short-range missile systems within three years, bans future production, and establishes provisions for verification of compliance. The United States is to remove its 108 Pershing II's, 64 Cruise Missiles, and 72 Pershing I's (totals 436 nuclear warheads); the USSR is to remove 441 SS20s, 112 SS4s, 120 SS22s, and 20 SS23s (totals 1,575 nuclear warheads). In INF terms, "intermediate-range" missiles are those with a range of six hundred to thirty-four hundred miles; "shorter-range" cover three hundred to six hundred miles. Still, the INF does not de-nuke the European theater. NATO will still have 4,000 "battlefield" nukes. Also, Britain and France have their own independent nuclear arsenals.

2. Both nations must trade data on the specific locations of all missile sites covered under the treaty. (The United States

gave the USSR much of these data before the treaty was signed; it also halted deployment of missiles).[4]

3. "Resident" inspection teams will be stationed at all sites covered by the treaty including twelve sites in the continental United States; the Soviet team inspected Magna, Utah, missile facilities during the summit even though the treaty has yet to be ratified by the United States Senate. "American inspectors will keep watch on the doors of a factory in Votkinsk that produces both intermediate-range SS20 missiles and intercontinental SS25 missiles; their mission will be to ensure that the factory produces only missiles that can reach the United States."[5]

4. Mr. Reagan agreed the United States would abide by the 1972 ABM treaty (which Senate has not ratified and which the USSR has repeatedly violated); thus, Strategic Defense Initiative components (SDI-Star Shield) will not be tested for eighteen - months and the shield not deployed for seven to ten years, if ever.

5. The United States and the USSR scheduled another Summit in Moscow to pursue START talks (Strategic Arms Reduction Treaty) with a goal of 50 percent reduction in long-range intercontinental missiles.

The INF treaty deals with only one type of missile. It does not stipulate destruction of nuclear warheads on those missiles. Mrs. Jeanne Kirkpatrick, former United States Ambassador to the United Nations, cautions: "Don't overestimate the importance of the INF treaty." She says the removal of intermediate- and short-range weapons "will leave western Europe marginally more vulnerable, the Soviet Union marginally less vulnerable and the NATO alliance marginally weaker. . . . it leaves western Europe with fewer options for self-defense and the Soviet Union with less to defend against."[6]

Some two hundred signatories from NATO countries urged rejection of the treaty. They warned, "We see the acute danger that the ability of the West to defend itself is being irreversibly negotiated away for the sake of short term political expediency. If the West proceeds to disarm itself while Moscow continues to build . . . a few years down the road, Moscow will be capable of taking Western Europe, with the help of radio frequency and other such weapons based on 'new physical principles'. . . and western Judeo-Christian civilization will have gone under. . . .

Pearl Harbor Day must not become the day on which the West disarmed itself."[7]

Jane's Defense Weekly, the preeminent authority on military affairs, warned: "The INF treaty bares Europe to the Soviets." *Jane's* believes the elimination of INF systems "will badly hurt NATO's deterrence and ability to block the Soviet advance" and "will not reduce the Soviet capabilities in any significant way." *Jane's* concluded: "The anticipated elimination of the INF in Europe would significantly improve the Soviet ability to conduct its favored form of [conventional] warfare in Europe. . . . the Soviets seem to be willing to absorb [the impact of the few nuclear weapons in Europe] in order to get the technological and industrial assets of Western Europe intact."[8]

A member of the United States Armed Forces in Western Europe wrote:

> Two primary viewpoints [here]: One . . . NATO got exactly what we wanted: a withdrawal of Soviet medium-range nukes. Thus, it is considered a major diplomatic/political victory. The other side of the coin is the feeling that we have been sold "down-river." The nuclear deterrent that we have is being withdrawn and there is no reason for the Soviets to fear to attack our numerically inferior forces. It is a scary feeling for me to watch across the border and know that there is nothing to really withstand the godless communist hordes. . . . we have lowered the nuclear threshold while simultaneously raising the probability of a conventional war.[9]

With regard to conventional forces, Senator Sam Nunn (Georgia) said that "if the United States had wanted to enhance European security, it would have banned tanks, not missiles."[10] The INF treaty does not alter the balance of conventional forces in Europe. "The specter that some troubled European soldiers see through the dust of those departing cruise and Pershing missiles is the Soviet bloc's superiority in many ordinary kinds of military power."[11] Opponents of the INF treaty warn that the results will leave Western Europe hostage ("dangerously exposed") to the USSR's vastly superior conventional forces. "In every field of conventional arms, the Western democracies are outnumbered two-to-one, heavily increasing the likelihood of a Soviet invasion sometime in the 1990s."[12]

The Soviets' Warsaw Pact Nations (WPN) have seventy-two combat divisions (725,000 men); the free world's NATO (North Atlantic Treaty Organization) has fifty-three divisions (580,000 men). The WPN have 24,200 battle tanks; NATO, 8,799; the WPN have 2,997 combat aircraft; NATO, 1,834. The International Institute for Strategic Studies paints a grim picture: WPN uniformed manpower, 6.3 million; NATO, 5.1 million; WPN reserves, 8.2 million; NATO, 6.3 million; WPN main battle tanks, 52,200; NATO, 22,200; WPN artillery, 37,000; NATO, 11,100; WPN armed helicopters, 1,630; NATO, 780; WPN combat aircraft, 7,963; NATO, 3,889.[13]

Representative James Courter (New Jersey) warned that the Soviets are building 3,700 tanks a year, "almost four times as many as NATO," are out-producing NATO twelve-to-one in anti-aircraft artillery, hold a nine-to-one advantage in surface-to-air missles, and have stockpiled three million metric tons of ammunition along the NATO border. "After their massive build-up over the past twenty years, the Soviets are likely to overwhelm NATO's conventional defenses with wave after wave of thirty-division assaults."[14] "Recent military studies indicate that NATO probably would lose a conventional war with the Soviet bloc, but only after a prolonged struggle."[15] Mr. Courter labels as "downright scary" the United States State Department's view that the INF treaty makes "Europe safe for conventional war."[16]

British Secretary of State for Defense, George Younger, warned, "It is impossible for deterrence to rest on conventional forces alone."[17] France remains suspicious of the Soviet intentions; its military leaders are dismayed by Mr. Reagan's vision of a nuclear-free Europe: "Nuclear weapons are not evil. Peace in Europe depends on the existence of nuclear weapons."[18]

With regard to a shift in the balance of power, Sir James Goldsmith also warns of the potential consequences of the INF treaty. Goldsmith cautioned, if the INF is followed by a 50 percent cut in strategic weapons as Mr. Reagan seeks, the United States "will have abandoned your capacity to intervene. . . . you will become isolated on your own continent. . . . you will be forced to withdraw from Europe. Thereby the Soviets will have accomplished their primary objective — the decoupling of Europe and America." Goldsmith suggests, "the Republican administration has lost its nerve and seeks popularity instead of respect." His fear is that "it is not impossible that our civilization, the European and American civilization, is in the process of transferring world leadership to others."[19]

> [The] first, and most immediate danger of the INF treaty, bitterly opposed by Pentagon leaders, is that it leaves Western Europe, that vast storehouse of industry, resources, technology and three hundred million people, naked to Soviet conventional attack. . . . In every field of conventional arms, the Western democracies are outnumbered two-to-one, heavily increasing the likelihood of a Soviet invasion sometime in the 1990s. It is extremely unlikely, in the circumstances, that the Europeans would be so foolish to resist Soviet domination.[20]

The United States General Bernard Rogers, immediate past commander of NATO forces, is highly critical of the INF treaty (the White House "retired" General Rogers because of his criticism). Rogers fears the link between the United States and Western Europe will be broken. "The Soviet Union's objective is the intimidation, coercion and blackmail of Western Europe." "The Soviets have expanded their conventional arms advantage and want the pact to pave the way for a nuclear-free Europe that would be safer [for the Soviets] for conventional war."[21]

With regard to verification, Mr. Reagan insists that the treaty contains the "most stringent verification regime in arms control history." He said the basis of the INF treaty is "trust but verify." Defense hard-liners challenge the verification protocol. They insist, "There is no conceivable way to account for non-deployed SS20s." They estimate there could be as many as two thousand of those. Inter-agency intelligence warned the President, "However many there are, the missiles are stashed out of sight, absolutely beyond discovery — unless the Kremlin chooses to uncover them."[22] George Carver, of the Center for Strategic and International Studies, wrote "It is true that there have been a lot of verification procedures, some of them unprecedented. But it is also true that the SS20 is a highly mobile missile, easy to cache in forests."[23] Virginia I. Postel wrote in *Reason*, "The treaty has a loophole: the Soviets can transfer their warheads to long-range missiles aimed at the same targets in Europe" now bracketed by INF intermediate- and short-range missiles.[24]

James P. Rubin of the Arms Control Association studied the treaty and concluded: "All the administration's talk about perfect verification turns out to have been empty rhetoric, and rightly so."[25] Neither side can offer complete assurance that stored missiles have been eliminated, simply because hiding them is too easy and finding them too hard.[26]

The likelihood of verification must be weighed against the Soviet's long and consistent record of violating treaties. "The Soviet government has broken its word to virtually every country to which it ever gave a signed promise" (United States Senate Judiciary Committee; Internal Security Subcommittee, 1956). The Soviets have signed sixty-six major treaties with the United States and other nations since 1917 and has violated every one of them[27] including: Biological & Toxic Weapons Convention (1972), Threshold Test Ban Treaty (1974), Helsinki Final Act (1975), Salt I (1973), Salt II (1976), and the ABM treaty (1972). Critics point out that the United States did little or nothing (but talk) about past violations. What, they ask, will the United States do if Soviets violate the INF treaty?

What were Gorbachev's two principal objectives at the Washington summit?: (1) killing the Strategic Defense Initiative, and (2) getting United States taxpayers and corporations to help finance his reconstruction (*perestroika*) program. Soviet watchers say the USSR's economy is a basket case; Gorbachev knows it must be bailed out before the people revolt.

With regard to SDI, Mr. Reagan insists that his commitment is "non-negotiable" — "it is not a bargaining chip." Yet, some insist he has cheapened the value of the "chip" by "agreeing in principle" to abide by the 1972 ABM treaty for another seven to ten years. The United States would forego space-testing of SDI components for eighteen months and would hold off deployment of the Star Shield for seven to ten years. Further, the United States and the USSR have "agreed to disagree" and postpone the hard decisions on SDI. That, assert Max Kampelman, Geneva negotiator, and Senator Samuel Nunn, is "the worst, and probably most dangerous, of all worlds."[28] Calling the INF and ABM decisions "a calamitous and astonishing debacle," High Frontier's Lt. Gen. Daniel O. Graham, one of SDI's originators, charged "non-deployment of SDI for seven to ten years will kill that program."[29]

Some observers believe Mr. Reagan has been outfoxed by Gorbachev who "is taking a shrewd gamble, one he is likely to win."[30] Sensing that congressional Democrats would kill SDI by postponement, Gorbachev dropped his demand that the United States shelve SDI as the price for a 1988 Moscow summit. Also, he knows that Secretary of State Shultz and White House Chief Howard Baker have agreed with Democrats on a "narrow" interpretation of the ABM treaty; that puts tight restrictions on the testing and deployment of SDI. Columnist William Safire suggested that Gorbachev thus dusted off an old Russian proverb: "Don't murder a man who is committing suicide." He has agreed to seek a separate treaty on strategic missiles "and let the American political process kill SDI for him."[31] Caspar Weinberger resigned as Secretary of Defense in part because of his opposition to the INF treaty. Weinberger advised the media that at the same time Moscow was demanding that the United States drop SDI, it was spending about $200 million on the development of its own strategic defense system.[32]

While in Washington, Gorbachev acknowledged that the USSR was actively engaged in SDI research and testing. And Soviet Chief of Staff Sergei Akhromeyev warned about the Soviet's "unpleasant" response should the United States launch SDI: "If the United States deploys a shield in space, the Soviet Union will have several options, none of what Washington would wish. . . . The Soviet Union will very quickly find a response of which the United States has no inkling as yet."[33]

With regard to an economic bailout, "Gorbachev pushed American businessmen, Reagan, Shultz, Verity, etc., for greatly increased US-Soviet trade, most-favored-nation trade status, membership in the International Monetary Fund (IMF), World Bank, and GATT (General Agreement on Tariffs Treaty). All are expected to be granted."[34]

Top Soviet trade advisers joined with Gorbachev to court a select group of corporate leaders and members of the Council on Foreign Relations. Their quest? "A $100 billion bailout of the Communist bloc."[35] Also, "To drum up takers for Soviet offers to form joint business enterprises."[36] Secretary of State George Shultz; Secretary of Defense Frank Carlucci, who unilaterally cut the United States defense budget by $33 billion and invited a top Soviet general into the most secret rooms of the Pentagon,[37] newly-appointed Secretary of Commerce William C. Verity, Jr., former co-chairman of the US-USSR Trade and Economic Council — USTEC which is a "hotbed of industrial sabotage"; Dwayne Andreas, Archer Daniel agribusiness magnate and "Gorbachev's best friend in America"; Armand Hammer, long-time Soviet emissary to the United States; and David Rockefeller, international banker, all met with Soviet traders to lay plans and map a campaign for increasing trade relations, lifting embargoes on hi-technology, and the granting of low-interest loans.

Howard Phillips, president of the Conservative Caucus, reported that "President Reagan has [already] substantially increased our economic assistance to the 'evil empire' and its allied despotisms."[38] Will that increase even more? Consider this: since the Washington summit, "more than a dozen United States firms have signed large contracts for joint ventures with the Soviets. . . . since early November, there has been a 'gush of applications' for export licenses, roughly 'double or triple' the same period a year earlier. . . . [And] for every firm that has signed with Gorbachev Incorporated . . . there are now several companies in line. . . . Gorbachev saw to this in a series of meetings with the leaders of United States culture from novelists to business leaders."[39]

The United States has bailed out the USSR three times in the past: in the 1920s after the Communists overthrew the Kerensky government; in the 1940s through lend-lease, and in the 1970s via "détente." Now, writes columnist Patrick Buchanan, "*glasnost* is yet another change of the Communist face, masquerading as a change of heart. Together they (*glasnost* and *perestroika*) are *maskirovka*, a strategic deception to dupe the West. . . . This time, we ought not to lift a hand. As Nietzsche reminded us — 'When you see something slipping, push it.' "[40]

Consider the Biblical Principles

Christians should view issues such as the INF treaty on two bases. First, what does God's Word require? In all things we must give Him and His Word preeminence (Deuteronomy 8:3; Matthew 4:4). And second, how can we insure the security of the nation?

First things first: what does the Lord God demand of His people in regard to those nations and forces which are His enemies — those who have set themselves against Him in their national policies and programs? "Should you help the ungodly, and love them that hate the Lord? Therefore is wrath upon you before the Lord" (2 Chronicles 19:2). "Surely Thou will slay the wicked, O God: depart from me therefore, you bloody men. For they speak against Thee wickedly, and Thine enemies take Thy name in vain. Do I not hate them O Lord, that hate Thee? Am I not grieved with those that rise up against Thee? I hate them with a perfect hatred: I count them mine enemies" (Psalm 139:19-22).

God's written Word is clear: His people are not to be yoked with or to trust in His enemies or those who covenant and compromise with His enemies. To do so is to make "a covenant with death and with hell" (Isaiah 28:15); (see also Exodus 23:32; Deuteronomy 7:2; 2 Corinthians 6:14). "I have hated them that regard lying vanities: but I have trusted in the Lord" (Psalm 31:6). "It is better to trust in the Lord than to put confidence in man. It is better to trust in the Lord than to put confidence in princes (ungodly rulers and leaders)" (Psalm 118:8, 9). "So are the paths of all that forget God; and the hypocrite's hope shall perish: whose hope shall be cut off, and whose trust shall be a spider's web" (Job 8:13, 14).

The Communist position is clear: the state is god. Communism is an enemy of the Lord God. As Otto Scott has written, "Did not Mikhail Gorbachev affirm that Christianity is the enemy, that Christianity must be destroyed?"

Believers are not to do business or make covenants with God's enemies. God's people must not even condone covenants with His enemies; the cost of doing so is to have God's wrath upon them. To be yoked with the forces of evil in any manner is to disobey God. Such alliances and agreements deny His supreme sovereignty, mock His Word, place trust in pacts and treaties of fallen men and place such alliances ahead of the covenant with the King of kings; they deprive themselves and their families of the assured fruits of obedience to Him.

Ahab, king of Israel, was threatened by Benhadad, king of Syria, who demanded tribute (1 Kings 20-21). The elders and people of Israel urged Ahab not to succumb to Benhadad's demands because he had mocked the Lord. Ahab resisted Benhadad and, despite the superior size and power of the Syrian forces and that of the thirty-two kings allied with him, God gave the tiny army of Israel a mighty victory. Why? "So that you shall know that I am the Lord" (1 Kings 20:28).

But following the victory, Ahab covenanted with Benhadad (1 Kings 20:34). Ahab wined and dined Benhadad, and set him free to return to Syria; he did not destroy him and his forces as the Lord God had commanded (1 Kings 20:42). As a result, Ahab was eventually slain in battle and the Israelites were captured (1 Kings 20:42).

Consider, also, Hezekiah, a man who had walked with the Lord and had been greatly blessed. Sadly, though, in victory and vanity, Hezekiah entertained God's enemies and showed them his armory (2 Kings 20:12-17). Thus saith the Lord: "Behold, the days come, that all that is in your house, and all that which your fathers have laid in store unto this day, shall be carried into Babylon; nothing shall be left." This story is remarkably relevant in light of the fact that the Secretary of Defense of the United States recently took a top Soviet general into the top secret chambers of the Pentagon.

And hearken to the case of Asa, king of Judah. Asa made a covenant with the king of Syria, an idolater who loved not the Lord. Because of that, God condemned Asa and his people to a time of wars (2 Chronicles 16:3-9). God will not be mocked; not by individuals, not by nations (Galatians 6:7).

What must God feel—what must the world think—about a nation which can declare 1983 as the year of the Bible and five years later enter into a covenant with an "evil empire" which is led by a man who declares Christianity "the enemy" which must be destroyed?

Second, consider the security of the republic: ultimately, the security of any nation depends upon the people's obedience to and trust in the Lord God. "Some trust in chariots, and some in horses; But we will remember the name of the Lord our God. They have bowed down and fallen; But we have risen and stand upright" (Psalm 20:7, 8).

Today's Christians must be like the "men of Issachar, who understood the times and knew what Israel should do" (1 Chronicles 12:32). We must be filled with the knowledge of God and His Word, lest we perish at the hands of false prophets and misguided leaders (Hosea 4:6). And we must know the ways of the enemy — his subtleties, his deceptions, his tactics, and his goals. "And this is the spirit of the Antichrist, which you have heard was coming, and is now already in the world" (1 John 4:3). We must become as adept at holding forth the Word of God as we are in exploiting the weaknesses of the enemy. All this we must weigh in the light of God's counsel. "An appalling and horrible thing has happened in the land. The prophets prophesy falsely, and their priests rule at their direction. My people love to have it so, but what will you do when the end comes?" (Jeremiah 5:30, 31).

We must not forget that the over-arching battle is a spiritual battle against the forces of Satan (Ephesians 6:12). As Christians, we recognize (or should recognize if we do not already) the nature of Marxist doctrine and the goal it seeks to achieve. Because of this, we have a responsibility to the Lord and to our nation to take the lead in the battle against the evil, anti-God empire.

The way to deal with evil, to overcome Satan, is to resist. "Be sober, be vigilant, because your adversary, the devil, as a roaring lion, walks about seeking who he may devour. Resist him, steadfast in the faith" (1 Peter 5:8, 9). "Submit yourselves, therefore, to God. Resist the devil and he will flee from you" (James 4:7). It is only when we are apart from God and therefore weak that Satan gains power. "Get thee behind Me (away with you), Satan, for it is written that you shall worship the Lord thy God, and Him only shall you worship" (Matthew 4:10).

For the Christian, there can be no neutrality in this battle: "He that is not with Me is against Me" (Matthew 12:30). Not only must we resist, we must go on the offense. Rather than rely on the words of men, we must rely on "the sword of the spirit which is the Word of God" (Ephesians 6:17). We must stand firm against the forces of evil — whether that be an individual, a group, or an "empire." We must proclaim the Word of the Lord — and lay bare the record of the enemy. Few state-controlled schools and few members of the media will do that job; the task is ours — with facts and figures concerning the Soviet's past and continuing bloody record.

And, with all of this, we must press for a strong defense for this republic: strong spiritually, strong militarily, and strong economically, keeping in mind that "if God is for us, who can be against us" (Romans 8:31).

Rev. Joseph C. Morecraft, III, reminds us that Romans 13:3, 4 "clearly indicates that the maintenance of a strong defense program, sufficient to protect the citizenry from any lawless enemy, is essential to godly rule. To do otherwise—to allow the nation's families to stand in a vulnerable position—is irresponsible and immoral. A nation that sheaths that sword (Romans 13:4) because of partiality . . . that sheaths it because of humanistic sentimentality . . . stands condemned before God. And, a nation that undermines its own defenses by making and permitting covenants with God's enemies will be held accountable just as surely as were Ahab, and Asa, and Hezekiah—and their people."

How then shall we, who seek to serve and obey the Lord, find true security? With whom shall we make a covenant for peace and safety? "Now know I that the Lord saves His anointed; He will hear from His holy heaven with a saving strength of His right hand" (Psalm 20:6). "But if you shall indeed obey His voice, and do all that I speak, then I will be an enemy unto your enemies, and an adversary unto your adversaries" (Exodus 23:20-22).

JUSTICE AND
THE COURTS

Our Founding Fathers never intended that the Judiciary be the superior branch of government. But many believe it has taken imperial powers unto itself.

Background Briefing

We thank you for the flowers so sweet,
We thank you for the food we eat,
We thank you for the birds that sing,
We thank you, God, for everything.

A simple little quatrain, yes? Hardly a threat to the republic, right? Well, when it comes to the public schools of this land, it is deemed improper, offensive. It's not allowed. In 1967 a United States Federal Court of Appeals prohibited a kindergarten teacher from using it in her classroom ever again.[1]

Take the case of Donald Thornton. He was demoted for refusing to work on the Lord's Day. Since Connecticut law required that employers give workers one day a week off to practice their religion, Thornton figured the law had been violated and his rights had been stomped on. He filed a law suit against his employers. The United States Supreme Court disagreed with Thornton; it held that the Connecticut law was unconstitutional. The ACLU and the Americans for Separation of Church and State cheered the decision.[2]

In 1973, in *Roe v. Wade*, the United States Supreme Court decreed that the Constitution guaranteed the "right of privacy" for women and that preempted the right to life for pre-born children. That "judicially ordained death warrant" has so far resulted in the slaughter of abortion for some twenty million babies.[3]

> And the [Supreme] Court has construed the equal protection clause of the Fourteenth Amendment so as to mandate a massive dose of racial integration as a supposed cure for racial segregation in public schools. In consequence, communities all across the land have seen their public schools come under the imperial dominance of federal judges who enjoy lifetime appointments and who have no responsibility to pay for or live with the implementation of their decisions.[4]

What's going on? Some call it "judicial supremacy." Others condemn it as the work of an "imperial court" grown far too powerful and exercising powers never intended by the framers of the federal Constitution.

> Judicial supremacy (sometimes called judicial review) is the belief that the Judicial branch of government has the supreme and sole right to interpret the Constitution and to bind that interpretation on the Legislative and Executive branches, as well as all citizens.[5]

The arrogance of "judicial supremacy" is not confined to the United States Supreme Court. A case in point: In 1980 a federal judge ruled that the city of Parma, Ohio, must provide three hundred units of low-income housing each year. The taxpayers could pick up the tab. The case was termed "the first federal takeover of a city."[6]

Another case in point: In 1980, Judge John F. Dooling, Jr. struck down as unconstitutional the Hyde Amendment limiting Medicaid abortions and ordered the federal government to pay for all Medicaid abortions.

Congressman Bob Dornan and Csaba Vedlik wrote:

> Three facts concerning Judge Dooling's decision are indisputable: (1) Congress did not appropriate funds for the abortions in question; (2) the Constitution in Article I, Section 9, Clause 7 clearly states that "no money shall be drawn from the Treasury, but in consequence of appropriations made by law" [i.e. by the

legislature]; (3) as Congress has the sole power over the purse, Judge Dooling's ruling . . . was a flagrant usurpation of the legislature's constitutional powers.[7]

Judge Dooling's decree was overturned by the United States Supreme Court. That did not deter a federal judge sitting in Kansas City, Missouri. He demanded that Kansas City increase its tax rates and levy new taxes to fund an overhaul of its school system including new recreation facilities.

Federal judges now regulate many activities of our lives that once were felt to be none of their business. As examples, courts have ruled that females must be allowed to compete with males in athletics, halted construction of a dam to preserve an endangered species of fish, banned school dress codes and blocked suspension of students. Courts have taken over the operation of . . . prisons in Alabama. In short, decisions and regulations once considered the province of legislators and executives are increasingly made by the courts.[8]

Concern over power grabs by the federal courts is increasing. "Within that system is a growing tendency to abrogate powers reserved to other branches of government — and to the states, and to the people." Professor Charles E. Rice, Notre Dame University School of Law, sees it as "a judicial activism through which the Court acts as an agent of social as well as constitutional change."[9]

This explains the angry reaction of Americans when federal courts allow a governmental agency in Michigan to distribute contraceptives to minors without parental notice, but prohibit the Gideons from giving out Bibles in Florida's public schools.[10]

"[The courts] are reaching into areas once considered the preserve of legislators, administrators, and the family." For example, a federal judge arbitrarily took over Boston schools and virtually controlled them for years until he was satisfied that the schools complied with his plan for desegregation. Example: a federal judge in Louisiana overruled an elected state judge who tried to uphold the right of parent and child to attend school on the basis of proximity to residence.

"By 1907, Darwin's concept of evolution and the Church's impotence in and retreat from the public arena were expressed when Chief Justice Charles Evans Hughes said that the Constitution [and thus the law] is what the judges say it is."[11] When Edwin Meese, III, United States Attorney General, had the temerity to remind the American Bar Association that the Constitution, and not the Supreme Court, was the law of the land, he was met with a storm of protest.

Back in 1835 Alexis de Tocqueville, the French statesman and author, saw it coming. In his book, *Democracy in America*, he wrote: "If I were asked where I place the American aristocracy, I should reply without hesitation that it is not composed of the rich . . . but that it occupies the judicial branch and bar."[12]

Such power, now increasingly exercised by federal courts, was never intended by the framers of the Constitution. To prevent accumulation of power by federal courts, the framers added Article III, which reads in part:

> In all cases affecting Ambassadors, other public ministers, and Consuls, and those in which a State shall be party, the Supreme Court shall have original Jurisdiction. In *all the other cases* before mentioned, the Supreme Court shall have appellate Jurisdiction, both as to Law and Fact, with such exceptions, and under such regulations as the Congress shall make (emphasis added).

Checks and balances are essential to the maintenance of justice. Thus, Congress reserved the right to restrict and, if need be, eliminate the power of the Supreme Court to hear cases other than those few situations allowed under its original jurisdiction.

Alexander Hamilton is generally acknowledged as one of the early advocates of increased judicial powers. But in his early writings, in Federalist Paper No. 18, Hamilton argued that the Court

> has been carefully restricted to those causes which are manifestly proper for the cognizance of national judicature; that in the partition of this authority, a very small portion of the original jurisdiction has been preserved to the Supreme Court, and the rest to subordinate tribunals.

James Madison, who is rightly called "the architect of the Constitution," made it clear that judicial imperialism "was never intended and can never be proper." In Federalist Paper No. 51, Madison emphasized that "in republican government, the legislative authority necessarily predominates."

And Abraham Lincoln in his first inaugural address asserted, "If the policy of the government, upon vital questions affecting the whole people, is to be irrevocably fixed by decisions of the Supreme Court . . . the people will have ceased to be their own rulers, having to that extent practically resigned their government into the hands of that eminent tribunal."

But the devotees of Chief Justice Hughes have engineered a change since those days. "Forsaking the 'higher law' philosophy of the Founding Fathers, they became caught up in the new philosophy of pragmatism which asserted that there are no moral absolutes, and legal positivism which rejected the notion that there is a law transcending all human laws. To the positivist, it is purely up to man to decide for himself what laws he wishes to have."[13] Law was not to be fixed on principle as was the case at the birthing of the republic. "Law had come to be seen as a fluid mix of established principles and changing social values."[14] And gradually the "established principles" gave way.

"The judge's purpose had changed as well. No longer did judges see themselves as those who discover God's Law and apply it, but 'as persons who make law by creating new principles, often in response to changes in social values.' "[15] "Former Supreme Court Justice Oliver Wendell Holmes said that law was made by the expression of social consciousness and social experience."[16] The principles which had distinguished the American revolution from the French rebellion were fading. The courts junked the law of nature and nature's God, and the writings of Montesquieu and Blackstone, and began basing their decisions on the rubber yardsticks of sociologists, psychologists, and other "social experts."[17]

In 1937 Justice Felix Frankfurter wrote President Franklin Roosevelt: "People have been taught to believe that when the Supreme Court speaks it is not they who speak but the Constitution; whereas, of course, in so many vital cases, it is they who speak and not the Constitution."[18]

In the past the Supreme Court has recognized Congress's authority over its power to decide issues. In *Wiscart v. D'Auchy*, the

Court held that "the Constitution distributing the judicial power of the United States vests in the Supreme Court an original as well as appellate jurisdiction. . . . Here, then, is the ground and the only ground on which we can sustain an appeal. If Congress has provided no rule to regulate our proceedings, we cannot exercise our appellate jurisdiction; and if the rule is provided, we cannot depart from it."[19]

Even though he stressed the importance of checks and balances, James Madison nevertheless wrote that "in republican government, the legislative authority necessarily predominates"— since it is the closest to the people and theoretically is the most responsive to their will. Clearly, then, it is up to the elected representatives in Congress to regulate and control the courts.

Today, however, Congress backs away from its responsibility in this regard. Generally, Congress will not even vote on a bill if its members think the Supreme Court might rule the proposed legislation unconstitutional. Thus, it is the Court that bridles the Congress! And, thus, the all-important system of checks and balances is jeopardized.

The answer, in the American constitutional system, is for the Congress to step forward. In this way, the courts can be prevented from becoming the engines of tyranny.

Congress would do well to enact legislation to return jurisdiction over the First Amendment cases to the states where they properly belong. This is the strategy suggested by Senator Jesse Helms (North Carolina). Senator Helms points out that "the Framers never envisioned that the main congressional remedy for judicial abuse of power would be a constitutional amendment. The Framers would then have made the Court not only the most dangerous branch . . . but also the supreme branch of the whole Federal government."[20]

Consider the Biblical Principles

In His infinite wisdom and justice, the Lord God gave man the pattern for right civil government. It was this form of civil government which was, in large measure, the matrix for the American republic designed by our Founding Fathers. ("We have this day restored the Sovereign to whom all men ought to be obedient. And, from the rising to the setting of the sun, let His kingdom come" [Samuel Adams, July 9, 1776].)

In the Hebrew republic, as in ours, there were three branches of government: the executive, the legislative, and the judicial (see Isaiah 33:22). As was the case when our nation was founded, God was acknowledged as the Supreme Sovereign. His laws were law, spiritual and civil; they were the fundamental for the laws and statutes enacted. Each of the twelve tribes was sovereign in its own right, as were the original thirteen states. The twelve tribes were a union (one nation) under God; there was unity in God and in matters of national import; yet, no tribe could trespass on the sovereignty of another.

Within this structure, and at each level, the Lord God commanded there be established a system of checks and balances, since He above all others was aware of the sinful nature of man. The authority of the judges was checked by the senate (comprising the leaders/princes) of the tribes. The power of the senatorial council was checked by the power of the judicial, and the power of the people. And the whole was under the restraint and constraint of the Divine Constitution (Covenant) established by the Lord God and accepted by the people at Mount Sinai (Exodus 20; see also Deuteronomy 5:3, 27).

When God permitted the people to have earthly kings (1 Samuel 8), the kings were required to "write him a copy of this law in a book and read therein all the days of his life" (Deuteronomy 17:18, 19).

Consider, now, the judicial system (justice) as God ordained it in that first republic—and note the similarities to that which was part of this American republic.

Through Moses, God established a system of superior and inferior and circuit courts (Exodus 18:21; 1 Samuel 7:15), with a supreme court to hear matters of dispute between the tribes and such matters of national importance that might come before it. God also set forth the requirements (attributes) of those who should be elected judges (Exodus 18:21, 22)—men who fear God, men who are able, men who love truth and hate covetousness.

Under God's perfect plan, the courts were readily available to every man without going far to obtain justice, and without waiting long to secure it (fair and speedy trial):

> Judges and officers shalt thou make thee in all thy gates, which
> the Lord thy God giveth thee, throughout the tribes; and they
> shall judge the people with just judgment (Deuteronomy 16:18).

As a protection against hasty decisions, the individual had
the right to appeal his case — in some instances all the way to the
highest court in the land (Deuteronomy 7:8, 9).

All justice was to be based on righteous judgments (Deuteronomy 25:1; Psalm 82). The corruption of justice is an abomination to the Lord (Proverbs 17:15), and perverted justice is not
justice but is against God's will (Isaiah 59:14). Justice is to be
meted out equally and even-handedly. No man is above the law,
no man is below the law (Deuteronomy 1:16,17; John 7:24).

In God's eyes, justice is synonymous with righteousness;
where there is no righteousness, there is no justice. When man
disobeys God, when he denies God and refuses God's laws, he
spurns justice and encourages sin. Man without God can only
produce sinful (ungodly) laws (Habakkuk 1:4). Thus, "to restore
justice, we must restore God to His rightful place in our personal
and national lives."[21]

Further, we must restore God's laws as the law of the land
and determine that those who are entrusted with the powers of
the judicial system are men who adjudicate the laws faithfully in
obedience to the Word of God. Those who are to judge must judge
righteously, according to His Word, without fear or favor . . .
faithfully, and with a perfect heart (2 Chronicles 19:6-9).

EIGHTEEN

LIBERATION THEOLOGY
(The Gospel According to Marx)

This attempt to forge an unholy marriage between Marxism and Christianity has been called one of the most dangerous movements in today's world.

Background Briefing

Dr. David Breese describes it as "the single most critical problem that Christianity has faced in all of its 2000 year history."[1] Why? Because, under the guise of theology, this spreading cancer seeks to make Marx the Messiah and the *Communist Manifesto* the new "Gospel" for mankind.

Dr. Lester DeKoster, former editor of *The Banner*, calls it "a remarkably brazen and cynical perversion of the Gospel . . . [it] keeps God on hand to wrap the mantle of the Church about its shoulders, and to beguile the innocent."[2]

Ray Hundley, professor at OMB Biblical Seminary, Medellin, Colombia, calls it "one of the most dangerous movements in the world."[3]

But, Rev. Harry Cox, Harvard Divinity School professor, boasts that the movement springs from the New Testament accounts of Jesus ministering to the poor. Cox says it has helped create vibrant new religious communities in Latin America.[4]

What is this movement which some extol and others tag as evil and anti-Christian?

Dr. DeKoster writes, "Liberation theology is neither liberating nor theology! . . . Or, to put it another way, if liberation theology were 'Christian,' then Marx and Engels were the original liberation theologians."[5]

Liberation theology is an attempt to forge an unholy marriage of Marxism and the Christian faith, a program to subvert Christianity and to advance the dominion of Marx, thus to replace Christianity with communism. Liberation theology sings songs to "peace" and "justice" but the "peace" it promotes is not the peace which comes through Christ Jesus; it is rather the "peace" of the Gulag. The "justice" it proclaims is not God's justice (based on righteousness) but the "justice" of subjugation or extermination for all who oppose communism. "When Marxism controls the entire world, the final stage of communism will be ushered in. In the terminology of liberation theology, this is designated, 'the Kingdom of God on earth.'"[6]

Rev. John Richard Neuhaus, Center for Religion and Society, calls liberation theology "a tired and tattered re-run of some very old Christian heresies." By promoting Marxism, said Neuhaus, liberationists help bring communist dictatorships to power.[7]

Indeed, University of Mexico Professor Jose Miranda, an ardent liberation theologian, insists: "The Bible teaches communism. . . . Communism is obligatory for Christians."

"No one can take the Bible seriously without concluding that . . . the rich, for being rich, should be punished."[8] Miranda asserts that all who are "wealthy" (those with property in excess of a lowest common denominator) are guilty of "mass murder" (gaining wealth by oppressing others). Miranda calls for execution of the wealthy. "This is violence," he acknowledges, "and it is not only permitted, it is commanded by the one true God. The human community has to defend itself from its attackers."[9]

Author David Chilton writes, "In the name of Jesus Christ, the advocates of liberation theology are preaching envy, theft, and mass extermination. Liberation theology is a theology of mass murder."[10] "Yet," asserts Chilton, "it is taught, in some form, as part of the official curriculum of almost every evangelical seminary in the United States (usually in the Missions department)." And, warns Chilton, many Christian leaders are either swayed by liberation rhetoric, or unable to answer it.[11]

Liberation theology has spread throughout Latin America (Cuba, Nicaragua, El Salvador, Brazil, Guyana, Colombia,

Argentina, Uruguay, Chile, and Mexico). Where it is, there also is communist subversion through which the Soviet Union acts to conquer the "soft underbelly" of the United States. Assistant Secretary of State Elliott Abrams labels liberation theology a front for Marxist ideology. "It is clear that they [the USSR] are exploiting liberation theology as a means of subverting the churches of the West."[12]

Pastor Alberto Ramirez, a Nicaraguan in exile in Guatemala, reports, "A Bulgarian-trained Sandinista officer admitted to me . . . that there is a concerted plan to eliminate the Church in Nicaragua. He boasted that in ten years there will not be one Evangelical left in the country. Their plans are well laid, and as soon as they have exterminated the Contras, they will come after the Christians."[13] Secretary Abrams denounces Catholic priests serving in the Sandinista regime as "accomplices to persecution."[14]

Liberation theologians are pushing on all fronts. "At the present . . . [liberation theologies] are collaborating with Marxist terrorists to bring down [the] governments of the Philippines, South Korea, Taiwan, El Salvador, Guatemala, and South Africa (in South West Africa, three top members of SWAPO [Marxist liberation front] hold senior positions in the Council of Churches of Nambia)."[15] In Marxist Zimbabwe, President Canaan Banana (an ordained Methodist minister and former World Council of Churches official) declared: "Every time I see a guerrilla, I see Jesus Christ."[16]

Enrique T. Rueda, a Catholic scholar who escaped from Castro's Cuba, defines liberation theology as "an attempt to reinterpret Christianity using Marxist concepts. . . . It is an attempt to blend the false liberation of Marx with the true liberation of Jesus. . . . The language [of liberation theology] is full of references to God, the Church, the Gospel, good works, and concern for the poor . . . but if you read carefully you will see that what is being presented is Marxism."[17] Professor Rueda emphasizes that Christianity and Marxism are totally incompatible. " 'Liberation theology' attempts to reinterpret the Christian message to suit Marxist polemics and make the Christian Gospel conform to them." But, warns Rueda, when Marxism is used to interpret Christianity, one ends up a Marxist—not a Christian. He predicts, "As Marxists consolidate their power (as in Nicaragua), they will discard the Church and use it only as a front for the sake of appearance."[18]

Is the United States devoid of liberation theologians? No. Professor Rueda lists several United States "centers" of liberation theology: Eighth Day Center for Peace and Justice (in Chicago), Network, Center for Concern, Quixote Center (Washington, D.C.), Maryknoll Fathers, and some "Sanctuary" groups.[19] Among the publicists for liberation theology are Ronald J. Sider (author of *Rich Christians in an Age of Hunger*), Jim Wallis (*Sojourners* magazine), and *Christian Century* magazine. "Wallis writes longingly of the day when 'more Christians will come to view the world through Marxist eyes.'" He thinks that day is inevitable. "It will," he writes, "even be predictable among the so-called 'young evangelicals' who, for the most part, have a zeal for social change that is not yet matched by a developed socioeconomic analysis that will cause them to see the impossibility of making capitalism work for justice and peace. . . . The foundation for the Christian Marxism that he [Wallis] recommends looks to be about as solid as quicksand."[20]

Sider, who is president of Evangelicals for Social Action, believes the state should control virtually every aspect of the economy—that any Christian who takes for himself more than the "plain necessities of life" has "gained riches and hell-fire."[21] He sums up his view of liberation theology: "God acts in history to exalt the poor and oppressed and to cast down the rich and oppressive." What is the basis for Sider's claim? The "Exodus Thesis" (see Biblical Principles, below). Sider insists: "God's people, if they are truly God's people, are also on the side of the poor and oppressed."[22]

Consider the 120-page pastoral letter on social justice issued by the American Roman Catholic Bishops (November 11, 1984). It smacks of liberation theology. Archbishop Rembert Weakland, chairman of the committee on Catholic Social Teaching and American Economy, argues that the document "urges a stronger sense of solidarity within our nation."[23]

The Bishops' pastoral letter terms America's "economic failures" as "massive and ugly"; it suggests Caesar should be the keeper of the poor and the creator of new jobs; it calls for a downward redistribution of wealth. At a time when the government already consumes 40 percent of the total national income, the bishops demand more and greater government welfare and decry the United States "militarization" (about one-sixth of the federal budget goes for defense).

William E. Simon, Catholic lay leader and former Secretary of Treasury says, "The bishops seem to believe that government should control and direct the economy and have a government solution for every economic woe with total disregard for the cost."[24] Columnist James J. Kilpatrick concluded: "So the bishops would redistribute the wealth, taking from the productive and giving to the unproductive. Perhaps that is economic justice in the ecclesiastical view, but it looks like spinach to me."[25]

Dr. Ronald H. Nash reduces liberation theology to two basic theses: (1) its economic thesis—capitalism is evil and socialism is good, and (2) its theological thesis—God is on the side of the poor and oppressed. Dr. Nash comments, "few liberation theologians hesitate to call themselves Marxists." But, liberationists insist that the Soviet brand of communism is a heresy and not true Marxism. They contend that "true Marxism" resembles Christianity. In fact, Professor José Miranda's book, *Marx Against The Marxists,* is subtitled "The Christian Humanism of Karl Marx." Miranda, who revises God's Word to fit his Marxist presuppositions, also revises the words of Marx to "use" Scriptures. Miranda proclaims that Karl Marx was not really an atheist; he was a Christian![26] (Marx boasted he was an atheist.) Perversions such as Miranda's are essential in the liberationist strategy to make a Marxist revolution acceptable in the eyes of the Christian Church.

Liberationists rant that a small minority of the world's population has control of most of the world's resources. Brazilian Archbishop Dom Herder Camara complains that 80 percent of all resources are at the disposal of 20 percent of the population.[27] Michael Novak, Roman Catholic author and philosopher, responds:

> Material remains inert until its secrets are discovered and a technology for bending it to human purposes is invented. . . . Protestant European culture, in particular, has been exceedingly fertile in the discovery of such resources and in the invention of such technologies. . . . Nothing prevented Brazilians from in-

venting the combustion engine, the radio, the airplane, penicillin, and other technologies. . . . Although Brazil is apparently one of the most richly endowed of all nations in material resources, neither Brazil nor other Latin American nations have so far provided a system favorable to invention and discovery. . . . Those cultures which value the intelligent and inventive use of God's creation are far better off than those which do not.[28]

Liberation theologians have another notorious failing—their exclusive preoccupation with Latin America. Walter Benjamin underscores their selective sympathy. "Too often, victims of Soviet oppression and their Eastern satraps, Boat People, Afghan rebels, the Kurds and Bahaists of Iran, Cuban political prisoners and exiles, and black victims of black dictators in Africa are ignored because the choice of underdog is . . . rooted in ideological criteria, . . . liberation theologians . . . cannot admit injustice or oppression in Vietnam because, by definition, socialist countries cannot oppress."[29]

What are the "roots" of liberation theology? The teachings of Dietrich Bonhoeffer, Jurgen Moltzmann, Karl Barth, Oscar Cullman, and Johannes Metz among others. Liberation theology emerged from Germany as the "theology of hope" looking to a collectivist transformation of the world. Friedrich Engels, a collaborator with Karl Marx, slid that "theology of hope" into the structure of communism ("the true Christianity of the early Church . . . had been similar to modern Communism"). Engels saw Christianity as a tool for communism's class struggle. During the '30s, efforts were made in France and Belgium to reconcile Christianity and Marxism; the hammer and sickle were superimposed on the Cross of Christ.[30]

Liberation theology spread to Latin America through Spanish missionaries who had been expelled by Franco. *A Theology of Liberation*, by Peruvian priest Gustavo Gutierrez, is widely considered the "Bible" of liberation theology.[31] For Gutierrez, "theology" is no longer the science or study of God but "man's critical reflection on himself, on his own basic principles." According to Gutierrez, the root cause of man's ills is not sin (man's transgression of God's Laws), but United States capitalism. The solution? A communist revolution.[32] In the eyes of liberation theologians, man—not Christ—is the redeemer of mankind.

Rev. Ray Hundley sees the genesis of liberation theology's subversion of Latin America Protestantism in the 1962 meeting of Church and Society in Latin America. Clergy there agreed that revolution (not Christ) was the only answer to the ills of Latin American society. Their conclusion: "Marxism was the only effective strategy for revolution. . . . they proclaimed that God was using the Marxist revolutionary movement to establish His Kingdom." Says Hundley: "This theology is now propagated in most of the major Protestant and Roman Catholic seminaries of Latin America."[33]

The French Jesuit Teillhard de Chardin was one who promoted liberation theology.[34] Also, the writings of Lutheran Paul Tillich, who rejected the doctrines of the Holy Trinity, Christ's virgin birth and physical resurrection, and the idea of a personal God. Tillich was a spiritual father of the "God is dead" theologians. He spurned the message of the Reformation and saw himself as being closer to Marx than Martin Luther.[35] Some claim that liberation theology was propagated in Moscow, that it was conceived by the Kremlin through its spokesman, Metropolitan Nikodim, who represents the Russian Orthodox Church in the World Council of Churches (WCC). Nikodim promoted liberation theology at the Fifth World Assembly of WCC under the title "Peace and Justice." Nikodim's thesis was accepted at the WCC's Nairobi session and he was named one of six presidents of the WCC.[36]

Consider the Biblical Principles

The Fall of Man (The First Adam). Christians recognize the fallen nature (innate depravity) of man. "As by one man sin entered into the world, and death by sin; and so death passed upon all men, for that all have sinned." "By the offense of one judgment came upon all men to condemnation" (Romans 5:12, 18). "For all have sinned and come short of the glory of God" (Romans 3:23). (See also Genesis 3:1-19; Psalm 14:1; Ecclesiastes 7:20, 29; Isaiah 64:6; and John 3:19.)

Most liberation theologians reject the doctrine of man's fall; they reject the first Adam. In the historical determinism of Marx, man transforms himself by conquest of his own liberty.

To the liberationist, redemption comes through violent revolution. If man is to redeem himself, the doctrine of man's innate depravity must be discarded (depraved man can hardly redeem himself). Further, Marxists cannot "presume to diagnose and prescribe a cure for man's ills if Marxists, too, were corrupted by inherent depravity."[37]

Salvation Through Christ (The Second Adam). God's Word makes it clear that salvation comes by believing on the Lord Jesus Christ. "Therefore as by the offense of one judgment came upon all men to condemnation; even so by the righteousness of one the free gift came upon all men unto justification of life" (Romans 5:18). "Neither is there salvation in any other: for there is none other name under heaven given among men, whereby we must be saved" (Acts 4:12). "For as in Adam all die, even so in Christ shall all be made alive" (1 Corinthians 15:22). (See also John 3:16-18; Ephesians 2:5, 8; 2 Timothy 1:9, 10; 1 Thessalonians 5:9, 10.)

The liberation theologian, having rejected the first Adam, must also reject the Second Adam. Thus, "the whole Biblical structure is shattered" — thrown out is the Biblical context for vicarious atonement and the substitutionary death of Jesus Christ.[38]

Regeneration ("New" life in Christ Jesus). As the Apostle Paul wrote, "Therefore, if any man be in Christ, he is a new creature: old things are passed away; behold all things are become new" (2 Corinthians 5:17). (See also Colossians, chapter 3.)

For liberation theologians, conversion and regeneration come not through the grace of the Sovereign Triune God; for the liberation theologian, man regenerates himself. "To be converted is to commit oneself to the process of liberation of the poor and the oppressed . . . with an analysis of the situation and a strategy of action" (Gutierrez). Liberation theology preaches man is made "new" through radical liberation and violent revolution.[39]

Sin. "Whosoever committeth sin transgresses also the Law: for sin is the transgression of the Law [lawlessness]" (1 John 3:4). "All unrighteousness is sin " (1 John 5:17). (See also Matthew 15:19 and John 8:44.) For the liberation theologians, sin is not "transgression of God's Law." Sin is no longer personal but "social and historical" — the absence of "love" in the relationships of society.

And, love. Our Blessed Savior sets forth two great commandments: "You shall love the Lord your God with all your heart and with all your soul and with all your mind. This is the first and great commandment. And, the second is like unto it, You shall love your neighbor as yourself" (Matthew 22:37-39). "If you love Me, keep My commandments" (John 14:15). "By this shall all men know that you are My disciples, if you have love for one another" (John 13:35). What is love? Paul lists the attributes, the all-encompassing spectrum, of love in 1 Corinthians 13:1-13 and emphasizes: "And though I bestow all my goods to feed the poor, and though I give my body to be burned, and have not love, it profiteth me nothing (v.3)."

What is love to Gustavo Gutierrez, the liberation theologian? To him, love must be defined in the context of dialectical materialism. Love? Yes. "But, to accept class struggle means to decide for some and against others. . . . To love all men does not mean avoiding confrontation. . . . One loves the oppressor by liberating them . . . by liberating them from themselves [translation by robbery and murder]. . . . To participate in class struggle is today the necessary and inescapable means of making this love concrete."[40] Thus, from Gutierrez's dialectical thinking comes his logic: love is to liquidate, to exterminate — not out of hate, but out of love. Of such is the logic of "theological reflection."

Consider now two primary Biblical concepts advanced by the liberation theologians: the "Exodus Thesis" and the "Ananias Thesis."

First, the "Exodus Thesis":

As articulated by Ron Sider, the Exodus of the Israelites from Egypt demonstrates the liberation theology contention that God "historically" sides with the poor and oppressed. Sider's argument is that because the Israelites whom God delivered from Egypt were poor and oppressed slaves, God's only reason for liberating them was their poverty and slavery. That, Sider proclaims, provides Christians with a "divinely inspired precedent for liberating the oppressed people of the world through political action." But, as Dr. Ronald Nash points out, God's reasons for the Exodus transcended poverty and oppression.[41]

Examine the Scriptures: "And the Lord said, 'I have seen the affliction of My people who are in Egypt'" (Exodus 3:7-8). Notice that "*My* people" is a specific and personal pronoun. God's redemption of the Israelites was not some general liberation movement (no doubt at that time there were other poor and oppressed people in Egypt). As David Chilton emphasizes, "They [the Israelites] were His people, who cried out to Him. The Exodus was not a freeing of slaves in the abstract, but a special redemptive, covenantal event in fulfillment of God's oath to Abraham, Isaac and Jacob" (Exodus 3:7, 8; see also Deuteronomy 7:6-8). Israel was unique; it was His, and for that reason God redeemed it.[42]

Second, the "Ananias Thesis":

In Acts 5:1-11, Luke recounts an incident involving Ananias and his wife, Sapphira, who "sold a possession and kept back part of the price . . . and brought a certain part, and laid it at the apostles' feet" (vv. 1, 2). Liberation theologians (and other socialists) insist that Ananias was struck dead because of his greed, and his refusal to share all with other believers (Acts 4:31-37).

Examine the Scriptures. Peter pinpointed the sin: "Why hath Satan filled thine heart to lie to the Holy Ghost. . . . you have not lied unto men but unto God" (vv. 3, 4). The sin was deceit, lying to God (as did Sapphira also — vv. 8-10). Further, Peter made it clear that the property in question belonged to Ananias and was his to do with as his chose (v.4). Thus, Peter clearly underscored the principle of private property (held in stewardship and accountable to God), not property that was collective as under communism. (See Exodus 20:15, 17, wherein God affirms private property and prohibits theft, greed, envy, and covetousness. See also Luke 12:13, 14 wherein Christ Jesus refuses to compel one brother to divide with another.)

In summary, God judges men not by their wealth or lack of it but by their obedience to Him (Deuteronomy 1:1-17; Romans 2:11; 1 John 2:3, 4). Our Lord tells the United States that we as His are to succor those in need and to help those in distress (Matthew 25:31-46). This is both a personal mandate and a mandate to His Church; a fast pleasing to Him (Isaiah 58:1-12). We are to do so in His name, for His glory, in keeping with His immutable Word (Matthew 4:4). We are not to promote Marx, not to build an ungodly system or follow a false prophet. To God be the glory! (Matthew 5:16).

NINETEEN

PARENTAL ABUSE

"For years we didn't find child abuse when it was there. Now we are in danger of finding it when it is not there."

Brain Taugher [1]

Background Briefing

Psychologist Lawrence Speigel parks his car and starts for his office. Two plainclothes detectives approach him, handcuff him, place him in their patrol car, and inform him that he is under arrest. The charge: "sexually abusing his two-and-a-half-year-old daughter." Speigel is indicted by a grand jury. He faces up to fifteen years in prison. For two years, he is forbidden to see his daughter. Eventually, he is declared "not guilty." What was the basis for the unfounded charge against him? Accusations by his ex-wife during a custody battle. [2]

It is three days before Christmas. Margaret "Doe" and her husband are seated in their living room. There is a knock on the front door. Four policemen enter and hand them a petition charging them with child abuse. The officers take their two daughters, ages two and four, first to a "shelter," then to a relative's home. Sixteen days later the girls are returned to their parents. No charges are ever filed. The basis for the violation of the parents' constitutional rights? A neighbor reported that the children exhibited behavior which "suggested" sexual abuse (the two-year-old had unbuttoned his shirt; the four-year-old had climbed onto his lap). [3]

In Houston, Jean Coyle's baby grandson is stung by a wasp and has an allergic reaction. It raises welts on the child's body. Jean's daughter takes the child to the hospital emergency room.

She is told the boy will be all right. The next day she takes him to an allergy specialist who reports the mother to the Department of Human Resources. Months later, the mother regains custody of her child. No charges are ever filed.[4]

Isolated cases and events? Not so!

In 1984 some 1.5 million cases of child abuse or neglect were reported, a 10 percent increase over 1983 and ten times the cases reported in 1963. Some observers believe such totals to be grossly and often purposefully exaggerated estimates. Further, they point out, 65 percent of the reports were totally unfounded.[5]

Most social workers have been trained under the theory that "children do not make up stories asserting they have been sexually molested. . . . [they] do not have the sexual knowledge necessary to fabricate such allegations."[6] One writer has likened the modern social workers to the colonial witch-hunters from Salem.[7]

> The suggestibility of children is a matter of great concern in cases where child sex abuse is alleged, because the child is usually questioned by a social worker who believes such allegations are true, neither the accused nor his attorney is present, and no videotape or tape recording is made. In such a setting, the social worker is able to lead a child into making a response that the social worker wants.[8]

Basing her research on data from the American Humane Association, Mary Pride concludes:

> You wind up with, in the entire U.S.A. out of a child population of over seventy-two million, less than ten thousand cases of major physical injury, a few thousand of actual incestuous rape, and a few thousand more of serious starvation and other genuine serious neglect.

"It's not great that several thousand North American children are severely harmed each year, but" stresses Mrs. Pride, "that's a far cry from the supposed millions of child abuse cases." Exaggerated data is part of what Mary Pride calls "The Child Abuse Industry."

According to Mrs. Pride, in 1985 "over one million North American families [United States and Canada] were falsely accused of child abuse." Some merely went through an interrogation and were "cleared" (though the names of many were kept on the files as suspected child abusers). Others were compelled to attend counselling programs. "Still others lost their houses and emptied their bank accounts fighting these unjust charges. Many lost their jobs. Others, saddest of all, lost their children."9

Douglas J. Besharov, J.D., LL.M., of the American Enterprise Institute for Public Policy Research, points out that labeling a parent as "abusive" or "neglectful" "authorizes public agencies to intervene into a family . . . even if the parents object, and it authorizes courts to impose treatment services, to remove a child from the home, to terminate parental rights and to impose criminal sanctions."10 Mrs. Pride emphasizes that once you are "hot-lined" you are guilty until proven innocent; once children are taken from the home the average time until they are returned is almost two years for whites and more than four years for blacks "even in cases where it is conceded that they were taken wrongly."11

Dr. Besharov believes that "we now face an imminent social tragedy: the nationwide collapse of child protective efforts caused by a flood of unfounded reports." "More troubling, the determination that a report is unfounded can only be made after an unavoidably traumatic investigation that is, inherently, a breach of parental and family privacy."12

> Each year, over five hundred thousand families are put through investigations of unfounded reports. This is a massive and unjustified violation of parental rights.13

Lottie Beth Hobbs, in *The Family Educator,* wrote:

> A network of federal, state and local agents is snatching children right out from under their parents' noses. This is the child abuse industry and every year it threatens more and more families. Here's how it works: It defines "abuse" so vaguely that all families are "guilty." It operates hotlines that are open invitations to malicious slander. It denies due process and a fair trial to those accused of child abuse. It grants immunity to hotline callers and welfare bureaucrats. It allows those parents who really are abusing their children to stay in their home, if they cooperate and undergo "therapy."

Author Linda Gordon observes that "child protection work was an integral part of the feminist [movement] as well as the bourgeois program for modernizing the family." She emphasizes that "the very undertaking of child protection was a challenge to patriarchal relations" in the traditional family structure.[14]

In 1974 Congress enacted the Child Abuse Prevention and Treatment Act. To obtain federal grant money under the act, states were required to meet certain eligibility requirements. By 1978 forty-three states had established comprehensive child protective systems.

> [Today,] almost all states have laws which require the reporting of suspected physical abuse, sexual abuse, and exploitation, physical neglect and emotional maltreatment. Although these terms are never adequately defined, state laws impose civil and criminal penalties on medical, education, social work, child care and law enforcement professionals who fail to report suspected child abuse. . . . These laws also have provisions which encourage all persons — including friends, neighbors, and relatives of the family — to report suspected maltreatment. In fact, nineteen states require all persons to report suspected child abuse.[15]

Some twenty-five states give child welfare workers authority to remove a child from the home without a court order if abuse is suspected.

In an important study on child abuse, Giovannoni and Becerra observed: "Many assume that since child abuse and neglect are against the law, somewhere there are statutes that make clear distinctions between what is and what is not child abuse and neglect. But, this is not the case. Nowhere are there clear-cut definitions of what is encompassed by the terms."[16] Thus, a major cause of excesses and decision-making problems is the vagueness and overbreadth of the legal standards.

Goldstein, Freud, and Solnit claim the existing definitions "delegate to administrators, prosecutors and judges the power to invade privacy almost at will" and invite "the exploitation of parents and children by state officials."[17] Yet, challenges on constitutional grounds have been denied.

Bureaucrats seek to defend such broad and open-ended or non-existent definitions. They insist they need freedom to exercise their sound judgment.[18] Those alarmed at the excesses and violations of family and parental rights on the basis of "suspicion and anonymous allegations" challenge their claims. They cite numerous cases where such ambiguities have provided open doors and invitations for zealous "social reformers" who view the traditional family unit as outmoded. In his *Don Bell Reports,* Don Bell writes: "The designs of this child abuse industry are meant to gain state control over every child under the humanistic doctrine that children are the property of the state. . . . this child abuse industry concentrates especially on home schools where parents believe that government begins with the family, not with state bureaucrats; and on families with children in Christian schools where the local church has assumed the responsibility of caring for its own."[19]

Boston Herald columnist Don Feder, whose wife was reported for "disciplining" an unruly child, gets to the ideological roots of the parent-abuse industry. He cites *A Social History of the American Family,* an influential social service textbook written by Arthur W. Calhoun:

> The view is that the higher and more obligatory relation is to society rather than the family; the family goes back to the age of savagery while the state belongs to the age of civilization. The modern individual is a world citizen, served by the world, and home interests can no longer be supreme.
>
> In general, society is coming more and more to accept as a duty the task of guaranteeing wholesome upbringing of the young. . . . the child passes more and more into the custody of community experts who are qualified to perform the complexer [sic] functions of parenthood.[20]

"In other words," snorts Don Feder, "ordinary parents are idiots. It's up to the planners and the bureaucrats to save children from their families and parents from themselves." He continues:

> Social theorists and their child-saver shock troops came to view the average family as incapable of adequate child-rearing, sorely in need of professional intervention. Social workers, many of

whom had power complexes to begin with, needed little encouragement to play God.

In her book, Mrs. Pride lists some of the categories considered child abuse "crimes": inappropriate punishment, lack of supervision (permissiveness), scolding, spanking, withholding TV privileges, raising your voice in anger, emotional neglect, and teaching children religious beliefs such as the "rapture."[21] In a number of states, emotional abuse is defined to include "the failure to provide a child with 'adequate love.'"

Dr. Besharov, a former director of the United States National Center on Child Abuse and Neglect (1975-79), reports that during the past twenty years there has been a nationwide expansion of child protection programs.

> However, in the rush to deal with this long-ignored problem, the public, the policy-makers, and the politicians have overreacted. They have sought to protect all children in possible danger of future maltreatment, as if this were even remotely possible. Through a combination of laws, agency policies, and public pronouncements, they have fostered the idea that all children coming to the attention of the authorities can be protected from future abuse. . . . [Thus] child protective professionals . . . intervene into private family matters far more than necessary, often with demonstrable harmful consequences for the children and the parents involved.[22]

Further, asserts Besharov, the extreme policies have been counterproductive. Not only have they invaded the home and ignored and violated legitimate parental rights, "the system is so overburdened with cases of insubstantial or unproven risk to children that it does not respond forcefully to situations where children are in real danger."[23]

Mrs. Pride points out that many who are the most militant and vociferous in regard to "child abuse" condone and promote the most prevalent and violent child abuse of all — murder by abortion (1.5 million children each year). While the "child protectors" savage parents for a reported "scratch on the arm" or "welts caused by allergy" or a spanking, they do nothing to halt abortions which "by definition causes the baby to be torn apart while alive, cut to pieces, or burned to death in a saline solution."[24]

Annually, some one thousand children die from child abuse. Each year, 35 to 55 percent of all child abuse fatalities involve children previously known to the authorities. Tens of thousands of other children suffer serious injuries short of death while under child protective agency supervision. What are the contributing factors? The flood of unfounded allegations is overwhelming the limited resources of the agencies, and child welfare agents are "running around after cases which don't belong in the system."[25]

Federal child abuse laws are now being reviewed by Congress. Family and parental rights groups urge tighter reporting laws to make clear what should and should not be reported; repeal or revision of laws which penalize negligent failure to report abuse while granting immunity for incorrect reports, thus creating incentive to make unfounded reports; requiring child abuse hotlines to screen reports for lack of credibility or maliciousness; and more stringent criteria for assessing the validity and appropriateness of reports.

> A lot of the graphic horror stories in the press are little more than child porn, published or broadcast because editors and producers want to titillate. And when they're not being salacious, the media is being mawkish, which sells almost as well.[26]

Consider the Biblical Principles

"Lo, children are a heritage of the Lord: and the fruit of the womb is His reward. As arrows are in the hand of a mighty man; so are children of thy youth" (Psalm 127:3). Jacob speaks of children as those "which God has graciously given thy servant" (Genesis 33:5). Children belong to God, not to the state; God entrusts them to the parents He chooses, not to Caesar (Genesis 4:1). God's Word makes it clear: parents are to care for the children placed in their trust.

Fathers are to raise their children in the Lord: "And, you fathers, provoke not your children to wrath: but bring them up in the nurture and admonition of the Lord" (Ephesians 6:4). Fathers are to be sure that the children in their trust are properly guided and governed (Galatians 4:1, 2). Mothers are to love their children (Titus 2:4), to prepare them for a life in and for the Lord: "But Hannah [the mother of Samuel] went not up [to offer the yearly sacrifice]; for she said unto her husband, I will not go up until the child be weaned, and then I will bring him, that he may appear before the Lord, and there abide forever" (1 Samuel 1:22).

Parents are to discipline their children; it is a sign of love: "My son, despise not the chastening of the Lord, nor faint when you are rebuked of Him: for whom the Lord loves He chastens, and scourges every son whom He receives." "Furthermore, we have had fathers of our flesh which corrected us, and we gave them reverence: shall we not much rather be in subjection [submission] unto the Father of spirits, and live?" (Hebrews 12:7, 9; see also Proverbs 12:28; 13:24). Parents are to practice the fruits of the Spirit in raising their children: love, joy, gentleness, goodness, temperance (Galatians 5:23). Fathers, while invoking authority which is their responsibility, are to do it in a godly manner (Colossians 3:21).

Child abuse is wrong; it is evil. It violates God's Laws and flaunts Christ's teachings (Matthew 18:6-10; Mark 10:14). Defenseless children must be protected from the immoral, the drunkard, the irresponsible. The abusers must be punished. That, however, is no excuse for trampling on the God-given (and constitutional) rights of the parents and the sanctity of the family. As for all areas of life, God's Word provides the proper solutions and right actions for parents, His Church, and civil authorities.

In cases of apparent or evident child abuse, close relatives should become involved in looking into the situation, counselling the parents, praying with them, and, if necessary, volunteering to care for the children temporarily. Should there be no close relatives, the body of Christ (the local church) should extend a loving and helping and guiding hand. It is the proper function of the congregation to help build, protect, and preserve strong, loving, Christ-centered families. Finally, should all else fail, local authorities should be contacted (and monitored) for the safety and well-being of the children. Should a "foster" home be advisable, members of the congregation should volunteer to fill that need rather than risk the possibility of placing the child in an ungodly environment.

Immunity for false witness is improper. Those who knowingly make unfounded reports concerning child abuse should know that they will be held to answer, especially if it can be shown that such reports were malicious or frivolous. God's Word makes it clear: false witness is a sin. "You shall not bear false witness against your neighbor" (Exodus 20:16). "You shall not raise a false report: put not your hand with the wicked to be an unrighteous witness" (Exodus 23:1; see also Deuteronomy 5:20). "He that works deceit shall not dwell within My house" (Proverbs 24:28). Unfounded, often spurious, reports of child abuse do great harm both to the innocent parent and to the child; they divert attention from serious abuse and provide bureaucrats with opportunity for capricious actions. As the Scriptures tell us, "Where no wood is, there the fire goes out: so where there is no talebearer, the strife ceaseth" (Proverbs 26:20).

Perjury is a serious offense, under both God's Law and man's: "If a false witness rise up against any man to testify against him that which is wrong . . . then you shall do unto him as he had thought to have done unto his brother: so shall you put the evil away from among you" (Deuteronomy 19:16-20).

Depending on only one witness is also unscriptural. "One witness shall not rise up against a man for any iniquity, or for any sin that he sinneth; at the mouth of two witnesses, or at the mouth of three witnesses, shall the matter be established" (Deuteronomy 19:15; see also 2 Corinthians 13:1).

TWENTY

PORNOGRAPHY

"The fight over what to do about pornography is basically a fight about whether the Ten Commandments still should govern our lives."

William Stanmeyer

Background Briefing

In 1979 Jimmy Carter created a Presidential Commission on Obscenity and Pornography. The commission held two public hearings, and declined to consider real-life police cases of the connection between pornography and sexual violence. Then it issued its finding: pornography is benign; there is no relationship between exposure to erotic material and subsequent antisocial behavior.

Rev. Morton Hill, a member of the commission, strongly disagreed. Rev. Hill called the report a "Magna Carta" for the porn industry. He was correct. The commission's report opened the flood gates to a profusion of debauchery, debasement, rape, sexual assault, and child abuse. In the years from then until 1987, it left thousands, if not tens of thousands, of innocent victims in its wake.

March Bell, legislative counsel for the National Freedom Institute, described the 1970 report as "a manifesto for aspiring playboys, neo-Marxists, Donahue guests and suburban swingers."[1]

In 1984 President Ronald Reagan announced the creation of the United States Attorney General's Commission on Pornography. The members of the 1984 commission spent more than one year wrestling with the issue of pornography. They received no remuneration. They reviewed the hard-core pornography in

2,735 magazines, 1,725 books, and 2,370 films; held two-day public hearings in six major cities; listened to 224 witnesses, and inspected sixteen porn outlets in seven major cities.[2]

As a result of the most extensive study of pornography ever, the commission concluded: "A causal link exists between sexually violent materials and antisocial acts of sexual violence." Psychiatrist David Scott testified before the commission that "half the rapists studied used soft-core pornography (read *Playboy* and *Penthouse*) to arouse themselves immediately prior to seeking out a victim."[3]

The commission found the combination of sex and violence explosive and prevalent in pornography. It also found that "nonviolent materials depicting degradation, domination, subordination, or humiliation" bears "causal relationship to the level of sexual violence, sexual coercion, or unwanted sexual aggression in the population so exposed."

Even before the commission's final report was issued in 1986, the porn industry launched a million dollar "big lie" campaign against it. It formed a "Media Coalition" of porn publishers and producers (films and video), hired the largest public affairs firm in Washington (Gray and Company, headed by a personal friend of President Reagan), launched a front group called "Americans for Constitutional Freedom," and set out to smear the commission and belittle its findings.[4]

The thrust of its campaign was censorship and an attempt by religious extremists to foist their values on the American public. (Three independent surveys found that the American public definitely favored stronger government action against pornography. In 1985 a Gallup poll reported that 75 percent believed that sexually explicit magazines, movies, and books lead to rape or sexual violence, and 73 percent favored a total ban on magazines that depicted sexual violence.)[5]

Subsequently, *Playboy* magazine filed suit against the commission (*Playboy, Inc. vs. Ed Meese et al*).[6] *Playboy* charged its business was hurt because of the commission's report. The Southland Corporation, for example, removed *Playboy* and *Penthouse* magazines from its forty-five hundred 7-Eleven stores and urged its franchisers to do the same. Although there is no doubt that the commission's report influenced Southland's decision, pressure had already been brought against the company by several Christian groups including the National Federation for Decency.

There is nothing of censorship in the commission's final report. (Censorship, as defined by the Supreme Court, is of First Amendment rights by the government.) There was no suggestion that the government exercise prior restraint against the pornographers; they remain free to produce what they wish. Enforcement, as recommended by the commission, would occur if the material produced for commercial distribution is deemed obscene — and thus, illegal.[7]

However, the porn-peddlers procured the support of the liberal media by obfuscating the issue of pornography and cloaking it with the First Amendment freedom of the press.

Obscenity, in a similar vein to libel, perjury, and contempt of court, has never been considered a First Amendment right.

The American Civil Liberties Union (ACLU) gave the porn groups wholehearted support. New York City *Tribune* columnist, Betty Wein, wrote, the ACLU "seems to be suffering from a severe deficit of common sense. The present ACLU, a captive of radicalism, would squander away America's investment in their children under the guise of protecting the First Amendment."[8]

Nicholas von Hoffman, himself a liberal columnist, was moved to chastise his peers: "Why it is that liberals, who believe 'role models' in third-grade readers are of decisive influence on behavior when it concerns racism or male chauvinist piggery, laugh at the assertion that pornography may also teach rape?" "If textbooks, those vapid and insipid instruments of such slight influence, can have such a sweeping effect, what are we to surmise about the effects on the impressionably young of an R- or X-rated movie, in wide-screen technicolor, with Dolby sound and every device of cinematic realism?"[9]

The commission members unanimously urged that the highest priority be given to child pornography. Fifty of the commission's eighty-two recommendations addressed the protection of children from the abuses of pornography.

Based largely on the recommendations of the 1984 commission, the Reagan administration has introduced the Child Protection and Obscenity Enforcement Act of 1987. It seeks to crack down hard on the producers, distributors, and retailers of child pornography and obscene materials. The act seeks to tighten the existing law in eleven basic areas under three specific categories: Sexual Exploitation of Children through Child Pornography, Obscenity, and Child Protection Acts. It would include child pornography under the Racketeer Influenced and Corrupt Organizations (RICO).

It would prohibit the use of federal roads, interstate railroads, motor vehicles, boats, and planes in the transporting of obscene materials across state lines, and it would permit the government to confiscate the ill-gotten gains from the production, distribution, or sale of obscene materials. (The United States Attorney General's office estimates that organized crime controls 85 percent of the $7 to $10 billion annual porn revenues.)[10]

On a related front, United States Senator William Armstrong (Colorado) has urged President Reagan to issue an executive order banning the sale of pornographic materials from retail shops in federal buildings and military installations throughout the world.[11]

The Reagan administration's agenda and the 1986 commission final report are important steps in the battle against pornography. However, much remains to be done: while the cancer of child pornography has been given the high priority it demands, the pervasive scourge of hard-core pornography continues virtually unabated.

There are still those who claim that pornography is a "victimless crime." That is a lie. Anyone who harbors such misconceptions would do well to read the Victimization section of the commission's report. Here are a few of the "milder" cases of violence related by witnesses:

A juvenile girl was gang raped by six adolescent boys who used a pornographic magazine's pictorial and editorial layout to recreate the rape in a woods outside their housing development. A woman related that her husband had a number of pornographic magazines around the house. The final episode, which ended their marriage, was when she was forcibly stripped, bound, and gagged and, with the help of her husband, raped by a German shepherd dog. Sara was a runaway forced into prostitution; the pimps used pornography to train and hold the girls. She told the commission members, "Pornography and prostitution are two sides of the same coin." Evelyn told how her husband became obsessed with *Playboy*, cheap paperbacks, obscene playing cards, and X-rated movies. Her husband wanted her to perform what he saw in pornography, and even wanted her to exchange sex partners and participate in orgies. A psychiatrist examined a man who had committed a brutal rape-murder following nineteen to twenty-four other sexual assaults on women. The doctor described how pornography was an essential part of the criminal's development. He needed pornography to commit sexual assaults. A mother told how her son died from imitating the autoerotic asphyxiation technique graphically depicted in an article in *Hustler* magazine called "Orgasm of Death." A young woman told how a respected family friend and lawyer sexually abused her, starting with showing her *Playboy* and *Penthouse.* She attempted suicide. Too frightened to tell her parents, she told the family doctor, and he assaulted her and abused her for two more years. Innocent victims of "victimless crime."

Por-nog-ra-phy — from the Greek, *pornographos* (writing of harlots). "Pornography is the theory and rape the practice" (Feminist Robin Morgan).

In the United States, it's a $10 billion a year industry.[12] "The types of material which have been found to violate federal and state obscenity laws are now distributed in drug stores, grocery stores, convenience stores, gas stations, video stores . . . in neighborhood shopping centers and malls, on cable TV and over the telephone."[13] And, now, there is "computer porn."

It's not just the explosion of availability and sales; it's also the increase in depth and range of filth and degradation and the mounting emphasis on violent sex, sadism, and vicious bestiality. Increasing callousness demands the portrayal of more and more explicit, depraved, and savage sex. "No serious research scientist today questions that the portrayal of violence in the media contributes to subsequent antisocial attitudes and behavior by its viewers."[14] "The same is true for research into sexual violence, particularly the sexual violence depicted in aggressive or violent pornography."[15]

When did the porn explosion begin? Experts say 1957, 1967, and 1970. In 1957 the United States Supreme Court decreed material could be ruled obscene only if it could be shown to be "utterly without redeeming social importance." Justice Hugo Black commented that this definition was "about as clear as the composition of the Milky Way." In 1967 the Supreme Court reversed several obscenity convictions and virtually licensed pornography. In 1970 the President's Commission on Obscenity and Pornography concluded that there was no relationship between exposure to erotic material and subsequent antisocial behavior. The commission's report opened the floodgates for pornographic materials of all types.

Research clearly demonstrates a direct link between pornography and bizarre antisocial behavior (sexual aberration, sexual violence, pedophilia [sexual abuse of children]).[16]

FBI investigations, plus records of many law enforcement agencies, testify that pornographic materials are "found data" (i.e., involved) in large numbers of "lust murders," autoerotic fatalities, mutilations, rapes, and ravages of women and children.[17] One state police investigative unit reported that "some 41 percent of thirty-eight thousand sexual assault cases on file involved pornography 'just prior to or during' the commission of the crime."[18] FBI agent Roger Young testified that every time a child has been molested, the person committing the crime "has been discovered to have read child pornography."[19] A study of 114 rapists convinced sociologist Diana Scully that scenes depicted in violent porn are duplicated in rapists' crimes.[20]

Police also find such materials intimately connected with recruitment/abduction of children into prostitution, pornography rings, alcohol/drug use, etc.[21] Vice squads report 77 percent of boy molesters and 87 percent of girl molesters admit patterning their actions after pornographic materials.[22] Each year, one million children, ranging in age from less than a year to sixteen, are sexually molested and then filmed or photographed.[23] There are between one hundred thousand and two hundred thousand children engaged in the child prostitution/pornography trade. "Many of them lead lives nasty, brutish and short."[24] Porn merchants are now emphasizing materials involving children less than five years old — some victims as young as six months. "It is clear . . . that the problem of child pornography is a by-product of child molestation and that the relationship child pornography has to child molestation is a greater threat to children than had been previously considered."[25] Testimony before United States Senate hearings revealed that the United States is the world's largest consumer of child pornography (85 percent of imported porn comes from the Netherlands and Denmark).[26] Los Angeles and New York are the major porn centers in the United States.

Since 1984 some twenty thousand stores have removed porn magazines (Eckerd Drug Co. removed *Playboy* and *Penthouse* from its 1,140 stores; Kroger Co. threw smut and sex magazines out of over six hundred Superex drug stores).[27]

David Scott, psychotherapist and expert on pornography, reported that the porn industry is an "integral" part of nationally organized crime groups, especially the Mafia (La Cosa Nostra). A nationwide consortium of five Mafia families controls the "lion's share" of the distribution of porn books, magazines, films, video tapes, and paraphernalia through more than fifteen thousand "adult" bookstores and five hundred theaters.[28] Scott stated that the Mafia's multi-billion annual take from porn business provides the perfect vehicle for laundering money from drugs, gambling, etc.[29]

Americans complain about the rising tide of rapes, sex violence, and child molestation — but a poll says that majorities approve of the sale of X-rated movies, sexually explicit magazines, etc. Fifty-two percent oppose stricter regulations on sexually explicit material (magazines and movies) — but 75 percent agreed such material encourages rape and sexual violence and 76 percent feel porn leads to loss of respect for women. Sixty-seven percent say porn brings a breakdown of public morals — but only 47 percent favor a ban on magazines that show adults having sexual relations.[30]

Purveyors of pornography hide behind the First Amendment (freedom of press and speech); and, in the main, courts have supported them. In 1982 the United States Supreme Court added child porn to a minuscule list of "unprotected" speech. Psychologist Samuel Janus insists that "porn merchants" are not only perverting the intent of the First Amendment, "they are ignoring one of the most basic human rights of man: the right not to be exploited."[31] In *Miller v. California*, the Court held that "to equate the free and robust exchange of ideas and political debate with commercial exploitation of obscene material demeans the grand conception of the First Amendment and its high purpose in the historic struggle for freedom."[32] Obscenity and pornography were virtually non-existent when the United States was founded; the issue was not raised in constitutional debates.

Some successes are coming now via different avenues: (1) child protection laws and (2) sex discrimination laws (violation of women). Legislation controlling distribution of porn material to children on the basis of its being "harmful to children" has been upheld by federal and state courts. Also, in recent years, laws prohibiting the production of child porn materials have also been upheld. The Protection of Children Against Sexual Exploitation Act (1977) combats child pornography. The Child Protection Act (1984) tightens laws against child porn and increases fines and prison terms.

There are between fifteen and twenty thousand "adult" bookstores in the United States — that's about three times the number of McDonald's restaurants. States with the highest readership of "men's magazines" (e.g., *Hustler, Playboy, Penthouse,*) had the highest incidence of reported rapes according to one survey. (Alaska is first, Nevada second; Arizona, California, and Colorado are in the top ten. North Dakota ranked lowest.) Some 350 child-pornography magazines are published in America. It's estimated that the porn industry grosses about $8 billion a year. One wrinkle though: "Dial-a-porn." Callers can have a sexually explicit (erotic) conversation by dialing porn phone numbers. Every major city has such an operation. Mothers complain dial-a-porn numbers are being passed around even in elementary schools. In New York City, there are an average of five hundred thousand such calls a day; daily revenues for the phone company average $25,000. (Auditors at the United States Department of Defense estimated that $300,000 of the Pentagon's huge phone bill went for dial-a-porn calls.) Phone companies say they can't refuse the "business" (First Amendment/free speech). But, the United States Court of Appeals upheld a lower court allowing telephone companies to deny dial-a-porn service. President Reagan's Child Protection and Obscenity Enforcement Act of 1987, which nails interstate commerce involving pornography, will be of assistance in that area.

Every week, at five hundred "adult" theaters Americans buy two million tickets to X-rated movies (annual box office take,

$500 million). Video Cassette Recorders (VCR) have opened a new field for porn peddlers. It is estimated that one-fifth of all video tape sales are X-rated movies. About 9 percent of all Americans (about 40 percent of VCR owners) bought or rented X-rated tapes during 1984. In New York, bestiality video cassettes are sold over the counter. Direct mail sales of pornographic material zoomed from $500 million to $3 billion annually. Now, there is even a "computerized" sex service; SEXTEX offers an "electronic orgy" to anyone with a computer.

Between 1979 and 1982, United States Customs agents seized more than 247,000 pieces of pornographic material; 70 percent of that contained material involving children. In Washington, D.C., within blocks of the Department of Justice, there are thirty-seven "adult" bookstores, eight X-rated theaters, fifteen topless bars.

Even the Coca-Cola Company, through its subsidiary Columbia Pictures, produces and distributes pornographic films.

The largest consumers of pornography are teenage boys and girls; almost 90 percent of all adolescents between the ages of thirteen and fifteen have examined pornographic material. Seventy-two percent of all junior high boys said they wanted to try some of the sexual behavior depicted in hard-core porn. Fifty-one percent of the males at UCLA who were shown pictures of women being raped said they would commit rape if they were not punished. So, 28 percent of college women have been raped or had it attempted since they reached age fourteen.

Consider the Biblical Principles

The battle against pornography is part and parcel of the total war between the flesh and the spirit, the dead word of man versus the Living Word of the Lord God. Pornography is Satan's fruit, bitter and poisonous but enticing to those who are corrupted by the lusts of seduction (Ephesians 4:18-22). Pornography is of an evil heart. "For from within, out of the heart of men, proceed evil thoughts, adulteries, fornications, murders, thefts, covetousness, wickedness, deceit, lasciviousness, an evil eye. . . . all these things come from within and defile the man" (Mark 7:21).

Pornography is born of lust; it thrives on lust. "Then when lust hath conceived, it bringeth forth sin: and sin, when it is finished, bringeth forth death" (James 1:15).

Pornography degrades that which God created in His image (Genesis 1:27). It brings man, created a little lower than the angels (Psalm 8:5), down to the level of animals. Pornography is an affront to the Lord God; all that pornography glorifies (promotes) is in direct and open violation of God's Law. For example: adultery (Exodus 20:14; Proverbs 6:32), carnal desire (Ecclesiastes 9:9; Ephesians 4:17-19, 21, 22; Matthew 5:28), bestiality (Deuteronomy 27:21; Leviticus 8:23), incest (Leviticus 18:6-9; 20:11-14), rape (Deuteronomy 22:25-27), Sodomy (Leviticus 18:22; Romans 1:26, 27), child molestation (Matthew 18:10).

Pornography is a cancer that gnaws at America's vitals because she has embraced the false religion of humanism which "changed the glory of the incorruptible God into an image made like to corruptible man. . . . Wherefore God also gave them up to uncleanness through the lusts of their own hearts, to dishonor their bodies between themselves . . . and even as they did not like to retain God in their knowledge, God gave them over to a reprobate mind to do those things which were not convenient [proper]" (Romans 1:23-32).

The battle against pornography must be waged on two fronts: internally (self-government — self-discipline — through oneness with Christ) and externally (civil government).

First, we must exercise Christ-centered self-government (Colossians 3:10; Ephesians 4:23-25). We must put off the "old" which is corrupt and put on the "new" "which is renewed in knowledge after the image of Him that created" our new self. It is fraudulent, and ineffectual, to demand civil action against pornography if the Christian's self-government is not obedient to the Lord God.

God's Word is clear: we are to abstain from any and everything that even appears to be evil (1 Thessalonians 5:21-22). We are not only to refrain from the evil act, but also the evil thought (the seed) that produces the evil deed (Matthew 5:28). We are to promote and support that which is true, honest, pure, lovely, and of good report (Philippians 4:8).

Christians are to shun—shut out, stay away from, resist without compromise—the heathen whose blinded hearts have prompted them to surrender themselves to licentiousness. We are not to be a "partaker of other men's sins: keep yourself pure" (1 Timothy 5:22b). We are not to be associated with, or condone, the peddlers of corruption and their wares. "Be not deceived! Evil communications corrupt good manners!" (1 Corinthians 15:33).

Jesus taught, "Blessed are the pure in heart, for they shall see God" (Matthew 5:8). If we truly seek to follow Jesus and serve Him and "see" Him, we must strive through the power of the Holy Spirit for purity of heart. If we are to be His we must be Christ-hearted. "As a man thinketh in his heart, so is he" (Proverbs 23:7). We are to censor our thoughts and think on ("Let your mind dwell on") that which is honest, just, pure, lovely, of good report, and virtuous (Philippians 4:8, 9; 2 Timothy 2:12). We are to reject (withstand, fight against) ungodliness and worldly lusts and live righteously in this world.

Second, we must exercise godly civil government. It is a proper (a mandated) function of civil government to protect the innocent from the onslaught of evil. Magistrates (public officials) are to be the ministers or servants of God to the people for good (Romans 13:4; Psalm 100:5; Matthew 19:17).

Under civil government as ordained by God (Genesis 9:5; Isaiah 33:22; Romans 13:1-7) and in keeping with His laws that magistrates are to enforce (Exodus 18:15-23; Romans 13:6, 7), we have a right to expect (require) that government will strive to remove or punish evil-doers in society, to preserve law and order, and to promote godliness and tranquility. And, who but the godly shall rise up to demand that civil magistrates fulfill the requirements of the One Who ordained them? "For the throne is established by righteousness. Righteous lips are the delight of kings [heads of government]; and they love him that speaketh right" (Proverbs 16:12, 13).

Thus, both the censure and censorship of pornography are imperative. "Where there is no counsel, the people fall" (Proverbs 11:14a). Dr. Francis Nigel Lee reminds us that Jesus censured evil spirits (Mark 5:2-13). The apostles condemned peddlers of pornography (Ephesians 4:29; 5:6; Jude). John forbade Christians to receive immoral heretics into their pulpits (2 John 7-11). Further, we are our brother's keeper (Genesis 4:9); as Paul wrote, we should be vigilant to oppose all that which "puts a stumbling block or an occasion to fall in his . . . way" (Romans 14:13b). True Christian love does not leave the stranger lying in the gutter of sin—whether it be the gutter of drugs or the gutter of "legal" pornography.

A *Newsweek* cover story on pornography concluded, "Any adult American has a license the Lord never allowed the citizens of Sodom and Gomorrah." The Lord God did not license the people of Sodom and Gomorrah; He destroyed them because they "licensed" their lusts . . . even as America does now.

TWENTY-ONE

POVERTY AND WELFARE

Since its start in 1965, "the war on poverty" has cost trillions of dollars, but, "the poor are always with us." Why? Because the system is inefficient, sometimes counterproductive—and, because our culture and economy have changed.

Background Briefing

In 1960, 39.9 million persons (22.4 percent of the population) were reported to be below the poverty line which was then set at $3,761. In 1964, Lyndon Johnson declared "war on poverty." In 1965, total social welfare expenditures came to $77.2 billion (11.2 percent of the gross national product).

In 1966, 14.7 percent of the population was below the poverty line ($4,146). Since then, trillions of taxpayers' dollars have been spent on social welfare/public assistance programs. The entire public assistance system has grown by 625 percent, in dollars adjusted for inflation. Cash assistance benefits grew 305 percent while non-cash benefits jumped by 1,860 percent. Since non-cash benefits are not counted as income in measuring official poverty rates, that causes the problem of poverty to be overstated.[1]

Welfare spending increased from $127 billion in 1981 to $132.2 billion in 1985. Of the fifty-five major federal welfare programs, ten provide cash assistance; they total $32.2 billion a year. The Aid to Families with Dependent Children (AFDC) puts out $14.8 billion annually. AFDC was originally intended to provide for widows with children in order to keep the family intact; today, the program tends to support families whose fathers often leave home so the mother can receive the AFDC benefits.[2] Supplemental Security Income (SSI) accounts for another $10.9 billion, and six health programs total $48.6 billion. Medicaid, which pays for the medical care of AFDC recipients and other low-income persons, is the fastest growing welfare program; it spends more than AFDC, SSI, and food stamps, combined.[3]

Food stamps, which provide benefits to twenty million persons a month, cost about $12 billion a year and Housing Assistance comes to $13.7 billion annually.[4]

The welfare system in the United States is grossly inefficient. Consider the impact of the welfare spending in light of the "poverty gap," i.e., the amount of money it would require to raise the income of everyone on welfare up to the "poverty level." If public assistance were distributed with total efficiency, $51.6 billion would have raised everyone below the poverty line above it. However, the $59.2 billion spent in 1984, for example, still left a "poverty gap" of $19 billion.[5]

Since 1950 the number of persons receiving public assistance and social welfare payments has increased from 6 million to 18 million (in 1974) to 22.7 million (in 1986). AFDC payments soared from $3.5 billion in 1960 to $14.8 billion in 1986; the number of persons receiving food stamps increased from 4.3 million in 1970 to 19.3 million in 1984, and the federal budget for food stamps increased from $550 million to $20.4 billion. In 1984 (latest available data) all governments (federal, state, and local) spent $672 billion for public assistance and social welfare; that represented about 50 percent of all government spending and 18.2 percent of the gross national product.[6]

Between 1956 and 1977, Congress passed thirteen major acts expanding or liberalizing the social insurance programs. These included the disability program in 1956, Medicare in 1965, big benefit increases in the early 1970s, and automatic indexing of Social Security in 1972. Over these two decades an average of 80 percent of House Republicans and 90 percent of Senate Republicans voted for these expansions. It was a bipartisan enactment of Lyndon Johnson's "Great Society." During the Nixon-Ford era, education, social and health services, and job-training budgets soared and were more than double Johnson's final budget.

Federal payments to individuals in 1985 totaled $427.3 billion. President Reagan's proposed budget for 1989 ups that to $468.7 billion, 43 percent of an estimated $1.1 trillion total. The total spent (by all governments) on welfare in fiscal year 1987 is estimated to have been $642 billion.[7]

After all the trillions of dollars spent on welfare from 1965 to 1986, here are the results: after counting annual income from all sources, 16,927,000 persons are still below the poverty threshold (which was set at $10,990 for a family of four); that was 7.4 percent of the population of 227 million. In 1950, one in every twelve Americans was below the poverty line; in 1979, it was one-in-nine; today, one in every seven Americans is reported to be below the poverty line.[8]

Poverty is big business: about 530,000 government employees (federal, state, and local) are paid to staff the welfare machine. The monthly payroll is $600 million, $7.2 billion a year.[9] No one has yet computed the costs of offices, office equipment, telephones, and travel expense — or the welfare program vendors who profit from the problem.

The following are some of the problems involved in the welfare/public assistance system:

1. Break-up of the family. In 34 percent of the families receiving AFDC payments, no father is present; in 9 percent, only the father is present. The growth in single-parent families in poverty is most disturbing. "Recent research indicates that a change in family structure causes three-fourths of all new AFDC cases: 45 percent from divorce or separation; 30 percent from illegitimate births."[10] Births out of wedlock have increased more than 450 percent in just thirty years.[11] The records indicate that women aged twenty-five or less when they start receiving AFDC payments remain dependent on AFDC for long periods of time: more than one-third stay on for at least ten years. The problem of the one-parent home is the most severe among inner city blacks. One out of every two black children in the inner city grow up without a father in the home; if present trends continue, 70 percent of black families in the inner city will be headed by single women.[12] Twenty-five percent of all children born in the inner city are born to teenage girls (black teenage girls have the highest pregnancy rate in the industrial world).[13] With each newborn babe, the mother receives increased public assistance benefits. In the inner city, "Mother's Day" is the day the welfare check arrives.

2. *The increasing number of elderly over age eighty-five.* In general, poverty is declining for persons between sixty-five and eighty-five years of age, but climbing for the over-eighty-five group. This "very old" population is expected to increase fivefold by 2050.[14]

3. *Unemployment (and underemployment).* The nation is changing from an industrial to an information and service economy. In the information areas (tele-communications, computers, etc.), a whole new field of education has developed with unique demands. Many companies are shifting their manufacturing offshore to foreign countries (such as Mexico, Korea, Taiwan, Brazil). Also, there are increasing imports from cheap-labor countries. Basic industries such as oil and steel have been cut back; auto industry employment is down. Most electronic components are now made abroad and many are also assembled abroad. Many who were once employed in manufacturing are now out of work. Some (the younger ones) will be retrained for the new economy; many (older) workers may not be absorbed.

The greatest number of "new" jobs are in the lower-paying service industries; thus, underemployment becomes a problem. Men who once earned $15 to $20 an hour in industry now are earning $5 to $10 an hour in service work. (At $5 an hour, that's an annual gross income of about $10,400, just below the poverty line.

Another factor is lack of education and skills. Again, the number of uneducated is especially high among blacks (about 50 percent of young blacks drop out of school, and, lacking education and job skills, are unemployed).[15]

Then, there are the homeless, especially in and around major cities. No one really knows how large this problem is; estimates range from a low of 250,000 to a high of 2 million. There was a 50 percent increase in the number of homeless in Los Angeles in recent years. The number of homeless families in New York City rose 14.7 percent. There have been similar jumps in Houston, Boston, Seattle-Tacoma, Chicago, and Detroit. Families with children now represent about 28 percent of the homeless population; in some cities the percentage is even higher. One Philadelphia official said, "We are approaching a point at which almost 50 percent of the persons in shelters are families with children."[16]

The courts in several states have held that individuals have a "right to shelter." In Atlantic City, New Jersey, a judge held that the state public assistance law obliges the city to see that persons "may not suffer unnecessarily from cold, hunger, sickness, or be deprived of shelter." In New York, a trial judge held that the state constitution required the city of New York to provide shelter and food for homeless men and women. Critics label that this is "the worst kind of judicial activism."

Church missions and relief organizations cannot keep up with the increase in homelessness. Some sources say about 25 percent to 30 percent of the homeless are alcoholics, drug addicts, and mentally ill patients who were released from hospitals when the mental health system was "deinstitutionalized." Patrick Durkin, an investment banker and former speech writer for Donald Regan, said that about 75 percent of the homeless are "average Americans who have had normal jobs and have led normal lives — until they found themselves out on the street." The homeless also includes about one million teenage runaways; about 70 percent of them turn to crime (prostitution, drug-pushing, robbery) to earn a living.

Caesar's "war on poverty" is a no-win proposition! Charles Murray, in *Losing Ground*, asserts that federal programs of the past twenty years have not helped but have, by-and-large, compounded the welfare problems.

Milton Friedman has said that "if you pay people to be poor, they will be poor." That blunt assessment may have been based on the facts which show that welfare programs "are laced with incentives which encourage long-term dependency. Welfare often offers more usable income than many entry-level jobs."[17] In many cases "welfare provides benefits worth more than $14,000 annually. . . . to enjoy the same standard of living without welfare, [a] family would have to earn at least $18,000 a year."[18] Chuck Hobbs, Deputy Assistant to the President for Policy Development, cataloged fifty-nine different programs designed to alleviate poverty. He authored the White House report ("Up From Dependency") which indicates that the welfare system is a mess. Hobbs concluded that many programs "mistarget" benefits; about one-half of those on welfare had prewelfare incomes above the poverty line; that leaves 16.9 million below the poverty line *after* welfare benefits are distributed. His report urges the decentralization of welfare programs to state and local levels (which are closer to the recipients, more familiar with their needs and problems, and where there is less red tape and fewer delays — there are now some six thousand pages of federal welfare regulations).[19] He also urges that able-bodied recipients be required to seek employment (or job training) and be allowed to earn more before phasing out welfare benefits.

Some states have been taking the lead in welfare reform: thirty-nine have some form of workfare program. The California reform of the AFDC program (GAIN — Greater Avenues to Independence) requires all employable recipients to seek work or job training. West Virginia proposes using welfare benefits to reimburse employers who hire on-the-job trainees. Indiana would base teenagers' parental benefits on their living with their families and going to school.

Homeless advocacy groups are pushing for a "Homeless Persons' Survival Act." Their demands would establish the right to emergency shelter, allow the homeless to use shelters as permanent addresses (no address, no welfare benefits), and ease requirements for health and economic assistance. The Heritage Foundation, a Washington think-tank, urges an end to social and economic policies that aggravate homeless problems: rent control and urban redevelopment projects that destroy low-income housing districts in favor of commercial and recreational developments, etc. "Slum clearance, provided by the law's urban redevelopment program, may have worsened the housing problems of low-income households by destroying low-quality housing in the centers of cities."[20]

Consider the Biblical Principles

Our Savior and King said "you have the poor with you always." But, He never gave the task of caring for them to Caesar. He gave it to His sheep, His Church. Christ does not assign the work to Washington; He assigns it to us, those who are His. "Inasmuch as you do this unto one of the least of these My brethren you have done it unto Me" (Matthew 25:40).

Unfortunately, we have not done very well. God used the prophet, Isaiah, to give us a word picture of the true faith:

> Is it not to deal [share] your bread to the hungry, and that you should bring the poor that are cast out into your house? when you see the naked, that you cover him; and that you hide not yourself from your own flesh? Then shall your light break forth as the morning, and your health shall spring forth speedily: and your righteousness shall go before you; the glory of the Lord shall be your rearward [protection]. Then shall you call, and the Lord shall answer. . . . And the Lord shall guide you continually, and satisfy your soul in drought, and make fat your bones: and you shall be like a watered garden, and like a spring of water, whose waters fail not. And they that shall be of you shall build the old waste [deserted] places: you shall raise up the foundations of many generations; and you shall be called, the repairers of the breach, the restorer of paths to dwell in (Isaiah 58:1-12).

What a challenge! What a promise! What a way to glorify Him! What a reward! Praise God!

"Blessed is he that considers the poor: the Lord will deliver him in time of trouble. The Lord will preserve [protect] him, and keep him alive; and he shall be blessed upon the earth: and Thou [God] will not deliver him unto the will of his enemies" (Deuteronomy 15:7, 8; Psalm 41:1).

Who are "the deserving poor"? Not the slothful (Proverbs 21:25,26). Not the sluggard (Proverbs 10:4; 24:30-34; 19:15). Not the person who can but will not work (2 Thessalonians 3:10). Biblical Law severely condemns the lazy and the wasteful and the irresponsible. The husband and father who abandons his wife and children "is worse than an infidel" (1 Timothy 5:8). Thus, for those who are in dire straits because of their refusal to work or their irresponsibility with the fruits of their labors, we are to spell out God's laws and make clear the wages of sin — and seek to bring them into the saving grace and regenerative (life-changing) power of the Living God. Evangelism is a vital part of the Christ-centered task of reclaiming the destitute and helping them rebuild their lives.

God's written Word is equally harsh on those who fail to help the deserving poor (Exodus 22:22; Matthew 25:41-46). And His

Word makes it clear that when it comes to the deserving poor (the truly needy) — the unfortunate, the widow, the abandoned mother and children, those who through no fault of their own are unemployed and down-and-out — charity (love) is an essential and mandated part of our lifework for Him.

As George Grant emphasizes, God's Dominion Charter demands service. We, who profess we are His, cannot expect to gain dominion for Him, we have no right to claim dominion for Him, unless and until we faithfully demonstrate that we have been willing and capable to serve Him by serving others. Such service attracts not only attention and acceptance from others, it begets the bountiful blessings of the Lord God. "God is the One who awards power, wealth and dominion" (Deuteronomy 8:18); He awards it to laborers and diligent workers (Proverbs 10:4).

This nation is on the brink of fiscal bankruptcy because it is on the brink of spiritual bankruptcy.

Christ's Great Commission is most effective (is often only effective) when words (preaching the Gospel) are coupled with works: for of such are the fruits of grace! "Let your light so shine before men that they may see your good works and glorify your Father which is in heaven" (Matthew 5:16).

James faithfully echoed our Master's teachings when he stressed that "faith without works is dead." "[If] a brother or a sister be naked, and destitute of [without] daily food, and one of you say unto them, Depart in peace, be you warmed and filled; notwithstanding you give them not those things which are needful to the body; what does it profit?" (James 2:15-17). Faith without works is also deadly: when God's people profess their faith but fail to engage in His appointed works, Caesar moves in and takes over. Thus it is that we now have a civil government that consumes 45 percent of the total national personal income and 37 percent of the GNP. When we refuse to be slaves to Christ, we become slaves to Caesar; the level of taxation is often an accurate barometer of slavery.

How shall we, as Christians, implement God's "war on poverty"? We do it be obeying God's Word: His whole and seamless Word; His Law-Word and His Gospel. The Bible spells out the system and the strategy; it has the answers as it does to all of life.

We begin with the tithe, by tithing, as God requires (Leviticus 27:30, 31; Malachi 3:8-10; Matthew 7:21) and by making sure it goes only to His work. It was when Christians were sold the idea that tithing was no longer required that socialism began to sink its roots deep into the heart and soul of America. Then, the Christian faith (like Samson) lost the power and influence it once hand in this Bible-founded land.

Second, we make sure our own families are cared for (1 Timothy 5:8), including adequate life and medical insurance. If every Christian family would care for its own—including parents and grandparents—federal welfare programs could be reduced by 30 percent.

Third, we join with others in our local congregation to make sure that any family and any person in the covenant community who is in need is provided for in the spirit of brotherly love and compassion. As Pastor Joseph C. Morecraft, III, has pointed out, if every church in America would care for its own families, government programs could be cut another 12 percent.

Fourth, we work to revive and expand God's law of gleaning (Leviticus 19:9-10; Deuteronomy 24:17-22)—yes, even in this "modern" age. God's principle of sowing and reaping still applies.

Fifth, as individuals and as members of the local church, we search out and reach out to those in need in the local (secular) community. If every church would "adopt" one needy family in its community, the federal welfare dole could be eliminated. Thus, Christians could bring charity back where it belongs— home to the family and the church instead of Caesar's empire.

TWENTY-TWO

PRAYER IN SCHOOL

Along with dirty sneakers and pet frogs, God and his written Word has been banned from the public classroom. Is it coincidence that the nation is in the midst of moral, economic, and international crises?

Background Briefing

It was test time. The third grader silently bowed his head. When his teacher asked him what he was doing, the boy replied he was praying about the test. For that he was sharply reprimanded and compelled to write, five hundred times, "I will not pray in class." A silent prayer prohibited? You say it could never happen? It happened. In a public (state) school in Oklahoma City. Only when the Rutherford Institute moved to represent the child in court did the principal apologize.[1]

On no other "social" issue is the nation so united as on voluntary school prayer: the right to seek Divine Guidance in matters of class and extra-curricular activities. The massive majority of Americans support it. The latest Gallup poll found that the public favors prayer in schools by more than two-to-one. Even a slanted poll by Norman Lear's People for the American Way found that 52 percent of respondents favor organized group prayer in public school (the poll did not ask about voluntary prayer).[2]

The federal Constitution is clear; it is explicit: "Congress shall make no law . . . prohibiting the free exercise thereof [religion]." President Harry Truman once said, "We all can pray. We all should pray." But, says the United States Supreme Court: "Not in public schools." As Pastor Kent Kelly has written: "It should be apparent, beyond controversy, that we are in serious danger of losing our liberty with the sanction, rather than the protection, of the United States Supreme Court."[3] Consider the landmark Supreme Court decisions which resulted in virtually banning God and prayer and the Bible from the nation's 83,700 public schools (39 million students).[4]

Engel v. Vitale (1962): In 1951 the New York Board of Regents suggested that local school districts consider starting each school day with a non-denominational prayer: "Almighty God, we acknowledge our dependence upon Thee, and we beg Thy blessings upon us, our parents, our teachers, and our country." Students could be excused, if they so desired. New Hyde Park (New York) Union School district instituted the prayer and was taken to court. Eleven of thirteen lower court judges held the prayer to be constitutional. Nineteen state attorney generals petitioned the Court to approve the prayer, "Our Founding Fathers, together with the great and God-fearing leaders of the past century and a half, would be profoundly shocked were they to have been told in their day that . . . a voluntary non-denominational acknowledgement of a Supreme Being and a petition for His blessings recited [in the classrooms] is being seriously attacked as a violation of the Constitution." Yet, the majority of the United States Supreme Court ruled that prayer is unconstitutional. The Court also ruled that even if prayer were to be voluntary, it would violate the establishment clause of the First Amendment.[5]

School District of Abington Township v. Schempp (1963): A Pennsylvania school district began each school day with a reading of the Lord's Prayer over the public address system, followed by a student's reading ten Bible verses of his or her choice—without comment. Students were free not to participate, or to leave the room during devotions. The Court ruled that the prayer and Scriptures constituted the advancement of religion and banned it. With that decision the Court also decided *Murray v. Curlett*. Madelyn Murray had sued Baltimore public schools because the Lord's Prayer was recited and Bible verses read at the start of each school day.[6]

Justice Potter Stewart dissented on both decisions: "The Court has mis-applied a great constitutional principle. . . . there is involved in these cases a substantial free exercise claim on the part of those who affirmatively desire to have their children's school day open with voluntary prayer reverence."[7] Professor

Charles E. Rice, then of Fordham University Law School, commented: "The school prayer decisions, if followed, predictably will have the effect of raising agnosticism to the rank of the official public religion of the United States."[8] Following the *Abington* decision, Henry P. Van Dusen, then dean of Union Theological Seminary, wrote: "A consistent application of such a policy [prohibiting government's affirmative recognition of all religion] would involve a revolution in the Nation's habitual practice of religion. . . . Nothing less than this is at stake."[9]

On what do militant anti-prayer groups base their opposition? They raise four main objections. (1) "Kids can still pray — silently." (Courts have ruled otherwise.) Pro-prayer groups argue that what is at stake is not simply individual prayer but brotherhood of spoken prayer as befits a commonwealth raised by God's Providence (cf. Declaration of Independence, etc.). (2) "Whose prayer will be said?" Prayer advocates say reasonable Americans can come up with reasonable prayers to the Deity. Even non-denominational prayers have been ruled out by courts. (3) "You're intolerant; you would violate the minority's rights." Tolerance is (or should be) a two-way street; it isn't under present dictums. Who is more tolerant? The great majority which bows to demands of the small minority? Or the demands of a militant minority which deprives the majority of its constitutional rights? The late Erwin S. Griswold, former dean of Harvard Law School, wrote: "Must all refrain because one does not wish to pray?"[10] (4) "School prayer is demeaning." It is no more demeaning in public school than it is in the United States Senate (which starts its day with a prayer) or the state legislature, or on great public occasions such as the inauguration of the President.

In a nation whose motto is In God We Trust, it is the prohibition of school prayer which is truly demeaning — debasing of the great republic.

This, then, is the clear and certain purpose of most anti-prayer advocates: "We need only insure that our schools teach only secular knowledge. . . . If we could achieve this, God would indeed be shortly due for a funeral service."[11]

In Mumford High School, Detroit, the principal refused to sanction the Young Socialist Alliance. The Court decreed that the principal had violated the socialists' First Amendment rights and ordered the principal to grant full recognition and rights, "immediately." BUT, at Guilderland High School, Albany, New York, when Students for Voluntary Prayer sought recognition, the principal refused. The students sued the school and the Courts upheld the principal! It ruled that any approval of prayer meetings in public schools were "too dangerous to permit."

The head of a high school English department assigned the class a magazine article "which repeatedly used a vulgar term for an incestuous son" and led the classroom discussion focused on the word. The school suspended the teacher who then sought a preliminary injunction against the school. He claimed his suspension violated his First Amendment rights. The court granted the injunction. BUT, the Sixth Circuit Court of Appeals in Chicago decreed that a kindergarten teacher violated the First Amendment (so-called separation of church and state) because she led her students in a simple little prayer at the start of the day's classes.

In Chelsea, Massachusetts, the School Committee voted to remove a book containing "vile, profane language" from the high school library. A group of students and teachers sued the committee; they claimed the action violated their First Amendment rights. The Court agreed and ordered the book returned to the library. BUT, in Kentucky, when copies of the Ten Commandments were posted in school classrooms, the United States Supreme Court said such action was "threatening" and ordered the posters removed. Said the Court's majority opinion, "[the effect of posting the Commandments] will be to induce the school children to read, meditate upon, perhaps to venerate and obey, the Commandments."

In Indiana, the court held that a high school administration could not ban an underground student newspaper containing profanity, vulgarity, and indecencies. BUT, a Florida court ruled that it was unconstitutional to allow the Gideons to distribute Bibles on school property.

Anti-prayer judges and groups such as the American Civil Liberties Union (ACLU) and People for the American Way, rest much of their argument on a phrase used by Thomas Jefferson: "a wall of separation between church and state," which was used by him in a letter to an association of Baptists in Danbury, Connecticut. In 1947 the United States Supreme Court parroted that phrase, despite the fact that Jefferson's phrase was not and is not in the federal Constitution; Jefferson had nothing to do with drafting the Constitution. In 1948 Justice Reed took sharp issue with the Court's legitimizing Jefferson's words: "A rule of law should not be drawn from a figure of speech."[12] The Court liberals found it convenient to disregard Jefferson's statement in his second inaugural address: "In matters of religion, I have considered that its free exercise is placed by the Constitution independent of the powers of the general government."

When an irate United States Supreme Court majority overruled Judge Brevard Hand's refusal to ban prayer in the Mobile, Alabama schools, then-Associate Justice William Rehnquist issued a stinging dissent:

> It is impossible to build sound constitutional doctrine upon a mistaken understanding of constitutional history, but unfortunately the establishment clause has been expressly freighted with Jefferson's misleading metaphor for nearly forty years. [This clause] did not require government neutrality between religion and irreligion, nor did it prohibit the federal government from providing non-discriminatory aid to religion. There is simply no historical foundation for the proposition that the Framers intended to build a wall of separation. . . . [recent Court decisions] are in no way based on either the language or intent of the drafters.[13]

What was it those first Pilgrims sought when they went into exile and made their home in a wilderness? "The Pilgrim wanted liberty for himself and his wife and little ones and for his brethren, to walk with God in a Christian life as the rules and motives of such a life were revealed to him from God's Word." What is it that today's American Christians seek? It is, as Peter Ferrara has written, "that they and those who hold similar beliefs, be free to participate in the community on the same basis as everyone else, without discriminatory burdens or restriction, or the imposition of unwanted values upon them."[14]

Supporters of prayer in school seek to restore traditional values. They call for a constitutional amendment to reaffirm and re-establish the original intent of the religious freedom clause of the First Amendment, that which has been stolen, twisted, and used against them. The issue, they insist, is the guaranteed preservation of religious liberty. "If the Court will not speak for the people, the people must speak for themselves." They remind members of the media and free speech groups that the First Amendment is a seamless whole: when one right is violated, all rights are in jeopardy.

"The time has come for this Congress to give a majority of Americans what they want for their children . . . voluntary prayer in their schools" (President Reagan). A proposed Prayer Amendment has been drafted:

> Nothing in this Constitution shall be construed to prohibit individual or group prayer in public schools or other public institutions. No person shall be required by the United States or by any State to participate in prayer. Neither the United States nor any State shall compose the words of any prayer to be said in public schools.

There is little if any action on such a Prayer Amendment, now. The President and Congress are more concerned with other issues—which says volumes about our priorities and values.

Consider the Biblical Principles

The central issue involved goes far beyond the issue of public prayer or prayer in school. It goes to the heart of the Christian faith: the sovereignty of God. "The battle is more than political or legal: it is theological. The issue is Lordship: who is Lord, Christ or Caesar?"[15]

To decree and accept as national public policy the prohibition of prayer in public institutions including schools is to deny God's supreme sovereignty. "He rules by His power forever; His eyes behold the nations: Let not the rebellious exalt themselves" (Psalm 66:7). "Thine, O Lord, is the greatness, and the power, and the glory, and the victory and the majesty: For all that is in the heaven and in the earth is thine; Thine is the kingdom, O Lord, and Thou art exalted as head above all" (1 Chronicles 29:11). "By Me kings reign, and princes decree justice" (Proverbs 8:16).

God warns men—and nations: "All those who hate Me love death" (Proverbs 8:36). And, our Savior and King also made it crystal clear: "But, whosoever shall deny Me before men, him will I also deny before My Father which is in heaven" (Matthew 10:33; see also Luke 9:26; 2 Timothy 2:12b). There is no looking through a glass darkly there; it's as clear as a bell. And that bell is sounding a heavenly warning. Wake up, America!

As constitutional lawyer John W. Whitehead has written: "Forbidding prayer involves, besides the relationship of church and state, the direct relationship between the Almighty and this country. In times of peace, spiritual severance may seem of little moment, but in time of national emergency the nation may desire communication with God. The question is: Will He listen?"[16] (see 1 Chronicles 7:19-21; Proverbs 1:24-31).

Is it just coincidence that the degradation of America—its fiscal and moral crises, its decline in world stature, its seeming inability to cope with international problems, let alone be a leader—took hold and now accelerates because God's sovereignty has been rejected, and His Word has been banned from our public life and institutions? Does not His Word give clear and ample warning as to what happens when a nation turns its back on God? "And I will give children [immature, childish, willful individuals] to be their princes and babes [spiritual and moral infants] shall rule over them. . . . O My people, they which lead you cause you to err, and destroy the way of your paths!" (Isaiah 3:4, 12).

Public reverence is an essential mark of a godly nation; it is vital to its survival (Ezekiel 33:7, 8). It is particularly urgent in our schools and for our youth. "We must not therefore neglect the duty, lest the omission be a greater scandal than the observation of it" (Matthew Henry).

"The fear [respect] of the Lord is the beginning of wisdom" (Proverbs 16:1). "Hear me now, therefore, children, and depart not from the words of My mouth" (Proverbs 5:7). "Hear counsel and receive instruction, that you may be wise in your latter end" (Proverbs 19:20). "The preparation of the heart in man, and the answer of the tongue, is from the Lord" (Proverbs 16:1). "Remove not the ancient landmark which thy fathers have set" (Proverbs 22:28).

"From the discovery of this continent to the present hour, there is a single voice making this affirmation. . . . we find everywhere a clear affirmation of the same truth. . . . this is a Christian nation." Those are the words of the United States Supreme Court. Not the Court of this day, but the Court of 1891 when it handed down its decree in the case of *Holy Trinity v. United States*. On April 17, 1952, by Joint Resolution, the Congress of this nation called for an annual National Day of Prayer. Since then, every President has proclaimed such a day, resuming a tradition begun by the Continental Congress. Would that the present Congress would do it and mean it, as did the members of that Continental Congress!

We are summoned to dedicate all our acts (public and private) to the providence of a caring God, as did our forefathers. "I will, therefore, that men pray everywhere, lifting up holy hands without wrath or doubting" (1 Timothy 2:8). "Whatsoever you do in word or deed, do all things in the name of the Lord" (Colossians 3:17). "Whether you eat or drink or whatever you do, do all to the glory of God" (1 Corinthians 10:31). " To Him be the glory and dominion for ever and ever" (Revelation 1:5; Colossians 1:16-18).

As His, we are called to witness as well as to cherish the Name and presence of God. "Let your work appear unto your servants, and your glory unto their children" (Psalm 90:16). "Providing for honest things not only in the sight of the Lord but also in the sight of man" (2 Corinthians 8:21). "Show forth the praises of Him Who has called you out of darkness into His marvelous light" (1 Peter 2:9).

The true strength of a nation lies not in its gross national product or its military might—those things rust and moth will corrupt. Here is the secret of a powerful land: "Blessed is the nation whose God is the Lord" (Psalm 33:12). "Righteousness exalteth a nation" (Proverbs 14:34). "The Lord is my strength and my shield; my heart trusteth in Him, and I am helped: therefore my heart greatly rejoices; and with my song I will praise Him" (Psalm 28:7). "No good thing will He withhold from them that walk uprightly" (Psalm 84:11b). "The hand of our God is upon all them for good who seek Him; but His power and His wrath is against all them who forsake Him" (Ezra 8:22b).

We misread our dilemma—and hugely underestimate our peril, I fear—if we suppose that the nature of world struggle is geographic, or economic, or one system of government versus another. The conflict is between our Christian heritage and secular power, between keeping faith and having none, between God and clever monkeys who are astonished at their ability to add and subtract.[17]

TWENTY-THREE

RELIGIOUS LIBERTY

"Separation of church and state" was never intended by the First Amendment, but it is being used to chew away at freedom of worship.

Background Briefing

How does religious liberty fare in the United States today? Not very well.

Consider the so-called Civil Rights Restoration Act. Its forerunner was first introduced in 1984 by United States Senator Edward Kennedy (Massachusetts) — and introduced again and again. Now it's the Civil Rights Restoration Act of 1987, more commonly called the Grove City College bill. Fifty-one members of the United States Senate and a majority of the members of the House of Representatives support it. They believe that churches and church-affiliated colleges and universities — and other private institutions — should be monitored and controlled by the federal government.

Here's the background:

Grove City College (Pensylvania) is a small coeducational institution. It has never discriminated on the basis of race, religion, sex, or handicap. It has never accepted federal funds. In fact, it has consistently refused all federal funding, well aware of the fact that with federal funds comes federal control.[1]

In 1977 the United States Department of Health, Education, and Welfare brought suit against Grove City College (*Grove City College v. Bell*). The complaint was that the college refused to sign and submit federal forms stating that the school did not discriminate on account of sex.[2]

The Department of Education argued that since a few Grove City students had, as individuals, received government aid (a guaranteed student loan), the college itself was a "recipient" of federal monies. Thus, demanded the bureaucrats, Grove City must comply with the provisions of Title IX of the 1972 Education Amendments. Those regulations require that institutions receiving federal aid have to comply with federal non-discrimination requirements including affidavits of compliance. Grove City College continued to refuse and eventually the case reached the United States Supreme Court.

In 1984 the Court held that a college or university is deemed to be a "recipient" of federal funds if it enrolls a student who receives any kind of federal grant or federally guaranteed loan. However, the court also held that only the "program" or "activity" in which the student enrolled—and not the entire institution—is the "recipient" and subject to the Title IX regulations. Therefore, only the financial aid office at Grove City College was required to comply with those federal regulations.[3]

Those who support freedom were concerned about the Court's broad definition of "recipient." That decision "outraged feminists and civil rights organizations" and liberals in the United States Senate and House. They railed that the Court's decision subverted the purpose of existing civil rights and anti-discrimination laws. At that point, in 1984, Senator Edward Kennedy came up with the so-called Grove City College bill.

Since then feminists and civil rights activists have combined to make enactment of the bill their number one priority. Essentially, the bill, which has been greatly expanded since 1984, would bring all institutions receiving any form of federal funds (the entire institution) under federal civil rights laws.[4] The bill specifically covers "state and municipal departments and agencies, institutions and systems of elementary, secondary, and higher education, corporations, partnerships and other private organizations."[5]

Thus, the fifty-one sponsors in the Senate, and some two hundred members of the House, want to force all recipients of any kind of federal money (direct or indirect) to submit to federal regulations—"private schools, businesses, grocery stores, pharmacies, farms . . . the reach of federal control would thus be dramatically extended."[6]

Nobel Prize winner Dr. Milton Friedman said, "By this line of reasoning, the corner grocer and the A & P are 'recipient institutions' because some of their customers receive social security checks. *The New York Times* and *Chicago Tribune* are Federal contractors because welfare recipients buy papers."[7]

The legislation has been called "the most dangerous piece of legislation ever introduced into the United States Congress."[8] For churches and church-affiliated colleges, it could well be. Jack Clayton, of the American Association of Christian Schools, charged that it was an attempt to foist upon the nation "the left-wing ideology of social engineers who have wormed their way into the federal bureaucracy and judicial system."

Check these ramifications:

The legislation prohibits "discrimination." That means that in their hiring practices, churches and colleges could not discriminate against alcoholics and drug addicts.

The legislation also provides that an institution may not refuse to hire individuals with communicable diseases such as tuberculosis—and AIDS (since individuals carrying that virus have come under the definition of "handicapped"). "Our knowledge of mechanisms for transmitting [AIDS] is hardly complete enough to make us sanguine about the prospect of federally forced hiring of AIDS patients by university cafeterias and hospitals."[9]

It may also mean that churches and church schools would be forced to employ homosexuals since the legislation prohibits discrimination for reason of sexual preference. Further, any educational institution receiving federal monies might well be required to remove all religious symbols.

Assistant United States Attorney General William Bradford Reynolds (in a *New York Times* interview), speaking of the original Grove City College bill, said: "It rewrites four statutes to the point that the federal government would be involved in every facet of state and local activity."

In assessing the potential impact of the bill, Jack Clayton cautions that Christians must keep in mind a recommendation by the 1975 United States Commission on Civil Rights: tax exemption should be treated as federal financial assistance.

How pernicious and pervasive is the act, when coupled with other developments? Consider this on the scale of religious liberty: there is the growing pressure to consider any form of tax exemption to be federal financial assistance. Should that doctrine prevail, every church in the land could be forced to comply with the provisions of the so-called Civil Rights Restoration Act.

Do not rest in the belief that churches are immune because of the free exercise clause of the First Amendment. Under Section 86.12 of Title IX of the 1972 Education Amendments the federal government established itself as the judge of the validity of religious tenets. Thus, federal bureaucrats are empowered to determine which religious tenets are permissible under public policy — and which are not.[10]

Some other ominous developments during recent years:

The Internal Revenue Service decreed that Bob Jones University's ban on interracial dating and marriages had violated "public policy" and that the university's tax exempt status should be revoked. The United States Supreme Court agreed. BJU lost its tax exemption status. (See below regarding "public policy" and religious freedom.)

A proposal to provide a prayer and meditation room at the Illinois State Capitol was prohibited by the Northern Illinois United States District Court on the grounds it would violate the Constitution.[11] (Anti-Christians have already challenged the tradition of opening the sessions of Congress with prayer.)

A county circuit judge in Portland, Oregon banned prayers from the commencement exercises at David Douglas High School. He ruled that the prayers would violate the First Amendment.

The New Jersey legislature enacted a statute mandating a minute of silence for public school students at the beginning of classes ("for quiet and private contemplation or introspection"). A federal district court voided the law. The judge said that a moment of silence "jeopardizes" the religious liberties of the community.

The United States Court of Appeals in the District of Columbia held that Georgetown University, a Catholic institution, must comply with the District's gay rights ordinance and allow sodomites to organize on campus and use university facilities to hold their meetings. ("The District of Columbia's compelling interest in eradicating sexual orientation discrimination outweighs any burden . . . on Georgetown's religious exercise.")[12]

Congress passed a Social Security Reform bill, mandating that employees of churches and Christian schools must pay the FICA tax (Social Security), and that the church must pay the employer's share of the tax. President Reagan signed the bill into law. For the first time in the history of this nation, churches and church-connected schools are taxed by the federal government. (For further details see chapter 27 on "Social Security.")

Infringements on religious liberty? There's more.

On February 23, 1983, the United States Supreme Court in a unanimous decision, decreed that Edwin D. Lee, Amish carpenter/farmer, must pay social security taxes for his Amish employees even though to do so would violate his religious convictions and the convictions of his Amish employees. Lee, a member of the Old Order Amish, adheres to the Scriptural injunction that families and congregations are to care for their own (1 Timothy 5:8). He refused to participate in the Social Security system. The IRS took him to court.

The United States District Court held for Mr. Lee. It said the free exercise clause of the First Amendment prohibits compulsory payment of the tax if payment (and receipt of benefits) violates one's religious beliefs. The IRS appealed to the Supreme Court and it reversed the lower court's decision.

Listen to what then-Chief Justice Warren Berger proclaimed:

> Maintaining a sound tax system is of such high order, a religious belief in conflict with the payment of taxes affords no basis for resisting tax.

(The Scriptures are correct: "Where your treasure is, there will your heart be also." In Mr. Burger's view apparently nothing was more sacred than the federal treasury.)

Consider the ramifications of the Court's decision; they are ominous: they may well establish a pernicious precedent. What other "system," what other sacred cow or golden calf, may someday be employed by Caesar's magistrates to void religious liberty yet again — and again?

Mr. Lee's beliefs are based on the long and deeply held religious convictions of the devout Old Order Amish sect. His stand cannot be challenged as any expedient or malicious attempt to simply evade taxation. He sincerely (religiously) believes that arbitrary imposition of FICA taxes is against God's Word; thus, to force him to go against God's will is a violation of his faith — and also his First Amendment rights. Lee refused to withhold taxes for his Amish employees or to pay the employer's portion of those taxes. Lee was left with a choice: either abandon his religious principles or face prosecution by the United States government. The Internal Revenue Service, the taxing arm of Caesar, announced it would move to collect the taxes, plus penalties.

In that majority opinion, Chief Justice Berger wrote:

> The State may justify a limitation on religious liberty by showing it is essential to accomplish an overriding governmental interest.

Compare that with Thomas Jefferson's warning that to compel a person to pay taxes for that with which he disagrees is the worst kind of tyranny. And, compare it also with Sandinista (Marxist) "media law" in Nicaragua. It decrees that "the practice of journalism (i.e., free press) is subordinate to the defense of the principles of the revolution."[13]

Finally, the Chief Justice also held: "This mandatory participation (payment of the FICA tax) is indispensable to the fiscal vitality of the social security system." Was that not a double standard? A clear disregard for equal protection under the law (Fourteenth Amendment)? The Amish are compelled to submit to the Social Security system but neither the Chief Justice nor his associates, nor millions of others in government were at that time compelled to participate in the "mandatory" system. (Subsequently, federal judges and new federal employees were given a set time in the future to come under the Social Security system.)

Those who push for government control of religious institutions (churches, church-connected schools and colleges, etc.) insist that the First Amendment "has guarantee of religious belief, but does not prohibit government regulation of religious practices." They point to the prohibition of polygamy as one example of government outlawing a religious exercise. Those who firmly hold to religious liberty argue that right to believe without freedom to practice is not liberty. They emphasize that the First Amendment reads: "Congress shall make no law . . . prohibiting the free exercise" of religion. Further, when the Court did outlaw polygamy, it held "[it] is contrary to the spirit of Christianity" and "Christianity has produced [the civilization of] the western world."

How far would some extend control of religious practices? Then-United States Senator Charles Mathias (Maryland) said, "I don't think you can draw the line at race discrimination. . . . we must consider how many examples of discrimination there are to cover . . . race, sex, religion, age or others." Senator Mathias believed the 1964 Civil Rights Act is open-ended, broad enough to facilitate complete control: "When we start enumerating we run into danger that . . . something is overlooked." Apparently, in the Senator's mind, Caesar's reach has no limit.

Opponents to such open-ended interference and control ask: "Would a Jewish seminary be forced to admit Moslems, or forfeit tax-exemption?" "Would a Catholic seminary or convent be compelled to admit Black Muslims?" "Would a Christian college be forced to accept avowed atheists—or practicing homosexuals?" (Under Senator Kennedy's Civil Rights Restoration Act, the answer to that question is yes. Religious freedom is not to be included under the umbrella of "civil rights").

As John Baker, of the Baptist Joint Council on Public Affairs, warned: "If you allow the IRS to force you to choose between your tax exemption and your theology, it would have the power to destroy many churches."

Those who seek to use tax policy to force social revision and "reform" raise three arguments: (1) tax exemption is a form of subsidy, (2) tax exemption should be granted only to organizations that "further national policies," and (3) agencies of the federal government (such as the IRS) have authority to decide or interpret what national policy is and who or what does and does not conform to the policy.

1. To argue that tax exemption is a government subsidy is to assert that all property belongs to the government and that the individual whose labor or investment produced the property may keep only that which the government permits, and may spend it only on what the government approves. Thus, both the power to tax and the power not to tax would be the power to

control. A previous United States Supreme Court has held that granting tax exemption is an act of neutrality, not a subsidy (*Walz v. Tax Commission*, 1970).

2. The purpose of tax exemption (IRS Section 501(c)(3)) is to exclude from taxation institutions organized exclusively for "religious, charitable, scientific, literary or education purposes . . . [and to] foster [amateur] sports." To suggest that exemptions (and deductibilities) should go only to those who support "federal policies" is to require all such groups to be propaganda agents for (extensions of) the federal government.

Treasury officials have affirmed that the "IRS is without legislative authority to deny tax-exempt status . . . on the ground that their policies or practices do not conform to notions of national public policy."

Just what is "national public policy"? Representative Phillip Crane (Illinois) observed, "It is significant to note that many of the favored, established religious groups that would be allowed to retain their tax exemptions advocate abortions, homosexuality, and witchcraft." The late Representative John Ashbrook once charged that the IRS seeks to deny tax exemption to Christian schools "while leaving unhampered tax exempt organizations which practice or promote witchcraft, homosexuality, abortion, lesbianism, and euthanasia."

A poll taken for the Williamsburg Center Foundation and reported in *USA Today* in early 1988 reported that 48 percent of the respondents think churches should be forced to pay taxes on all their property. Is that "public policy"? Is that to become "public policy"?

3. The Constitution does not give agencies the power (authority) to rule by administrative fiat. Agencies are created (commissioned) by elected representatives of the people and as such are answerable to the representatives. They were never intended to become a "fourth branch" of government. Congressional oversight and control is vital; otherwise, what is left of the republic will be dominated by techno-bureaucrats. The Supreme Court has held that "courts are not arbiters of scriptural interpretation." Is the IRS or any governmental agency to be vested with such power?

Consider the Biblical Principles

First, consider the principle of God's sovereignty. "I am the Lord your God, which have brought you . . . out of the house of [civil] bondage. You shall have no other gods before Me" (Exodus 20:1-6). The Lord God's words in that instance have a direct reference to civil governance. (See also Deuteronomy 4:39; 10:17; 2 Samuel 7:22; Jeremiah 10:10.)

For the state to demand that a person who has made Christ Jesus King of all life must deny God and obey Caesar is to violate that individual's freedom of worship. And, to demand that the person who holds to the total sovereignty of God must put the state above God is to trample on that individual's religious convictions and abrogate God's dominion — thus putting itself above God. Such action by the state, or any of its agencies, does in fact force the individual to render unto Caesar those things that belong only to the Lord God. Further, to force an institution dedicated to the service of the Lord is to establish a "super-religion" controlling God's Church — that is, indeed, Moloch worship!

"One is your Master, even Christ" (Matthew 23:8-10). We must live according to His Word (Matthew 4:4; Ephesians 1:22; Acts 5:29). For there is, indeed, only one true King: Christ Jesus. The affairs of Christ's Church — including the peaceful and godly (God-serving) activities of its members — are not to be abridged by the rudiments of man (Colossians 2:6-8).

Second, consider the principle of personal property, that which has been entrusted to the individual by the Lord God who is the true owner of "the earth and the fulness thereof." "All the earth is mine," said the Lord (Exodus 19:5). "Behold, the heaven and the heaven of heavens is the Lord your God's, the earth also with all that therein is" (Deuteronomy 10:14). "All things were created by Him and for Him." (Colossians 1:16).

The Lord gives His property to those whom He chooses (Jeremiah 27:5); it is to be used to glorify Him, not the self, not the state — but Him. The individual gains temporal ownership (title or deed) of personal property by vesting time and labor and resources and talents in the development and fruition of that property; thus, property is consigned (by the Lord) to the individual as God's steward; it is not consigned to the group, not to the state. The individual is to have control over that property and is answerable to the Lord God for his or her stewardship. In that context, it is the God-given liberty of the individual (in free concert with others) to determine what portion of his property (earnings, holdings) he will contribute to the state for God-ordained (commissioned) functions of civil government (Romans 13:6, 7). God holds the individual accountable for the obedience (or disobedience) involved in the determination he or she makes.

For the state to decree that property belongs to the government, or to determine what the individual may keep, violates not only the individual but more importantly God's sovereignty and the God-commissioned principle of personal property. It is the individual who decides what will go to the state, not vice versa. The state creates no property, produces no property, should have only that which is voluntarily granted to it by its citizens. But today it goes beyond that to confiscate what it unilaterally demands — such a state is tyrannical and ungodly.

Conscience is the most sacred of all property. Christians must seek always to have a conscience void of offense toward God. Only then can they have a conscience that is truly void of offense toward men of good will. (Should one's conscience be void of offense toward God but offensive toward men, it is because such men are ungodly and perhaps to be counted as God's enemies.) If, for example, we seek to have a conscience void of offense toward men by taking a position offensive to the Lord God, we sin against God. As the Apostle Paul said, it is better to please God than men (Acts 4:19).

Those (including the state or its minions) who demand that the individual decide between obedience to God and prosecution by the state are offensive to God (Matthew 18:7).

Those who stand firm in the Lord are blessed of and to Him (Luke 7:23; 1 Peter 5:6-9).

Third, consider the principle of individual/family/church responsibility. The Christian should need no middleman (no Caesar's agency or agent) to do the Lord's work. We as His are charged as individuals, as family members, and as members of His Body (Church) to care for our own and for strangers (1 Timothy 5:8; James 1:27; Matthew 25:31-46; Luke 10:25-37). To invite, or permit, the state to assume these responsibilities, or to proscribe them, is to be guilty of forsaking Christ's teachings and God's commandments. We must stand firm in the faith, put our faith to His works, and resist the encroachments of government.

Fourth, consider the principle of separation. We are not to use our liberty in Christ as a cloak of maliciousness or slothfulness or greed, but as servants of God and followers of Christ (1 Peter 2:16). We are to be *in* but not *of* the world, to glorify Him in body and spirit (1 Corinthians 6:20), even if the world hates us for doing so (John 15:19).

We are to be separate from those and those things of the world which conflict with (deny) His Word (Galatians 5:1; 2 Corinthians 6:14). The affairs of Christ's Church are to be attended to by the members of His Church, not the secular courts (1 Corinthians 6:1-4). The works of faith are to be attended to by those in the faith (James 2:14-26). Our unity in Christ is to be the unity of faith in the work of His ministry. It is not to be based on thesis or anti-thesis or sin-thesis, but on His Word (Matthew 4:4); not on compromise, but on consecration and prayer (Psalm 1:1-3).

SCHOOL BASED HEALTH (SEX) CLINICS

A shocking rise in teenage pregnancies brought a push for so-called health clinics. Reports show they have increased pregnancies, use of contraceptives — and teenage abortions.

Background Briefing

The "sexual revolution" in the United States has brought a tragic increase in teenage pregnancies. "During the 1970s, the percentage of sexually active teens grew nearly 67 percent . . . there are more than eleven million sexually active teenagers in America today."[1] With that increase came a rise in the pregnancy rate for teenage females. Some 1.1 million teenagers between the ages of fifteen and nineteen become pregnant each year — that's one out of every eleven, three thousand each day. More than half of them get abortions.

"Babies are having babies. Or, killing them."[2] Only about 50 percent of the pregnant teenagers — 430,000 — were married.[3]

The teenage pregnancy rate in the United States is twice that in Great Britain, France, and Canada; three times that in Sweden; and seven times that in Holland.[4] Now, AIDS adds a new dimension: teenage "promiscuity could mean more than pregnancy — it could mean death."[5]

The rising alarm over such statistics has spawned an accelerated push for "public health clinics" to provide teenagers with birth control counselling and free contraceptives. Many of these clinics are located in or near public schools. The major pushers for such sex clinics are Planned Parenthood Federation and other population-control groups and "professionals" who see school children as a "captive audience" for their values in birth control, contraception and adolescent behavior."[6] Others who are promoting the clinics are organizations such as the Robert Wood Johnson Foundation (Johnson & Johnson Co., a major manufacturer of contraceptives). That organization gave $16.8 million for schools starting clinics.[7]

The majority members on the United States House of Representatives Select Committee on Children, Youth, and Families want more government funding of sex education and birth control programs. That committee studied the years from 1971 to 1982 and found that the number of sexually active teenage girls increased by 50 percent despite millions of local, state, and federal tax dollars which were spent on sex education and birth control programs. But, the committee's majority members argued that the number of births to unwed teens dropped during that period. They called for a nationwide taxpayer-funded program to establish "comprehensive health clinics" which would emphasize family planning and sex education in public schools.[8]

Minority members of the committee took issue with the report. Representative Daniel Coats (Indiana) was one who rejected their findings and proposals. Congressman Coats said:

> The report concludes that because the number of births has decreased, the programs providing sex education and contraceptives to young people are successful, but it makes no distinction between births and pregnancies. The statistics hide the fact that this decline in births is the result of a dramatic increase in abortions during the '70s and '80s.[9]

> Progressively over the last twenty-five years, we have, as a nation, decided that it is easier to give children pills than to teach them respect for sex and marriage.[10]

Programs used at the school based health clinics were found to promote promiscuity. Stanley Weed and Joseph Olsen, of the Institute for Research and Evaluation, reported that the number of teenage clients served by family planning clinics increased from 300,000 in 1970 to 1.5 million in 1981. "The number of teenagers using family planning services climbed 300 percent for blacks between 1969 and 1980 and 1700 percent among whites."[11]

It is estimated that the annual costs for such programs now total more than $500 million. Weed and Olsen stress that teenage involvement with family-planning programs may reduce teenage birthrates but not pregnancy or abortion rates; in fact, they assert, such programs must be recognized as a factor in the increase in promiscuity, contraception, and abortion.[12]

> The current belief that illegitimacy will be reduced if teenage girls are given an effective contraceptive is an extension of the same reasoning that created the problem in the first place. It reflects an unwillingness to face problems of social control and social discipline while trusting some technological device. . . . The irony is that the illegitimacy rate occurred precisely while contraceptive use was becoming more, rather than less, widespread and acceptable.[13]

Even Planned Parenthood (which in 1980 reportedly distributed some 2.5 million contraceptives to adolescents) admits greater teenage use of contraceptives has resulted in increased pregnancies. "More teenagers are using contraceptives . . . than ever before. Yet the number and rate of premarital pregnancies continues to rise."[14]

Encouraging teenage sex: In the face of such mounting tragedies, proponents of school based sex clinics advocate more of the same. They insist on even greater federal support and spending. "By increasing rather than decreasing federal support for clinics that provide teenagers with effective and confidential services, we would make it possible for more teenagers to get responsible advice . . . [and] make it possible for adolescents to exercise responsibility and competence in their sexual behavior."[15] Sylvia Hacker, who co-authored the key chapters in a manual to train teachers in sex education, stated: "The major task of . . . professionals is to move towards acknowledging and legitimizing the sexuality of young people." She insists that "values clarification" must be an integral part of sex education. "Only through raising and examining controversial issues . . . can we clarify where we are going in terms of a new sexual morality. We must adopt the view that sex education . . . represents an exciting opportunity to develop new norms."[16]

Eric Buehrer wrote in *Education Newsline:* "The proponents of school based health clinics draw simple conclusions from questionable research. . . . In their mind, it is better to give a child a pill than to teach that child an important character trait— self-control. There is definitely something wrong with a society that chooses such a synthetic option rather than provide moral courage."[17]

Children versus parents: In his rejection of the select committee's majority report, Congressman Coats warned: "The prevailing attitude in a number of government programs is that we have to get children away from home, away from parents. . . . I think this is going in exactly the wrong direction. We need to find ways to bring the family and its values into the system."[18]

United States Secretary of Education, William J. Bennett, insists that sex education programs must teach children not to fornicate. Mr. Bennett told a National School Boards Association meeting: "It is doubtful that much sex education is doing any good at all" because most programs do not teach moral values. An outspoken critic of school based sex clinics that distribute birth control pills, condoms, and other contraceptives, Bennett took strong issue with the National Academy of Science's Research Council for recommending that contraceptives be made available to teenagers at low or no cost. Said Bennett: "Sex education courses in which issues of right and wrong do not occupy center stage is an evasion and an irresponsibility."[19]

What is a school based clinic (SBC)? "The clinics offer adolescents pregnancy testing, psychosexual-interviews, contraceptive counselling and distribution, prenatal and postpartum care, treatment for venereal diseases, and abortion counselling, all within the general 'health' framework." Since clinics are not covered by school law, that "virtually eliminates any public or parental accountability."[20] The Michigan Family Alliance reports that "a child of fourteen or older can receive psychological or psychiatric treatment—without parental knowledge or consent."[21] "SBCs shall be in the school building or a viable location." The "local school district where [the] SBC is based must provide a degree of support. The clinic must be affiliated with the school."[22] "By definition, all of the clinics are involved in family planning."[23]

The University of Texas opened the first school based clinic in Dallas in 1970. St. Paul Ramsey Hospital (Minnesota) started a "health/sex" clinic at Mechanic Arts High School in 1973; it is generally considered the prototype. The idea spread to other cities. Since then, clinic proponents have sought to use the St. Paul experience as an example of their effectiveness. They claim a drop in teen births coincided with female patronage of the in-school clinics. However, independent researchers have challenged the validity of such claims. Research analyst Marie Dietz noted: "The widely publicized findings of the teenage contraceptive clinic which supposedly showed a drop in the birthrate are simply not supported by the data presented in the [St. Paul] research report."[24] Michael Schwartz in the *American Education Report* observed: "We still do not know whether the rate and/or number of pregnancies changed or how many students submitted to abortions."[25]

How widespread are SBCs? As of late 1986, there were sixty-six SBCs in twenty-eight cities in eighteen states (Arizona, California, Colorado, Connecticut, Florida, Illinois, Indiana, Maryland, Michigan, Minnesota, Missouri, Mississippi, New Mexico, New York, Ohio, Oregon, South Carolina, and Texas). Of those, forty-nine dispensed contraceptives or provided prescriptions for the Pill.[26] Pressures are now mounting for clinics at or near all public schools. Initial plans called for one hundred SBCs to be started during the years 1987-1990.[27]

The National Education Association (NEA) supports family planning including "community-operated, school based family planning clinics."[28] The National Association of Secondary School Principals has suggested the best location for such clinics would be in hospitals or county health facilities. "We would prefer that schools not be given another job."[29] Speaking before the Education Writers Association, Education Secretary Bennett remarked: "First of all, in my view this is not what school is for. . . . But even as an additional function of the school, it is my view that this response to teenage pregnancy . . . is the wrong kind of response to the problem. . . . it tends to legitimate the very behavior whose natural consequences it intends to discourage."[30]

Failure of SBCs: In a special report researched and written for the Family Research Council, Barrett Mosbacker concluded:

"Like past programs . . . school based health clinics fail to simultaneously reduce pregnancy, sexual activity, abortion and venereal disease among our young people. They fail because they are founded upon the same flawed presuppositions as previous programs: the reliance on birth control to reduce teen pregnancy, the myth of moral neutrality, and the 'kids are going to do it anyway' mentality." "A recent national study found that even today nearly half of all eighteen-year-old females have never had premarital intercourse. Moreover 20 percent of all sexually experienced teenagers ages fifteen to seventeen have had intercourse only once. . . . it would be short-sighted to conclude [that teen sexual activity] is an irreversible trend."[31]

What is happening in the land? In 1986 television programming, there were twenty thousand instances of "suggested sexual intercourse" without a single mention of birth control or danger of disease—let alone any reference to self-control or moral values. Public schools teach "situational ethics" and measure morality with a rubber yardstick. Teenagers are targeted by popular entertainers who glamorize promiscuity. They are subjected to TV commercials in which tails in tight jeans are wagged lasciviously.[32] There is no call for abstinence, no endorsement of morality in that electronic Hades!

Here is what Rockford Institute's Alan Carlson has to say:

> The United States is engaged in a great moral struggle, where traditional means of controlling teenage sexuality—parental regulation of dating and courtship, religious condemnation of sex outside of marriage, informal community controls such as the shame attached to an illegitimate birth—are being supplanted by a new social model. In this new scheme, children are cast as wholly independent moral actors, sexual activity is considered independent of marriage, and community use of stigma or shame is relabeled as illegal "discrimination." These two normative orders cannot co-exist: each necessarily undermines the other. Clearly, the post-1960 birth control movement has aligned itself with the latter model.[33]

Do you want to keep sex clinics out of your school? Erik Buehrer of the National Association of Christian Educators, makes these suggestions:

1. Be informed. Know the facts; they are in your favor.

2. Be organized in your efforts. Draw up a fact sheet; distribute it where it will have an impact. Stick with the facts, have a well-reasoned approach, and avoid emotion.

3. Don't let controversy become the issue. Keep the issue the issue. Get the media to report the facts.

4. Develop three or four solid arguments and stick with them when talking to school board members, opinion leaders, and media reporters.

5. Take your concern to local churches. Talk to pastors, Sunday school adult classes, women's Bible groups, etc.

6. Be alert. Health clinic advocates may quietly try to establish a "limited" program and then slide in a sex clinic. Watch out for "low key" starts and misleading program labels.[34]

As for legislative action, the Eagle Forum urges a push for laws to protect teenagers' health:

1. Amend health education laws to mandate teaching sexual abstinence.

2. Prohibit the installation in public schools of facilities which could dispense contraceptives and abortion referrals.

3. Require a copy of all public school textbooks to be placed in local school libraries (with citizen access).

4. Require AIDS blood tests prior to marriage license.

5. Require that persons in sensitive jobs be tested regularly for drug abuse and AIDS.[35]

How empty sex education is, the way it is taught—and, how glorious it could be! Why haven't we Christians drawn up a sex education course that glorifies God? Where have we been while others have made a mess of it? Let's not just come under condemnation—let's do something about it![36]

Are there alternative programs, resources which may help Christians reach teens with mature, positive sexual values? Yes. *Teen Aid: Sexuality, Commitment and Family* is a three-week course designed for junior and senior high students which promotes abstinence until marriage (available from W. 22 Mission, Spokane, WA 99201-2320). Christianity Womanity is another organization that promotes chastity as the solution to teen pregnancy. Their publications include *Not in the Public Interest: the Planned Parenthood Version of Sex Education* (available from Womanity, 2141 Youngs Valley Rd., Walnut Creek, CA 92596). *Sex Respect: The Option of True Sexual Freedom* is another program. It includes a two-week unit for junior and senior high. The course presents chastity as a positive alternative to the "contraceptive mentality" (available from Sex Respect, 1850 E. Ridgewood Lane, Glenview, IL 60025). Couple to Couple League International has available a slide film and audio program for teens. The program offers seventeen reasons for abstinence before marriage (grades seven through twelve). (Available from Couple to Couple League, 3621 Glenmore Ave., Cincinnati, OH 45211.)

Consider the Biblical Principles

Peter Frogley of Light Educational Ministries, Booleroo Centre, South Australia, says this:

> The Lord God made man and woman so that they would love each other (Genesis 2:24) and gave impetus to their love by creating in them physical attraction and physical expression of that love. So, in that deepest expression of love that husband and wife can experience, man and woman together bring about the act of creation (pro-creation) which brought great joy to God's heart in the first place (Job 38:7). In marriage, when two come together as husband and wife, God is able through His Spirit to reveal something of the depth of His love for us by the depth of the love we have one for the other—and by the depth of love in our being for that which is created through that act of love.
>
> Now, if you want to teach sex education, that is where it's at! If I had been taught sex education that way it would have been such a blessing! If you would teach children of the incredible fusion that takes place between husband and wife as they come together in marital intercourse (Mark 10:6-9), and the way that fuses their persons into one, and how that is reserved for marriage, we would have fewer people wanting to fool around before marriage.

Consider the following:

1. Sex education is a parental responsibility. "Train up a child in the way he should go: and when he is old he will not depart from it" (Proverbs 22:6). Sex education is an important part of the instruction parents are to impart to their offspring; it is a responsibility of parenthood. Surveys show that when parents educate their children about sex, there is far less likelihood that the teenager will engage in illicit sex. Parents rightly believe that in-school sex clinics usurp their authority and responsibility. At the same time, parents must accept and fulfill their responsibility; failure to do so invites outside sources and ungodly counseling. "And you shall teach them [God's words] to your children, speaking of them when you sit in your house, and when you walk by the way, when you lie down and when you rise up" (Deuteronomy 11:9).

2. Moral values must be based on God's Word, not situational ethics or secular norms. "Beware, lest any man spoil you through philosophy and vain deceit, after the traditions of men, after the rudiments of the world, and not after Christ" (Colossians 2:8). Paul's warning applies to parents as individuals seeking to live for Christ and also as mothers and fathers charged with the education of their children. As part of parental responsibility to "bring them up in the nurture and admonition of the Lord," parents have the responsibility to help their offspring form firm moral values based on Biblical teaching. "Be not conformed to this world: but be you transformed by the renewing of your mind that you may prove what is that good and acceptable and perfect will of God" (Romans 12:2). Parents are to guide their children in such a transformation: to send a child into the world without such power to withstand the tempter's snare (peer pressure, etc.) is to leave a mental and spiritual void to be filled by those who espouse the amorality of hedonism and humanism.

3. Sexual conduct should be an expression of the deepest love reserved for husband and wife; it is to be governed by God's commandments and Christ's teachings. "Have you not read that He which made them at the beginning made them male and female, and said, 'For this cause shall a man leave father and mother, and shall cleave to his wife, and the two shall be as one flesh?'" (Matthew 19:5). "I beseech you, therefore . . . that you present your bodies a living sacrifice, holy, acceptable unto God" (Romans 12:1). "That every one of you should know how to possess his vessel in sanctification and honor" (1 Thessalonians 4:4, 5).

4. Christians must stand firm against the onslaughts of an ungodly world. At the same time, evangelism which begets repentance, revival, and reform is the only effective solution to sexual degeneration. J. Edwin Orr, revival historian, writing of the Welsh Revival which started in 1904, notes the impact of that great spirit-fired event on sexual conduct in the area: "That revival also affected sexual moral standards. I had discovered through the figures given by British government experts that, in Radnorshire and Merionethshire, the actual illegitimate birth rate had dropped 44 percent within a year of the beginning of the revival."[37]

5. The Christian witness must shine through personal deportment as well as public works and words. We are to be living examples of the power of Christ within us, thus to present hope and counsel winsomely to those who are searching and confused. "You are the light of the world. . . . Let your light so shine before men that they will see your good works and glorify your Father which is in heaven" (Matthew 5:14-16).

TWENTY-FIVE

SEX EDUCATION AND VALUES MANIPULATION

When it comes to "sex" and "sexual mores" in the United States, the revolution was! It's one more of the bitter fruits of junking Biblical principles in the public schools.

Background Briefing

As Peter J. Leithart has pointed out in his essay, "Modern Sex-Speak," even the meaning of the word *sex* has been obfuscated today. "Two meanings are now in common usage. On one hand, *sex* refers to gender. . . . [But] most often, *sex* refers to sexual intercourse. . . . A *sexy* individual is not one who embodies the highest qualities of his or her sex, but rather, in everyday speech, someone who arouses lust in the opposite sex."[1]

Professor Allan Bloom suggests that a people's use of language is a key barometer of the moral health of a culture. According to Dr. Bloom, we have developed "an entirely new language of good and evil . . . preventing us from talking with any conviction about good and evil."[2] A prime example of this "sex-speak," as Leithart points out, is seen in the manner in which the media reports on the AIDS epidemic. According to the press, AIDS is a threat to anyone who is "sexually active." In reality, the threat is not only to those who are sexually active; the threat is to those who are promiscuous and perverted.

With such a perversion of language and morals, is it any wonder that American teenagers "do one thing better than their peers in any other Western land: make babies." The annual

United States teenage pregnancy rate (births plus abortions for women, ages fifteen to nineteen) is ninety-six per one thousand.[3]

The sexual revolution in America really took off in the 1960s. It raged during the '70s, slowed a bit but continues to spread in the '80s. The revolution soared on the winds of radical rebellion and a rising tide of nihilism and "Me-ism." That brought a rejection of traditional values and cultural restraints. Also, the sexual revolution was and is a travelling companion of drugs and the rock culture. Research has found that drugs, sexual promiscuity, and perversion go hand-in-hand.

But, a major instigator of the sexual revolution has been, and still is, sex education in the public schools. Sex education courses are filling many young people with all kinds of ideas: (1) that traditional values and Christian morality are "junk"; (2) that most parents are "ignorant, intolerant, irrational, and old-fashioned"; (3) that the Scriptures are "moralizing crap"; and (4) that the old "shalt nots" are simply no longer relevant.

Prior to the 1960s — when some semblance of Christian morality was extant in American classrooms, there were relatively few teenage pregnancies under the age of sixteen, and very little venereal disease among teenagers of any age. Today, after years of sex education (values manipulation), both are rampant. Now, with the specter of AIDS, there is an accelerated drive for school based sex clinics and more intensive public school instruction in "safe sex." Seldom, in these programs, are the words, *abstinence* or *chastity* invoked.

United States Education Secretary William J. Bennett has charged the programs and clinics "legitimate" sexual activity while encouraging teenagers to have "sexual intimacy" on their minds.[4]

Sex educators claim that the programs are "value free," dealing only with biology and physiology. But, audits of many of the courses show clearly that this is not true. Most programs deal more with "sociology" than biology and are largely concerned with values manipulation.

Author and editor Barbara Morris has warned, "The purpose of sex education is to eradicate Christian values and Christian behavior relating to sexual activity and to replace them with Humanist values and behavior."[5]

Mr. and Mrs. Ted Anderson, parents of three boys, attended a tenth grade biology class on sex education in Candler, North Carolina. They reported: "Right away the home was forgotten. All authority of parents was dismembered. The child became a business customer for the abortion clinic. All business to these clinics would be held highly confidential, not even a court order could reveal their business relationship between the child and the abortion clinic."[6]

Dr. Ralph Sexton, Sr. also attended a sex education class at the same school. He was stunned "to sit in that class and hear sex discussed, and see contraceptives displayed with what appeared to me to be only one thing in mind: 'Young people, go ahead and have sex, but here is how to keep from getting pregnant, and if you do, come by and we will abort "it" for a price.' "[7]

Following the infamous United States Supreme Court *Roe v. Wade* abortion decision in 1973, Dr. Alan Guttmacher, past-president of Planned Parenthood boasted, "The only avenue in which Planned Parenthood has to win the battle is sex education."[8]

Dr. Thomas Szasz agreed: "What sex educators want is not to impart information but to influence behavior." Dr. Szasz charged that "so-called sex education as practiced is a mass of misinformation and outright fraud."[9]

Thus, the underlying purpose and thrust of sex education programs cannot be fully comprehended unless it is recognized as one phase of a humanistic attempt to alter values of American youth.

And, that goes hand-in-hand with the promulgation of socialism.

> It is no accident . . . they supplement each other. . . . The socialist project of homogenizing society demands that the family be vitiated or destroyed. This can be accomplished in good measure by profaning [marriage love] and breaking monogamy's link between sex and loyalty.[10]

Margaret Sanger, founder of the National Birth Control League (which later became Planned Parenthood Federation) and "Humanist of the Year" in 1965, is often called the mother of sex education. Mrs. Sanger was one of the most radical feminists of all times. Her "creed" was free love, birth control, abortion, and the sterilization of those she considered inferior.[11]

The full legacy of Sanger's philosophy has been the sexual revolution of the 1960s and 1970s: abortion-on-demand, multiple
divorces, serial marriages, and a soaring rate of child abuse in
all countries where abortion is legal, and epidemics of venereal
and sexually transmitted diseases.[12]

When Margaret Sanger's International Planned Parenthood sex-
ologists first attacked America's . . . Christian foundation of
moral ethics, there was only one divorce in every eleven marriages. Now, 50 percent of all marriages end in divorce. . . . [13]

A major impetus for sex education was the 1961 Conference on
Church and Family called by the National Council of Churches.
Delegates from twenty-eight Protestant churches met with scientists and educators to discuss sex and marriage. They came up
with the assertion that "sex codes requiring too high a level of ethical sensitivity are harmful" and called for "understanding, tolerance
and reform as a meaningful Christian ethic of sexual behavior."
Any reference to Biblical mandates and principles was absent.[14]

One of the results of that conference was the founding of the
Sex Information and Education Council of the United States
(SIECUS) in 1964. SIECUS has been a major purveyor of "value
free" sex education programs in public schools along with Planned
Parenthood, the National PTA, and the National Education
Association (NEA).[15]

The dominating characteristic of the programs [pushed by those
agencies] is their obvious promulgation of the philosophy of humanism. Thus, there has been the elimination of any established
moral base, any traditional values, any Scriptural principles
that support a belief in absolutes declared by God in His Word.
All this is in a philosophical attitude of permissiveness.[16]

"Surprisingly, many churches readily abandoned Christian
principles. The United Methodist Church and the United Church
of Christ were soon receiving special praise from the experts for
their progressive sex curricula."[17] Most recently, the American
Catholic Bishops' Conference issued a controversial paper
approving of the distribution of condoms to school children.

In 1965 Isadore Rubin, managing editor of the magazine
Sexology wrote: "The beginning of wisdom for educators is the

recognition of the fact that the old absolutes have gone."[18] So much for the Biblical injunction that the beginning of wisdom is the fear (respect for and obedience to) God's Word. But then, God has been stricken from sex education in the same manner that He has been locked out of the public schools.

Writing in *Persuasion at Work: Pregnant Teenagers and Moral Civil War*, Allan C. Carlson suggests that the arguments of "these partisans of a new moral and social order" deserve attention "as a case study on how to conduct and win a moral revolution through the manipulation of words and ideas." He then spells out their seven-point strategy:

> First, declare the old morality dead. Second, destroy the residual influence of tradition and religion. Third, make everything relative by recasting the traditional as abnormal. Fourth, declare religious opinion unacceptable in any public moral debate, allowing only science to take part. Fifth, advocate "choice." Sixth, advance the "contraceptive" solution as the sole answer to our social problems. Finally, seize control of the schools and begin indoctrination of the young in the "new" code.[19]

To understand part of the task facing Christians, reverse the thrust of each of those seven facets. For example, declare the so-called new morality (which in truth is an old-and-once-discarded morality) deadly — present the hard facts of what it has produced in recent years.

"Sex education programs cause particular harm to children between the ages of six and twelve," warns Dr. Melvin Anchel, psychiatrist. During those years, he points out, a latent sex drive is sublimated into seeking personal achievements and feelings of compassion. When that latency is stimulated and diverted through sex education programs it can do irreparable harm and in later life often results in sex cruelty or perversion.[20] (Sex educators maintain there is no such thing as sex perversion; that the term is a manifestation of the "hang ups" caused by "religious bigotry and puritanical cultures.")

Sex education promoters claim that sexual activities among youth are natural and inevitable and should be made "safe" by arming children with information, contraceptives, and access to abortion. But, "William Marsiglio and Frank L. Mott found that teenagers who have had sex education have a higher probability of engaging in premarital sex at early ages — ages fifteen through nineteen — than youngsters who have not had the instruction."[21]

Deborah Anne Dawson, author of another study, reports "that one of her statistical models shows that 'prior contraceptive education increases the odds of starting intercourse at fourteen by a factor of fifteen' — that is, by 50 percent."[22]

Digging under the Guttmacher Institute's juggling of the findings of its 1985 report promoting "liberalized" sex education, Professor Jacqueline R. Kasun finds these to be significant factors: (1) having both parents in the home lessens the likelihood of a girl's having premarital intercourse (ages fourteen through sixteen); (2) a young woman who attends church one or more times a week is significantly less likely to engage in premarital sex at any age from fourteen through eighteen; and (3) the effects of regular church attendance are stronger than any other observed influences on the behavior of girls over the age of seventeen.[23]

Dr. Kasun's studies show that the "states which spend most heavily to provide free contraceptives and abortions have the highest rates of premarital teenage pregnancy." And the differences are major. The rate of premarital teen pregnancy is more than twice as high in California as in Idaho or South Dakota, and California spends more than four times as much per capita as the other two on free birth control. "Free birth control encourages sexual risk-taking and therefore a higher level of unintended pregnancy."[24]

Professor Kasun concluded: "The policy implications of these findings are obvious. If the intent is to reduce premarital sex activity and pregnancy among teenagers, there is no evidence that sex education will help. Church will. And so will a stable home environment."[25]

Professor Philip Cutright, Indiana University, observed, "In these younger groups we find no evidence that [sex education] programs reduced illegitimacy. . . . Venereal disease is actually found to increase . . . .the reason for negative results is that the programs stimulate much higher rates of sexual activity." Other studies show that when teens are "given information and access to contraceptives, they assume 100 percent freedom and safety in sex, and activity increases." In addition to seeking to replace traditional values with "there is no 'right' or 'wrong' but only what feels good for you," sex education programs often fail to stress to young girls the dangers of the intrauterine device and the Pill and the higher incidence of cervical cancer caused by premature sex and promiscuity.[26]

Phyllis Schlafly capsulized some of the data from the research of Dr. Kasun:

- Four states lead in public-funded birth control: California, Hawaii, Georgia, and New York. All four provide abortions at taxpayer expense and provide contraceptives and abortions without parental consent.

- California's rate was 150 percent of the national average of teenage pregnancies and abortions; New York's was 135 percent; Hawaii's, 134 percent, and Georgia's, 131 percent.[27]

When does sex education start in state schools? How long does it continue? Generally, it is a K-12 continuing program conducted under a variety of classes including family planning, health, biology, life sciences, social science, human sexuality, home economics, etc.

In the first grade, sex education may start with a "mixed-group" tour of restrooms and an explanation of male and female genitals. By fourth grade, many students receive a detailed description of human sexual intercourse. In many schools, seventh and eighth graders may spend one-fifth of the day for four weeks on sex education. Discussions center primarily around "values clarification." In all but a few instances, traditional values are debunked, sexual activity (how and with whom) is presented as "strictly a matter of personal preference," and sexual deviation (homosexuality, incest, etc.) is viewed as acceptable (see accompanying comparative chart). Love and marriage are largely ignored.

Taxpayers pay the largest part of the bill for sex education. Millions of our tax dollars flow to the program from federal agencies. However, several large foundations (the Rockefeller Foundation, Robert Wood Johnson Foundation, for example) pour millions more into sex education through such organizations as Planned Parenthood.

The time has come for the American public to demand that the public schools teach children to say *NO* to fornication as well as *NO* to drugs, and *NO* to alcohol. Any other instruction in the public schools about these three subjects is tantamount to lead-

ing children down the primrose path of behavior that is un-
healthy, emotionally traumatic, financially costly, illegal, and
possibly fatal.[28]

Biblical Principles v. Evils of Humanism

How do the Biblical principles of godly behavior compare
with the humanistic principles of ungodly behavior?

God's Word versus the Tenets of Humanism

"Teaching us that, denying ungodliness and worldly lusts, we
should live soberly, righteously,
and godly in this present world"
(Titus 2:12). "Because it is written,
be you holy; for I am holy" (I Peter
1:16). "Let us hear the conclusion
of the whole matter: fear [respect]
God, and keep His commandments: for this is the whole duty
of man" (Ecclesiastes 12:13, 14).

"Yeah, has God said . . . ?" (Genesis 3:1). "And even as they did not
retain God in their knowledge,
God gave them over to a reprobate mind, to do things which are
not convenient [proper/decent]"
(Romans 1:28).

Sexual Conduct

"Therefore shall a man leave his
father and his mother and shall
cleave unto his wife: and they
shall be one flesh" (Genesis 2:24).
"What, know you not that he
which is joined to a harlot is one
body? for two, says He, shall be
one flesh" (1 Corinthians 6:16). "I
beseech you, therefore . . . that
you present your bodies a living
sacrifice, holy, acceptable unto
God" (Romans 12:1). "Know you
not that you are the temple of God
. . . if any man defile the temple
of God, him shall God destroy" (1
Corinthians 3:16, 17). "Every one
of you should know how to possess
his vessel in sanctification and
honor" (1 Thessalonians 4:4, 5).

"In the area of sexuality, we believe that intolerant attitudes,
often cultivated by orthodox religions and puritanical cultures,
unduly repress sexual conduct."[29]

"Sex is fun and joyful, courting is
fun and joyful, and it comes in all
types and styles all of which are
okay. Do what gives pleasure and
enjoy what gives pleasure, and
ask for what gives pleasure. Don't
rob yourself by focusing on old-
fashioned ideas about what's 'normal' or 'nice'" (Planned Parenthood booklet for teenagers).

Moral Values

"Thy word have I hid in my heart, that I might not sin against Thee" (Psalm 119:11). "Let this mind be in you which was in Christ Jesus" (Philippians 2:5). "And herein do I exercise myself, to have always a conscience void of offense toward God, and toward men" (Acts 24:16). "Beware lest any man spoil you through philosophy and vain deceit, after the tradition of men, after the rudiments of the world, and not after Christ" (Colossians 2:8). "But, put you on the Lord Jesus Christ, and make not provision for the flesh to fulfill the lust thereof" (Romans 13:14). "Having therefore these promises, dearly beloved, let us cleanse ourselves from all filthiness of the flesh and spirit, perfecting holiness in the fear of God" (2 Corinthians 7:1).

"Moral values derive their source from human experience. Ethics is autonomous and situational, and needs no theological or ideological sanction."[30] "Parents with traditional values are intolerant, ignorant, bigoted. . . . Sex educators approach the following in 'openness' to 'relieve' the child's anxieties: non-marital sex, homosexuality, masturbation, abortion, contraception, and incest. Noticeably missing are God's plans for reproduction, the beauty of marital sex, and the value of abstinence until marriage."[31] "Schools must not be allowed to continue the immorality of morality. An entirely different set of values must be nourished" (*Sexuality and the School,* Marianne & Sidney Simon).

Parents and Family

"Train up a child in the way he should go: and when he is old he will not depart from it" (Proverbs 22:6). "You fathers, provoke not your children to wrath; but bring them up in the nurture and admonition of the Lord" (Ephesians 6:4). "And you shall teach them [The Lord's commandments] to your children, speaking of them when you sit in your house, and when you walk by the way, when you lie down, and when you rise up" (Deuteronomy 11:19).

"Parents are the worst source of factual information regarding sex" (Human Sexuality textbook). "DOP (*Dimensions of Personality*, a course used in many fourth, fifth, and sixth grades) demotes and patronizes the parent when it isn't showing them to be mean, lacking in sensitivity to the child's feelings . . . parents hold foolish and false values. Children are told their parents lack the skills to be good parents"[32]

Children

"Children, obey your parents in the Lord, for this is right. Honor your father and mother, which is the first commandment with a promise" (Ephesians 6:4). "My son, keep your father's commandments, and forsake not the law of your mother; bind them continually upon your heart" (Proverbs 6:20-23).

Planned Parenthood calls for compulsory sex education, K-12th grades.[33] "No religious views, no community moral standards, are to deflect [the child] from the overriding purpose of self-discovery, self-assertion, and self-gratification."[34]

Fornication/Adultery

"You shall not commit adultery" (Exodus 20:14). "Abstain from fleshly lusts that war against the soul" (1 Peter 2:11). "For this is the will of God, even your sanctification, that you should abstain from fornication. . . . For God has not called us unto uncleanness but unto holiness" (1 Thessalonians 4:7). "Now the works of the flesh are manifest, which are these: adultery, fornication, uncleanness, lasciviousness . . . that they which do such things shall not inherit the kingdom of God" (Galatians 5:19-21).

"Youth is led [through school sex education programs] to believe that carnality need not be sublimated; governing factors responsible for normal maturation are thereby excluded from their lives."[35] "Teachers must be alert to keep 'moralizing crap' [Christian morality] out of their work with values"[36] "A lengthy list of reasons why young people have sex . . . included such reasons as 'they want to prove their masculinity or femininity,' 'everybody else is doing it,' etc., without once mentioning love or marriage."[37]

Abortion

"You shall not commit murder" (Exodus 20:13). "If a man strive and hurt a woman so that her fruit depart from her [i.e. miscarriage] . . . and if any mischief [i.e. harm, loss of life to mother or child] follow, then you shall give life for life" (Exodus 21:22-25; see also Deuteronomy 22:6, 7; Isaiah 59:1-9).

Abortion is touted to young people as one more form of birth and population control. Planned Parenthood centers arrange for teenage abortions without parental knowledge or consent.[38] "What happens . . . if you get pregnant, what are the choices? Well, you can carry the baby or abort."[39]

Sodomy

"In the image of God created He him; male and female created He them" (Genesis 1:27). "You shall not lie with mankind as with womankind; it is an abomination. . . . Defile not yourself in any of these things" (Leviticus 18:22-24). "For this cause God gave them up unto vile affections: for even their women did change the natural use into that which is against nature; And likewise the men, leaving the natural use of the woman, burned in their lust one toward another . . . receiving in themselves that recompense of their error which was meet" (Romans 1:26, 27).

"The prevailing theme . . . children from the sixth grade on must come to accept it [homosexuality] as normal. . . . A good experience [is to] have two ten-year-old girls 'role play' two male lovers . . . Parents who quote Scriptures against homosexuality are 'irrational,' their minds are perverted."[40]

Perversion

"Wherefore God gave them up to uncleanness through the lusts of their own hearts, to dishonor their own bodies between themselves" (Romans 1:24, 28-31). "While they promise them liberty, they themselves are the servants of corruption; for of whom a man is overcome, of the same is he brought into bondage" (2 Peter 2:19). "Thus they were defiled with their own works, and went a whoring with their own inventions [ideas]. Therefore was the wrath of the Lord kindled against His people, insomuch that He abhorred His own inheritance" (Psalm 106:39-40).

"The many varieties of sexual exploration should not in themselves be considered evil. . . . Individuals should be permitted to express their sexual proclivities and pursue their lifestyle as desired."[41] "The influence of sex educators has the same effect as seduction, which can lead the young person into all kinds of sexual aberrations."[42]

SOCIAL SECURITY AND THE TAXING OF CHURCHES

As originally designed, the Social Security system was to be an actuarially sound trust fund to supplement retirement pensions. Now it is virtually a national welfare program with a voracious appetite and ever-increasing tax take.

Background Briefing

Congress passed the Social Security Act on August 14, 1935. As it was originally conceived, benefits under the program were not intended to be a full-scale retirement program but only a partial replacement of wages lost due to retirement.

In 1937, 1 percent of a worker's first $3,000 in earnings went to the federal old age insurance fund ($30 a year matched by tax on employer). Since 1937 Congress has expanded the program thirteen times; the tax rate has been increased seven times, and taxable earnings have been upped to about $45,600.

Don't let anyone tell you that Social Security is a trust fund; it isn't. Plain and simple, it is a non-deductible tax. As Dorcas Hardy, Commissioner of Social Security, has emphasied, "This isn't a savings account, it's a pipeline.[1] And," said W. Allen Wallis, former chairman of the Advisory Council on Social Security, "when you pay Social Security taxes you are in no way making provisions for your own retirement. You are paying the pensions of those who are already retired."[2] To which columnist

M. Stanton Evans added, "repeated references to Social Security as an 'insurance' or 'pension' program are a sham."[3]

In 1940 when the first benefits were paid, Social Security paid only retirement benefits; now, twenty-one general types of benefits are provided by Old Age Survivors, Disability and Health Insurance (OASDHI). Medicare hospital insurance was added to the system in 1965.

For 1988 the Federal Insurance Contributions Act (FICA) tax on both employee and employer is 7.51 percent on wages up to $45,600 (13.02 percent for self-employed). The maximum annual employee-employer tax is $6,800. Social Security (FICA) tax is scheduled to increase to 15.3 percent of wages up to $57,000 by 1990.

One in every six Americans receives a monthly Social Security check. Of those receiving OASDHI benefits, 60 percent are retired, 32 percent are spouses or children of retired, disabled or deceased workers, and 7 percent are disabled workers. Some 126 million people in the nation's workforce now pay into the system; that's about 95 percent of all workers in the United States.

About 33 percent of the federal revenues come from social insurance tax receipts; 42 percent of the federal budget goes from direct payments to individuals. Fifty-one percent of all Americans pay more FICA taxes than federal income taxes. More than 13 percent of the national payroll goes to OASDHI. In 1970 OASDHI expenditures took more than 18 percent of the federal budget; today, they take more than 27 percent. In 1970 OASDHI took about 4 percent of the gross national product (GNP); now it's approximately 7 percent.

From 1935 to 1982, Social Security taxes totaled $1 trillion. One trillion dollars in OASDHI benefits were paid out in the four years, 1981-1986. Obviously OASDHI is voracious. It can aggravate fiscal crises: a 1 percent hike in inflation ups OASDHI payouts $1.5 billion per year; a 1 percent increase in unemployment reduces OASDHI revenues by $2 billion. OASDHI tax hikes worsen unemployment. It is estimated that the Social Security tax increases since 1977 have cost at least half a million jobs: the funds could have gone toward plant expansion or equipment instead of OASDHI. Higher FICA taxes in the future may cause additional unemployment through 1990 as even more funds are poured into the system. OASDHI also lessens the ability and incentive for Americans to save (economists estimate a loss of 35 percent in savings); thus, the private sector is being decapitalized and the GNP vitiated.

During recent years, the Social Security system has been in a perilous financial condition. Increases in taxes, and the reforms of the Social Security Amendments of 1983, are calculated to keep the system in the black until about the year 2050. Some actuaries say that this is an optimistic estimate. They insist that as the system now operates, only a continual increase in the FICA tax rate on a higher tax base will keep the system solvent over a period of years.

Pete DuPont, former governor of Delaware, calls the Social Security system "a ticking time bomb." He warns that it may go broke by the time today's 77 million baby boomers reach retirement age. According to DuPont, the system "works today because 77 million are paying in and 36 million are taking out. When the 77 million retire sometime after the turn of the century, and there aren't enough workers to pay the benefits, there will be problems."[4] Further, the optimistic estimates foresee a continuing expansion of the economy with low inflation and high employment. Economist Michael Boskin warns: unless honest solutions are found and commitments honored, the nation faces the "greatest tax revolt and age warfare in [its] history."

Experts say the system may have a "quick fix" for now but, for the long haul, it remains a fiscal nightmare. The system's unfunded liabilities (to cover those now paying into the program) total more than $5.5 trillion — about three times greater than the rest of the federal debt.

What has caused the crisis in the Social Security program? Politics, mostly. First, the professional politicians have made the system a sacred cow — untouchable when it comes to cutting costs or balancing the federal budget. And, Congress buys votes with "liberalized" benefits; that depletes reserves (the average Social Security beneficiary receives about five times as much as he or she paid into system). In the face of the increased longevity of American workers, politicians have okayed earlier retirement (at age sixty-two at 80 percent of maximum benefits), eased requirements for disability benefits, and added hospital insurance, special student benefits, and other benefits.

When Social Security first took effect — in 1940 — the life span of the average American was sixty-three. Retirement at sixty-two or sixty-five put a limited burden on the system. Today, the average American can expect to live to age seventy-five; but, under the system, he can still retire at sixty-two with partial benefits and at sixty-five with full benefits. Thus, the longer period of benefit receipts puts an increased drain on the system. Starting in the year 2000, the age required for full benefits will increase one month each year so that by the year 2022, the full benefits will not be paid until age sixty-seven.

Also, the ratio of workers to recipients has declined drastically. In 1940 sixteen workers funded each Social Security recipient; today, it's about three-to-one with a projected ratio of two workers to each Social Security recipient by the year 2000.

By then, at present trends, OASDHI expenditures will be taking 10 percent of the GNP, 43 percent of the federal budget — and at least 30 percent of average worker's wages.

Is OASDHI a good deal? For some, yes. A person retiring now after making maximum contributions to the system for forty-five years will have paid in about $28,000. At the current maximum monthly benefit of about $800 he will get back his entire contribution in slightly more than three years — sooner if cost-of-living adjustments increase. If you retire at age sixty-five, actuarial tables suggest you will be collecting Social Security benefits for about fifteen years. That means that ultimately you will collect five times in benefits what you paid in FICA taxes. In a sense, it is a "legalized pyramid scheme."

But, for the young worker, it's a lousy investment (that is why participation is mandatory rather than voluntary; even the staunchest supporters of the Social Security system acknowledge that freedom of choice was thrown out the window — a "conscious" decision). A worker entering the system in 1980, earning average wages all his life and retiring at sixty-five, will probably pay more than $335,000 FICA taxes over the length of his working years (the actual amount will depend on future wage trends since the tax base is now indexed). But, he would receive OASDHI benefits of about $15,000 per year for himself and his spouse and thus would have to live to be almost ninety to have his benefits equal the taxes he paid. If, however, an amount equal to the FICA taxes he paid had been put into a private fund at 6 percent interest, he could retire at age sixty-five on $45,000 per year or could draw $28,000 per year and bequeath an estate worth $500,000.

OASDHI is now virtually a full-scale tax-funded welfare program; 97 percent of all Americans over the age of sixty-five depend on it for a large part of their income. Millions of dollars in Social Security benefits have gone to felons behind bars and some $500 million has gone to aliens—many of whom made minimal contributions to OASDHI and have returned to their native land.

In 1982 and 1983, the system teetered on the edge of bankruptcy. The Social Security Amendments of 1983 were intended to solve the pressing problems and prevent the system from going broke. Payroll taxes increased starting in January 1984. There are more hikes to come in both the tax rate and the base on which those FICA taxes are to be paid. These are among the other "solutions" enacted in 1983: cost of living adjustments (COLAs) are indexed to a 3 percent hike in the inflation rate (in 1986 the President and Congress anticipated that that hike would come in 1987 and announced a raise in the COLA just before the '86 elections); middle-upper-income retirees are taxed on their Social Security benefits; full benefits retirement age will be raised from sixty-five to sixty-seven; benefits for early retirement will be reduced (before age sixty-five); and benefits are increased if a later retirement is taken (after age seventy)—thus reducing the strain on OASDHI funds.

It is estimated that such revisions will save the Social Security system about $160 billion. Authors of the 1983 law claim that all that will insure the system's solvency into the twenty-first century. Others challenge that claim: they say it falls short of meeting what has to be done by about one-third; they point to Medicare's rapidly growing financial crisis which has not been addressed.

Incidentally, under the present law, elderly citizens between the ages of sixty-five and seventy, who draw Social Security and seek to supplement their benefits by working, now lose $1 in benefits for every $2 they earn over the allowed annual income of

$8,600. Social Security Commissioner Dorcas Hardy is pushing to have that penalty repealed. Former United States Senator Norris Cotton, who has long crusaded for such relief for the elderly worker, calls the existing penalty unfair, unjust, and demeaning.

So much for dollars and cents. Consider another important impact of the 1983 law which was passed by Congress and signed by President Reagan. It mandates that employees of non-profit organizations must be covered by OASDHI and must pay the FICA tax.

That means that for the first time in the nation's history, the federal government is empowered to tax religion. Church staffs (secretaries, sextons/janitors, and church [parochial] school teachers) must join Social Security, and must pay the FICA tax. The original "reform" provisions compelled churches to collect the employee's FICA tax and also pay the employer's tax. The estimated Social Security taxes under that law would have cost Christian schools about $240,000 a day.

The tax on religion has brought a storm of protest. Senator Tom Eagleton (Missouri) told the Senate Finance Committee, "Mandating participation of religious organizations in the tax system violates the constitutional principles of religious liberty required by the First Amendment."[5] A preeminent constitutional attorney, William B. Ball, warned: "[Congress] has not only said in effect that churches and other religious bodies must pay if they are to carry out their God-given mandate or else suffer persecution and penalties; it has also set the stage for further taxation."[6] Forest Montgomery, counsel to the National Association of Evangelicals, urged Congress to rescind the tax on churches and halt what he sees as "an inevitable confrontation between church and state."[7]

The National Council of Churches and the Lutheran Council in the United States oddly supported the mandatory tax. In fact, many of the National Council's member churches had already voluntarily joined the Social Security program in earlier years. The NCC announced that the solvency of the Social Security system is "a state interest that may outweigh any claims of religious liberty." Attorney Ball disagreed. He testified that there is no evidence whatever that "whether churches are in or out of the program will affect the health" of the Social Security program.

Dr. Gerald Carlson of the American Association of Christian Schools insisted that (1) government does not have the power to tax churches; (2) the Christian school is an inseparable part of the church ministry; and (3) the mandated payment of Social Security (FICA) taxes violates the time-honored principle of separation of church and state.[8] Kent Kelly, a local pastor and president of the Christian Schools of North Carolina, argued that it was not the function of the church to collect taxes for the state. To do so, argued Pastor Kelly, would give the Internal Revenue Service access to church records which, he maintained, would involve excessive entanglement.[9]

Christian attorneys warned that the IRS had the power to put liens and levies on church property and hold pastors, deacons, elders, or trustees involved responsible for any refusal to pay tax. More than eight thousand pastors vowed not to pay the FICA tax.[10]

Thousands of churches across the nation stood firm: they declared that they could not and would not pay the tax because of religious and Biblical convictions.[11] President Reagan remained adamant: he insisted that the Social Security Act of 1983 was "untamperable"; the churches must pay the FICA tax.

However, faced with the likelihood of thousands of pastors, church officers, and employees being indicted or jailed, or church properties being seized, Congress had second thoughts. On July 17, 1984, it passed the so-called Dole Amendment which repealed the direct FICA tax on church and church-controlled organizations. But, the Dole Amendment simply shifted the entire tax to church employees and classified them as "self-employed." In other words, the FICA tax is lifted but the Self Employment Tax Act (SETA) is enforced.

Churches were given until October 15, 1984, to make one-time irrevocable election to opt out of the Social Security system and shift the tax to their employees.

Must all church employees pay? No. Members of "religious orders" (nuns and priests) and Christian Science practitioners are exempted (evangelical ministers are considered "self-employed"; thus they pay the FICA tax on that basis).

Christian leaders considered the switch an unfortunate and unsatisfactory compromise. Clearly, the Dole Amendment simply switched the FICA levy on churches from direct to indirect taxation; and, they argue, a tax is still a tax—direct or indirect. Some churches refused to exercise the "election for exemption" option, or the requirement that employees pay the SETA tax. The members of Bethel Baptist Church, Sellersville, Pennsylvania, filed a lawsuit challenging the constitutionality of the 1983 law which mandated church participation in the Social Security tax system.

Dr. Richard Harris, pastor of the church, and president of Keystone Christian Education Association, explained why his congregation has agreed to take the lead in the battle:

> (1) Congress continues in its purposes to tax churches, even if indirectly. (2) Since church employees are part of the church, and indispensable to the church's ministry, a tax on them is a tax on the church. (3) If the church accepts the "exemption," it permits the federal government to change the relationship between the church and its employees [i.e., church staff members would then be considered "self-employed"] and that would constitute federal entanglement in the affairs of the church. (4) The Bethel Baptist case [to be argued by attorney Ball] would test both the constitutionality of taxing the church or the church employees. (5) To accept this provision [i.e., the "election of exemption"] the church is further silenced instead of raising its voice in opposition to the continuing and expanding intrusion of the federal government into [the church] family's affairs.[12]

To date, the courts have refused to hear the Bethel Baptist case holding that "the government's social policy supporting the Social Security system overrides the First Amendment religious liberty concerns of the church." Bethel Baptist members have voted to appeal to the United States Supreme Court so that the constitutional issues can be argued.[13]

Should Christians go to court in such matters? Yes! The purpose of civil government is to be a servant (minister) of God through ministry of justice. And, the Lord God, through Moses, ordained and established a system of courts to administer justice (Exodus 18:21; Deuteronomy 6:18; 7:8, 9). The Apostle Paul, a citizen of Rome, when charged with sedition because he preached the Word of God used litigation to defend himself (Acts 22:22-25; 25:10-12).

Consider the Biblical Principles

Social Security (OASDHI and its related programs and problems) is one more example of the rejection of God's sovereignty and disobedience to God's laws regarding the tithe, the family, the congregation of believers, the care of the elderly, and welfare programs.

By accepting Caesar as the major source of care for the aged, disabled, and survivors (widows and orphans), the nation continues its attempts to escape Biblically-mandated personal and family responsibilities. OASDHI makes Caesar "the great provider"; and that simply will not work (Matthew 7:24).

> "Cast me not off in the time of old age; forsake me not when my strength fails" (Psalm 71:9).

According to God's Word, individuals, families, and congregations are responsible for the care of the elderly and the needy. Is the heavy and intrusive hand of Caesar a punishment upon God's people who refuse to obey Him? The lighter we take God's commandments, the heavier God permits Caesar's hand to weigh upon the land (Deuteronomy 28:15-68; 1 Samuel 8:15; Malachi 3:8, 9).

Parents are to care for and provide for their children, including providing them with an inheritance (Deuteronomy 21:15-17; 2 Corinthians 12:14). In this manner, a godly culture or society is perpetuated through the generations, and God's will on earth is dynamically developed and extended. At the same time, children are to honor their parents (Exodus 20:12; Ephesians 6:2, 3); this includes caring for them in their old age if need be (Matthew 15:1-9). It certainly does not mean handing them over to Caesar's tax-supported and often dehumanizing care. The son or daughter who fails to care for his or her parents in need is cursed and considered worse than an infidel (Deuteronomy 27:16; 1 Timothy 5:8). One of the "bloody abominations" of ancient Jerusalem was the failure of the people to obey the Lord God in that respect (Ezekiel 22:7).

In God's order, the family is the basic unit; it is the foundation of society (Genesis 2:24; Numbers 1:1-3; Matthew 19:4-6); its God-ordained functions are both spiritual and material (economic). Children who view care of their parents to be an option or a "gift" rather than a God-mandated responsibility, deny the Word of God. Notice that Jesus made sure His earthly mother would be cared for after He departed (John 19:26, 27).

When the family cannot provide care of the elderly, widowed and orphaned, needy and disabled, the responsibility rests with the congregation, the local assembly of believers (Galatians 6:2; Romans 5:1; James 2:8)—thus, it falls on each one of us as a part of our lifework for Him (Matthew 25:31-36). It must be a personal work, an individual responsibility, as Jesus commands— not a program under Caesar. In a very real sense, expecting the state to assume duties which our King has assigned to His own is to "render unto Caesar" those things which belong to God and His people. In strict economic terms, Caesar's legion of horrors costs four to five times as much—thus taking in taxes those funds which could better be spent to serve others, the work of His people for the Lord. (On this see George Grant's very helpful books on Biblical Charity: *Bringing in the Sheaves: Transforming Poverty into Productivity* and *The Dispossessed: Homelessness in America*.)

Those who preach/teach a "dialectical gospel" in which the state and its institutions are the instruments of first resort for welfare are at odds with God's Word (1 Samuel 8:7, 18). They magnify Caesar and diminish the flow of God's bounty in and through the lives of those whom He expects to fulfill His Royal Law (Matthew 22:37-40). Thus, tithing (of time and money) is a rudimentary requirement if we will obey the Lord and seek to serve Him by serving others (Leviticus 27:30-33; Deuteronomy 14:22-29). Should anyone question the sufficiency of His funds, let him remember God's promise in Malachi 3:10. Who dares to suggest the hand of the Lord waxes short (Numbers 11:23)?

Consider now the most basic principle of all: God's supreme and total sovereignty.

· Taxation is an assertion of sovereignty, an assumption of power to control. It is a claim of preeminence. Thus, when the state taxes the church, as it does under the Social Security Reform Act of 1983, it asserts its sovereignty over Christ's Church and takes unto itself the right to control it. The Congress and Chief Executive have placed the state (the federal government) above the sovereignty of God. They have made of the state ("public policy") a god and put it above the One True God; thus they violate God's First Commandment (Exodus 20:3-5).

Even pagan Artaxerxes, king of Persia, acknowledged the sovereignty of God and sanctity of God's house and holy servants. Mark these words in the letter of authority and credit which king Artaxerxes gave to Ezra (an able scholar in the law of Moses who was chosen by God to restore the temple):

> Whatever is commanded by the God of heaven, let it be diligently done for the house of the God of heaven: for why should there be wrath against the realm of the king and his sons? Also, we certify to you, that touching any of the priests and Levites, singers, porters [doorkeepers], Nethinim, or ministers of this house of God, it shall not be lawful to impose toll, tribute or custom upon them (Ezra 7:23, 24).

That which is "devoted" to the Lord (i.e., established or operated or maintained by tithes and gifts to worship and serve God) is "most holy unto the Lord"—it is not to be taxed, incumbered, or decapitalized (Leviticus 27:28-34). To tax such property—such holy estate—is to tax the Lord God just as the state taxes the individual when it taxes his property. For the Church to pay tax to the state is to agree that it exists by the grace of the state rather than the grace of God and is a subject of the state rather than of the Lord God. That the Church of Christ cannot do; for, the Church is Christ's body, not Caesar's.

What does the Psalmist say of those who would appropriate God's property?

> O, my God, make them like a wheel; as the stubble before the wind. As the fire burneth a wood, and as the flame setteth the mountain on fire; so persecute them with Thy tempest and make them afraid with Thy storm. Fill their faces with shame; that they make seek Thy name, O Lord. Let them be confounded and troubled forever; yea, let them be put to shame, and perish: that men may know that Thou, whose name alone is Jehovah, art the Most High above all the earth" (Psalm 83:13-18).

God's people cannot accept any law, any regulation, that places the sovereignty of man or state above the sovereignty of God. Those who accept or condone such laws that are illegitimate in the eyes of God are as guilty as those who originated and enforced the illegality. Thus says the Word of God (Psalm 50:18).

What, then, shall we do? The proper course is not anarchy, not revolution, but a revival of the tithe while using the God-ordained court system to end the violation. The tithe advances God's Kingdom on earth; God means it to be used to create His order. It is incumbent upon the individual and the congregation to be about His works and to enlist others in them, keeping in mind always that all we do must honor and glorify Him. Ezra, who was used mightily of God, "prepared his heart to seek the Law of the Lord, and to do it, and to teach in Israel statutes and judgments" (Ezra 7:10). Thus could the Lord use Him—even as He would use us, now.

TWENTY-SEVEN

SODOMY (HOMOSEXUALITY)

They represent at most 5 percent of the population, yet their ungodly forces have declared war on America. Their goal: to overturn the nation's religious and moral values.

Background Briefing

Listen to the words of practicing homosexuals:

> We shall sodomize your sons. . . . we shall seduce them in your schools, in your dormitories, in your gymnasiums, in your locker rooms, in your sports arenas, in your seminaries, in your movie theater bathrooms, in your army bunkhouses, in your truck stops, in your all male clubs, in your houses of congress. . . . your sons will do our bidding. They will be recast in our image. They will come to crave and adore us.[1]

> There has come the idea . . . that all gay males should give blood. . . . whatever action is required to get national attention is valid. If that includes blood terrorism, so be it.[2]

The gay community has declared war on America and that declaration "is comprehensive confronting every aspect of our life and culture. It is most clearly reflected in the political maneuvering by homosexual pressure groups to get AIDS carriers 'handicapped' status. They want to break the backs of churches by forcing them to hire avowed homosexuals or lose their tax exempt status for going against public policy."[3]

> This movement is stronger, more widespread, more skillfully structured than most Americans realize. It reaches into our media, our political institutions, our schools, even into main-line churches. It has already come closer to achieving its goals than most Americans know. Today, throughout the United States, our children are being subjected to homosexual propaganda to an extent that would have been unthinkable just a few years ago. Moreover, this is being done in ways most people of the United States consider repugnant. For the homosexual movement is nothing less than an attack on our traditional pro-family values. And now this movement is using the AIDS crisis to pursue its political agenda. This, in turn, threatens not only our values but our lives.[4]

In city after city, and in some states, they and their ultra-liberal allies have succeeded in forcing the enactment of laws which prohibit landlords and realtors from refusing to rent or sell apartments and houses to homosexuals. They claim for themselves the same anti-discrimination rights as racial minorities. In fact, recently in Houston, during a tempestuous campaign over a gay rights referendum, the mayor labelled those opposed to the bill as "bigots."[5]

Now the homosexual and lesbian forces are actively pursuing the passage of a so-called Gay Bill of Rights in the United States Congress. Among other things, the bill would: (1) legalize homosexuality and lesbianism; (2) make it a criminal offense for churches, schools, businesses, and local and state and federal agencies to refuse to hire homosexuals for any reason; (3) make it a crime for any individual to refuse housing accommodations to homosexual or lesbian couples; and (4) set a precedent by which the homosexual and lesbian sub-culture can legally repeal all sodomy laws governing the age of consent, allow the legal marriage of homosexual and lesbian couples and their adoption of children, and require all public schools to create sex education courses taught by homosexuals to show their lifestyle as a moral, healthy, normal alternative to heterosexuality.[6]

It is clear that the sodomites are using sympathies engendered by the AIDS crisis as a launching pad for their legislative goals. As Ralph Diamond, a gay activist suffering from AIDS boasted,

"Don't call us AIDS victims. AIDS is not my weakness. AIDS is my strength."[7]

In the United States, the opposition to the homosexual ideology and lifestyle is widespread. It crosses all social, economic, and ethnic groups. The rejection is based mainly on religious and moral grounds — which is why the sodomites see the Church as their biggest single obstacle to winning their "war." A nationwide poll found that 71 percent of the people interviewed believed that male homosexuality was morally wrong; 70 percent held that female homosexuality was morally wrong. (The higher the level of "religious commitment," the stronger the opposition to homosexual behavior.)

It is estimated that only about 4 percent of the nation's adult population are sodomites. Yet, despite that, and in the face of society's overwhelming disapproval of sodomy, sodomites are becoming increasingly militant. As homosexuals become more brazen, and while a disapproving but timid or "tolerant" majority remains silent, other sexual deviates are becoming more daring.

For example: NAMBLA (the North American Man Boy Love Association) openly procures and seduces young boys as homosexual partners and prostitutes. Authorities believe that many of the nation's "missing" young boys have fallen into the grasps of such perverts. "Thousands of children are stolen from parents to meet the sexual needs of homosexuals."[8]

> This sexual desire constitutes the first great danger of the homosexual to society. Young pre-teen male children have the characteristics so prized by many male homosexuals. It explains, too, why so many homosexual pornographic magazines are so profusely illustrated with sex acts involving pre-teen male children.[9]

Under the Carter administration, several gay rights groups gained 501(c)(3) tax exempt status. During the 1977 Dade County, Florida, campaign against a gay rights ordinance, the White House sent the chief of its liaison office to work with and for the sodomites. In the 1986 election campaigns, "gay-PACS" raised millions of dollars and openly supported candidates for state and federal offices. United States representatives who had co-sponsored federal gay rights bills were their chief beneficiaries; most of them were re-elected. Two members of the Massachusetts congressional delegation, Representatives Gerry Studds and Barney Frank, are avowed homosexuals. It is generally acknowledged that there are others in the House and Senate—of both genders—who qualify for membership in the gay community. "When placed in public positions of power and importance . . . the homosexual gains tremendous personal prestige. From these positions he can easily influence and recruit others into homosexuality."[10]

In Arizona the 1988 successful impeachment and recall movement against Governor Evan Meachem was started and liberally funded by an avowed homosexual. Why? Because he was incensed by the Governor's expressed disdain for the gay lifestyle. Gay-panthers are now active in the 1988 political campaigns: the Massachusetts homosexual alliance has endorsed Rev. Jesse Jackson in his quest for the Democratic presidential nomination. Jackson supports a bill which would add sexual orientation to Title VII of the 1964 Civil Rights Act.[11]

Are sodomites making progress in campaigning to force acceptance of an immoral lifestyle? Today virtually all states have granted the sodomites protection either by legislation or court action. And, many of the nation's major cities have enacted pro-sodomy laws, or their executives have issued orders including gays with other minorities protected by anti-discrimination ordinances. In New York, Mayor Edward Koch ordered that job discrimination on the grounds of sexual preference (a euphemism for homosexuality) would result in the loss of city contracts. As a result, the Salvation Army and the Catholic Charities organizations—major segments of the city's welfare effort—refused to sign for their day care centers, foster care homes, and adoption programs. As severe as the potential loss of city funding was, neither organization would agree to hire homosexuals. Faced with a fiscal crunch, Koch backed down.

Wisconsin passed a Fair Employment Law in 1982 which bars job discrimination based on sexual orientation. In 1987, the state began requiring subsidized children's programs to sign statements that they would abide by the law or lose their licenses. The state moved against the Rawhide Boys Ranch because the Ranch required that its houseparents be married and that the marriage partners be of the opposite sex. The twenty-two-year-old organization provides educational, recreational, and vocational programs to court-referred boys with long delinquency backgrounds. The environment emphasized Biblical moral values and had a 90 percent success rate.

Homosexual advocacy groups demanded the Ranch comply or lose its license. Rawhide officials signed the required statements under protest hoping that legislation would exempt the nondenominational organization. The legislation failed.[12]

In the 1988 race for partisan presidential nominations, most of the Republican candidates opposed special "rights" or public approval for homosexuals and lesbians. George Bush: "I don't think we need a codification—putting a stamp of approval on that lifestyle. That's not what our society should be asked to do." Jack Kemp: "The Constitution or the law should not endorse a lifestyle that is at odds with the Judeo-Christian value system." Pat Robertson: "I don't see that we should give those engaging in aberrant behavior any kind of a protected status whatsoever."[13]

By contrast, the Democratic candidates were unanimous in their support of pro-gay legislation: Massachusetts Governor Michael Dukakis spearheaded and signed the State House of Representatives gay rights bill which the gays had been promoting for fourteen years. Representative Richard Gebhardt attacked Rev. Jerry Falwell's description of homosexuality as a "perverted lifestyle." United States Senator Albert Gore said, "I do not agree on a personal level with any discrimination based on someone's sexual preference." And Senator Paul Simon, a Lutheran lay leader, is a co-sponsor of federal lesbian and gay rights legislation.[14]

The Democratic National Committee has a lesbian and gay men's party caucus and gives it equal status with its black and Hispanic caucuses. A former Democratic Party national vice chairman, Ann Lewis, has asserted, "Human rights, and that includes gay rights, is no longer a debatable issue within the Democratic Party."

In June 1986 the United States Supreme Court upheld a Georgia statute which makes it a criminal offense to commit sodomy. In *Bowers v. Hardwick* the justices stated, "the Fourteenth Amendment does not confer any fundamental right on homosexuals to engage in acts of consensual sodomy." The gay community reacted with anger. Its members claimed the right of privacy had been violated.

But, as Charles Colson wrote, "The Supreme Court decision had nothing to do with these issues. . . . The Court simply stated that it could find no constitutional right to sodomy, conduct uniformly outlawed when the Constitution was adopted." Justice Byron White wrote, if the Court creates some new right, "the judiciary necessarily takes to itself further authority to govern the country without express constitutional authority."[15]

> Now many Christian officials are climbing aboard yesteryear's bandwagon, advocating the ordination of gays and the legitimation of homosexuality as an "alternative lifestyle."[16]

Within the ecclesiastical community, the National Council of Churches, the United Presbyterian Church, and the United Church of Christ have all endorsed gay rights legislation. The Evangelical Lutheran Church in America "has recently produced a report which essentially affirms the agenda of Lutherans Concerned, a homosexual advocacy group." *Newsweek* magazine estimated "that 30 percent of Roman Catholic Clergy and an even higher percentage of Episcopalian [Clergy] are actively homosexual."[17] Thankfully, though, those data are believed to be unsupported by convincing evidence.

Even so, the fact that the sodomites are seeking to subvert the Church is beyond doubt.

> There is no question that the main stumbling block in the theoretical and practical acceptance of homosexuality by American society has been traditional religion. This has been perfectly understood by the leadership of the homosexual movement. For many years systematic efforts to utilize religion in support of homosexuality have been implemented not only by the founding of religious organizations which cater almost exclusively to homosexuals while purporting to justify their sexual propensities and activities, but also by the establishment of organizations within other religious institutions for the purpose of using them for the promotion of the homosexual ideology.[18]

Proponents of gay rights bills say they are strictly a matter of civil rights. Opponents counter: Civil rights must not be based on sexual appetite, and do not include a license to promote perversion or corruption of children. Further, opponents insist that the government has no right to force employers and homeowners to accept sodomites as employees or tenants if that violates their religious beliefs or moral values. Taxpayers, they say, should not be coerced into subsidizing sexual deviates. Federal, state, and local taxes fund as much as one-half of all homosexual organizational budgets. In 1984 the United States Department of Human Services granted sodomites more than $11 million for just one project.

Proponents of gay rights bills demand a favored status as a "minority." Opponents retort that that is an insult to those legitimately deemed to be minorities (on basis of race, color, national origin, religious conviction, etc.). Sexual perversion, they insist, is a sin—not grounds for special treatment.

Some avid backers of gay rights legislation profess to be Christians. They say, "God made us the way we are" and that it may be wrong for heterosexuals to indulge in homosexual acts but it is all right for homosexuals to do so. Further, they label anti-homosexual Christians as homophobic and un-Christian, accusing them of rejecting God's handiwork. By accepting the homosexual and his lifestyle without judgment, they argue, one may "move into the full light of God's love and grace." In San Francisco, which is the "citadel of sodomy," the Roman Catholic archdiocese has taken the position that "homosexual orientation is not held to be a sinful condition." (The Diocese report did, however, encourage homosexuals to resist promiscuity by forming a "close relationship with [only] one person.") It was reported that, prior to the AIDS plague, homosexuals led incredibly promiscuous lives. They often had as many as fifteen hundred different "partners" during their active sex lives.

Friends of sodomy cite Christ's forgiveness of the woman taken in adultery (John 8:4-11) as a reason that Christians should not judge or reject sodomites. Opponents point out that the Bible makes it clear that God created humans to be heterosexual; that the Lord God consistently and specifically (through His prophets and judges and apostles) condemns sodomy as a capital sin. As for the John, chapter 8 passage, Christ's parting words to the woman were, "Go, and sin no more." Thus, the

Savior, while forgiving the woman her past sins, admonished her to repent — to put an end to her adultery: He loved the sinner but hated the sin.

Just as gay-panthers push for political clout, they also push for influence in mainline religious groups. There are about 350 homosexual congregations now reported in the United States, including ninety-three Roman Catholic, thirty-seven Episcopal, twenty-one Jewish, sixteen Lutheran, and at least a dozen United Methodist. The core of the homosexual "ecclesiastical community," however, is the Universal Fellowship of Metropolitan Community Churches with about 100 congregations. Gays now have influential caucuses in United Methodist, United Presbyterian, Episcopal, Friends Society, American Baptist, Unitarian Churches, United Church of Christ, National Council of Churches, National Federation of Priests' Council, Union of American Hebrew Congregations, and the General Convention of the Episcopal Church.

Sodomites argue that their sexual tastes are their own business, do not hurt others, and should not be the concern of others. They argue "right of privacy" between consenting adults. But, the homosexual "reproductive" process depends on recruitment. There was little public opposition to homosexuals until they "came out of the closet" and started militantly trying to force their lifestyle as an acceptable alternative to traditional values.

As Rev. Enrique Rueda emphasizes in his landmark book, *The Homosexual Network*, "The transformation of the schools according to the needs of the homosexual movement is a major goal of the homosexual leadership." Rueda points out that the gay rights platform demands "federal and state encouragement and support for sex education courses, prepared and taught by gay women and men, presenting homosexuality as a valid, healthy preference and lifestyle and as a viable alternative to heterosexuality."[19] They insist on having textbooks that encourage students "to explore alternative lifestyles including lesbianism."

Also, after a comprehensive study of "sexually flavored" mass murders, Dr. Paul Cameron, of the Institute for Scientific Investigation of Sexuality, reports that the homosexual murder rate is fifteen times higher than that for heterosexuals. The likelihood that a murderer is a homosexual is twelve times greater in most mass homicides.

Also, the emerging specter of rampant homosexually transmitted disease is giving the public great cause for concern. With only 4 percent of the adult population, it is estimated that sodomites account for 75 percent of AIDS fatalities, 49 percent of all syphilis, 51 percent of throat gonorrhea, and 53 percent of lower intestinal infections.[20] As columnist Jeff Hart wrote: "The homosexual's lifestyle may turn out to be his 'deathstyle.'" San Francisco (Sodom-by-the-Bay) passed a gay rights ordinance in 1978; since then, "sex diseases" have risen some 2,400 percent.

"Make no mistake about it — AIDS is one of the most serious incurable diseases we've come up against," warned Dr. Leonard Feldman of the Centers for Disease Control in Atlanta. Because of that fact, Dr. Cameron was prompted to ask: "By what logic does the [federal] Health Service not condemn homosexuality even as it condemns smoking? Why do they not immediately warn homosexuals to stop homosexual activity? We are paying our taxes to be protected and they are risking the lives of the rest of the citizenry not to offend homosexual activities. . . . that is patently criminal."

Consider the Biblical Principles

Leaders of the gay rights movement see religious beliefs (traditional Christian teachings) as the greatest single force causing universal disapproval and rejection of homosexual behavior. Thus, there is an all-out effort to overcome, subvert, or discredit religious organizations that hold fast to Biblical truths. They seek to do this by (a) revising ("modernizing") the Scriptures, and (b) subverting mainline denominations and then using them as launching pads for attacks against Bible-teaching churches.

Rev. Cecil Williams, of the far-left, pro-gay Glide Memorial Church, San Francisco, had testified before a congressional hearing saying, "There are no absolutes. All absolutes have to be . . . reinterpreted, revised. That is why you have revised versions of the Bible." Williams also told the hearing, "The Bible is not the Word of God but the word of men in which the contemporary word of God comes to men. . . . A Bible passage is to be interpreted in terms of experience." How far will homosexuals and pro-gay groups go to revise God's Word? William R. Johnson, the first ordained homosexual minister in the United Church of Christ proclaimed "gay liberation is a movement of the Holy Spirit."

Gay Bible "scholars" suggest that David and Jonathan were homosexuals (1 Samuel 18:1-4; 20:16-18), and that the Apostle Paul's "thorn in the flesh" was his homosexuality (2 Corinthians 12:7). Finally, they infer (even assert) that Jesus and John the Apostle were homosexual lovers because John is referred to as "the beloved Apostle" (John 13:23; 20:2). Apparently, homosexuals are willing to go to any length to distort the Bible to accommodate their ungodly and wicked lifestyle.

According to the Bible, homosexuality and lesbianism are abominations in the sight of the Lord God—perversions of the creature He made in His image: "male and female created He them [heterosexuals]" (Genesis 1:27). Sodomy is a sin of the gravest and most serious consequences. In Romans 1:28 Paul wrote that sodomy is one of two sins for which God abandoned sinners—the other being the sin of blaspheming the Holy Ghost (Matthew 12:31, 32).

God warns man against the sin of sodomy: "Thou shalt not lie with mankind, as with womankind: it is an abomination" (Leviticus 18:22). "Defile not yourselves" in this sin, commands the Lord God (Leviticus 18:24; see also Deuteronomy 23:17). "If a man also lie with mankind, as he lieth with a woman, both of them have committed an abomination: they shall surely be put to death; their blood shall be upon them" (Leviticus 20:13). In setting forth God's laws of human relations, Moses made it clear there were to be no sodomites in Israel (Deuteronomy 23:17).

Sodomy brings catastrophic consequences upon the city or nation that approves of it or condones it or fails to stand against it: "The land is defiled: therefore I do visit the iniquity thereof upon it, and the land itself vomiteth out her inhabitants" (Leviticus 18:25).

Did God really mean what He said? This nation—and many cities and states—would do well to consider the fate of Sodom and Gomorrah (Genesis 19:1-29; see also 2 Peter 2:6-10; Jude 7). The wickedness of sodomy brought forth the wrath and curse of the Lord God. Because sodomy was so prevalent—"all the people, from every quarter" (Genesis 19:4, 5, 28,)— God destroyed both cities: "all the inhabitants of the cities, and that which grew upon the ground . . . and lo, the smoke of the country went up as the smoke of a furnace" (vv.24, 25). Jude wrote that the destruction of Sodom and Gomorrah (and adjacent towns that likewise gave themselves over to sensual perversions) was not only a punishment but also "set forth as an example" (Jude 7). Homosexual and pro-homosexual clergy argue that Sodom's sin was not sodomy but being unkind to the strangers who visited the city.

The people of ancient Canaan were completely submerged in depravity (Genesis 13:13). Homosexuality was so prevalent it was made a religious rite. For such abominations God sentenced the Canaanites to death (Leviticus 18:22-29; Deuteronomy 9:1-3). God warned the Israelites that when He had delivered the wicked Canaanites before them (Deuteronomy 8:5) they were to make no covenant with them (Deuteronomy 7:2-4). Israel's failure to execute the judgment God demanded ultimately became its own judgment (Deuteronomy 7:1-5; Leviticus 18:28, 29; Judges 2:9-15; 4:1-3).

Sodomy promotes idolatry, invites false gods, and nurtures apostasies. It spawns additional perversions; it gnaws at the vitals and rots the soul—first, the souls of those who indulge in its lusts and evils and, ultimately, the soul of the nation which permits it to continue unchallenged. Historically, rampant homosexuality has been one of the social malignancies that preceded the fall of nations and empires (Greece, Rome, etc.).

So final and so awful are the consequences of sodomy that the Lord God, in His grace, grants time for cleansing, and He commends and rewards those who work to rid the land of the evil. "And Asa did that which was right in the eyes of the Lord, as did David his father. And he took away the sodomites out of the land, and removed all the idols that his fathers had made" (1 Kings 15:11, 12; see also 1 Kings 22:46; 2 Kings 23:3, 7).

The Apostle Paul minced no words about sodomites. He wrote to believers in Rome that if sodomites refuse to repent and change their wicked ways, God abandons them to "uncleanness through the lusts of their own hearts, to dishonor their own bodies between themselves."

> Who changed the truth of God into a lie [a false religion] and worshipped and served the creature more than the Creator,

Who is blessed forever. Amen! For this cause God gave them up to vile affections: for even their women did change the natural use into that which is against nature [exchanged their natural function for an unnatural and abnormal one]: And likewise also the men, leaving the natural use of the woman [turned from natural relations with women] burned in their lust for one another; men with men working that which is unseemly [committing shameful and indecent acts with men], and receiving in themselves that recompense that was meet [suffering in their own bodies and souls the inevitable consequences and penalties of their wrong-doing]. Even as they did not like to retain God in their knowledge [since they did not choose to acknowledge God or consider Him worth knowing] God gave them over to a reprobate [base] mind to do those things which are not convenient [things not proper or decent but loathsome] . . . Who knowing the judgment of God, that they which commit such things are worthy of death, not only do the same [persist in doing such things] but have pleasure in [approve and applaud] them that do them (Romans 1:25-32).

In 1 Corinthians, chapter 6, Paul includes homosexuals — "abusers of themselves with mankind [sodomites]" — among those who shall not inherit the kingdom of God (vv.9, 10). In his first letter to Timothy (1 Timothy 1:9-10), Paul writes that the Law is made for the lawless, the disobedient, and the ungodly sinner including "them that defile themselves with mankind [sodomites]."

Is there a cure for sodomy, a way in which to break the bonds of appetite and passions of this awful and unnatural desire? There is, indeed! Through the redeeming love of Jesus Christ.

Dr. Rod Mays of Family Counselling and Resources reminds us that the homosexual can experience the forgiveness of God. But, repentance is mandatory. Those who will turn to Christ, and accept Him as their Savior and Lord, will find power to repent and resist (Philippians 4:13; Colossians 1:13). The power of Christ can cleanse the vilest mind, cure the most evil heart (1 John 1:7; 1 Thessalonians 5:23). The individual who scorns and rejects Christ is lost, dead in sin. But, whoever shall turn to Christ, and believe on Him, shall become a new person, redeemed, born again, justified, and sanctified.

TWENTY-EIGHT

STRATEGIC DEFENSE INITIATIVE ("Star Shield")

Thanks to a mad policy, the United States is naked before a nuclear attack. SDI, however, could close that "window of vulnerability."

Background Briefing

On April 2, 1984, the Soviet military commander at Yurya missile complex ordered the launch of six SS20 missiles on a trajectory toward the United States. The missiles were destroyed over the polar region of the Barents Sea.[1]

In September 1986 a Soviet SSN8 submarine-launched missile strayed 1,400 miles off course; its dummy warhead landed near the Soviet-Chinese border. Question: How effective would the United States missile defense have been in intercepting and destroying the SS20 missile or the SSN8? One hundred percent? Seventy-five percent? Fifty-percent? Twenty-five percent? Answer: ZERO. The USA has no strategic anti-missile defense. None.

Why? Because in 1972, the President of the United States and the Congress went MAD: They signed an agreement with the USSR to keep America defenseless. That Anti-Ballistic Missile (ABM) treaty is part of the original SALT accords negotiated by Mr. Nixon and then-Secretary of State, Henry Kissinger. It remains legally binding and pledges the United States will not defend itself against incoming Soviet missiles. It says that both nations agree to keep its people undefended against nuclear attack by the other side.[2]

Mr. Reagan has proposed that the ABM treaty be extended for five to seven years. The USSR wants to extend the treaty fifteen years and ban or curtail the deployment of space-based defenses. The ABM treaty is based on the concept that "mutual assured destruction" (MAD) would keep both nations from a nuclear "first strike." "This doctrine . . . [is] a cruel policy, because it leaves the American people open to incineration by Soviet nuclear weapons, and only offers the incineration of the Soviet people as a deterrent to that dreadful act."[3]

The United States has abided by the ABM agreement. In 1975, after spending $7 billion on it, Congress ordered the dismantling of the Safeguard Anti-Ballistic Missile system. Since 1972, the United States has spent virtually nothing on civil defense against nuclear attack. America's civilian population has been deliberately left defenseless, exposed to nuclear attack. Says retired Lt. Gen. Daniel O. Graham, "We are a nation of nuclear nudists, and our allies are no better off."[4] Nevertheless, the Reagan administration feels the nuclear threat is great enough to warrant the appropriation of $1.5 billion to protect elected officials in Washington, D.C.[5]

And the Soviets? They have undertaken to do exactly what they agreed not to do. "The Soviet Union is pursuing large programs for defending its citizens from nuclear attack, for shooting down American missiles, and for fighting and winning a nuclear war."[6] Since 1973 the Soviets have not hesitated to exceed ABM limits. In fact, Moscow is now protected by the world's only operational antimissile defense — an Anti-Ballistic Missile radar network, complexes with nuclear-tipped Galosh and Gazelle interceptor missiles, and satellites with over-the-horizon radar, etc. The CIA reports that in the past ten years the Soviets have spent nearly $150 billion on strategic defense and by the 1990s will have an SDI defending Moscow and key targets in the Western USSR and east of the Urals.[7] The Soviets now spend $1 billion a year on laser weapons[8] and have more than doubled the number of nuclear warheads aimed at the United States since President Carter signed Salt II. The USSR has built and deployed (and now constantly expands and modernizes) an extensive anti-ballistic missile air defense and fighter-interceptor system. "Soviet air defenses, comprising over 2,000 fighters, 7,000 radars, and about 10,000 surface-to-air missiles, are the most massive in the world."[9] The USSR is pushing forward on particle beam and laser weaponry to make outer space a vital part of their military doctrine.[10] It has launched 533 rockets into space in the past six years (compared to 98 for the United States). The authoritative *Jane's Space Flight Directory* reports that "the Soviets are so far ahead of the United States in space experience that they are almost out of sight."[11] Dr. Edward Teller reports that the Soviets have spent more than $100 billion on civil defense and are now spending some $5 billion a year to provide protection for its civilian population.[12]

What are the fruits of the MAD policy? In 1978 Marshal Nicolai Orgarkov, Chief of the Soviet General Staff, boasted to a United States congressional delegation: "Today, the Soviet Union has military superiority over the United States. Henceforth, the United States will be threatened. It had better get used to it."[13]

In 1984 United States Secretary of Defense Caspar Weinberger acknowledged, "the Soviet military buildup, both quantitative and qualitative, has produced a major shift in the nuclear and conventional balance."[14] In 1985 the United States Joint Chiefs of Staff stated: "The Soviets have now developed strategic offensive and defensive capabilities that erode the credibility of the United States deterrent and increase the risk that Soviet leaders would consider launching a surprise nuclear attack."[15]

The Soviet's continued violations of the SALT and ABM treaties shows "deterrence" is a perilous concept. United States Senator Patrick Moynihan (New York) sees the MAD concept as a disproven theory which produced "the greatest peril our nation has faced in its two-hundred-year history."[16]

Can nuclear war be made obsolete? Leading scientists say yes. MAD's "balance of terror" can be replaced by a "shield of defense." With Star Shield in place "the window of vulnerability" could be slammed shut.

"Research based on the new technologies of missile defense — the ultra-compact computer, the laser, and other sophisticated devices — offers the promise of an end" to the nightmare.[17] As a package, this is known as the Strategic Defense Initiative (SDI) — "High Frontier," "Star Shield," and (derisively by opponents)

"Star Wars." Conceived in the late 1960s by General Daniel Graham, Dr. Robert Jastrow, Dr. Edward Teller and others, it was supported early-on by Senators Garn (Utah), Hollings (South Carolina), Laxalt (Nevada), Wallop (Wyoming) and others. Mr. Reagan embraced the concept on March 23, 1983, and offered the vision of a defensive "Star Shield." He called upon scientists to develop a system to "put a shield between the United States and its enemies to protect us from their deadly weapons." After its initial support, a majority in the Congress has consistently whittled away at the funds required for sustained research for the project.

What is the Strategic Defense Initiative? Technologically, it is a synergistic three-layered non-nuclear defense system designed to destroy enemy missiles in flight. "It would give the United States the ability to checkmate a Soviet first strike by interdicting Soviet missiles over Soviet airspace shortly after launch," or during their twenty-five-minute trajectory, or in the terminal phase as they approach their target. "The Soviet Union is absolutely paranoid about the United States deployment of Star Wars."[18] They fear its reality could turn their nuclear missiles into duds.[19] They "see SDI as a device that could wipe out all their gains since the Cuban missile crisis and put them back into the condition of inferiority."[20] The Soviets fear the start of a new technological race with the United States: "If SDI is not slowed down, it will produce lots of technology with all kinds of military applications—it will shift the competition between the Soviet Union and the United States to a hi-tech area where the United States has a considerable advantage."[21] Further, the Soviet economy is a basket case; the added expense of a hi-tech race could increase problems, forestall economic reforms, and generate civil unrest.

Cynics tag Star Shield as "sci-fi" fantasy, an expensive system that could not provide 100 percent protection. Columnist Thomas Sowell retorts, "Those who sneer at Star Wars fail to understand its purpose. The purpose of a defense against nuclear missiles is not to win World War III, but to prevent [it]. . . . Star Wars does not have to achieve perfection to deter an attack. All it has to do is increase the uncertainty of the outcome to the point that makes a nuclear 'first strike' a bad gamble. . . . the Soviets have never been reckless gamblers, much less suicidal."[22] Even if SDI were only 50 percent effective, the Soviets would think twice about a "first strike."

Designers of Star Shield assert that proven technology is now available to permit the attack of ICBMs through most of their trajectory. A three-layered ballistic missile defense would afford multiple opportunities for the interception and destruction of the missiles. As planned, the ultimate system would include (1) a ground-based, terminal phase intercept, (2) a ground-based mid-course intercept, and (3) a space-based early intercept (during boost stage). ICBMs not intercepted by the initial layers would be attacked again and again by successive layers so, if missiles are not destroyed during the boost stage, they would be attacked during their twenty-five-minute mid-course trajectory; and, if the missiles elude the first two intercepts, they would be attacked again during a terminal phase.

The Star Shield System

1. The *terminal defense layer* is quickly deployable with off-the-shelf technology. It would be installed to defend military sites (ICBM silos and command posts). This layer would employ kinetic energy (the tremendous energies produced by the collision of two high-velocity bodies). A high-velocity cloud of thousands of dense metal alloy fragments or "swarms" of one-inch rockets would destroy the enemy missile on impact with no explosives involved. This first phase could be operative within three years at a cost of less than $3 billion.

2. A *mid-course defense* at Grand Forks, Nebraska would consist of one hundred launchers and would provide population protection for most of the North American Continent. Additional launch sites on the East and West coasts would give further defense against submarine-launched missiles. This phase of the system would employ either Lockheed's ERIS homing interceptor or Vought/Martin-Marietta's VM-3 interceptor rocket (both have been successfully tested). Star Shield backers say it could be in place in five years at a cost of about $5 billion.

3. The *early trajectory (boost stage) defense* calls for space-based, orbiting non-nuclear satellites with early warning sensors armed with interceptor rockets and "pellet cloud guns." This would be

lifted into space orbit by either Saturn rockets or the Space Shuttle and would provide from 50 to 70 percent effectiveness against a full-scale attack (at least fourteen hundred USSR missiles). It could be in place in seven to eight years. The cost for one thousand Star Shield satellites is about $25 billion.

In summary, Star Shield is the development and deployment of all three defense layers over seven and a half years at a cost not exceeding $30 billion with annual maintenance expenditures after that not exceeding $6 billion (about 2 percent of the annual defense budget). Its advocates say it could provide 80 to 90 percent protection from enemy nuclear missiles.

For the fiscal year 1987 Mr. Reagan budgeted just under $5 billion for SDI research and development. Congress slashed that to $3.5 billion (less than 1 percent of the defense budget). Opponents say the plan is "unworkable," "risky," and "destabilizing." They insist that the United States continue its MAD policies and programs, and maintain "equivalency" with the USSR. SDI proponents point out that under "equivalency" the USSR has built and modernized its military strength and is using nuclear blackmail to expand its "evil empire"—Angola in 1975; Ethiopia and Mozambique in 1977; Afghanistan in 1979 and now Central and South America (Nicaragua, Panama, El Salvador, and Chile).[23]

As for SDI's being "risky," the SDI supporters argue it is the MAD mentality which is risky; it leaves the United States in real peril. Further technological advances make MAD obsolete, and suicidal. They argue, it is not a question of "if" SDI can be done but "when" it will be done and who will do it — the United States or the USSR. After a tour of SDI research facilities, United States Senator Pete Wilson (California) said the missile defense system is possible by the mid-1990s.[24] The George C. Marshall Institute believes that the SDI system could be in place by 1994 and could be as much as 93 percent effective against ten thousand warheads and one million decoys.[25] On-going scientific breakthroughs are rapidly fitting into place and underscore the feasibility of Star Shield. For example, the electro-magnetic rail-gun can propel plastic projectiles at speeds up to two miles per second—fast enough to penetrate four one-inch plates of tank armor.[26] Also, there are now sophisticated sensors that can distinguish between decoys and nuclear missiles, and ultra high-speed computers that can handle billions of pieces of data per minute.[27]

The debate surrounding SDI is no longer scientific; it is political. SDI opponents are mostly from the ranks of the old anti-Vietnam, "nuclear freeze," and MAD groups: Carl Sagan, Rev. Robert Drinan, Robert McNamara (father of the Edsel auto and the MAD concept), Senators Biden (Delaware), Glenn (Ohio), Kennedy (Massachusetts), Kerry (Massachusetts), Leahy (Utah), Wirtz (Colorado), the League of Women Voters, National Council of Churches, Common Cause, Americans for Democratic Action, SANE, the *New York Times*, American Friends Service Committee, the Campaign to Save the ABM Treaty, and the Union of Concerned Scientists.[28] Also opposing Star Shield are some Pentagon officials who fear that budgets for SDI would cut support for their pet projects (shades of Billy Mitchell's fight in the 1930s to get the Army to recognize the potential of air power!). And then there's the United States State Department. When asked if he thought the State Department was trying to get Mr. Reagan to negotiate away the deployment of SDI, Representative Jack Kemp (New York) responded: "The answer to that clearly is 'Yes,' and this is my warning." Kemp commended Mr. Reagan for refusing to abandon SDI at the Iceland meeting with Gorbachev: "If we had agreed to do this, the Soviet Union would enjoy a monopoly in strategic defenses . . . and they would still have their current nuclear and conventional offensive advantage."[29] However, many believe that Mr. Reagan softened his support of SDI at the 1987 Washington summit. He agreed to slow down research and delay deployment.

Has ideology distorted the anti-SDI claims made by opponents? Consider the Union of Concerned Scientists (UCS), generally recognized as an ideologically committed left-wing group. Originally, the UCS insisted it would take 2,400 SDI satellites to protect the United States against Soviet missiles. When their data were challenged, they corrected that to 800, then to 300. Finally, the UCS group lowered their estimate to 162. Pro-SDI scientists then pointed out that they had always stated the number needed is approximately 100. The UCS also insisted that the neutral particle beam for SDI's space-based tier would require orbiting a linear accelerator weighing forty thousand tons. The actual weight required is twenty-five tons (less than the shuttle's average payload of thirty-three tons). And, the UCS declared it would take 280,000 "smart missiles" for the ground-based terminal tier (phase of SDI) but the actual total required is about 5,000. The Office of Technology Assessment of Congress declared that the USSR could protect its missiles with lead shields one-tenth of an inch thick. Research has demonstrated that it would, in fact, require lead shields at least one and a half inches thick — too heavy for the Soviets to launch the missile.[30] The UCS says it has recruited seven thousand scientists who pledge not to do research on SDI. Meanwhile, in the USSR, ten thousand of their colleagues are working on SDI projects at R&D facilities and test ranges. Science writer, Ben Bova, pointed out that virtually every major United States scientist opposed to Star Shield has been or is employed on nuclear weapons and strategies. "They are emotionally set against an idea that might make nuclear weapons useless."[31]

American citizens favor Star Shield. Polls, following both the Reykjavik and Washington summits, indicated SDI had the support of 71 percent of the American public. At the same time that the public gave its qualified approval to the dismantling of intermediate-range nuclear missiles, it said it wanted Washington to get on with developing Star Shield.[32]

Despite proven technological capabilities and public support for Star Shield, backers fear that time is running out; they are afraid the project is doomed unless Mr. Reagan moves now to make the initial (ground-based) system operational as soon as possible. If the Democrats should gain control of the White House, as well as both houses of Congress, they fear the program would be scuttled. Led in the Senate by Daniel Quayle (Indiana), conservatives succeeded in including in the defense authorizations the requirement that the Pentagon report on a speed-up of the program. In the House, another group headed by Representatives Kemp and James Courter (New Jersey), and joined by Dr. Teller and former Secretary of State Alexander Haig and others, are pressing Mr. Reagan to push for an SDI system that could be operational by the early 1990s and would protect civilian population centers as well as military targets.[33]

Consider the Biblical Principles

Biblical Christians must understand these United States are in serious peril. Polls show that 60 percent of all Americans do not realize that we have no defense against nuclear missiles. As a nation, we are in a position similar to that described by Hosea: "My people perish for lack of knowledge," knowledge, first, of His Word and His will and knowledge, second, of the forces at work in the world (Hosea 4:6).

Thus, we must be like the "men of Issachar, who understood the times and knew what Israel should do" (1 Chronicles 12:32). As Christians, we are told how to deal with evil: "Be sober [serious], be vigilant [alert], because your adversary, the devil, as a roaring lion walks about [in fierce hunger] seeking whom he may devour [seize upon]. Resist him, stead-fast [firmly established] in faith" (1 Peter 5:8-9).

First of all, we must stop making covenants with evil.

> Therefore, hear the Word of the Lord, you scoffers [scornful men] who rule. . . . You boast, "We have entered into a covenant with death, with the grave [Sheol] we have made an agreement. When an overwhelming scourge sweeps by, it cannot touch [will not come to] us, for we have made a lie our refuge and falsehood our hiding place." So this is what the Sovereign Lord says: "See, [Behold] I lay a stone in Zion, a tested stone, a precious cornerstone for a sure foundation; the one who trusts will never be dismayed [act hastily to make expedient, ungodly pacts]. I will make justice the measuring line and righteousness the plumb line; hail will sweep away your refuge, the lie, and water[s] will overflow your hiding place. Your covenant [with death] will be annulled; your agreement with death [Sheol] will not stand; When the overwhelming scourge sweeps by, you will be beaten down by it." (Isaiah 28:14-19).

Second, as we resist evil, so also we must take the offense against it.

> Therefore take up the whole armor of God, that you may be able to withstand in the evil day, and having done all, to stand . . . with truth . . . righteousness . . . the Gospel of peace . . . the shield of faith with which you will be able to quench all the

fiery darts of the wicked one. . . . take the helmet of salvation
. . . and the sword of the Spirit, which is the Word of God"
(Ephesians 6:13-17).

The Lord will cause your enemies who rise against you to be
defeated before your face; they shall come out against you one
way and [shall] flee before you seven ways (Deuteronomy 28:7).

We must reject the ploys of containment and "equivalency"
and go forth with God's truth, and also tell the world the truth of
the horrors of the "evil empire"—its global designs, its violations
of human rights, its disregard for national sovereignty, its goal to
be a god. We must stop supporting its economy with trade and
low-interest (taxpayer subsidized) loans. "Should you help the
ungodly, and love them that hate the Lord? Therefore is the
wrath upon you from before the Lord" (2 Chronicles 19:2b).

Third, we must act now to build and repair the nation's defenses.

So I sought for a man among them who would make a wall,
and stand in the gap before Me on behalf of the land, that I
should not destroy it; but I found no one. Therefore I have
poured out My indignation on them; I have consumed them
with the fire of My wrath, and I have recompensed their deeds
on their own heads (Ezekiel 22:30-31).

Fourth, we must be alert to innovation which, as a fruit of
fervent prayer and faith, often comes by inspiration.

And the Lord said unto Joshua, See, I have given into your
hand Jericho. . . . And you shall compass [go around] the city,
all your men of war, and go round about the city once. You
shall do thus six days. . . . And it shall come to pass, that
when they make a long blast with the ram's horn, and when
you hear the sound of the trumpet, all the people shall shout
with a great shout; and the wall of the city shall fall down flat
(Joshua 6; see also the fall of Ai [Joshua 8]; and Gideon's
defeat of the Midianites [Judges 7]).

Fifth, we must seek and support and work with the Ezras
and Nehemiahs of this day. Ezra was the most learned inter-
preter of God's Word whom He used to rebuild the temple and

reshape the nation as the people of "the Book." Nehemiah was the builder who was used of God to motivate and mobilize the people in the task of rebuilding the gates and the wall. As Dr. D. James Kennedy has pointed out, SDI—Star Shield—can be the modern-day wall to protect this nation using God's laws of nature and science (physics, engineering, electronics, astronomics, etc.), thus to preserve its mission to be a light unto the world for Him.

And foremost and always, we must have utter delight (and faith) in His Word and complete consecration to His will. "Unless the Lord builds the house, they labor in vain who build it; unless the Lord guards the city (nation) the watchman stays awake in vain" (Psalm 127:1).

Francis A. Schaeffer once wrote, "The world quite properly looks back to the Church in Germany during the early days of Hitler's rise and curses it for not doing something when something could have been done." We who are His are to be His watchmen, to sound the trumpet and warn the people.

> When I say unto the wicked, O wicked man, you shall surely die; if you do not speak to warn the wicked from his way, that wicked man shall die in his iniquity; but his blood will I require at your hand (Ezekiel 33:8).

TWENTY - NINE

SUICIDE

The so-called Great Society of humanism, drugs, faceless crowds, and god-less technology — a society which teaches "suicide education" in its public schools — is reaping a mounting whirlwind of teenage death.

Background Briefing

Every twenty minutes, somewhere in the United States someone commits suicide. That's eighty lives taken each day, more than twenty-nine thousand every year.[1]

What is even more tragic is this: every minute an adolescent attempts suicide. That's two million a year.[2] Once every one hundred minutes, a young person between the ages of fifteen and twenty-four succeeds in taking his or her life. That's about six thousand a year.[3] About eighteen hundred were still in their teens. Suicide is not confined to the young; an increasing number of the elderly are taking their own lives, too. Some experts believe that more than 40 percent of the suicides in the United States are older adults.[4]

Suicide is the third leading cause of teenage death (after accidents and homicides). Many authorities say it probably should be ranked second. Mitch Anthony, executive director of the National Suicide Help Center, claims: "The actual suicide rate is much higher than six thousand — I would estimate it at more like twenty thousand. This is because many accidents [auto, drug overdose, etc.] — currently the leading cause of death among teenagers — are really suicides."[5] Thirty to 50 percent of teen suicide victims were drug or alcohol abusers.[6]

Since 1970 the number of teen suicides more than quadrupled for boys and doubled for girls.[7] More girls than boys attempt suicide but more boys die. An article in *The Duquesne Law Review* reported that the number of suicides among those aged ten to fourteen jumped 100 percent between 1968 and 1976.[8] The National Center for Health Statistics reports that teen suicides peaked during 1977 and dropped 9 percent between 1977 and 1983. But the Center estimates that the totals increased again in 1985 and 1986. Private psychological practitioner Toni Davis warns, "It [suicide] is a growing problem."[9]

The typical teenage suicide victim is white and is from a middle or upper-middle class family. What makes it four times more likely that a teenager will try to kill himself or herself in 1988 than in 1955? The reasons are complex. Experts point to a number of social factors: the breakdown of the family, drug and alcohol abuse, and increased influence of the mass media (some rock songs, such as AC/DC's "Shoot To Kill," actually encourage suicide; and suicide is sometimes romanticized when it is dramatized on television or in the press).[10]

Mitch Anthony "points to another change that the news media often ignore: increasing sexual activity at ever-younger ages. When a teenager breaks up with someone he or she was sexually involved with, it's like a divorce. . . . for kids it can be devastating."[11]

Tom Burklow, the director of Pastoral Counselling Services, a division of Youth For Christ, warns that even some Christian teenagers, whose faith is in its early stages, may be susceptible to suicide. "Christian kids may feel like they want to be in heaven with Jesus or with a loved one who died. Or, their sensitized conscience may lead them to feel so bad about themselves because of their sins that they begin to believe they deserve to die."[12]

There have been about eighteen "cluster" suicides in the past few years. In Bergenfield, New Jersey, in March of 1987, four teenagers "put three dollars worth of gasoline in their car, drove into a garage, closed the door, and let carbon monoxide snuff out their lives."[13] In Omaha, Nebraska, five teenagers in the same high school attempted suicide and three succeeded. Upper-middle class Plano, Texas, had eight teen suicides in sixteen months in 1983-84. Students and parents in Plano responded to that tragedy with BIONIC (Believe It Or Not I Care), SWAT (Students Working All Together), and a hotline for troubled teenagers.

Some critics assert that media sensationalism is partly responsible for copycat suicides. There was, for example, a 12 percent jump in suicides in the weeks after movie actress Marilyn Monroe apparently took her own life. David P. Phillips, a guest editorialist in *USA Today*, reminded the media that "shortly after four teenagers asphyxiated themselves in a Bergenfield, New Jersey garage, two other teenagers attempted suicide in the same way in the same garage. A day after the Bergenfield bodies were found, two teens in Illinois committed suicide in the same way. Two days later a Chicago teen was found dead in his garage poisoned by exhaust fumes. Under his bed were found newspaper clippings describing the earlier teen suicides."[14]

Margaret A. Bocek, a former member of the Arlington County (Virginia) School Board, puts a share of the blame on death and suicide teaching in the public schools. "Since the advent of death education more than a decade ago, the rate of suicide among children has increased and is occurring at ever-younger ages."

Mrs. Bocek said:

> Death education is not simply a matter of a teacher helping a child through a crisis. Programmed repetition of death, despair, and personal evaluation of self-worth in these programs may be turning our children into suicide victims. While educators profess the need for facts and knowledge about death, they are in fact using psychological techniques aimed at the subconscious rather than the conscious. An eighth-grade English text advises, "Write a suicide note.". . . a Health education questionnaire requires children to choose "one of five reasons that would cause them to commit suicide" and list ten ways of dying . . . in order of "most to least preferred."[15]

And, after years of "suicide education" in many public schools, research by Dr. David Shaffer of Columbia University indicates that those teens which are suicide-prone are most likely to be upset by such programs. "If we are upsetting the most vulnerable kids, it may not be best to intervene in this way." In 1986 there were one hundred suicide prevention programs in sixteen schools, involving 150,000 students.[16]

Is the suicide rate highest in underdeveloped nations? No. Suicide is a major problem in industrialized nations. Hungary has the highest suicide rate (forty-five per one hundred thousand people). The *1987 Statistical Abstract* reports that Denmark, with one of the most "advanced" social welfare programs in the world and a high standard of living, has the highest suicide rate in the free world (thirty per one hundred thousand people). Nearly twice as many Danes die by suicide as die by auto accidents. Then comes Austria (27.3 over-all, but among those aged seventy-five and over, the suicide rate was reported to be an amazing 99 percent), Finland (24.0), Japan (20.7), and Sweden (reputedly a worker's paradise with complete sexual license, had a suicide rate of 18.7). The United States ranked sixteenth (12.1 per 100,000 people).[17]

In most of those nations, the suicide rate among males, ages fifteen to twenty-four, is even higher. For example: Austria, 40 for every one hundred thousand in that age bracket; Denmark, 37.1; West Germany, 28.5; Sweden, 27.8; Japan, 27.6, and the United States, 19.2.[18]

By contrast, consider some "have not" nations where poverty is rampant and little hope is held for the future. There, the suicide rate is the lowest: Chile (0.4), Egypt (0.2), Ecuador (2.7), Guatemala (1.2), Jamaica (1.0), Panama (2.0), Peru (1.4), Spain (4.1), and Venezuela (4.6).[19]

What accounts for the increase in suicides and attempted suicide? Psychologists say mostly socioeconomic factors including: pressures to do well in education and business; rejection by family or peers; parents too busy with their own problems; drug and alcohol abuse; divorce and broken homes; fear of nuclear war; a sense of futility; desperate financial straits (e.g., farmers faced with loss of their homes and land); worries about the future; and severe depression.

Mental health practitioners see suicide as "a cry for help, attention." Barb Wheeler, suicidologist, says that "suicide is the ultimate form of communication."[20] Patrick Cox, a political analyst, believes "suicide is the ultimate withdrawal from human jurisdiction."[21] Kenneth Snow, Greater Manchester (New Hampshire) Mental Health Center, says, "Usually, it is an attempt to tell someone how they are feeling." Snow suggests most suicidal teenagers are looking for an opportunity to talk out their problems to someone who will listen.

All that may be true *but* those are merely surface symptoms and causes, say Christ-centered psychologists and counselors. There are more and deeper (root) causes. According to Bill Blackburn in *What You Should Know About Suicide,* two of the most solid and dependable sources of support for adolescents are no longer solid and dependable. Those two sources are: "A society where moral guidelines are firm and a family you can depend on."[22] Thus, as Christian writers have pointed out, values clarification and situational ethics are not "victimless crimes"; they take a heavy toll.

Columnist Cal Thomas adds, "[Suicide] prevention begins in the family where Mom and Dad had better think about reordering some of their priorities."[23] Here, a major result of inflation is highlighted: when both parents must work to make ends meet, "latch-key" children return home from school to a parentless house and are robbed of parental time and guidance. Today, about 60 percent of married women work outside the home.

And, writes Thomas, "Teenage suicide can only be dealt with in a culture that values life." In today's materialistic, hedonistic society, life has been — and continues to be — devalued.

When preborn babies are considered "garbage" and tossed in dumpsters, and abortion is condoned (or even promoted) by the courts, media, educators, TV and movie entertainers, and liberal clergy . . . When convicted premeditated murderers escape capital punishment, and auto drivers high on drugs or drunk on alcohol are given light or suspended sentences for vehicular homicide and return to the highway . . . When a TV network airs programs publicizing pro-suicide groups such as the Hemlock Society and Exit, and those pro-suiciders publish "do-it-yourself suicide guides" and claim suicide is "a civil right". . . When state-controlled education teaches that man evolved through a chain of bio-chemical accidents, and the religion of humanism champions the "right to suicide". . . And when the governor of Colorado calls upon the aged to take their own lives and depart from the scene because they are a drain on society, wasting taxpayer funds . . . When life is held to be so cheap, thoughts of suicide are more easily entertained — especially by the young and impressionable.

United States Surgeon General C. Everett Koop recalled that in one two-week period he noted articles on euthanasia in ten major newspapers. The hype on euthanasia, said Dr. Koop, is abroad in our land and is little more than a promotion on how to prepare for suicide. Citing one article in the *Wall Street Journal* ("Can't We Put My Mother to Sleep"), Dr. Koop mentioned that the writer started the column by recalling that in his youth his pet dog was put to sleep and that many were now suggesting the same procedure for the elderly.[24]

Secular psychologists see suicide as an act of self-hate. Dr. Rod Mays, pastor and the editor of *Restoration: A Publication of Family Counselling and Resources*, disagrees. He asserts that *selfishness* is the major cause of suicides, a product of the "Me" generation of recent years.

Dr. Mays writes,

> Our culture is being plagued by an unhealthy emphasis on *selfism*. Books, pamphlets, magazine articles, seminars, film series—all are propagating self-esteem, self-assertion, self-admiration, self-indulgence, self-confidence, self-pleasing, self-determination, and self-satisfaction.
>
> One of the real dangers of the "third force" or humanistic psychology is its emphasis on self-love [narcissism]. Such an emphasis on selfism [e.g. doing for oneself, loving self, looking out for number one, etc.] causes one to "feel" badly if he is not measuring up. This leads to suicidal tendencies. What must be confronted here is that suicide is a very selfish act and often committed because the person loves himself too much and doesn't want to continue to live [face life's problems]. Therefore, he considers only self [selfism] and no one else.[25]

Dr. Mays refers to the many modern churches which accommodate "pop psychology." He asserts that the selfism ministry of those churches is "baptized" secularism. He points to *Self-Esteem: The New Restoration*, the recent book by Robert Schuller, pastor of Crystal Cathedral in Garden Grove, California. Such a ministry, warns Dr. Mays, draws Christians' attention away from Jesus Christ to the theories of Erich Fromm, Abraham Maslow, or Carl Jung. Pastor Mays reminds Christians, especially clergy and counselors, that they are called to confront today's problems with God's Word, not with the religion of pop psychology.

Consider the Biblical Principles

"Know you that the Lord He is God: it is He that has made us, and not we ourselves; we are His people, and the sheep of His pasture" (Psalm 100:3). Since we are not our own, but God's, for a person to take his or her own life is to destroy His property. It is to make self sovereign rather than God.

Man is created in the image of the Creator; to dishonor or destroy our bodies is to dishonor Him. "What? know you not that your body is the temple of the Holy Ghost which is in you, which you have of God, and you are not your own?" (1 Corinthians 6:19).

God is the giver of all life both for "here" and for "eternity" (Genesis 1:26, 27; Psalm 8:5; 24:1; John 1:3; 3:16; 10:10; 11:25, 26). It is He who sets the bounds, He who sets the span and nature of being, and He who has established the laws of life for here and for eternity (Job 7:1).

Neither love of life nor desire for death may be placed before (above) God; to do so is to give the god of self preeminence. Thus is the First Commandment violated: "Thou shalt have no other gods before Me" (Exodus 20:3).

Consider, also, this: "Thou shall not kill [murder]" (Exodus 20:13). Suicide is self-murder. Thus, those who commit suicide violate God's Sixth Commandment. "And surely your blood of your lives will I require [hold you responsible for]; at the hand of every beast will I require it, and at the hand of man; at the hand of every man's brother will I require the life of man" (Genesis 9:5). "All who put an end to their own lives . . . are murderers, whatever coroners' inquests may say of them," (Adam Clark). Matthew Henry comments, "Man must not take his own life. . . . Our lives are not our own as that we may quit them at our own pleasure, but they are God's."

Christ, our Savior and our King, our Master and our example, was in all things tempted, even as are mortal men. "For we have not an high priest which cannot be touched with the feeling of our infirmities; but was in all points tempted like as are we, yet without sin" (Hebrews 4:15). There on the pinnacle of the temple in Jerusalem, did not Satan tempt Jesus, urging Him to commit suicide? "If you are the Son of God, cast Thyself down from hence" (Luke 4:9-11). And did not Christ rebuke him? "It is said, You shall not tempt [test] the Lord thy God" (Luke 4:12).

Suicide is not a problem of pathology. It is not a problem of the mind. It is a problem, a sickness, of the soul (Isaiah 1:5, 6) devoid of the saving, healing power of Jesus Christ. Sin is the source of suicidal inclinations. When the soul is without Christ, the mind is corrupted, hopeless, lost. Those without Christ are lost in more ways than one. "There is a way that seemeth right unto a man, but the end thereof are the ways of death" (Proverbs 16:25).

It is the Savior who heals the broken heart and sets at liberty them that are bruised (Luke 4:18). There is a balm, a refuge, for the heavy heart and desperate soul. "Come," said Jesus, "Come unto Me, all you that labor and are heavy laden, and I will give you rest. Take My yoke upon you, and learn of Me: for I am meek and lowly in heart, and you shall find rest unto your souls" (Matthew 11:28-30). In an uncaring world, it is Christ who hears, cares, heals, and saves. It is He who can transform a death-wish into a joyous song for life.

Christ is indeed the answer — yes, even for those bent on suicide. And, if we are His, it is our task to bring the wounded, the sick, the despairing, the desperate to Him for love, understanding, mercy, grace, and peace.

Consider the Apostle Paul (2 Corinthians 1:8-10). He was "pressed out of measure" and "despaired even of life." Yet, through the grace of God and the power of the Holy Spirit, he learned "in whatsoever state I am, therewith to be content. . . . I can do all things through Christ which strengthens me" (Philippians 4:11-13).

Thus we return to the sins of the modern Church. A watered-down religion, devoid of the healing power of the blood of the Lamb, is not sufficient unto the tasks and pressures of the times. A religion that preaches self-centeredness rather than Christ-centeredness, that teaches self-satisfaction rather than self-denial, that teaches psychology rather than theology, is conformed to this world. Such a religion is based on the word of man rather than the Word of God. It is more in tune and in step with "pop" psychology than it is with the saving power and love and truth of the Triune God. It is, in fact, a pagan religion — the offspring of humanism. Devoid of the Kingdom Gospel, it is lacking Christ's great mandates, oblivious to God's Laws for life, easy pickings for a wily Satan, and an abomination before the sight of God.

In such a religion there is no healing, no power to transform, no power to reform, no power to save. No power to offer "a life of hope through the resurrection of Jesus Christ" (1 Peter 1:3); no power to inspire, to repent and sustain reformation through the Holy Spirit. (For additional Scriptures see the Book of Job; Numbers 11:15; Deuteronomy 27:24, 25; Psalm 32, 38, 51; Jeremiah 8:3; Jonah 4:8; Acts 16:27; 2 Corinthians 5:28; Philippians 1:20-23; and Revelation 9:6.)

T H I R T Y

TAXATION

God requires that His people tithe (all told about 16 percent). Caesar now takes 47 percent of the total national personal income. What's gone wrong with the tax system?

Background Briefing

Taxes (federal, state, and local) take the biggest chunk of the average person's income, about $200 billion more than all we spend on food, clothing, and shelter. The Tax Foundation reports that in 1987 the typical American worker labored 123 days to pay his taxes. Figuring 260 working days in a year, that means about 47 percent of our work days go to finance Caesar and his state and local nephews.[1]

United States Senator Robert W. Kasten, Jr., has pointed out that over the past twenty years, 1967 through 1987, federal taxes have skyrocketed from about $148 billion a year to $854 billion.[2] In 1987 (latest hard data available), total federal tax receipts were about eight hundred fifty four billion dollars. Tacked on to that came about $150 billion in deficits.[3] (A deficit can be considered a delayed tax plus interest.)

All told, in 1987, total government expenditures (federal, state, and local) came to $1.5 trillion. That amounted to 35 percent of the gross national product.

It is estimated that the federal tax take for 1989 will total almost $1 trillion by itself. Total federal spending is projected at more than $1.5 trillion—and that does not include an expected deficit of between $130 billion and $176 billion; the taxes for that will come later.

The direct tax bill in 1989 will look something like this: $414 billion in individual income taxes; $349 billion in social insurance taxes; $120 billion in corporation taxes; and about $439 million in excise taxes and other fees.[4]

On a per capita basis, those taxes will average about $3,500 for every man, woman, and child in America. But, of course, lots of folks don't pay taxes—kids, for example. So, figure the tax burden per worker—and that will average out to more than $8,000 depending on the number of employed. If you think that's an exaggeration, remember that every day you pay many hidden taxes. About 125 different taxes make up a lot of the dough in the price of a loaf of bread!

Incidentally, the term *corporate tax* is a snare and a delusion—corporations don't pay taxes, people do. When it comes to taxes, the corporation basically serves as a transfer agent. It includes the cost of taxes along with its other costs, adds it to the price of its product or service, collects it from the customer, and transfers that amount to Uncle Caesar.

In 1981 the Economic Recovery Tax Act (Kemp-Roth) was enacted with the boast that over eight years (1981-1989), it would mean a cumulative reduction in federal taxes of $1.5 trillion. But, Congress "giveth" and Congress also "taketh" away. Federal tax increases since that 1981 tax cut will add up to over half a billion dollars by the end of 1989.[5] The taxpayer is left holding a one-half-million-dollar bag.

From 1981 to 1989, the biggest tax hike ($650 billion) came through "bracket creep"—as wages and salaries rose to keep up with inflation, many taxpayers moved up to higher tax brackets and thus higher taxes. In many instances, the increase in taxes wiped out the increase in earnings. Thankfully, "bracket creep" was ended in 1985 by indexing incomes to inflation.

Social Security (FICA) taxes will take an increased $377 billion during the 1981-89 period as the combined employee-employer rates climb to 15 percent of base earnings of $45,600 in 1988 and are scheduled to rise again to about 15 percent on a base of $57,000 by 1990. And, the 1987 "deficit-reduction" legislation will mean another $23 billion in tax take in addition to a $101 billion in additional taxes already set for the next two years (1988-1989).[6]

These were some of the major tax hikes enacted since 1981: the $100 billion Tax Equity and Fiscal Responsibility Act (1982); the Highway Revenue Act (1982); the Social Security Amendments (1983); the Railroad Retirement Act (1983); the Deficit Reduction Act (1984); the Consolidated Omnibus Budget Resolution Act (1984); the Omnibus Budget Reconciliation Act (1986); The truth in labelling law does not apply here. Not one of the laws was tagged for what it was — a tax increase.

According to the Reagan administration, over the five-year period, 1986 through 1990, those "tax reform" measures will raise $500 billion in taxes.[7] The politicians in Congress play fast and loose with statistics — and your taxes. Daniel Mitchell explains that "Congress claims taxes will increase only $9 billion in [1989]. In reality, taxes were already estimated to increase $44 billion next year. The new taxes will make the overall increase $53 billion, but Congress can say there is only a $9 billion increase because the current services budget already plans on the forty four billion dollar increase."[8] That old shell game is not confined to the sidewalks of New York; it flourishes in the halls of the political kings.

Check the tax overhaul ("reform") law of 1986. It was supposed to simplify the tax codes. Ask your accountant about that! The law totaled two thousand pages (and already the Senate Finance and House Ways and Means Committees have introduced a five-hundred-page package to make hundreds of "corrections"). The first revised Form 1040 had to be recalled; not even the IRS people could figure it out. But, the "reform" law will bring in about $54 billion in net tax boosts over the ensuing three years (it pulled in $11 billion in extra revenues in 1987 as deductions ended before lower rates went into effect).

It did replace fifteen progressive tax brackets with two tiers (15 percent and 28 percent plus a 5 percent surtax on incomes from $71,000 to $214,000). At the same time, the law eliminated or phased out various deductions (state and local sales taxes, increased capital gains tax) and took six million low income persons off the tax rolls. Middle and upper-middle income taxpayers were hit the hardest while several special interest groups received $11 billion of relief in "transition benefits."

During the Reagan administration, federal revenues have increased from $517 billion in 1980 to $854 billion in 1987. That's an average rise of more than $250 billion a year. And, while the federal revenues increased 50 percent from 1980 to 1986, federal spending rose by more than 67 percent.[9]

Now, new calls for additional taxes are sounded by those who argue an increase in federal revenues is needed to reduce the deficit. History attests to the fact that an increase in taxes does not reduce deficits; it increases spending. A congressional Joint Economic Committee study found that a $1.00 increase in taxes leads to a 58-cent increase in the deficit. In other words, for every $1.00 increase in taxes, federal spending went up $1.58.[10]

A number of other tax increases are being discussed for our future: oil import fees, gasoline taxes (each 1-cent increase in gas tax generates $1 billion in new revenues), increase in excise taxes (tobacco and alcohol and certain luxury items), and taxes on Social Security benefits for upper income retirees, etc.

A value added tax (VAT) has also been proposed. Proponents estimate that VAT could put about $150 billion a year into the federal collection plate. They propose that a portion of that be used to reduce other taxes and that the remainder go to reduce the deficit. Opponents argue that VAT is nothing but a regressive federal sales tax, one more hidden tax. VAT would place a tax (say 10 percent) on the value added at each stage of production, manufacturing and sales. The cumulative VAT would be added to the final price to the consumer or taxpayer.

Another proposal is a "flat tax." That would be a federal income tax applied at the same rate on all taxable income. Basic exemptions for head of household and dependents would be kept but all other deductions or exclusions would be dropped. A simplified tax form would be about four lines long and fit on a postcard. Proponents claim a flat rate tax of 15 percent would produce about the same revenue as now collected and would get the tax system back to raising revenue instead of forcing social reforms via redistribution of the wealth.

The inherent danger in any new legislation labelled "tax reform" is that it most often ends up being one more gimmick to increase the tax take.

As of now, the federal tax take alone comes to about 23 percent of the gross national product. Add state and local taxation, and the total take runs around 35 percent of all the goods and services produced. J. Peter Grace, former chairman of the President's Private Sector Survey on Cost Control emphasized, "Suppose we just confiscated everything over $75,000 not already taxed. What does that give us? It gives us enough money to run the federal government for ten days."[11] And Gail Foster of the Senate Budget Committee adds, "The rhetoric suggests that there's a pot of gold out there. . . . There's no pot of gold."[12]

In 1862, the first federal income tax was enacted. It lasted for ten years and hit a top tax rate of 10 percent. In 1895 a federal income tax was declared unconstitutional. In 1913, the Sixteenth Amendment established a federal income tax. During the debate, opponents voiced the fear that tax rates might eventually go as high as 10 percent. Congress okayed a 1 percent individual income tax with a maximum of 7 percent. In 1943 the withholding of taxes from paychecks was enacted as a temporary measure; it's still there.

Of the more than 1.5 trillion tax dollars spent in the United States in 1986, about 65 percent went to Washington, 20 percent went to the states, and only 16 percent stayed at the local level. (Some of the "federal" money did finally come back to the states and local levels in various federal revenues having programs — minus a "handling" fee.)

The total tax take has just about quadrupled since 1970. Federal spending zoomed from about $195 billion in 1970 to $1 trillion in 1987. That's more than a fivefold increase while the population of the nation was increasing about 20 percent. Uncle Caesar is a heavy eater: the federal tax take in 1987 consumed more than 22 percent of the net national product created by United States capital and labor, and that does not include the "tax" of inflation. The tax take has been increasing at an average of 10 percent per year while federal deficits have been increasing at about 9 percent a year.

There are some eighty thousand governmental bodies in the United States financed by sixty-eight different types of taxes. Indiana taxes ice for alcoholic beverages but not for soda pop or watermelons. New York taxes caramel-popcorn but not salted or buttered popcorn. In 1960 "Tax Freedom" day came on April 15 (from January 1 until then, a worker's total earnings equaled the amount taken from his income by taxes). In 1987 "Tax Freedom" day came in May. Look at it this way: the first two hours and forty-five minutes of each day, you're working for Uncle Caesar. About 50 percent of the working men and women in America pay out more in Social Security taxes (FICA) than they do on their federal income taxes.

Total government spending averaged out to $7,000 per person and $19,000 per household. Ninety-three percent of the income tax is paid by 50 percent of the taxpayers: those earning between $20,000 and $70,000 a year.

Consider that it would take all the personal incomes of all the folks in all the states west of the Mississippi River, plus seven states east of that river, to equal the total tax revenues extracted by the government (and that does not include the most insidious tax of all — inflation). Color those states red; color the taxpayer blue.

Consider the Biblical Principles

Taxation is an exercise of power, a manifestation of sovereignty. That which is sovereign has the power to tax (i.e., require contribution under threat of penalty or punishment).

Godly Christians must consider taxation within the context of God's supreme and total sovereignty (God is the God of all). "I am the Lord: That is My name: and My glory will I not give to another, neither My praise to graven images" (Isaiah 42:8). If an individual (or nation) acknowledges God's sovereignty, then he must know God for what He is and obey Him in every area of life. God's sovereignty is not piecemeal; it is total.

When a people reject God — and when God's stewards fail to render unto God His required tithes — they invite Caesar to assume ungodly power and take coercive dominion over the property and affairs which have been assigned by God to His people.

"Nowhere in the Old Testament before the era of the kings do we find even a hint that the tithe or half shekel offerings were forcibly levied. . . . payment of the tithe was voluntary. Sufficient revenues were thereby generated for public needs." As

Christian economist Tom Rose points out, "The rise of all-powerful civil governments . . . and the oppressive levels of taxation which are eventually imposed on the people by secular governments [1 Samuel 8:11-18] are evidences of God's judgment on an apostate people who failed to govern themselves according to Biblical principles."[13]

Under God, the state's power (including its power to tax) is to be restricted lest it magnify itself above God rather than serve as God's minister to the people for good (Romans 13:1-4). Excessive taxation casts the state in the role of master and shepherd.

Our Lord commands that we are not to covet our neighbor's property (Exodus 20:17). We are not to do this as individuals or gangs or corporate bodies politic. The godly Christian must oppose (and seek lawfully to change) any tax system which arbitrarily takes (plunders) a person's property (Leviticus 24:22). We are not to steal (Exodus 20:15); stealing is stealing whether it is done on an individual or collective basis under the aegis of the state. The anonymity of the gang (even an elected body) cannot legitimize crime or excuse sin.

Withholding of wages or earnings to pay taxes is un-Biblical. The first fruits of our labors (and the return on our investments) belong to and should go to the Lord (Exodus 22:29, 30; Romans 11:16). We are not to give God our leftovers. The offering of the first fruits to God is a symbolic offering of a part which represents the whole — and the whole belongs to God (Psalm 24:1; 1 Corinthians 10:26, 28).[14]

Withholding a person's earnings before he can tithe puts the Lord in second place — behind the state. Thus, God's sovereignty is denied (rejected) and the state is deified; that is a modern form of worship (Exodus 20:3; John 19:15).

We are instructed by God's Word to support the proper and necessary functions of civil government. The Apostle Paul wrote that as Christians we are to pay tribute (tax) to support the persons and programs exercising the civil authority ordained by God to be ministers of justice and defense (Romans 13:6, 7). But, when civil magistrates use taxes to go beyond their assigned and proper role as set forth by God, Christians must work lawfully to remove them from office and to restore adherence to Biblical principles. To do so is to honor God and welcome His sovereignty (Exodus 20:3; Acts 5:29). To fail to do so, especially under a representative form of government, is to be a party to dishonoring God.

Proportional taxation (taxing an equal portion from all, regardless of wealth or position) is a basic Biblical principle. God does not require a greater percentage for a tithe from a wealthy person than He does from the man who may have less. We are told to neither thwart nor favor any person because of their economic status; we are to be even-handed (Exodus 23:2, 6). "The rich shall not give more and the poor shall not give less" (Exodus 30:14, 15). Progressive or regressive rates violate that principle. "Our modern graduated income tax is totally foreign to the Scriptural model which designated an equal tax for all. . . . Dr. R. J. Rushdoony comments: 'By means of this stipulation of an equality of taxation the law was kept from being unjust.'"[15]

May we not take the tithe (a "flat tax") as a basic principle of taxation? A flat tax of about 16 percent would seem to be close to the Scriptural precept.

All adults should share in the cost of government, even if it is just a token payment. Here, too, the widow's mite is as important as the merchant's gold. To remove a class of citizens from the tax rolls is to put them into an inferior status.

Hidden taxes, such as one which politicians shift to business firms knowing that it will be "hidden" in the price of the product, are also a fraud and a deceit (Psalm 10:7; Job 24:16).

Property is basic to the perpetuation of the family and the prosperity of the nation. It is to be handed down in the family from generation to generation. A tax on land would seem to be anti-Biblical ("The earth is the Lord's and the fullness thereof"). It is what the land or property produces which may be taxed, not the land or property itself. Also, because property is pro-family, a tax on inheritance is improper (1 Kings 21:3).

It is not only suicidal but sinful to tax the "seed corn" which, when combined with labor, produces economic well-being for the family and the nation.

1 Samuel, chapter 8 seems to make it clear that, under God, the state's power to tax is to be restricted lest the king (civil government) magnify himself rather than serve God. When the Israelites rejected God and "demanded a king to judge us like all

the nations," Samuel could accurately warn that the people would not only be compelled to pay a simple tithe, they would also be forced to give the "king" a tenth of virtually everything they had (even their sons and daughters). In fact, warned Samuel, things would become so oppressive that the people would cry out because of the king they chose over the Lord God (1 Samuel 8:9-18).

Is there not a modern-day parallel here? Has not this nation rejected the Lord God? Have we not run after other gods and other laws and standards? Do not many consider the state their shepherd? And, like Israel of old, do we not now pay a horrendous price? Are not the destructive, malignant tax system and the corrosive Babylonian debt-economy part of that price?

In a very real sense, the tax system of this nation today may be seen as part of the fruitage of fiscal rebellion against the Lord. True tax reform will come only when we obey God's "tax system" and render unto God that which is His. Then the tithe will advance His kingdom, not Caesar's (Malachi 3:7-9).

THIRTY-ONE

TUITION TAX CREDITS AND CHRISTIAN EDUCATION

Parents who send their children to Christian schools bear a double finan-cial burden; they pay taxes for public education in addition to the costs of tuition. Some propose a tuition tax credit. But, would that invite govern-ment's increased control of private and parochial schools?

Background Briefing

About 5 million students are enrolled in some 21,000 private schools (K-12)—about 4.5 million (85 percent) are in 16,000 sec-tarian (mostly Christian) schools. The average tuition at church-related day schools is $1,000 a year (higher at private Christian day schools—$1,200 to $1,500). An estimated $13.5 billion was spent in 1986 to send students to church-related and private Christian day schools (K-12).

Parents are turning from tax-funded state schools in increas-ing numbers. Parochial schools (mostly evangelical or funda-mental Christian) are growing at a rate of more than 100,000 students per year. A Gallup poll found that 47 percent of public school parents would shift their children to a private school if cost were not a factor. Another Gallup poll reported that 49 per-cent of the public believe the increase in non-public schools was a "good thing"; 30 percent thought it was a "bad thing;" 21 per-cent had no opinion.

In 1986, $148 billion went to tax-supported schools; $105 bil-lion went for K-12. Parents sending children to private schools help pay those billions. Thus, they carry a double burden: paying taxes for state-controlled public schools and the tuition for a private school education. For several years, private groups have pushed for tax relief on those double costs. Mostly, the effort has been for federal tuition tax credit (TTC), a dollar amount which would be subtracted from the bottom line of the income tax form.

One of the first in Congress to seek TTCs was Representative Phil Crane (Illinois). He introduced such a bill in 1969. In 1976 both major party platforms supported TTCs. In 1980 President Reagan made tuition tax credits a campaign promise. By 1988 the support for tuition tax credits divided along party lines among the candidates for President. The Republicans favored the tuition tax credit plan while the Democrats opposed it, primarily on the basis of opposition from the National Education Association (NEA).

Mr. Reagan's proposed legislation, which was submitted to Congress in 1983, is an example of how the tuition tax credit system might work. The Educational and Opportunity Equity Act was introduced by Senator Robert Dole (Kansas). The bill contained the following basic features: (1) It would have permitted a tax credit for tuition paid by parents of a child attending a tax-exempt private school (K-12) which did not follow a "racially discriminatory policy." The tax credits would have been for one-half of the tuition with a maximum credit of $300 per child; (2) The credits would have been phased in ($100 the first year, $200 the second year, and the $300 maximum in the third year and from then on); (3) The credit allowed could not have exceeded the parent's tax liability, and would have applied to families with adjusted gross incomes under $40,000; and (4) The bill stipulated that the tax credits "shall not constitute federal financial assistance to educational institutions or to the recipients."

The supporters of tuition tax credits believe the United States Supreme Court's five-to-four ruling upholding Minnesota's state tax deductions for parents' school expenses enhances their cause (about 95 percent of the private schools in Minnesota are sectarian). However, the Court in upholding that law pointed out that Minnesota law provides tax deductions for both public and private school expenses; thus it dealt with the secular nature of education. Opponents of the 1983 Dole bill emphasized at that time that it would have provided tuition tax credits for parents of private school children only. And, they emphasized, the Court did not disturb its 1973 ruling in which it found that a New York statute providing tax benefits to parents of private school children was unconstitutional.

Proponents of TTC argue that by sending children to private schools they reduce the taxes (costs) for public schools. If, for example, all the K-12 students now in private schools were to enroll in public schools, that would up the cost to the nation's taxpayers by more than $13 billion. If students in parochial schools (K-12) alone descended upon public schools, the additional tax cost would be about $10 billion.

Opponents complain that the tuition tax credit plan would cost the federal government millions in lost revenue at a time when the debt and deficits are already soaring and more funds are needed. Senator John Chaffee (Rhode Island) once argued that such diversion of funds to private schools would fly in the face of fiscal crises in the public schools. A Joint Congressional Committee report estimated that the TTCs would have cost more than $700 million in 1986, 1987, and 1988. Supporters of tuition tax credits contend that even $800 million a year would represent only 0.8 percent of the money spent on public education. That, they say, is practically nothing compared to the billions that private school parents save the public system.

The backers of tuition tax credits believe the plan would promote (at least, make possible) freedom of choice in educating children and enable many more families to send their children to private schools. They note that nothing in the Constitution gives the state an exclusive educational fiat. Compulsory education, coupled with economic burdens, hands the state education a monopoly that destroys choice, smothers competition, and stifles the pursuit of excellence (Philippians 1:10).

The opposition claims that most private schools are primarily efforts to escape government mandated integration of schools, and that private schools are in the main "subterfuges of segregation." Private schools and their supporters reject that argument, saying that the facts indicate that very few Christian schools were started for that reason. According to a 1982 survey (the Coleman Report) there is less segregation (racial and/or economic) in religious schools than in public schools. In recent years, they emphasize, private schools were started because public schools were undesirable and unsupportable. Most private schools (especially Christian day schools) are run for and by parents who seek quality education for their children. What they seek to escape is violence, drugs, sexual promiscuity, low moral and academic standards, lack of discipline, and biased humanistic curricula that deny or belittle God. Also, they object to the subtle drumbeat that works to separate children from parental values.

According to a report by Mel Gabler, an educational research analyst, in the 1940s the most prevalent offenses in public schools were talking, chewing gum, making noise, running in the halls, and getting out of turn in line. In the 1980s, wrote Gabler, the most prevalent offenses in public schools were rape, robbery, assault, burglary, and arson.

Opponents of tuition tax credits assert that the state has the responsibility to set "minimum" standards, and that tuition tax credits would encourage the spread of schools without or below such standards. Supporters of TTCs reject that argument. They say such centralized standards destroy diversity (pursuit of truth and excellence) and are usually bureaucratic and often humanistic. Besides, by any measurable criteria, most Christian schools not only meet but surpass the academic standards set for state schools.

Groups against TTCs charge that the plan would violate the First Amendment by using government funds to subsidize religious schools. Liberals use a double standard in this argument. For example: when demanding tax monies to subsidize abortions for poor women, liberals insist that use of federal funds does not imply approval of abortion but simply allows for freedom of choice. Apparently freedom of choice is acceptable for abortions but not for education.

Those who support TTCs argue that the tuition tax credit is in the same league with tax deductions allowed for contributions to church, missions, etc. Further, argue the proponents, food stamps are not restricted to government stores, and Medicare benefits are not confined to government hospitals. Why, then, should the benefits of taxes paid for education be available only at government schools?

The opposition claims that TTCs would benefit only the upper-middle and upper classes, but advocates say the records show the contrary is true. Of those parents who send their children to private schools, 62 percent have an annual income of $25,000 or less. And, in the inner city, where minority parents send their children to private schools, 72 percent earn less than $15,000 a year. CORE (Congress On Racial Equality) charges that the state school monopoly locks black parents into inferior schools in the ghetto.

Teachers' unions charge that tuition tax credits would destroy the state school system. They say it would take away funds and reduce support for tax-funded schools at a time when they are struggling to make ends meet. TTC advocates respond, Not so! TTCs are not tied to a reduction in funds for public schools (those tax monies have increased during recent years even while enrollment has decreased). The loss of support for state schools, say TTC groups, was brought on by state bureaucrats and union establishments. They suggest that experience in other nations indicates that TTCs bring competition to education and force the public schools to be more responsive to public and parental desires. They point to Western Europe and other English-speaking nations, claiming that the government support of a dual-educational system (public and private schools) has forced state schools to try harder to achieve excellence.

Not all opposition to tuition tax credits comes from groups hostile to private or Christian education. And not all support is without reservation.

United States Senators Orrin Hatch (Utah) and Jesse Helms (North Carolina) both support TTCs. But, both express concern that tax credits might become "a lever" for federal control of private education.

Bill Billings, formerly with the National Christian Action Coalition (NCAC), warned of proposed amendments to any tuition tax credit bill which might open the door to federal control of Christian education: "It would be better to have no bill than a bad bill."

The 1983 Dole bill provided that tuition tax credits would be denied if an educational institution "follows a racially discriminatory policy." Many educators worried about that provision.

They insisted the issue involved was not approval or disapproval of racial discrimination. The issue is control. If prohibition of racial discrimination is not a control then the question arises: When is a control not a control? The answer seems to be: When a control enforces "public policy." In view of recent Court actions, what new "public policies" lie ahead?

Federal court decisions do raise questions and do cause concern that TTCs might become the bait to snare Christian schools into a federal trap. In 1982 the United States Supreme Court unanimously held that Amish employers must pay Social Security tax even though that violated a long-held Amish religious belief (1 Timothy 5:8). Chief Justice Warren Burger wrote: "Religious belief in conflict with the payment of taxes affords no basis for resisting the tax" which is public policy. In a case involving Bob Jones University, the majority on the United States Supreme Court held that "entitlement to tax exemption depends on meeting certain common law standards . . . namely that an institution seeking tax-exempt status . . . not be contrary to established public policy." Justice Powell concurred with that decision but expressed fear it might invest the IRS "with authority to decide which public policies are sufficiently 'fundamental' to require denial of tax exemption." Justice Powell's concern is shared by many who would otherwise support tuition tax credits.

Barbara Morris, in "Tax Tuition Credits: A Responsible Appraisal," warns: "TTCs are the camel's nose under the private school's tent." With public funds goes public control—that's what the Supreme Court has said. She emphasizes that since TTCs concern federal income tax, TTCs would be scrutinized by the Internal Revenue Service. Any on-going IRS harassment of Christian churches and schools should be a big red flag to supporters of tuition tax credits.

As for Western European nations, Mrs. Morris reminds us that France recently took over all private schools and integrated more than nine thousand religious schools into the public school system because the schools receive state aid. In the Netherlands, extolled by TTC advocates, the government does support private schools and also determines the curricula and teacher qualifications.

According to Mrs. Morris, the supporters of the Minnesota law providing tax deductions for parents admitted "it was designed primarily to rein in a rash of tiny 'home schools' set up by fundamental Christians." Citizens for Educational Reform, a major supporter of tuition tax credits, also suggests that tuition tax credits could reduce the number of Christian home schools.

Consider the Biblical Principles

The responsibility to educate children rests not with the state but with parents. It is the responsibility of parents to bring up children in the fear and love of God (Proverbs 22:6; 1 Peter 2:2). Parents are to make sure that children receive an education based upon God's written Word (Isaiah 28:10), in "the nurture and admonition of the Lord" (Ephesians 6:4; see also Deuteronomy 6:5-9; Proverbs 1:7; and Matthew 4:4).

Albert Shanker, president of the American Federation of Teachers, asserts, "Public schools exist to create citizens." That was also Hitler's view. It is the Soviet plan. But it definitely is *not* the purpose of education for godly Christian parents who know that children are to be educated so they will grow to be God's servants and, first and foremost, citizens of His Kingdom. Thus, Christians must resist, and separate themselves from, anything that will or even might interfere with such a God-given blessing and responsibility (Job 8:14).

We must shun that which might spoil not only ourselves but also our children (Colossians 2:8). If it appears that tuition tax credits might be a carrier of such a deadly seed, we must shun it. We dare not risk any venture, any alliance, any gift (real or false) that makes us wards of the state (Isaiah 42:17). Paul warns us, "Let no man deceive you with vain words: for because of these things cometh the wrath of God upon the children of disobedience. Be ye not partakers with them" (Ephesians 5:5, 6).

We must never forget: the Caesar that grants tax credits is the same Caesar that levied an improper tax in the first place. The Caesar that bears "gifts" is the same Caesar that banned our God from the schools we are compelled to support with our taxes—the same Caesar that opened public schools to the gods of humanism.

Consider the purpose of taxation. As set forth in God's Word, it is to support the civil authorities (powers) in their proper duties as magistrates (ministers) of God so that we may live peaceful, productive, and godly lives (1 Timothy 2:2; Romans 13:6, 7). God's Word does not tell us to pay taxes for social reform. It does not give Caesar the power to tax for education of our children. Such work is to be done by the Church, and to support that work we are to pay the tithe. We may be compelled to pay taxes for programs that are ungodly, but we must never voluntarily seek or support tax programs that invite or enable Caesar to trespass on areas that are not his. That would be to place a very small price on our faith. To do so would be to trust in man rather than God. If we are persuaded that He is able to keep that which we have committed unto Him (2 Timothy 1:12) we will not seek gimmicks or gadgets or favors from the state (Philippians 4:19; Psalm 118:8, 9). Rather, we will tithe to educate our children in God's house, work to redress the proper balance between church and state, and realign man's laws with God's. Only then, when we obey God, will Caesar stop infringing upon those rights and duties which belong to Christians.

THIRTY-TWO

UNITED NATIONS AND WORLD PEACE

What was envisioned as "man's last best hope for peace" has degenerated into a bloated bureaucracy dominated by anti-USA blocs.

Background Briefing

In Moscow, on October 19-30, 1943, an agreement for the United Nations Organization was reached by the big four allied powers: the United Kingdom, the United States, the USSR, and the Republic of China. Each member nation was given one vote except the Soviet Union, which was given three votes in the General Assembly—one for the USSR, and one each for the Ukraine SSR, and the Byelorussia SSR.

In San Francisco, June 26, 1945, representatives of fifty nations signed the United Nations (U.N.) Charter. On July 28, 1945, the United States Senate ratified the U.N. Charter, 89-to-2. Senators William Langer (R—North Dakota) and Henrik Shipstead (R-Minnesota) voted "Nay." Langer warned the Senate, "[the United Nations] is fraught with danger to the American people and to American institutions." On October 15, 1945, the U.N. charter was ratified by a majority of signatory nations.

Mindful of the horrors and devastation of World War II, the nations involved saw the United Nations as "man's last best hope for peace" and ignored the implicit dangers. In the United States, the vast majority of the populace welcomed the organization. Even in 1959, Gallup reported that eight-seven percent of Americans thought the U.N. was doing a good job. Since then, the United States public has lost confidence. In 1985, polls found eighty-one percent of those Americans polled thought the United States should stay in the U.N. but fifty-four percent were highly critical of its operations: only twenty-eight percent thought it was doing a good job.[1]

There are those who feel that if the United States Senate were voting on U.N. membership now, the vote would be very close, perhaps negative. After drawing up a "balance sheet" on the U.N., Dr. Juliana Geran Pilon of the Heritage Foundation concluded, "There are questions . . . as to whether the United States is benefiting from its U.N. membership, given the paralysis of the Security Council and the anti-American, anti-Western, anti-industrial, anti-capitalist majority in the General Assembly." Charles Lichenstein, former deputy Ambassador to the U.N., argues, "I think if the United States were fully serious about what it is attempting to do in the world it would have nothing to do with the U.N."[2] And, columnist Patrick Buchanan condemned the U.N. as a "cathedral to a dead religion."

What is the purpose of United Nations? To keep world peace. But what is "peace"? To the Soviets, peace is not the absence of war, it is the absence of resistance. Has the U.N. achieved its purpose? Supporters say " Yes." They boast that "because of the U.N. no major wars have been fought since 1945." They call Korea and Vietnam "police actions." Critics of the U.N. disagree. They say the charter calls for the U.N. to uphold the right of self-determination of small nations. Yet, since the start of the U.N., hundreds of millions of once-free persons have been taken over by anti-Christian communists. The absence of "major" wars, they argue, is due to restraint between the super-powers, not because of the U.N. As a peacekeeper, they contend, the U.N. has been mostly "all mouth and no muscle."

British Prime Minister Margaret Thatcher once pointed out that between 1945 and 1983 there had been "140 conflicts in which up to ten million people have died." Between 1945 and 1987, the United Nations has been totally inept and ineffective in regard to at least ninety-three conflicts.

It did little or nothing about the Soviet invasion of Hungary (1956), the war between the Netherlands and Indonesia (1962), the Soviet invasion of Czechoslovakia (1968), or the Vietnam wars (1945-1975). It was also ineffective regarding the Ethiopian war against Somali (1977), and has been a virtual non-entity during the Vietnamese invasion and slaughter in Cambodia (1977 to present), the Soviet invasion of Afghanistan (1979 to present), the Iran-Iraq war (1980 to present), Qadhafi's invasion of Chad (1983), or the continuing fighting in Lebanon.

Pro-U.N. groups insist the organization is important for world dialogue. Their argument is that "talking is better than fighting." Former United States Ambassador to the United Nations, Jeanne Kirkpatrick described the U.N. as a "forum for airing ideas." "Yes," say those who are negative about the U.N., "but most of those ideas are anti-USA. Essentially the U.N. is a forum for attacking America." And, they quote Stalin's statement: "Words must have no relation to action."

Critics say the U.N. maintains a double standard in that it has a "consistent record of exploiting and exaggerating the problems of the West while remaining silent regarding the flagrant, often heinous violations of human rights by the Soviet bloc nations." The bloc of ninety-three Third World nations branded the United States as the "only" threat to peace and prosperity in the world. Critics charge that the U.N. fuels violence and legitimizes terrorism by recognizing such groups as the Palestine Liberation Organization (PLO) and the South West Africa People's Organization (SWAPO). The PLO was an international non-entity until the U.N. invited Yassir Arafat to address its General Assembly. The non-member PLO has observers at the General Assembly and representatives on several United Nations' agencies — a courtesy extended to no other non-member, including founder-nation, Free China Taiwan.

Burton Pine, head of the Heritage Foundation's United Nations Assessment Project, charged that the U.N. increases tensions, politicizes non-political issues and provides a United States base for USSR espionage. The Soviets keep a staff of two hundred seventy five at the Soviet, Ukrainian and Byelorussian missions in New York. In addition, four hundred eleven Soviets work at the U.N. Secretariat.[3] According to former Under-Secretary-General Arkady Shevchenko, the majority of those Soviets report regularly to the KGB. In 1985, the United States Senate Intelligence Committee identified one of the two special assistants to the Secretary-General as a KGB agent.[4] Shevchenko, himself an ex-KGB agent, was the highest-ranking Soviet official at the U.N. prior to his defection to the United States.[5] He revealed that the opportunity for a spy nest in New York was one reason the USSR always insisted that the United Nations be located in the United States.

Supporters say the U.N. is needed to protect human rights throughout world. Again the record does not support that assertion. The U.N. did little or nothing about Idi Amin's policy of genocide in Uganda. It did little or nothing about Pol Pot's slaughter of three million in Cambodia. And it was silent in the face of the continued violation of human rights in the USSR and Soviet bloc nations. It has said little and has done nothing about the Soviet's use of germ and bio-chemical warfare in Afghanistan and Cambodia. Critics also point to the vicious war that the United Nations' troops waged against the black, anti-Communist government of Katanga. That, indeed, was a gross violation of human rights: U.N. forces bombed hospitals, shelled ambulances, destroyed churches, murdered non-combatants, and slaughtered women and children.

Observers insist that the U.N. had a built-in bias against the Western world (and especially the United States) from the beginning. From Alger Hiss to Kurt Waldheim, the U.N. Secretary-Generals were either communists or socialists. Hiss, FDR's key adviser on the U.N., was quietly selected at Yalta to act as interim Secretary General until the U.N. charter was ratified. Andrie Gromyko, USSR Ambassador to U.N., led the campaign for Trygve Lie, the first elected Secretary-General. Lie was a high-ranking member of Norway's Social Democratic Labor Party, a spin-off from The Communist International. Lie was succeeded by Dag Hammarskjold, a Swedish Socialist and admirer of Red China's Chou Enlai. Hammarskjold once wrote, ". . . I was twelve years old when I had a very strong feeling that I am a new Jesus." He was succeeded by U Thant of Burma, an avowed Marxist and vocal anti-American. U Thant appointed a Soviet KGB officer as his personal aide. He was followed by Kurt Waldheim, Austria's Socialist representative at the U.N. Waldheim, a Nazi lieutenant during W.W. II, appointed a KGB agent as the United Nation's personnel director.

Communists have always held the most sensitive post in U.N. Secretariat: Under-Secretary for Political and Security Council Affairs. Of the thirteen who have held the post, twelve were Soviets and one a Yugoslav. How sensitive is that office? It handles all matters concerning military, territorial, and jurisdictional disputes, thus virtually controling the way in which the U.N. Secretariat approaches regional conflicts, deploying and directing the use of its military forces and missions. The United Nations officer in charge of military operations in the Korean war was a Soviet. He was privy to all U.N. plans and strategies against Soviet supported North Korea.

The total annual budget for the U.N. and its various agencies and commissions is approximately four billion dollars.[6] The United States supplies about twenty-five percent of that or about one billion dollars.[7] From 1945 to 1965, the United States taxpayers paid forty percent of the U.N. budget. The level of that assessment was gradually reduced to twenty-five percent by 1974 and is now about twenty-one percent. Since the United Nations was founded in 1945, the taxpayers of the United States have poured about fifteen billion dollars into its coffers.[8]

The USSR's assessment is less than thirteen percent; Japan's, ten percent; West Germany, eight percent; Great Britain, five percent. In 1986, fifteen nations headed by the U.S., Japan, and the Soviet Union carried roughly eighty percent of the U.N.'s operating budget. "Of the one hundred fifty nine member states, one hundred eleven accounted for two percent of the total budget. The majority of those contributed the bare minimum, one-tenth of one percent or roughly sixty seven thousand dollars. The rest of the member nations pay the remaining thirty-nine percent of the budget. Oil rich Saudi Arabia pays just over one-half of one percent. The bloc of one hundred twenty Third World and non-aligned nations contributes nine percent of the total budget — but, that bloc has three-fourths of the vote in the U.N. General Assembly."[9]

For years, the United States personnel at the U.N. have criticized its bloated staff and budgets. In 1948, there were four thousand employees at the Secretariat. Today, there are fifty-two thousand. There are twenty-eight Under-Secretary-Generals and twenty-nine Assistant Secretary-Generals with annual salaries higher than those paid to a United States Senator. The U.N.

staff personnel are paid salaries which are more than 12 percent higher than the salaries of equivalent civil service personnel in Washington. U.N. professional employees based in New York start at a salary of more than thirty-five thousand dollars. And, U.N. pensions are substantially higher than those in the United States Civil Service.[10]

The Kassebaum-Solomon Amendment mandates a reduction in United States support of the United Nations from twenty-five percent to twenty percent of its budget until reforms are made and operating costs are cut. So far, the only effect has been talk but no real cuts.[11] In fact, the U.N. plows ahead with its plan to build a seventy-five million dollar "U.N. Center" in Addis Ababa, in Marxist and famine-ridden Ethiopia.

Now, the U.N. wants more money from the United States. But, as Allan L. Keyes, former assistant Secretary of State for International Organization Affairs, warns: "the United Nations has reached a time of judgment." Unless necessary changes are made, there is little doubt the United States Congress will slash contributions further.[12] It cannot condone waste in the U.N. when it is face-to-face with mandatory slashes in its own budgets and deficits.

In the U.N. General Assembly, the policy is for every nation to have one vote. That means forty-four thousand inhabitants of St. Kitts-Nevis have a vote equal to the United States with a population of two hundred thirty-five million. Small nations, paying only three percent of the U.N. budget, comprise the majority in the General Assembly.

The Heritage Foundation has pointed out that the United States is also shortchanged when it comes to staffing of the Secretariat and its agencies. The Third World nations are vastly over-represented. So for example, while United States payments and contributions total about twenty-five percent of all U.N. spending, only about eleven percent of the U.N. professional staff is American. African nations pay less than two percent of the U.N. budget but have nearly fourteen percent of the high level posts; Latin Americans pay less than four percent, but hold nine percent of the jobs. Middle Eastern countries pay about two percent, but hold seven percent of the senior top-level spots.[13] The "tone and thrust and strategies" of the United Nations are set by the Secretariat bureaucrats. It is a truism of government: "Those who administer policy end up making policy." Thus, the United States is locked into a minor role.

Underway in the U.N. (by bloc of one hundred twenty nations) is a drive for a New International Economic Order (NIEO); in other words, global socialism. Among NIEO's stated goals are to redistribute the United States' wealth on a global scale, regulate United States business and industry (use of raw materials, production, etc.), force the United States to share technologies, weaken protection provided by patents, allocate ocean floor mining sites, levy taxes on ocean-mining, regulate per capita consumption, and make the World Health Organization (WHO) the enforcement agency overriding the United States Food and Drug Agency, etc.

As Senator David Patrick Moynihan, former United States Ambassador to the United Nations, warned, the U.N. is "a dangerous place" for the United States—in those halls it is becoming "an endangered species."

Now a new danger has arisen: the United States Constitution states that treaties have the force of law; that they are co-equal and are as binding as the provisions of the federal Constitution.

In the past, when the United States delegates to the U.N. voted for a resolution which contained elements at variance with United States policy, they were careful to include a declaration which disassociated the United States from the objectionable parts of the resolution and any possible legal effect. Now, based on the World Court's 1987 decision in favor of Nicaragua (Nicaragua v. United States), the United States must "support fully every aspect of every resolution for which it votes—or risk being accused of violating international law."[14]

As The Heritage Foundation warns, "A world court decision allows the U.N. to impose laws on the United States."[15] Senator Langer was correct: "The United Nations is fraught with danger to the American people and to American institutions."

Consider the Biblical Principles

The Lord God is man's best (and only) hope of peace. Christ Jesus is the Prince of Peace (Isaiah 9:6).

World peace is certainly a condition to be desired. But, neither the prince of this world, nor all his agents or agencies—human and inhuman—can bring it to pass. A messianic state, national or supra-national, is not an instrument of peace; it can only be an instrument of coercion. Unless the Lord God build the house, politicians and diplomats labor in vain (Psalm 127:1).

Men would make of the United Nations a god. It is, in a sense, the ultimate expression of humanism, as if man could save the world. Yet, men would lift it above the Lord God. His sovereignty is spurned (Exodus 20:3). In the U.N. "meditation room," other gods are placed on a par with the One True God. That individual or institution that denies God will be denied by the Lord God (Matthew 10:33; 2 Chronicles 7:19).

Men may reject God, and they may seek to create a god-state and worship it. Yet even in their hardness of heart, some desire what only He can provide (Isaiah 26:3). In the U.N. park across the street from the U.N. tower, this Scripture is written in the marble. ". . . they shall beat their swords into plowshares, and their spears into pruning hooks. Nation shall not lift up sword against nation. Neither shall they learn war any more (Isaiah 2:4)."

Consider what was omitted on that U.N. wall. Ignored and rejected is the very basis, the central, unyielding requirement, of that blessed hope:

> And it shall come to pass in the last days, that the mountain of the Lord's house shall be established in the top of the mountains (i.e. above all other nations, above all other kingdoms) and shall be exalted above the hills; and all nations shall flow into it. And many people shall go and say, Come ye, and let us go up to the mountain of the Lord, to the house of the God of Jacob; and He will teach us His ways, and we will walk in His paths: for out of Zion shall go forth the law, and the word of the Lord from Jerusalem. And He shall judge among the nations, and shall rebuke many people, and "O house of Jacob, come ye, and let us walk in the light of the Lord (Isaiah 2:2-3)."

Man may seek to pick and choose what they desire from God's Word, but it won't work. God's Word is a seamless whole. Man's spiritual and geopolitical myopia not withstanding, it is the Lord's house, to which the nations shall come; the Lord God that shall establish peace; God's Law, and God's Word that shall prevail, and God's ways, and God's paths (not the U.N.'s) that nations shall travel to find true and lasting peace.

We are not to follow false gods or make idols of institutions. We are to stand firm in the faith, meek (obedient) before Him. Then, surely, we shall delight in the abundance of peace (Psalm 37:11). Blessed are such peacemakers for they do love the Lord (Matthew 5:9).

Consider the tower of Babel (Genesis 11:1-9). It, too, was an affront to God, a rebellion against God by those who thought themselves wiser than God. It was not a tower of worship. It was a war tower against the Lord. Did not Nimrod seek to establish a universal monarchy, to challenge the Supremacy of God—even as the U.N. seeks to be a god and establish one world government? And, did not the Lord God confound the language of those who would have built a high tower to be on a level with Him? Does not controversy and strife and babble rage in the U.N. today? Is it not a Tower of Babel? Never have so many words accomplished so little.

And, even as the builders of Babel quit building because of confusion, is not the U.N. self-destructing because of confusion and stalemate and hostility? Those who would have built the tower of Babel had no rock, they made their own brick. They used slime for mortar. Those who would build the U.N. have no Rock, they have rejected the Keystone. They use hatred for mortar and they build on the sands of man. They are destined to despair and destruction (Matthew 7:24-27). "Come out of her, My people, that ye be not partakers of her sin and ye receive not of her plagues" (Revelation 18:4).

Rev. Joseph C. Morecraft, III, sums up the anti-Christian foundations of the United Nations by saying that it is: messianic (sees itself as the savior of the world); legalistic (holds to the doctrine of salvation through works of man); humanistic (its faith rests in man); egalitarian (it holds that all religions are equal); and it is totalitarian (it seeks to establish an absolute order binding upon all mankind). But, concludes Morecraft, "We must obey God rather than men" (Acts 17:7).

THIRTY-THREE

VIDEO WITCHCRAFT AND SATANISM

Across the nation parents, police, and clergy have a growing concern about the increase of Satanism and the spread of demonic "fantasy" games.

Background Briefing

On Thursday, February 18, 1988, residents of the quiet town of Revere, a suburb of Boston, were shocked to learn that the headless carcasses of a lamb, several chickens, and a duck had been found on the town beach. The creatures had been drained of blood and were neatly arranged in what appeared to be a calculated geometric design.[1]

Some authorities saw it as one more piece of evidence — albeit comparatively mild — of an increasing "self-styled Satanism laced with drugs, savage rock music, and a mish-mash of symbols and rituals . . . among teenagers caught up in the occult."[2]

In one three-year period, California reported more than one hundred murders which were related in one way or another to occult rituals. In 1987 three Missouri teenagers were charged with first-degree murder for beating a classmate with baseball bats and dumping the body down a cistern along with a bludgeoned cat.[3] In Denver, Satanism and drugs propelled a youth gang into burglary, suicide, attempted suicide, auto theft, and rituals in which they drank blood and burned dogs with acid. Some of the "Purple Knights" were as young as twelve.[4]

"Three years ago, nobody wanted to hear about it, nobody believed it was real," said San Francisco police detective Sandi

Gallant, who receives four calls a day from around the country on crimes with satanic or occult overtones.[5]

The Chicago-based "Cult Awareness Network" reports that every month brings more news of a teenager involved in crimes which seem to be linked to devil worship. The Network's executive director, Cynthia Kisser, says "I suspect we're only getting the tip of the iceberg."[6]

Since the 1960s Satanism has been making a comeback in the United States. In recent years, there has been a spate of movies focussed on Satanism and the demonic (*Rosemary's Baby, The Exorcist, The Amityville Horror, Poltergiest,* to name a few). More and more TV programs are also preoccupied with the occult.

"Fantasy" games and interactive video sports such as *Dungeons & Dragons, Tunnels and Trolls, Chivalry and Sorcery, Rune Quest,* and *Hellpits of Nighfang,* many of them delving into the occult, continue to be big sellers in many toy and department stores. Teenagers comprise a major share of the market. Selections range from coloring books for younger children to high-priced role-playing games complete with guide books for "dungeon masters." Many fantasy games have been adapted for personal (home) computers. Also, home TV game video cassettes (for VCRs) have become a staple item in video rental stores. These involve hunt and chase and murder fantasies, etc. One video game producer boasted about his X-rated cartridge, "Custer's Revenge," that has as its object taking a naked male figure through a maze of obstacles to rape an Indian maiden tied to a post.

The games are merchandised as "fun and fantasy." But, there seems to be increasing evidence that the games often open the door to the occult and to Satan worship. Players compete to "summon demons to defeat opponents," to "employ dark forces to win battles," etc. Some of the games have been used in public school classes for gifted children.

In Montpelier, Virginia, the parents of a sixteen-year-old student brought suit against the principal and two teachers at their son's high school. They charged that they were responsible for the boy's suicide because they permitted *Dungeons and Dragons (D&D)* to be an organized school activity. Hours before Bink Pulling's suicide, a "curse" was placed on him by a teacher conducting the *D&D* game. Police, investigating the death, found that the boy's room was filled with *D&D* paraphernalia. Subsequently, the boy's mother, Mrs. Patricia Pulling, founded BADD (Bothered About *Dungeons & Dragons*).[7]

Some law enforcement officials downplay the impact of the video witchcraft games. They term such activities "youthful fascination," insisting that the kids are only "dabblers," and that only about 5 percent of the teenagers get deeply involved in violence. Mrs. Pulling responds, "The dabblers are the ones committing the crimes. They're kids, and they're killing people." Sean Sellers, an intense, intelligent, lonely twelve-year-old was fascinated with *D&D*. Now, at age seventeen, he is the youngest inmate on death row at the Oklahoma State Penitentiary. In 1986 Sean murdered his parents and a convenience store clerk.[8]

It's part of a big and mushrooming business. Even *Time/LIFE Books* has entered the market. It offers *The Enchanted World* series — books about "that strange, alluring world that exists alongside our mortal world . . . wizards and witches . . . giants, ogres . . . avenging child spirits . . . awesome poltergeists . . . macabre grinning skulls . . . red-eyed banshees . . . all conjured up . . . in [this] vividly illustrated" series. All that, proclaims *Time/ LIFE,* makes the series a "magnificent home library that will enchant your family for years!"[9]

Millions of Americans (mostly teenagers and young adults) comprise the growing market and literally are enchanted with these "games" and books about the occult. The sale of such materials grossed about $500 million in recent years. But, is it all "fun and games"?

Some may think the games and books are harmless, that they are strictly for fun, fantasy, and entertainment. Beware! They are not! Parents who buy or allow such games and books and tapes are playing with dynamite — and their children's souls. They open their homes, and their children, to the subtle introduction of the occult, to Satanism and the malignant world of psychotherapy (mind alteration, values modification). There is nothing benign about these games; they are part of the increasing spread of Satanism and various forms of the occult, a push that will increase in tempo and fervor as Satan's time grows shorter.

TSR, Inc., producers of *Dungeons and Dragons*, created a *D&D* cartoon to run as part of the CBS Saturday morning lineup of children's programs. "Charges that the game inspired occult-related violence in a macabre trail of suicides and murders convinced CBS to take the cartoon off the air after three years."[10]

Gail Sanchez, at one time a game designer for TSR, Inc., has acknowledged that *D&D* is heavily occult. He related that he had seen the black magic practices in the game and had urged TSR to create new games that would not deal with historical occultism.[11] Rosemary Layacono, mother of a player who committed suicide, insists *D&D* seduces its players into Satanism.[12]

Helmut Thielicke suggests that "the nearer we come to the end of this present age, the more energetically the Adversary mobilizes his last reserves, until the demonic excesses reach their climax and Christ returns and the new age of God begins."[13]

Anton La Vey, author of "The Satanic Bible" and for years one of the more prominent proponents of Satanism, once boasted that he had ten thousand members in his San Francisco First Church of Satan. Others estimate that the Satanist movement has about one hundred thousand adherents throughout America.

One of the more notorious members of the Satanist cult is Charles Manson. Manson, the leader of a cult-crazed group now imprisoned, was convicted of multiple murders. During the orgies of violence and death performed by Manson and some of his followers, they used the blood of their victims to paint satanic messages on the walls of the homes they invaded. One of the victims was actress Sharon Tate.

In his book, *The Truth about Witchcraft,* Hans Holzer writes that "the devil-worshipers were reversing the symbols and rites of Christianity purely because they believed that these symbols and rites had power and in reversing them the power would go to them, into their ritual, rather than flow out toward the God of the Christians."[14] Sexual rites are often added to emphasize their blasphemy. When their rites conclude, they are closed with a curse rather than a blessing.

Games such as *D&D* may not be religious in themselves but they do teach principles and terms and rituals of occult forms of religion. One school board member based his objection to *D&D*'s being in public schools on the contention that "[it] is clearly religious in nature . . . [and] the Supreme Court has already barred religious activity from public facilities."[15]

As Peter Leithart and George Grant point out in their book on the subject, the various facets of the occult games include: death, deities, prayer and fasting, Satanism, human sacrifices, murder, cannibalism, defilement, and defecation. The "games" purposefully and constantly use Biblical terms and phrases blasphemously. Dr. Gary North has said, "After years of study of the history of occultism, after having researched a book on the subject, and after having consulted with scholars in the field of historical research, I can say with confidence, these games are the most effective, most magnificently packaged, most profitably marketed, most thoroughly researched introduction to the occult in man's recorded history."[16]

John Torell, of Christian Life Ministries, reached this conclusion about *D&D*: "Instead of a game, [it's] a teaching on demonology, witchcraft, voodoo, murder, rape, blasphemy, suicide, assassination, insanity, sex perversion, homosexuality, prostitution, Satan worship, gambling, Jungian philosophy, barbarism, cannibalism, sadism, desecration, demon summoning, necromantics, divination and many more teachings brought to you in living color direct from hell!"[17]

The Capsule, a Christ-centered newsletter for parents, educators, and pastors, asks: "Is this the 'toy industry' of tomorrow?"[18] The letter warns,

> The forces which affect a child's training also influence his imagination. They include his parents, toys, television, school, church, movies, books, magazines, music and peer pressure. . . . Every day children are being exposed to the occult more and more. Television cartoons and movies openly present the practice of the occult. Toys are patterned after television cartoons and have the capacity for promoting occult practices in the play of children.[19]

Psychiatrists assert it is reasonable to assume that such interactive games (i.e, the player not only plays a role but assumes the identity of the character he creates and lives in a created "reality") are fraught with peril. They are, or come very close to being, part and parcel of a program to teach the (religious) principles and rituals of witchcraft (occultism). And, Dr. Thomas Radecki, chairman of the National Coalition on Television Violence, is concerned that children who become increasingly expert at blasting spaceships into electronic oblivion (via video games) may lose the ability to distinguish between fantasy and reality. Says Dr. Radecki: "Violent games do tend to increase the tendency to violence in other settings. . . . We are training our next generation to be a barbaric, warrior society."[20]

United States Surgeon General C. Everett Koop warns that "more and more people are beginning to understand the adverse mental and physical effects of video games on pre-teenage and teenage children. . . . There is nothing constructive in the games. . . . Everything is eliminate, kill, destroy."[21]

Many newer video games are more sophisticated — and more cruel. In the rulebook which accompanies the *Arduin Grimoire* game, a "critical hit" table is included for the players: "Dice roll: 37-38, hit location: crotch/chest; results: genitals/breast torn off, shock . . . Dice roll: 95; hit location: guts ripped out . . . "[22] The National Institute of Health reports it has found a correlation between TV and movie violence and many of the crimes that are being committed today.

Examine the dangerous (fantasizing) component of these games. Role-playing is a subtle, sugar-coated form of psychodrama adapted to humanistic designs for sensitivity training and values modification. Some Christians may view role-playing as harmless. The fact is that it is a first-step form of psychotherapy that seeks to destroy what humanists call "the God syndrome" (i.e., belief in God). In other words, it is the first step toward subtly inducing the child to reject the religious training of home and church.

Highly directed and sophisticated sociodrama or psychodrama (psychotherapy) can destroy traditional values and imprint the young person's mind with "new" or no values. Lavrenti Beria, Soviet master-manipulator, used such methods to develop the USSR's psychopolitical warfare (also termed psychopolitics and brain-washing).

Psychodramatic techniques were introduced in the early 1900's by Dr. Jacob L Moreno, a contemporary of Sigmund Freud. Moreno wrote that his objective was to develop "a positive religion" (for evidence of how his work has been implemented and is being implemented, see *Humanist Manifesto I*, and *Humanist Manifesto II*). Such a "positive" religion, wrote Moreno, would be expanded and improved by science while making use of "insights" of Marxism.

In his 1932 book, *Who Shall Survive*, Moreno wrote that through psychodrama with role-playing "we will destroy the God syndrome." He set forth his intentions: "The idea was that if you can 'play a role' — for instance, the role of God — and develop that role and stop its playing at will, you will begin to learn how not to be possessed of that role. . . . The only way to get rid of the God syndrome is to act it out."[23]

Values clarification, "sensitivity training," and role-playing, have been going on in the United States for decades. Evidence continues to suggest that it is part of a program to remold American traditions and values through generational-revision (Judges 2:10). The seemingly innocuous games of "fantasy" would seem to be a part of that strategy.

Consider the Biblical Principles

"Finally, my brothers, be strong in the Lord, and in the power of His might. Put on the whole armor of God, that you may be able to stand against the wiles of the devil" (Ephesians 6:10, 11).

Participation in the occult is strictly forbidden by God. Trafficking (even trifling) with the occult — demons, witchcraft, dark forces (ouija boards, tarot cards, astrology, fortune telling, charms — is pagan idolatry. It is anathema — an abomination — to the Lord God.

> Neither shall you use enchantment [sorcery], nor observe time [astrology]. . . . regard not them that have familiar spirits, neither seek after wizards, to be defiled by them (Leviticus 19:26).

> When thou art come into the land which the Lord thy God giveth thee, thou shalt not learn to do after the abominations of those nations. There shall not be found among you any one that makes his son or his daughter to pass through fire, or that uses divination, or an observer of times, or an enchanter, or a witch. Or a charmer, or a consulter with familiar spirits, or a wizard, or a necromancer. For all that do these things are an abomination unto the Lord . . . (Deuteronomy 18:9-12).

And the soul that turns after such as have familiar spirits and after wizards, to play the harlot after them, I will even set My face against that soul and will cut him off from among his people (Leviticus 20:6; see also Isaiah 47:12-14; Jeremiah 10:2).

Demons are unclean spirits (Matthew 10:1), evil spirits (Acts 19:12), fallen angels who rebelled and are now in darkness unto judgment (Jude 6); their power is limited but not ended (2 Peter 2:4); they serve the prince of darkness, the prince of this world (Matthew 12:24; John 12:31).

The Bible teaches that God's own people are not to fear Satan or his demons, but to stand against him and be firm in the Lord God who has the power to cast out demons and who causes devils to tremble: "Thou believest that there is one God; thou doest well: the devils [demons] also believe, and tremble" (James 2:19; see also Matthew 8:28-32).

Occult practices are a sin; they honor Satan rather than God; they make God's enemies the guiding force, the hope and source of knowledge. How can we live in and for Christ Jesus and traffic with Satan? We must not depart "from the faith" or give heed to "seducing spirits and doctrines of the devil" (1 Timothy 4:1). Once a person's delight (interest) is in the occult rather than in the love and Law and prophets of the Lord God, a door is opened to Satan. "Know you not that to whom you yield yourselves servants to obey, his servants you are" (Romans 6:16).

We must not be preoccupied with thoughts or fears of Satan or his demons; but, certainly we should be aware of, and on guard against, such forces. How are we to shun, to overcome, such evil entities? God's Word counsels us: "Submit yourselves therefore unto to God. . . . Resist the devil and he will flee from you" (James 4:7, 8).

Role-playing or psychodrama (assuming another's identity and values as contrasted with legitimate dramatic arts)[26] is ungodly, dangerous — and deadly. What is the first recorded case of role-playing? Eve, in the Garden of Eden when Satan tempted her into trying to play the role of a god (Genesis 3:5).

Mrs. F. C. Bosworth, of the Pro-Family Forum, has set forth two basic premises on which psychodrama (role-playing) must be opposed: "(1) the root determines the fruit (Matthew 7:17);

the root of role-playing is humanistic psychology with the intent to 'play God out of one's life,' and (2) the method is the message, and there is no way to use the psychodrama (role-playing) method in a Christian way, because the underlying message of role-playing will always be the message of humanism."

"For as he thinketh in his heart, so is he" (Proverbs 23:7). "Keep thy heart with all diligence; for out of it are the issues of life" (Proverbs 4:23). "The fool hath said in his heart there is no God" (Psalm 14:1). Satan boasted that he would be like God (Isaiah 14:14). Surely it must be clear that Christians must have no part of those who deny God or would play God or be a god. We must not fall prey to their schemes and devices. "Learn not the way of the heathen" (Jeremiah 10:12).

In addition to its other insidious evils, role-playing invites (encourages) escapism, nihilism, and situational ethics. It paves the way for values modification and manipulation. It suggests that the absolutes of God's truth must give way to the "electives" of humanism. Against such things we are to be on guard (Ephesians 4:14, 15).

END NOTES

Chapter 1—Abortion

1. Alisa Samuels, "When Babies Become Disposable," *New Hampshire Sunday News*, December 13, 1987.
2. Ibid.
3. Joseph Scheidler, "Don't Let Clinics Advise Anyone About Abortion," *USA Today*, February 3, 1988; see also, "Block Passage of Planned Parenthood's Bill to Fund School-Based Clinics and Abortion Pills," *National Right to Life News*, February 25, 1988.
4. "101 Uses For A Dead (or Alive) Baby," Olga Fairfax, *A.L.L. About Issues*, February, 1985.
5. "Pro-Life Suit Seeks Ban on California Abortion Funding," *A.L.L. News*, January 1, 1985, p. 1.
6. George Grant, *Grand Illusions: The Legacy of Planned Parenthood*, (Brentwood, TN: Wolgemuth & Hyatt, Publishers, 1988) p. 39.
7. Judie Brown, "And Now It's More Than 18 Million," *A.L.L. News*, January 18, 1985, p. 3.
8. C. Everett Koop, *The Right to Live, The Right to Die*, (Wheaton, IL: Tyndale House, 1976).
9. Michael R. Gilstrap, *The Phineas Report* (Geneva Divinity School, May, 1983).
10. *Bering v. Share*, 106 Wn. 2d 212 721 P. 2d 918 (1986).
11. *National Right to Life News*, August 2, 1984, p. 13.
12. "Our Throwaway Society," Right to Life of Kansas.
13. United Press International, Peking, November 11, 1982.
14. "A.L.L. About Issues," American Life Lobby, June 1983, p. 31.
15. "Induced Abortion: A World Review," (New York: The Population Council, 1983).
16. Interview with Dr. Bernard Nathanson, *Human Events*, May 7, 1983, pp. 13, 14.
17. United Press International, Washington, February 14, 1984.
18. Jeffrey Hart, syndicated column, August 4, 1984.
19. *Human Events*, May 7, 1983, pp. 13,14.
20. Letter from Dr. Bernard D. Nathanson to Michael Quinlan, McDonald's Corporation, Oak Brook, IL, December 30, 1987.
21. Brief of The Rutherford Institute, Amici Curiae, *United States Catholic Conference et al., v. Abortion Rights Mobilization, Inc., et al.*, February 1988.
22. "Baby Bodies and Billions," Olga Fairfax, *Right to Life Defender*, January 1988, p. 6.
23. Matthew Clark, "Should Medicine Use the Unborn?" *Newsweek*, September 14, 1987, pp. 62, 63.
24. Ibid.
25. Ibid.

26. *Newsweek*, September 14, 1987, pp. 62, 63.
27. Ibid.
28. Patrick J Buchanan, "Dr. Mengele, Call Your Office!" *Manchester (NH) Union Leader*, January 8, 1988, p. 29.
29. Matthew Henry, *Commentary on the Whole Bible*, ed. Leslie F. Church (Grand Rapids, MI: Zondervan Publishing House, 1961).
30. C. Everett Koop and Francis A. Schaeffer, *Whatever Happened to the Human Race* (Westchester, IL: Crossway Books, 1979, 1983).

Chapter 2 — AIDS (Acquired Immune Deficiency Syndrome)

1. As quoted by Reed Irvine, "Notes from the Editor's Cuff," *AIM Report*, April 1987.
2. Bob Greene, "What Is the Most Devastating News Story of The Decade?" *Chicago Tribune*, August 8, 1985.
3. Jack D. Amis, M.D., in letter to Plymouth Rock Foundation, December 17, 1985.
4. Donald D. Schroeder, "Even You Could Be Infected," *Plain Truth*, November-December 1985, p. 5.
5. Steven Findlay, "What Doctors Don't Know Worries Us," *USA Today*, December 10, 1985.
6. *AIM Report*, April 1987.
7. *AMA News*, November 22, 1985.
8. Joyce Brothers, "Voices from Across the USA," *USA Today*, December 13, 1985.
9. "150 Nations Attend AIDS Summit," Associated Press, Washington, D.C., January 26, 1988.
10. Ibid.
11. Ibid.
12. "AIDS Cases Near 55,000," *USA Today*, March 3, 1988.
13. Larry Thompson, "AIDS and Minorities," *Washington Post*, August 11, 1987.
14. Kim Painter, "AIDS Tally: 50,265, 400 each Week," *USA Today*, January, 13, 1988.
15. Sam Ward, "AIDS: A Look into The Future," *USA Today*, June 1, 1987.
16. "Viral Mutation Rate Alarms AIDS Researchers," *New Scientist*, June 4, 1987, p. 28.
17. Ibid.
18. Ibid.
19. Michael Specter, "AIDS Carriers May Be Increasingly Infectious," *Washington Post*, June 4, 1987.
20. Lewis J. Lord, "The Staggering Price of AIDS," *U.S. News & World Report*, June 15, 1987, pp. 16-18.
21. David Holzman, "New AIDS Victim: Hospital Budgets," *Insight*, August 25, 1986, pp. 54-56.
22. *U.S. News & World Report*, June 15, 1987, pp. 16-18.
23. Ibid.
24. Ibid.
25. Fern Schumer Chapman, "Don't Rob Other Medical Research," *USA Today*, March 3, 1988.
26. "White House Is Told AIDS 'Most Significant' Disease U.S. Has Faced," Associated Press, Washington, D.C., December 3, 1987.
27. Ibid.

28. "Don't Rush to Pass More AIDS Laws," *USA Today*, January 7, 1988.
29. Gary North, "Bad News on The AIDS Scene," *Remnant Review*, May 15, 1987, p. 8.
30. Ibid.
31. Ibid.
32. "Covering Up The Blame for AIDS," *The Forerunner*, May 1986, p. 20.
33. Ibid.
34. Ibid.
35. Ibid.
36. Ibid.
37. Kirk Kidwell, "The Protected Plague," *The New American*, April 13, 1987, p. 43.
38. Ibid.
39. Ibid.
40. "The Deadliest Cover-Up," *AIM Report*, April 1987, p. 4.
41. Ibid.
42. *AIM Report*, April 1987.
43. Senate Special Hearing on Funding AIDS, Dr. William A. Haseltine, Dana-Farber Cancer Institute, Harvard Medical School.
44. *AIM Report*, April 1987.
45. "An AIDS Report Urged," *Wall Street Journal*, February 25, 1988.
46. Patricia McCormack, "Poll: Parents Say Identify AIDS Children," *New Hampshire Sunday News*, February 21, 1988.
47. Donald Boys, "Fear Is Well-Founded; So Is Discrimination," *USA Today*, December 3, 1986.
48. Ibid.
49. Thomas Sowell, Hoover Institute, Stanford University, as quoted in *GEM News*, January 1986.
50. David Chilton, *Power in the Blood: A Christian Response to AIDS* (Brentwood, TN: Wolgemuth & Hyatt Publishers, 1987).

Chapter 3 — Capital Punishment

1. Paul Reidinger, "A Court Divided," *ABA Journal,* January 1, 1987, p. 47.
2. Ibid.
3. Samuel Meddis, "Executions No Longer a Rarity," *USA Today*, September 28, 1987.
4. Ibid.
5. Ernest van den Haag, "New Arguments Against Capital Punishment?" *National Review*, February 8, 1985, p. 33.
6. Stephen Goode, "Few on Death Row Face the Executioner," *Insight,* October 26, 1987, p. 60.
7. "Child Killer Reported Resigned To Die in Gas Chamber Today," *Manchester (NH) Union Leader.*
8. *ABA Journal*, January 1, 1987, p. 50.
9. *USA Today*, September 28, 1987.
10. Ibid.
11. "Cons Favor Death Penalty," *USA Today* Nationline, December 1986.
12. Isaac Ehrlich, *American Economic Review*, June 1975, as cited by Ernest van den Haag in "Death and Deterrence," *National Review*, March 14, 1986, p. 44.
13. Stephen K. Lawson, *Southern Economic Journal*, July 1985, as cited by Ernest van den Haag, "Death and Deterrence," *National Review*, March 14, 1986, p. 44.

14. Ernest van den Haag, "Death and Deterrence," *National Review,* March 14, 1986, p. 44.
15. Charles E. Rice, "Capital Punishment: An examination of its purpose in serving justice," *The New American,* June 8, 1987.
16. Ibid.
17. Lawrence W. Johnson, "The Executioner's Bias," *National Review,* November 15, 1985, p. 44.
18. Ibid.
19. *USA Today,* September 28, 1987.
20. Tony Mauro, "Okla Case Could Decide Fate of 31," *USA Today,* November 9, 1987.
21. *USA Today,* November 9, 1987.
22. "States with Capital Punishment," *USA Today,* September 28, 1987.
23. David E. Goodrum, "God and Capital Punishment," *The Counsel of Chalcedon,* February 1987, p. 12.
24. Francis Nigel Lee, "Communism and Christianity On The Death Penalty" (a paper to Mt. Olive Tape Library, Mt. Olive, MS), 1987.
25. Ibid.

Chapter 4 — Child Abuse

1. John Demos, *Past, Present and Personal: The Family and Life Course in American History,* (New York: Oxford University Press, 1986), pp. 68-91.
2. Ibid.
3. Ruth C. Blanche, "The Nightmare of the Sexually Abused Child," *USA Today,* November 1985.
4. Ibid.
5. Ibid.
6. Curtis J. Sitomer, "Americans Cope with Sensitive Subject," *Christian Science Monitor,* February 18, 1986, pp. 3, 7.
7. Judith Reisman, "The Porno Industry: Giving Child Molesting Its Stamp of Approval," *The Rutherford Institute,* January/February 1986, pp. 10, 11.
8. Ibid.
9. Ibid.
10. Ibid.
11. Ibid.
12. *Christian Science Monitor,* February 18, 1986, pp. 3, 7.
13. Phyllis Schlafly, ed., *Child Abuse in The Classroom,* (Alton, IL: Pere Marquette Press, 1984).
14. Ibid.
15. Ibid.

Chapter 5 — The Cost of Government

1. Unless otherwise noted, all statistical data is from U.S. Bureau of the Census, *Statistical Abstract of the United States* (Washington, D.C.: Government Printing Office, 1987) or "Federal, State, and Local Expenditures," Tax Foundation Facts and Figures of Government Finances, February 1988.
2. *Time,* June 15, 1987, p. 66.
3. Stephen Moore, "New Taxes To Cut The Deficit: Another Congress Bait-and-Switch Ruse," *The Heritage Foundation,* July 6, 1987, p. 3.

4. "Economists Growing Uneasy Amid Omens of New Inflation," *Insight,* May 11, 1987, p. 38.
5. Ibid.
6. "Federal, State, and Local Expenditures," Tax Foundation Facts and Figures of Government Finances, February 1988.
7. Edward Meadows, "Peter Grace Knows 2,478 Ways To Cut Deficit," *National Review,* March 9, 1984, p. 28.
8. Ibid.
9. Patrick J. Buchanan, "The 'Wild Pigs' Win Another One," *Manchester (NH) Union Leader,* January 17, 1988.
10. Glenn Simpson, " 'Goodies' Bills: A Legislative Coup," *Insight,* February 1, 1988, pp. 22, 23.
11. "Amid Budget Cuts, Congress Ups Outlays for its Expenses," *The Roll Call Report,* Washington, D. C., December 26, 1986; see also Bill Whalen, "Congress Figures a Pay Raise's Cost," *Insight,* February 2, 1987, pp. 18, 19.
12. Ibid.
13. Jim Drinkard, "146 Dairy Owners Will Get More Than $1 Million Each," *Manchester (NH) Union Leader,* December 24, 1986, p. 44.

Chapter 6 — Crimes Against Property (Retribution or Restitution?)

1. Jack E. Yelverton, "Prisons: A Sound Social Investment," *The Prosecutor,* Winter 1987, p. iv.
2. Ibid.
3. "Justice System Expenditures by Level of Government, 1985," *Bulletin, United States Bureau of Justice Statistics,* March 1987, p. 2.
4. "Justice System Employment and Payrolls, October 1985," *Bulletin, United States Bureau of Justice Statistics,* March 1987, p. 2.
5. U.S. Bureau of the Census, *Statistical Abstract of the United States,* (Washington, D.C.: Government Printing Office, 1987).
6. "Population as a Percentage of Reported Capacity for State and Federal Prisons, 1983-1985," *Bulletin, United States Bureau of Justice Statistics,* June 1986, p. 9; see also, "Crime and (Surer) Punishment, *U.S. News & World Report,* October 13, 1986, p. 10.
7. Op. cit., "Most jurisdictions are operating above capacity," p. 6.
8. Andrea Neal, "Uprisings, Homicides Plague United States Prisons," UPI, *New Hampshire Sunday News,* February 23, 1986.
9. Charles Colson, "Of Mice and Men," *Eternity,* March 1987, p. 11.
10. Ibid.
11. Ibid.
12. Ibid.
13. Ted Gest, "Searching for solutions," *U.S. News & World Report,* June 9, 1986, p. 73.
14. Samuel Meddis, "Crime Study Projections: USA 'Crisis'," *USA Today,* March 9, 1987.
15. Daniel W. Van Ness, "Restoring Crime's Victims," *Eternity,* March 1987, p. 9.
16. Lori Santos, "Average Jailbirds Free After a Year," *Manchester (NH) Union Leader,* December 31, 1987, p. 68.
17. *Eternity,* March 1987, p. 9.
18. Ibid.
19. Ibid.

Chapter 7 — Debts and Deficits

1. Alfred L. Malabre, Jr., *Beyond Our Means,* (New York: Random House, 1987), p. 4.
2. "Reagan's Budget to Project Deficits Exceeding Target," *Wall Street Journal,* February 12, 1988.
3. Lawrence Patterson, "U.S. Government Debt Held by Foreigners," *A Monthly Lesson in Criminal Politics,* February 1988, p. 7.
4. "U.S. Is World's Biggest Debtor," *United Press International,* June 24, 1987, p. 36.
5. Ibid.
6. Louis J. Richman, "The Japanese Buying Binge," *Fortune,* December 7, 1987, pp. 77-94.
7. Truman Clark and Arthur B. Laffer, "We Won't Have to Tax More If We Cut More," *USA Today,* April 15, 1987.
8. Ibid.
9. "Reagan's Budget to Project Deficits Exceeding Target," *Wall Street Journal,* February 12, 1988.
10. Gary North, "7 Lies You've Been Told," *Special Report,* January 1988.
11. Malabre, p. 4.
12. John M. Berry, "Surprisingly Enough, the Big, Bad Federal Deficit Has Gone on a Diet," *Washington Post National Weekly,* November 16, 1987, p. 19.
13. A. J. Lowery, "National Deficit Spending Week," *The American Sunbeam,* November 18, 1984, p. 2.
14. John P. McManus, "America, Look What They're Doing to the Land of the Free," *The New American,* January 5, 1987, p. 27.
15. John Seigenthaler, "Cutting the Deficit Will Require Pain," *USA Today,* January 8, 1988.
16. "Congressional Advisory Survey on Slashing Government Spending," The Heritage Foundation, January 1988.
17. Truman Clark and Arthur B. Laffer, "Tax Hikes Are Wrong Way to Cut Deficit," *USA Today,* December 9, 1987.
18. "Go For It, Mr. Bush," *Wall Street Journal,* February 12, 1988.
19. Senator Strom Thurmond, "Balanced Budget Amendment Is Crucial," *Human Events,* August 22, 1987, p. 11.
20. "Gramm Proposes Saving $285 Million," *Human Events,* June 20, 1987, p. 18.
21. Malabre, p. 4.

Chapter 8 — Dealing with God's Enemies

1. W. A. John Johnson, "USTEC Scandal Needs Investigation," *Daily News Digest,* October 14, 1987.
2. Anthony Harrigan, "A Right To Know Who's Selling Us Out," *Manchester (NH) Union Leader,* June 25, 1987, p. 40.
3. *Daily News Digest,* October 14, 1987.
4. *Insight,* September 14, 1987, p. 18, as cited by Johnson in *Daily News Digest,* October 14, 1987.
5. *Daily News Digest,* October 14, 1987.
6. Miles M. Costick, "The Economics of Détente and United States-Soviet Grain Trade," The Heritage Foundation, 1976, p. 102.
7. Douglas A. Harbecht, "Export Controls: The Political Winds Are Shifting," *Business Week,* February 16, 1987, p. 31.

8. Ibid.
9. Don Bell, "Not 'If' but 'When'," *Don Bell Reports,* November 4, 1983.
10. Ibid.
11. Mel Thompson, "Traitors' Trade Aids Enemies," *Manchester (NH) Union Leader,* December 2, 1983.
12. Gregory A. Fossedal, "Man of the Year Should've Been Leonid Brezhnev," *Manchester (NH) Union Leader,* January 5, 1988, p. 24.
13. Ibid.
14. "Shultz Critical of Grain Sale To the Soviets," Associated Press, Washington, August 6, 1986.
15. James Reston, "The Allies Doubt the U.S. . . . ," *The Virginian-Pilot* and *The Ledger-Star,* June 14, 1987.
16. Jeanne Kirkpatrick, ". . . and Mistrust Reagan," *The Virginian-Pilot* and *The Ledger-Star,* June 14, 1987.
17. "US Leaves Freedom Fighters in Lurch," *Aida Parker Newsletter,* January 28, 1987.
18. Lawrence J. Brady, "Soviet Empire Funded By Western Banks," *Manchester (NH) Union Leader,* January 6, 1988, p. 11.
19. Ibid.
20. R. E. McMaster, Jr., " 'Amerika' Today: The Reality," *The Reaper,* February 25, 1987.
21. *Manchester (NH) Union Leader,* January 6, 1988, p. 11.
22. Ibid.
23. Ibid.
24. *Manchester (NH) Union Leader,* January 5, 1988, p. 24.
25. Ibid.
26. Radio Leningrad, August 27, 1950.
27. Lunarcharsky, Russian Commissioner of Education, quoted in the *United States Congressional Record,* 77:1539-1540.

Chapter 9 — Evolution vs. Creation

1. Paul Reidinger, "Creationism and The First Amendment," *ABA Journal,* January 1, 1987, p. 35.
2. "Equal Time in the Christian Schools," *Washington (D. C.) Times,* undated article on file.
3. Jerry Bergman, "Contemporary Censorship of Creation Thought," *Contrast,* May-June 1987, p. 1.
4. Ibid.
5. Ibid.
6. Ed Garrett, "The Evolution of A Monster!" *Creation Ex Nihilo* 8:4, p. 33.
7. Ibid.
8. Tom Willis, "Is Evolution Science?" *Bible-Science Newsletter,* February 1987, pp. 4, 5.
9. *ABA Journal,* January 1, 1987, p. 35.
10. John G. Leslie and Charles K. Pallaghy, "The Religious Nature of Evolution Theory and its Attack on Christianity?" *Ex Nihilo,* 7:4, p. 43.
11. Charles Cook, "Evolution: A Powerful Delusion," *Bible-Science Newsletter,* April 1987, pp. 1, 5.
12. Ibid.
13. Ibid.
14. Ibid.

15. Ibid.
16. Ibid.
17. Pierre P. Grasse, as quoted in Paul Kroll, "Why Science Questions Evolution," *The Plain Truth,* May 1986, p. 20.
18. Ray Waddle, "ACLU Alarmed at Formation of Speaker Group," *Nashville Tennessean,* August 10, 1986.

Chapter 10 — Executive Orders and the Constitution

1. Don Bell, "Out of the Closets," *Don Bell Reports,* July 10, 1987, p. 1.
2. Archibald Roberts, "Colonel North Plots To Suspend Constitution," *Bulletin, Committee To Restore The Constitution,* September 1987, p. 1.
3. "Constitutional Celebration?", Associated Press, Washington, July 16, 1987.
4. *Bulletin, Committee to Restore the Constitution,* September 1987, p. 1.
5. Archibald Roberts, *The Republic: Decline and Future Promise* (Ft. Collins, CO: Betsy Ross Press, 1975), p. 5.
6. *Don Bell Reports,* July 10, 1987, p. 1.
7. Ibid.
8. Robert McCurry, "Civil Government at Every Level Conspires to Suspend Constitution," *Temple Times,* August 17, 1987, p. 2.
9. *Federal Register* 51:219 (November 13, 1986).
10. T. Robert Ingram, Rector, St. Thomas Episcopal Church, Houston, as quoted in *The Committee To Restore The Constitution Bulletin,* November 1987, p. 6.

Chapter 11 — Farms and Families

1. Allan C. Carlson, "The Moral Backbone of the Nation," *USA Today,* December 18, 1985.
2. Unless otherwise noted, all other data is from U.S. Bureau of the Census, *Statistical Abstract of the United States* (Washington, D.C.: Government Printing Office, 1987).
3. James Bovard, "The Time Has Come to Cut Off Farm Aid," *USA Today,* December 18, 1985.

Chapter 12 — Gambling (and State Lotteries)

1. Robert K. Landers, "State Lotteries," *Editorial Research Reports,* February 27, 1987, pp. 90-99.
2. Ibid.
3. Ibid.
4. Ibid.
5. "Six More States Cash in On NH's Lottery Genius," February 15, 1988, p. 1.
6. Sally Ann Stewart, "Lotteries Growing Fast on Wave of Respectability," *USA Today,* February 16, 1987.
7. Richard Mackenzie, "Lottery Madness," *Insight,* March 17, 1986, pp. 6-15.
8. Ibid.
9. *USA Today,* February 16, 1987.
10. Ibid.
11. *Insight,* March 17, 1986, pp. 6-15.

12. Sarah B. Ames, "Addiction Risk Linked to Lottery," *The Oregonian,* February 1, 1987.
13. "News You Might Have Missed," *Editorial Resources,* March 1987, p. 11.
14. *Editorial Research Reports,* February 27, 1987, pp. 90-99.
15. "Texans, Listen to This Expert," *The Family Educator,* Pro-Family Forum, Fall 1987, p. 1.
16. Kerby Anderson, "Lotteries Bring Problems," *Dallas Morning News,* May 19, 1984.
17. *The Oregonian,* February 1, 1987.
18. Ibid.
19. Ibid.
20. Mary Beth Murphy, "Church Groups Campaign Against Lottery," *Milwaukee Sentinel,* March 14, 1987.
21. *"Lotteries: A Big Payoff For the States,"* *Business Week,* September 8, 1986, p. 15.
22. "Lotteries Are A Bad Bet," *Concerned Women of America* newsletter, June 1987, p. 7.
23. Charles Colson, "The Myth of the Money Tree," *Christianity Today,* July 10, 1987, p. 64.
24. *Editorial Research Reports,* February 27, 1987, pp. 90-99.
25. Ovid DeMaris, "Why Casino Gambling Is a Bad Bet," *Parade,* May 11, 1986, pp. 12, 13.
26. Ibid.
27. Ibid.
28. Ibid.

Chapter 13 — Home Schools and Christian Education

1. "The Freedom Report," as quoted in Christians for Freedom of Education in Wisconsin, April 1984, p. 2.
2. Louis De Boer, "Resistance VI — Public Schools," *The Pilgrim,* June 1974.
3. R. Berenda, "The Influence of the Group on the Judgments of Children," as cited by Dave Haigler and Bill Ambler in *Home School Defense Manual,* 1982, pp. 11-27.
4. Court cases cited in *The Home Study Journal,* Christian Liberty Academy, 1982, p. 3.
5. *The Home Study Journal,* p. 4.
6. "The C.L.A.S.S. Review," Christian Liberty Academy Satellite Schools, 1984. p. 4.
7. William David Gamble, "The Conflict in Education: Christianity vs. Secular Humanism," *On Teaching,* American Reformation Movement, April 1984.
8. "The Parent As Tutor," *Home Education Resource Center,* Winter Bulletin no. 14, 1984.
9. Ibid.
10. *On Teaching,* American Reformation Movement, April 1984.
11. Ibid.
12. John Dunphy, "A Religion for a New Age," *The Humanist,* January/February, 1983.

Chapter 14 — Humanism

1. As quoted in "People & Events," *Christian Life,* July 1984, p. 26.
2. Paul Baldwin, *The Social Sciences* (New York: Harcourt, Brace, and Jovanovich, 1970), p. 210.

3. John Dunphy, "A New Religion for A New Age," *The Humanist,* January/February 1983.
4. Gary K. Griswold, "Religion: An Obstacle to a Better World?" *The Humanist,* March/April 1987, pp. 18, 44.
5. Devin Carroll, "The Humanist Family and Moral Education," *The Humanist,* March/April 1987, p. 35.
6. *The Humanist,* January/February 1983.
7. Steve Hallman, "Christianity and Humanism," National Federation for Decency, 1984, p. i.
8. Laurain Mills, "Humanism's Influence on Charismatic Christians," *World Map Digest,* p. 14, 23.
9. As cited in *Presidential Biblical Scoreboard,* 1984, p. 10.
10. James J. Kilpatrick, "Judge Hand on Target: A Belief in No God Is a Religion, Too," *Keene Sentinel,* March 23, 1987; see also, Russell Kirk, "Militant Secularism on Trial," *The World & I,* June 1987, pp. 114-121.
11. *Keene Sentinel,* March 23, 1987.
12. *The Humanist,* January/February 1983.
13. Neal Frey, "Getting The Humanism Out of The Teaching and Writing of History," *Education for Eternity,* Christian Heritage College, August-September 1981, p. 4.

Chapter 15 — Inflation

1. Mark Memmott, "'88 inflation: An '87-size bite," *USA Today,* January 21, 1988.
2. Gary North, "Negatrend fl2: Inflation," *Remnant Review,* October 3, 1986, p. 9.
3. "Dollar Power: Going . . . Going . . . Gone!" Financial Timing, Inc., December 1986.
4. Matthew Yancey, "Pay Raises Lag Behind Inflation," Associated Press, Washington, D.C., January 30, 1988.
5. Matthew Memmott, "Disposable Income Rises Just 1.2% in '87," *USA Today,* January 29, 1988.
6. Daniel Seligman, "Journey to the Past," *Fortune,* March 1987.
7. As quoted by R. E. McMaster, Jr., "Money Chickens; Coming Home to Roost," *The Reaper,* May 3, 1984, p. 1.
8. John Maynard Keynes, "The Economic Consequences of Peace," 1919.
9. Otto J. Scott, "Paper Money in Colonial America," *Chalcedon Report,* June 1984.

Chapter 16 — The INF Treaty (Strategic Arms Talks)

1. "Work with Soviets to Make World Safe," *USA Today,* December 14, 1987; see also Don Bell, "The Orchestration," *Don Bell Reports,* December 4, 1987.
2. Sir James Goldsmith, "America, You Falter," *Wall Street Journal,* November 12, 1987.
3. As quoted in the *Aida Parker Newsletter,* November 1987, p. 4.
4. *Don Bell Reports,* December 4, 1987.
5. "Heavy Metal Treaty," *Wall Street Journal,* December 9, 1987.
6. Jeanne Kirkpatrick, "INF Treaty Won't Change World," *Manchester (NH) Union Leader,* December 6, 1987, p. 13.
7. "An Urgent Appeal To Prevent The INF Treaty," *Manchester (NH) Union Leader,* December 4, 1987, p. 35.

8. Yossef Bodansky, "Jane's: Treaty Bares Europe to Soviets," *Jane's Defense Weekly*, London, November 28, 1987.

9. Letter from U.S. Army Captain to Plymouth Rock Foundation, January 6, 1988.

10. Daniel J. Sobieski, "Nuclear Weapons Aren't Threat To Peace, But Soviets Are," *Manchester (NH) Union Leader*, January 12, 1988, p. 28.

11. "Western Europe Needs to Rearm," *The Economist*, London, as reprinted in *The World Press*, November, 1987, pp. 17, 18.

12. "Détente: Defeat for the West," *Aida Parker Newsletter, December 1987, pp. 1, 3.*

13. *Henry Trewhit, "Arms Control: Is It Good for Us?" U.S. News & World Report*, December 14, 1987, pp. 24-32; see also John Barry and Russell Watson, "Can Europe Stand on Its Own Feet?" *Newsweek*, December 7, 1987, pp. 31-37.

14. Henry Mohr, "State Department: Soviets Are Defensive," *Human Events*, December 19, 1987, p. 7.

15. *Newsweek*, December 7, 1987, pp. 31-37.

16. *Human Events*, December 19, 1987, p. 7.

17. "British Say Conventional Deterrence Is Impossible," *High Frontier*, 4:15, December, 1987.

18. Madeline C. Kalb, "The French and the Fear of a Denuclearized Europe," *The Washington Post National Weekly Edition*, January 4-10, 1987, p. 25.

19. *Wall Street Journal*, November 12, 1987.

20. *Aida Parker Newsletter*, December 1987, pp. 1, 3.

21. Ibid.

22. J. W. McQuaid, "A Terrible Treaty," *New Hampshire Sunday News*, November 29, 1987.

23. V. H. Krulak, "Soviets and INF: Question of Trust," *Manchester (NH) Union Leader*, January 14, 1988, p. 42.

24. Virginia I. Postel, "Gorbomania," *Reason*, February 1988, p. 8.

25. R. Jeffrey Smith, "A Treaty That Beats Weapons Into Waste," *The Washington Post National Weekly Edition*, December 31, 1987, pp. 6-8.

26. Ibid.

27. Donald S. McAlvany, "A Special Report, Betrayal and Surrender: The Reagan Sellout To The Soviets," *The McAlvany Intelligence Report*, December 1987, p. 10.

28. Samuel Nunn, "Renegotiate The ABM Treaty," *U.S. News & World Report*, December 14, 1987, p. 30; see also "Put the Right Men in the Right Place," p. 23.

29. In a letter to President Reagan, November 19, 1987.

30. "But Will We Still Love Him Tomorrow?" *U.S. News & World Report*, December 21, 1987, p. 21.

31. William Safire, "Secrets of the Summit," *New York Times*, December 6, 1987.

32. Herbert M. Hart, "Military Buildup Contradicts Soviet Talk," *ROA National Security Report*, May 1987, p. 2.

33. *The McAlvany Intelligence Report*, December 1987, p. 10.

34. Patrick J. Buchanan, "Will We Bail Out the Deadbeat Empire?" *Manchester (NH) Union Leader*, December 6, 1987.

35. Michael Mandelbaum and Strobe Talbot, "Superpowers in Sync," *U.S. News & World Report*, December 21, 1987, p. 23.

36. Howard Phillips, "Dealing with Soviets Makes World Unsafe," *USA Today*, December 14, 1987.

37. W. A. John Johnson, "USTEC Scandal Needs Investigation," *Daily News Digest*, October 14, 1987, pp. 1-4.

38. *Manchester (NH) Union Leader*, December 6, 1987; see also Buchanan, *The McAlvany Intelligence Report*, December 1987, p. 10.

39. Patrick J. Buchanan, "What A Friend We Have in Gorby," *Manchester (NH) Union Leader,* January 12, 1988.
40. Ibid.

Chapter 17 — Justice and the Courts

1. Michael Ford, "Raw Power: Isaiah the Supreme Court Playing God?" *New Wine,* November 1983, pp. 11, 12.
2. "Court Rules Sabbath Observance Unconstitutional," *Keene Sentinel,* June 26, 1985, p. 2.
3. Charles E. Rice in Foreword of Bob Dornan and Csaba Vedlik, *Judicial Supremacy: The Supreme Court on Trial,* (Plymouth, MA: Plymouth Rock Foundation, 1986), p. xi.
4. Ibid.
5. "How is Judicial Supremacy Affecting You and Your Family?" *Pro Family Forum,* Fort Worth, TX, n.d.
6. Ibid.
7. Bob Dornan and Csaba Vedlik, *Judicial Supremacy: The Supreme Court on Trial,* (Plymouth, MA: Plymouth Rock Foundation, 1986), p. 3.
8. Ibid., Foreward.
9. Ibid.
10. *New Wine,* November 1983, pp. 11, 12.
11. Ibid.
12. Alexis de Tocqueville, "Democracy in America," 1835. Arlington House edition.
13. Mary-Elaine Swanson, "How Supreme Is the Supreme Court?", *The Mayflower Institute Journal,* November 1984.
14. *New Wine,* November 1983, pp. 11, 12.
15. G. E. White, University of Virginia, quoted from "Moses, Blackstone, and The Law of The Land," in *Christian Legal Society Quarterly,* n.d.
16. *New Wine,* November 1983, pp. 11, 12.
17. Ibid.
18. Cited in Raoul Berger, *Government by Judiciary: The Transformation of the Fourteenth Amendment* (Cambridge, MA: Harvard University Press, 1977), p. 281.
19. As cited by John W. Whitehead, "Justice and The Courts," *FACSheet* No. 19, Plymouth Rock Foundation, 1982.
20. *The Mayflower Institute Journal,* November 1984.
21. R. J. Rushdoony, *Law and Liberty* (Tyler, TX: Thoburn Press, 1977), p. 5.

Chapter 18 — Liberation Theology
(The Gospel According to Marx)

1. "Dr. David Breese Reports," KYFC-TV, September 28, 1979, as quoted in "Humanism, Liberation Theology or The Economic Gospel," *The Capsule,* January 1980, p. 5.
2. Lester DeKoster, "Is Liberation Theology Christian?" *The Christian News,* October 15, 1984, p. 11.
3. "Cambridge Scholar Exposes Liberation Theology," *Christian Inquirer,* March 1985, p. 20.
4. Lawrence Fienberg, "Discussion of Liberation Theology Examines Catholics and Communism," *Washington Post,* November 3, 1984.

5. DeKoster, *The Christian News,* October 15, 1984, p. 11.
6. Ibid., p. 2.
7. Ibid., 4.
8. José Miranda, *Communism in the Bible,* (Orbis Books, 1982), pp. 6f.
9. Ibid., pp. 8, 74.
10. David Chilton, "Ronald Nash's Liberation Theology," (Tyler, TX: Institute for Christian Economics, 1984), p. 14.
11. Ibid., p. 10.
12. "Liberation Theology Marxist Front" *Christian Inquirer,* January 1985, p. 14.
13. "Christians Say Contras Have Protected Church in Nicaragua," *The Forerunner,* August 1985, p. 5.
14. Ibid., p. 12.
15. "The New False Christ," *Signposts,* 3:4, 1984, as cited in *Focus,* February 1985, p. 3.
16. Ibid., p. 15.
17. John Rees, "Father Enrique T. Rueda," *The Review of the News,* March 14, 1984, as cited in *The Christian News,* March 19, 1985, pp. 7, 8.
18. *The Christian News,* March 19, 1985, p. 17.
19. Ibid.
20. Ronald H. Nash, *Social Justice and the Christian Church,* (Milford, MI: Mott Media, 1984), p. 158.
21. David Chilton, *Productive Christians in An Age of Guilt Manipulators* (Tyler, TX: Institute for Christian Economics, 1981), p. 116.
22. Ibid., pp. 21, 56.
23. Rembert Weakland, "Make This Nation More Just and Caring," *USA Today,* November 15, 1984.
24. William E. Simon, "Bishops' Pastoral Is Santa Claus Wish List," *USA Today,* November 15, 1984.
25. James J. Kilpatrick, "The Bishops' Letter: A Bit 'Barmy'" *Keene Sentinel,* November 17, 1984.
26. Nash, pp. 20, 157.
27. Chilton, pp. 3, 10.
28. Ibid.
29. Nash, pp. 20, 160.
30. DeKoster, p. 2.
31. Ibid.
32. Ibid., p. 32.
33. Ibid.
34. "Paul Tillich, A Great Philosopher But No Christian Theologian," *The Christian News,* October 22, 1984, p. 17.
35. "Paul Tillich—The Adulterer and the Non-Christian," *The Christian News,* October 22, 1984, pp. 17, 18.
36. Ibid., p. 12.
37. Ibid., p. 32.
38. Ibid.
39. Ibid.
40. Ibid.
41. Nash, pp. 20, 164.
42. Chilton, pp. 10, 57.

Chapter 19—Parental Abuse

1. As quoted by William Slicker, "Child Sex Abuse: The Innocent Accused," *Case and Comment,* 91, (November/December 1986): 12.
2. "All Things Considered," National Public Radio, March 1987.

3. Ibid.
4. Lisa Pope, "Families Protest 'Kidnapping' by Welfare Agencies," *Dallas Times Herald,* May 13, 1985.
5. Douglas J. Besharov, " 'Doing Something About Child Abuse': The Need to Narrow The Grounds for State Intervention," *Harvard Journal of Law & Public Policy,* 8:3, (Summer 1985), p. 556; see also Besharov, "Unfounded Allegations — A New Child Abuse Problem," *The Public Interest,* No. 83, Spring 1986, p. 19.
6. *Case and Comment* 91 (November/December 1986): 12.
7. Ibid.
8. Ibid.
9. Mary Pride, *The Child Abuse Industry* (Westchester, IL: Crossway Books, 1986), p. 29.
10. Ibid., p. 13.
11. *Harvard Journal of Law & Public Policy,* p. 567.
12. Pride, p. 15.
13. *The Public Interest,* pp. 22, 23.
14. Linda Gordon, "Family Violence, Feminism, and Social Control," *Feminist Studies,* 12:3 (Fall, 1986), pp. 453-477.
15. *Harvard Journal of Law & Public Policy,* pp. 543-544.
16. J. Giovannoni and R. Becerra, "Defining Child Abuse 2," as cited in *Harvard Journal of Law & Public Policy,* p. 567.
17. J. Goldstein, A. Freud, and A. Solnit, "Before the Best Interests of the Child," as cited in *Harvard Journal of Law & Public Policy,* p. 561, n.d.
18. *Harvard Journal of Law & Public Policy,* p. 568.
19. Don Bell, "The State of Our Apostasy," *Don Bell Reports,* February 13, 1987, p. 4.
20. *Don Bell Reports,* p. 4.
21. "Parent Abuse: A State-Sponsored Reign of Terror," Don Feder, *Human Events,* October 18, 1986, p. 918.
22. Pride, p. 21.
23. *Harvard Journal of Law & Public Policy,* p. 540.
24. Pride, p. 33.
25. Besharov, *The Public Interest,* p. 25.
26. Ibid.

Chapter 20 — Pornography

1. Betty Wein, "A Call to Action," *The World & I,* February 1987, p. 434.
2. Ibid.
3. John D. Beckett, "Routing the Philistines," *Intercessors for America Newsletter,* 13:7 (July 1986).
4. Phyllis Schlafly, *The Phyllis Schlafly Report,* April 1987, p. 3.
5. National Reports, *Intercessors for America Newsletter,* July 1986.
6. "Lawsuits Against Pornography Commission Continue," *Family Protection Report,* July 1986, p. 6.
7. *The World & I,* February 1987, p. 434.
8. Ibid.
9. William Stanmeyer, "The Pornography Commission Report: A Plea for Decency," *The Benchmark, Center For Judicial Studies,* September-December 1986, p. 9.
10. "President Issues New Port Initiatives," *Family Protection Report,* The Free Congress Research and Education Foundation, December 1987, pp. 1, 3, 4.

11. "Armstrong Urges Halt To Porn Sales," *Family Research Today,* May/June 1987, p. 4.
12. *The Phillis Schlafly Report,* April 1987, p. 3.
13. "Legal Aspect," Citizens for Decency Through Law, Phoenix, AZ, 1985, p. 7.
14. "Symposium on Media Violence and Pornography," Ontario Institute for Studies in Education (OISE), February 5, 1984.
15. Ibid.
16. Edward Donnerstein and Daniel Lutz, "Sexual Violence in the Media: A Warning," *Psychology Today,* January 1984, pp. 14, 15.
17. "Research Professor Receives Grant To Explore Role of Pornography in Family Violence, Sexual Abuse and Exploitation, and Juvenile Delinquency," The American University, Washington, D.C., March 12, 1984.
18. Idem.
19. R. L. McCollum, III, "Officer Returns for Pornography Talk," *New Haven News Review,* May 7, 1979 (quoting Michigan State Police Detective Lieutenant Darrel Pope).
20. "Nevada Activists Fight Child Pornography: Bill Passes Unanimously," *Family Protection Report,* November 1983, p. 19.
21. Aric Press and Tessa Namuth, "The War Against Pornography," *Newsweek,* March 18, 1985, p. 65.
22. Paul C. McCommon, III, "Pornography, 1984: Its Pervasive Presence in American Society," Citizens for Decency through Law, Inc., 1985, p. 3.
23. Ibid.
24. Seth L. Goldstein, "Investigating Child Sexual Exploitation: Law Enforcement's Role," *FBI Law Enforcement Bulletin,* January 1984, p. 24.
25. *Intercessors for America Newsletter,* February 1, 1985, p. 4; see also "Fact Sheet," Citizens for Decency through Law, Inc., 1985.
26. "The Problem of Pornography," *Faith Family Forum,* March 1985, p. 1.
27. "An Interview with David Scott, Psychotherapist and Expert on Pornography," *Family Protection Report,* January 1985, pp. 8-12.
28. Ibid.
29. *Newsweek,* March 18, 1985, p. 65.
30. Haven Bradford God, "Child Pornography Linked to Sexual Abuse," *Human Events,* January 7, 1984, p. 13.
31. "The Problem of Pornography," *Faith Family Forum,* March 1985, p. 1.
32. Bruce C. Hafen, "The First Amendment and Obscenity," *Vital Speeches of the Day,* January 15, 1987, pp. 210, 211.

Chapter 21—Poverty and Welfare

1. "Up From Dependency: A New National Public Assistance Strategy," Report to the President by Domestic Policy Council, December 1986, p. 23.
2. Mary P. Lewis, "Welfare Reform Debate: Pro-Family Voices Heard," *Family Protection Report,* March 1987, p. 6.
3. "Up From Dependency," Report to the President by Domestic Policy Council, December 1986, p. 25.
4. Ibid., p. 26.
5. Ibid., p. 24.
6. Statistical Abstract of the U.S., Social Welfare Expenditures Under Public Programs, p. 356.
7. Johanna Neuman and Richard Wolf, "Budget Gets Qualified Support," *USA Today,* January 6, 1988.

8. Longitudinal Research File, 1983-84, Domestic Policy Council, December 1986.
9. Government Employment & Payrolls, Statistical Abstract of the U.S., p. 284.
10. "Up From Dependency," Report to the President by Domestic Policy Council, December 1986, p. 24.
11. "The Family: Preserving America's Future," Report of the White House Working Group on the Family, November 1986.
12. David Whitman and Jeannye Thornton, "A Nation Apart," *U.S. News & World Report*, March 17, 1986, pp. 18-21.
13. Ibid.
14. Ibid.
15. Luis Overhea, "Conservative Professor Challenges Fellow Blacks on Power Concepts, Moral Values," *Christian Science Monitor*, February 7, 1986, pp. 1, 36.
16. Robert K. Landers, "Low-Income Housing: Problem Isaiah Getting Worse," *Editorial Research Report*, May 8, 1987, p. 211.
17. "Up From Dependency," Report to the President by Domestic Policy Council, December 1986, p. 24.
18. Ibid.
19. Ibid.
20. *Editorial Research Report*, May 8, 1987, p. 214.

Chapter 22 — Prayer in School

1. The Rutherford Institute, July 1986.
2. Data from Liberty Alliance, September 1986.
3. Kent Kelly, *The Separation of Church and Freedom* (Southern Pines, NC: Calvary Press, 1980).
4. The National Center for Education Statistics, cited in *USA Today*, 1986.
5. John W. Whitehead, *The Separation Illusion* (Milford, MI: Mott Media, 1977).
6. Peter J. Ferrara, *Religion and The Constitution* (Washington, D.C.: The Free Congress Research and Education Foundation, 1983.)
7. Robert G. Howes, "School Prayer," (an unpublished paper), Youngstown, OH, August 1985.
8. Ibid.
9. Ibid.
10. Ferrara, *Religion and the Constitution.*
11. From "The American Atheist," as cited by Lynn R. Buzzard and Samuel Ericsson in "The Battle for Religious Liberty," as quoted by Ferrara, in *Religion and the Constitution.*
12. Ferrara, *Religion and the Constitution.*
13. Howes, "School Prayer."
14. Ferrara, *Religion and the Constitution.*
15. R. J. Rushdoony, "We Are at War" in *The Separation of Church and Freedom* (Southern Pines, N.C.: Calvary Press, 1980).
16. Whitehead, *The Separation Illusion.*
17. George Roche, "A World Without Heroes," *Imprimis*, 15:8 (August 1986).

Chapter 23 — Religious Liberty

1. Michael E. Hammond, "Grove City," *Family Policy Insights*, Child and Family Protection Institute, March 1987, p. 2.
2. Albert Veldhuyzen, "Federal Tyranny in the Name of Civil Rights," *Concerned Women for America*, newsletter, March 1987.
3. *Family Policy Insights*, March 1987, p. 2.

4. Ibid.
5. *Concerned Women for America,* newsletter, March 1987.
6. Ibid.
7. As cited by Dr. Dennis F. Kinlaw in "Christian Colleges — Will Bureaucrats Destroy Them?" *Asbury College,* March-April 1977, pp. 10-15.
8. Kent Kelly, "Disaster!" *Life & Liberty Letter,* 6:11 (February 1988), p. 5.
9. Jack Clayton, "Grove City Bill Must Be Defeated If Not Amended," American Association of Christian Schools (AACS), letter to members, February 13, 1988.
10. Ibid.
11. Stephen Goode, "Chapel Canned," *Insight,* January 19, 1987, p. 68.
12. AACS Washington Report, a newsgram, February 1988.
13. *World Press Review,* March 1982, p. 60

Chapter 24 — School Based Health (Sex) Clinics

1. Allan C. Carlson, "The Sensual School, Persuasion At Work," Rockford Institute, July 1986, p. 1; see also, Barrett Mosbacker, "Teen Pregnancy & School-Based Health Clinics," *Family Research Report,* Family Research Council, August 1986, pp. 3-6.
2. David Van Biema, "What's Gone Wrong With Teen Sex?" *People Magazine,* April 1987, pp. 111-121.
3. Eric Buehrer, "School-Based Health Clinics: Encouraging Children to Have Children," *Education Newsletter,* National Association of Christian Educators, undated, p. 1.
4. Patricia McCormack, "School-Based Contraceptives Create Major Controversy," United Press International, New York, October 23, 1986.
5. *People Magazine,* April 1987,pp. 111-121.
6. Newsletter, Michigan Alliance of Families, Flushing, MI, May 1987.
7. *Education Newsletter,* p. 1.
8. March Bell, "Teen Pregnancy Report Stirs Controversy," *Freedom Report,* Freedom Council, May 1986.
9. Ibid.
10. U.S. Congress, House, Select Committee on Children, Youth and Family, December 1985, p. 386.
11. Stanley E. Weed and Joseph A. Olsen, "Effects of Family Planning Programs on Teenage Pregnancy — Replication and Extension," *Family Perspective,* 20:3 (July 1986).
12. Ibid.
13. Kingsley Davis, "The American Family in Relation to Demographic Change," Research Reports, United States Commission on Population Growth & The American Future; see also James H. Ford, MD, and Michael Schwartz, "Birth Control for Teenagers: Diagram for Disaster," *Linacre Quarterly,* February 1979, pp. 71-80.
14. *Education Newsletter,* p. 1.
15. U.S. Congress, House, Select Committee on Children, Youth & Family, December 1985.
16. Newsletter, Michigan Alliance of Families, Flushing, MI, May 1987.
17. *Education Newsletter,* p. 1.
18. *Freedom Report,* Freedom Council, May 1986.
19. "Teach Against Premarital Teenage Sex, Bennett Urges," Associated Press, Washington, D.C., January 22, 1987.

20. Newsletter, Michigan Alliance of Families, Flushing, MI, May 1987.
21. Ibid.
22. Ibid.
23. Douglas Kirby, "School-Based Health Clinics: An Emerging Approach to Improving Adolescent Health & Addressing Teenage Pregnancy," Center for Population Options, April 1985, p. 8.
24. *Family Research Report,* Family Research Council, August 1986, pp. 3-6.
25. Michael Schwartz, "Lies, Damned Lies, and Statistics," *American Education Report,* March 1986, p. 4.
26. McCormack, "School-Based Contraceptives," UPI, October 23, 1986.
27. Newsletter, Michigan Alliance of Families, Flushing, MI, May 1987.
28. McCormack, "School-Based Contraceptives," UPI, October 23, 1986.
29. Ibid.
30. William J. Bennett, speech before Education Writers Association, as quoted by Eric Buehrer, in *Education Newsletter,* p. 1.
31. *Family Research Report,* Family Research Council, August 1986, pp. 3-6.
32. *People Magazine,* April 1987, pp. 111-121.
33. Carlson, "The Sensual School," Rockford Institute, July 1986, p. 1.
34. *Education Newsletter,* p. 1.
35. "Prescription for Teenage Health," Eagle Forum, Washington, D.C., 1987.
36. Peter Frogley, "Sex Education: The Christian Method," Light Education Ministries, Booleroo Centre, South Australia.
37. "It Has Happened Before," *The Standard,* May 1987, pp. 8, 9, 11.

Chapter 25 — Sex Education and Values Manipulation

1. Peter J. Leithart, "Modern Sex-Speak," *Chalcedon Report,* No. 270, January 1988, p. 1.
2. Ibid.
3. Ibid.
4. Phyllis Schlafly, "School-Based Sex Clinics vs. Sex Respect," *The Phyllis Schlafly Report,* June 1986, p. 1.
5. Barbara Morris, "Change Agents in the Schools," *Barbara Morris Report,* 1979.
6. Phyllis Schlafly, "What Sex Education Means," *Manchester (NH) Union Leader,* April 30, 1985, p. 23.
7. Ibid.
8. *Washington Star,* May 3, 1987, as cited in *Where There's God's Will There's A Way!* Belmont, CA, Gloria Dei Enterprises, Inc.
9. Murray Norris, "Weep for Your Children," *Christian Family Renewal,* 1979.
10. Joseph Sobran, "What Is This Thing Called Sex?" *National Review,* December 31, 1980.
11. Madeline Gray, *Margaret Sanger: A Biography of the Champion of Birth Control* (New York: Richard Marek, Publishers, 1979).
12. Elasah Drogin, *Margaret Sanger: Father of Modern Society,* (C.U.L. Publications, 1979), p. 71, as cited by Keith Bower and John F. Kippley, *Not in the Public Interest* (Cincinnati, OH: The Couple to Couple League, 1980).
13. *Where There's God's Will There's A Way,* (Belmont, CA: Gloria Dei Enterprises, Inc.).
14. Claire Chambers, "The Siecus Circle," *Western Islands,* 1977, as cited in *The Capsule,* (Cameron, MO: Caravans for Christ, January 1981).
15. Ibid.

16. Ibid.
17. Carlson, "The Sensual School," Rockford Institute, July 1986, p. 3.
18. Ibid.
19. Ibid., p. 3, 4.
20. Melvin Anchel, M.D., *A Psychiatrist Looks At Sex Education,* (Clovis, CA: Up With Families, 1981).
21. Jacqueline R, Kasun, "The Economics of Sex Education," no. 20, *Christian Economics,* New South Wales, Australia, October 1987, p. 1.
22. Ibid.
23. Ibid.
24. Ibid.
25. Ibid.
26. Philip Cutright, M.D., "Illegitimacy in the United States: 1920-1968," Research Reports, United States Commission on Population Growth and The American Future, Vol. 1, as cited by Bower and Kippley, *Not in the Public Interest.*
27. Phyllis Schlafly, "The High Costs of Free Sex," *The Phyllis Schlafly Report,* 20:7 (February 1987).
28. Ibid.
29. *Humanist Manifesto II,* (New York: Prometheus Books, 1973).
30. Ibid.
31. Karen Davis,Report on Sex Educators' Workshop, Washington, D.C., (Ft. Worth: Christian Women's National Concerns).
32. Rhonda Lorand, as quoted in Dr. Murray Norris, *Weep For Your Children* (Clovis, CA: Christian Family Renewal).
33. *Family Protection Report,* Washington, D.C., January 1981.
34. Jacqueline R. Kasun, "Turning Our Children into Sex Experts," *Sex Education and Mental Health Report,* (Clovis, CA: Up With Families).
35. Melvin Anchel, "A Psychiatrist Looks at Sex Education," (Clovis, CA: Up With Families).
36. Dr. Sidney Simon, as quoted by Farnum Gray in *Doing Something About Values.*
37. Kasun, "Turning Our Children into Sex Experts," *Sex Education and Mental Health Report.* Washington, D.C. (Ft. Worth: Christian Women's National Concerns).
38. Janis Sumpter, "A Mother Reports From The Battle Front," *Capsule,* (Cameron, MO: Caravans for Christ).
39. Tatum, Report on Sex Educator's Workshop.
40. Mary Lee Tatum, Report on Sex Educators' Workshop.
41. Lars Ullerstam, M.D., *The Erotic Minorities.*
42. Anchel, "A Psychiatrist Looks at Sex Education."

Chapter 26—Social Security and the Taxing of Churches

1. "This Isn't a Savings Account, It's a Pipeline," *USA Today,* June 24, 1987.
2. "Social Security Debt Far Greater Than Was Thought," *Manchester (NH) Union Leader,* February 5, 1984, p.2.
3. Harry Anderson, "The Crisis in Social Security," *Newsweek,* June 1, 1981, pp. 25-27.
4. John Distaso, "Kemp, du Pont Battle Over Social Security," *Manchester (NH) Union Leader,* January 22, 1988, p. 6.
5. "Greenspan Panel Ignored Conservative Solution," *Human Events,* January 29, 1983, p. 4.
6. John W. Whitehead and Tedd Williams, "The Social Security Amendments of 1983: Impact On and Response By Churches" (Manassas, VA: The Rutherford Institute, January 1984).

7. William Bole, "Evangelicals Warn Congress on Social Security Reforms," *Christian News,* December 26, 1983, p. 19.
8. Gerald Carlson, "The Social Security Threat," *The AACS Newsletter,* (Normal, IL: American Association of Christian Schools, January 1984).
9. Kent Kelly, "A Minority Report," Christian Schools of North Carolina, December 1983.
10. "Social Security Tax on Churches," *Freedom Defender,* (Harrisburg, PA: January 1984) Pennsylvanians for Biblical Morality, p. 3.
11. "Religious Groups Employees Protest Social Security Requirements," *Family Protection Report,* Washington, D.C., January 1984, p.5.
12. Dr. Richard Harris, "Memorandum," *The AACS Newsletter,* August 4, 1984, pp. 1-3.
13. "Bethel Appeals," *AACS Newsletter* as quoted in *Life and Liberty Letter,* (Southern Pines, NC: Calvary Press, January 1988), p. 6.

Chapter 27 — Sodomy (Homosexuality)

1. As cited by Gene Antonio in "AIDS: A Weapon In the Hands of Militant Homosexuals," *Intercessors for America Newsletter,* June 1987, p. 2.
2. As cited in "Homosexuality and AIDS National Disgrace and Curse," *Intercessors for America Newsletter,* September 1985, p. 3.
3. *Intercessors for America Newsletter,* June 1987, p. 2.
4. Enrique T. Rueda and Michael Schwartz, *Gays, AIDS and You,* (Old Greenwich, CT: The Devin Adair Co., 1987), p. viii.
5. Melvin Anchell, M.D., "A Psychoanalytical Look at Homosexuality," *Vital Speeches,* February 15, 1986, p. 286.
6. Don Bell, "That Sodomite International," *Don Bell Reports,* January 9, 1987, p. 2.
7. *Intercessors for America Newsletter,* June 1987, p. 2.
8. *Vital Speeches,* February 15, 1986, p. 286.
9. Ibid.
10. Ibid.
11. David Balsiger, "Presidential Biblical Scoreboard," *Biblical News Service* (Mott Media), Spring 1988, p. 31.
12. William North, "Wisconsin Boys Ranch Says No to Hiring Homosexuals," *Christianity Today,* March 6, 1987, p. 48.
13. *Biblical News Service,* Spring 1988, p. 31.
14. Ibid.
15. Charles W. Colson, "What the Sodomy Ruling Really Means," *The Constitution,* February 1987, p. 21.
16. "Homosexuality and the Clergy," *Religion and Society,* Institute for Religion and Democracy, June 1987, p. 7.
17. Ibid.
18. Rueda and Schwartz, p. 86.
19. Enrique Rueda, *The Homosexual Network* (Old Greenwich, CT: The Devin Adair Co., 1985), p. 20.
20. David Chilton, *Power in the Blood: A Christian Response to AIDS* (Brentwood, TN: Wolgemuth & Hyatt, Publishers, 1987).

Chapter 28 — Strategic Defense Initiative (Star Shield)

1. Robert A. Jastrow, *How To Make Nuclear Weapons Obsolete,* (New York: Little Brown & Co., 1985), p. 19; see also "The Near-Term Deployment of SDI," *National Security Record,* Heritage Foundation, October 1986, pp. 1-3.

2. Rus Walton, *One Nation Under God* (Nashville: Thomas Nelson Publishers, 1987), p. 177.
3. Jastrow, pp. 14, 15.
4. "Deploy Strategic Defenses Immediately," *Conservative Digest,* November 1986, p. 31.
5. Jastrow, p. 17.
6. Ibid.
7. CIA Deputy Director Robert M. Gates, as quoted in "Capital Briefs," *Human Events,* October 18, 1986, p. 2.
8. "The Soviets Have an SDI, Too," *U.S. News & World Report,* October 27, 1986, p. 22.
9. Jastrow, p. 21; see also United States Senator Malcolm Wallop, in an address before Conservative Political Action Conference, Washington, D.C., January 30, 1986.
10. George Wilson, "Soviets Reported Pushing Laser Arms," *Washington Post,* October 1986.
11. *The McIlvany Intelligence Report,* October 16, 1986.
12. Quentin Crommelin, Jr. and David Sullivan, "Soviet Military Supremacy: The Untold Facts About the New Danger to America," (Los Angeles, Defense & Strategic Studies Program, USC, 1986), pp. 52, 53.
13. Ibid., p. 62.
14. Ibid.
15. Ibid., p. 63.
16. Ibid.
17. "In the Realm of the Possible: the Work on Strategic Defense," *Insight,* November 10, 1986, pp. 56-61.
18. Daniel O. Graham, " Strategic Defense Development & Deployment (SD3)," *High Frontier,* October 7, 1986, pp. 6-14.
19. Secretary of State George Shultz, as quoted in "Is SDI a Poker Chip—or the Pot?" *U.S. News & World Report,* October 27, 1986, p. 19.
20. Joseph C. Harsh, "The Soviet SDI Debate: What It's All About," *Christian Science Monitor,* October 23, 1986, p. 14.
21. Arnold Horelick, RAND-UCLA Center for the Study of Soviet International Behavior, as quoted in *U.S. News & World Report,* October 27, 1986, p. 22.
22. Thomas Sowell, "Moscow Learned a Lesson at Iceland," *Manchester (NH) Union Leader,* October 29, 1986, p. 33.
23. *High Frontier,* October 7, 1986, pp. 6-14.
24. "Star Wars Feasible," *USA Today,* December 19, 1986.
25. "Star Wars Seen by 1994," United Press International, Washington, December 23, 1986.
26. "SDI Railguns Are Fast and Furious," *Insight,* October 20, 1986, p. 22.
27. "In the Realm of the Possible: the Work on Strategic Defense," *Insight,* November 10, 1986, pp. 56-61.
28. "Why the United States Should Pursue 'Star Wars,'" *Human Events,* November 8, 1986, pp. 10-12.
29. Ibid.
30. "Star Wars Bloopers," *Conservative Digest,* July 1985, p. 37; see also Jastrow, pp. 48-52.
31. "Author Says Opponents of SDI Have Stake in Nuclear Weapons," United Press International, West Hartford, Connecticut, September 8, 1986; see also, "The Nightmare of a Soviet Breakout," *National Security Record,* Heritage Foundation, November 1986, p. 3.

32. "Transcript of President Reagan's Interview with TV Anchormen, December 3, 1987," *USA Today,* December 4, 1988.
33. "Now the Right is Taking Pot Shots at Star Wars," *Business Week,* November 20, 1986, p. 39.

Chapter 29—Suicide

1. Division of Vital Statistics, National Center for Health Statistics.
2. Diane Eble, "Too Young to Die," *Christianity Today,* March 20, 1987, pp. 19-24.
3. "Teens Need Help to Solve the Problem," *USA Today,* February 26, 1986.
4. "Suicide is a Crisis We Must Confront," *USA Today,* March 20, 1987.
5. *Christianity Today,* March 20, 1987, pp. 19-24.
6. Laurie J. Storey, "Teenage Suicide: Growing Problem," *New Hampshire Sunday News,* February 25, 1986; see also statements by Dr. David Shaffer, Jane Brody, "Youth Suicide—A Common Pattern," *New York Times,* March 12, 1987.
7. *Christianity Today,* March 20, 1987, pp. 19-24.
8. Marzen, O'Dowd, Crone and Balch, "Suicide: A Constitutional Right?" *Duquesne Law Review,* 24:1 24, (Fall 1985), p. 3.
9. Leslie L. McCullough, "Suicide, Its Causes and Cure," *Plain Truth,* November-December 1982.
10. *Christianity Today,* March 20, 1987, pp. 19-24.
11. Ibid.
12. Ibid.
13. "Suicide Is a Crisis We Must Confront," *USA Today,* March 20, 1987.
14. David P. Phillips, "It's Time for the Media to Face Responsibility," *USA Today,* March 20, 1987.
15. Margaret A. Bocek, "Don't Let Death Education Backfire," *USA Today,* March 20, 1987.
16. Susan Hill, "Suicidal Teens Reject Prevention Programs," *USA Today,* October 22, 1987.
17. U.S. Bureau of the Census, *Statistical Abstract of the United States* (Washington, D.C.: Government Printing Office, 1987), table 1441..
18. United Nations Demographic Yearbook, 1984.
19. Ibid.
20. *New Hampshire Sunday News,* February 25, 1986.
21. Patrick Cox, "There Is No 'Crisis'; It's a Media Invention," *USA Today,* March 20, 1987.
22. As quoted by Cal Thomas, "Prevention Must Begin at Home," *USA Today,* February 26, 1986.
23. Ibid.
24. "Interview with Dr. Koop on Euthanasia," *Action Line,* Christian Action Council, July 12, 1985.
25. Rod Mays, "Selfism," *Restoration,* April 1984.

Chapter 30—Taxation

1. The Tax Foundation, "Pay for Your Lunch," *Leisure Weekly,* February 13, 1986, p. 35.
2. Robert W. Kasten, Jr., "A Boost in Taxes Won't Cure Nation's Deficit," *American Conservative,* October 1987, p. 1.

3. "Reagan Budget at a Glance," *Wall Street Journal,* February 19, 1988, p. 17.
4. Tom Raum, "Budget Proposal: $1,090,000,000,000," Associated Press, *Keene Sentinel,* February 18, 1988, p. 1.
5. "Don't Raise Taxes, Mr. President!" *Human Events,* October 31, 1987, p. 1, 7.
6. Daniel J. Mitchell, "A $124-Billion Tax Hike for Us All," *Human Events,* January 23, 1988, p. 20.
7. *Human Events,* October 31, 1987, p. 7.
8. Ibid., January 23, 1988, p. 2.
9. Ibid., October 31, 1987, p. 7.
10. *American Conservative,* October 1987, p. 1.
11. John Rees, "Peter Grace: An Interview," *The Review of the News,* May 30, 1984, pp. 39-52.
12. Karen Riley, "Congress Giveth Then Taketh Away," *Insight,* February 15, 1988, p. 20.
13. Tom Rose, *Economics: the American Economy from a Christian Perspective* (Mercer, PA: American Enterprise Publications, 1985), p. 68.
14. Joseph R. McAuliffe, "Dominion Work," *Chalcedon,* No. 2, December 1985, p. 1.
15. Ibid.

Chapter 31—Tuition Tax Credits and Christian Education

All statistical data from the Bureau of Labor Statistics, Statistical Abstract of the United States, (Washington, D.C.: Government Printing Office, 1987).

Chapter 32—United Nations

1. Adam Platt, "United Nations: Time of Judgment," *Insight,* November 17, 1986, p. 14.
2. Ibid.
3. Ibid.
4. Thomas E. L. Dewey, "U.S. Should Demand Meaningful U.N. Reforms," *Human Events,* June 20, 1987, p. 18.
5. Ibid.
6. Thomas E. L. Dewey, "The Legal Case for Cutting United States Funding for The United Nations," *Backgrounder No. 536,* The Heritage Foundation, September 26, 1986.
7. Ibid.
8. Ron Paul, "The United Nations," *Ron Paul Reports,* undated.
9. Dr. Juliana Geran Pilon, "The United States and the United Nations: A Balance Sheet," *Backgrounder No. 162,* The Heritage Foundation.
10. *Insight,* November 17, 1986, p. 14.
11. Charles M. Lichenstein, "United Nations Reform: Where's The Beef?" *Backgrounder No. 587,* The Heritage Foundation, March 10, 1987.
12. *Insight,* November 17, 1986, p. 14.
13. Thomas E. L. Dewey, "A World Court Decision Allows the U.N. To Impose Laws on the U.S.," *Backgrounder No. 37,* The Heritage Foundation, February 19, 1987.
14. Ibid.
15. Ibid.

Chapter 33—Video Witchcraft and Satanism

1. "The Evening News," WCB-TV, Boston, MA, February 18, 1988.
2. Lisa Levitt Ryckman, "Teenagers Caught Up in Satanism Worry Officials, Parents," *Keene Sentinel,* February 20, 1988.
3. Ibid.
4. Ibid.
5. Ibid.
6. Ibid.
7. Ibid.
8. Ibid.
9. "The Enchanted World," promotional letter, *Time/LIFE Books,* January 1985, and frequent TV commercials since then.
10. Richard White, "Dungeons & Dragons," *The Standard (CBN University),* December 1986, pp. 6, 7.
11. Ibid.
12. Ibid.
13. Helmut Thielicke, *Man in God's World,* as cited by William J. Peterson in *Those Curious Cults* (New Canaan, CT: Keats Publishing, 1975), p. 100.
14. Hans Holzer, *The Truth About Witchcraft* (New York: Doubleday & Company), as cited by Peterson *Those Curious Cults.*
15. "Dungeons & Dragons," *Christian Life Ministries* newsletter, undated.
16. "Living-Room Arcade," *The Capsule,* November/December 1982, p. 15.
17. "Dungeons & Dragons, Good or Bad," *Christian Life Ministries,* as quoted in *Dungeons & Dragons: Only A Game?* (Ft. Worth, TX: Pro Family Forum).
18. *The Capsule,* November/December 1982, p. 15.
19. "Toy-ology—The Nature of Toys," *The Capsule,* Cameron, MO, October/November/December 1986, p. 8.
20. Dr. Thomas Radecki, University of Illinois School of Medicine, as quoted in "Dungeons & Dragons Game Linked To 9 Suicides and Murders," National Coalition of Television Violence press release, undated.
21. United States Surgeon General C. Everett Koop, as reported in the *Washington (D.C.) Times,* November 10, 1982.
22. David Hargrave in "Rule Book, Arduin Grimoire," Vol. 1, p. 60.
23. As cited in "Dungeons & Dragons, Only a Game," (Ft. Worth, TX: Pro Family Forum).

SELECT BIBLIOGRAPHY

Inflation

Hazlitt, Henry. *What You Should Know About Inflation*. Irvington, NY: Foundation for Economic Education.

———. *The Inflation Crisis and How To Resolve It*. Irvington, NY: Foundation for Economic Education.

Hodge, Ian. *Baptized Inflation*. Tyler, TX: Institute for Christian Economics, 1987.

Rose, Tom. *Economics: The American Economy from A Christian Perspective*. Mercer, PA: American Enterprise Publications, 1985.

Rose, Tom and Robert Metcalf. *The Coming Victory*. Atlanta, GA: American Vision.

Sennholz, Hanz. *Inflation, or Gold Standard*. Irvington, NY: Foundation for Economic Education.

———. *The Age of Inflation*. Irvington, NY: Foundation for Economic Education.

Justice and the Courts

Dornan, Robert, The Honorable and Csaba Vedlik. *Judicial Supremacy: The Supreme Court on Trial*. Plymouth, MA: Plymouth Rock Foundation, 1986.

McGuigan, Patrick B. and Jeffrey P. O'Connell. "The Judges War." Washington, D.C.: The Institute For Government and Politics, Free Congress Research and Education Foundation, 1987.

Rushdoony, R. J. *Law and Liberty*. Tyler, TX: Thoburn Press, 1977.

Wine, E. C.. "The Hebrew Republic." Wrightstown, NJ: American Presbyterian Press.

Parental Abuse

Whitehead, John W. *Parents' Rights*. Westchester, IL: Crossway Books, 1985.

371

Pride, Mary. *The Child Abuse Industry.* Westchester, IL: Crossway Books, 1986. (Mrs. Pride's book includes a summary of Child Abuse Laws for the United States and territories as of July, 1985.)

Organizations actively combating parental abuse include the following:

Concerned Women for America, 122 C St., N.W., Washington, D.C. 20001 (202-628-3014),

Family Rights Coalition, P.O. Box 524, Crystal Lake, IL 60014 (815-455-2268).

Pro-Family Forum, P.O. Box 8907, Ft. Worth, TX 76112.

Missouri Parents and Children (MoPAC), Box 16866, Clayton, MO 63105.

Texas Parents and Children Together (T-PACT), P.O. Box 264, Rowlett, TX 75088 (214-475-1973).

Victims of Child Abuse Laws (VOCAL), 3711 Washburn Ave., N., Minneapolis, MN 55412 (612-588-6583).

Poverty and Welfare

Grant, George. *Bringing in the Sheaves.* Atlanta, GA: American Vision, 1985.

_____. *The Dispossesed: Homelessness in America.* Ft. Worth, TX: Dominion Press, 1986.

_____. *In the Shadow of Plenty.* Ft. Worth, TX: Dominion Press, 1986.

Religious Liberty

Brutus, Junuis. *A Defense of Liberty Against Tyranny.* Gloucester, MA: Peter Smith, 1689.

DeJong, N. and J. Van der Slik, *Separation of Church and State: The Myth Revisited.* Jordan Station, Ontario, Canada: Paideia Press, 1985.

Dornan, Robert, The Honorable and Csaba Vedlik. *Judicial Supremacy: The Supreme Court on Trial.* Plymouth, MA: Plymouth Rock Foundation, 1986.

Kelley, Kent. *Separation of Church and Freedom.* Southern Pines, NC: Calvary Press, 1980.

Whitehead, John W. *The Separation Illusion: A Lawyer Examines the First Amendment.* Milford, MI: Mott Media, 1977.

Rock 'n Roll: Drugs, Sex, and Rebellion

Babcock, Wendell K. "Music On The Rocks." Grand Rapids, MI: 1975.

Larson, Bob. *Rock and the Church*. Carol Stream, IL: Creation House, 1971.

Noebel, David, Ph.D. *The Marxist Minstrels: A Handbook on the Communist Subversion of Music*. Manitoba Springs, CO: Summit Ministries, 1974.

Peck, Richard. *Rock, Rock, Rock: Making Musical Choices*. Greenville, SC: Bob Jones University Press, 1985.

Seidel, Leonard. *God's New Song*. Tyler, TX, Thoburn Press, 1982.

Sex Education and Values Manipulation

Davis, Karen. *Sex Education in the Public Schools & Planned Parenthood*. Ft. Worth, TX: Christian Women's National Concerns.

Gow, Kathleen M., Ph.D. *Yes, Virginia, There Is a Right and Wrong*. Wheaton, IL: Tyndale House, 1985.

Marshner, Connie. *Decent Exposure*. Brentwood, TN: Wolgemuth & Hyatt, Publishers, 1988.

Norris, Murray, Ph.D. *Weep For Your Children*. Clovis, CA: Christian Family Renewal.

――――――――. *Turning Our Children Into Sex Experts*. Clovis, CA: Christian Family Renewal.

"Sex Education," *The Capsule*, 1205 W. 5th Street Terrace, Cameron, MO 64429.

For additional information regarding sex education in the State schools and what you can do about it, contact your local Pro-Family Forum, or write PACT (Parents and Children Together), 522 Hilaire Road, St. Davids, PA 19087.

Strategic Defense Initiative (Star Shield)

Jastrow, Robert. *How To Make Nuclear Weapons Obsolete*. Boston, MA: Little, Brown & Company, 1985.

Crommelin, Quentin, Jr. and David S. Sullivan, *Soviet Military Supremacy: the Untold Facts About the New Danger to America*. Los Angeles, CA: The Defense and Strategic Studies Program, USC, 1985.

Tuition Tax Credits and Christian Education

Morris, Barbara. "Tuition Tax Credits: A Responsible Appraisal." *The Barbara Morris Report,* Box 756, Upland CA 91786.

United Nations

Backgrounder series, "A United Nations Assessment Project." Washington, D.C.: The Heritage Foundation.

Lee, Robert W. *The United Nations Conspiracy.* Belmont, MA: Western Islands.

Roberts, Archibald E. *The Emerging Struggle.* Ft. Collins, CO: Betsy Ross Press.

Video Witchcraft: Dungeons and Dragons, Etc.

The Capsule. Caravans for Christ, 1205 W. 5th Street Terrace, Cameron MO 64429.

"Dungeons and Dragons Information, Handbook #23." Education Research Analysts (The Mel Gablers), P. O. Box 7518, Longview, TX 76702 (send contribution of $5.00 to cover costs of production and mailing).

"Dungeons and Dragons: Only A Game?" Pro Family Forum, P.O. Box 8902, Ft. Worth, TX 76124.

Leithart, Peter and George Grant. *A Christian Response to Dungeons and Dragons: The Catechism of the New Age.* Ft. Worth, TX: Dominion Press, 1987.

North, Gary. *Unholy Spirits: Occultism and New Age Humanism.* Ft. Worth, TX: Dominion Press, 1986.

Peterson, William J. *Those Curious Cults.* New Canaan, CT: Keats Publishing, 1975.

COLOPHON

The typeface for the text of this book is *Baskerville*. Its creator, John Baskerville (1706-1775), broke with tradition to reflect in his type the rounder, yet more sharply cut lettering of eighteenth-century stone inscriptions and copy books. The type foreshadows modern design in such novel characteristics as the increase in contrast between thick and thin strokes and the shifting of stress from the diagonal to the vertical strokes. Realizing that this new style of letter would be most effective if cleanly printed on smooth paper with genuinely black ink, he built his own presses, developed a method of hot-pressing the printed sheet to a smooth, glossy finish, and experimented with special inks. However, Baskerville did not enter into general commercial use in England until 1923.

Substantive editing by George Grant and Mike Hyatt
Copy editing by Lynn Hawley
Cover design by Kent Puckett Associates, Atlanta, Georgia
Typography by Thoburn Press, Tyler, Texas
Printed and bound by Maple-Vail Book Manufacturing Group
Manchester, Pennsylvania
Cover Printing by Weber Graphics, Chicago, Illinois

A Few Words About the

PLYMOUTH ROCK FOUNDATION

The Plymouth Rock Foundation has been called *"one of the premier educational institutions in the hand of God today."* John Beckett, president of Intercessors for America, has said that the Foundation is *"unexcelled in its ability to apply Biblical truth to contemporary issues."*

Plymouth Rock is an uncompromising advocate of Biblical principles of government, and Christ's perfect Law of Liberty, as the true basis for individual freedom and right civil government.

Since 1970, the Foundation has sought to serve Jesus Christ through serving His people. Its primary mission is to help its members develop a total Christian world and life view. Its work centers in the areas of research, education, publications and program development. The Foundation's materials focus on:

- Basic Biblical principles of government, education and economics.

- America's Christian history and the Biblical foundations of the American republic.

- Biblical principles concerning contemporary issues of importance to godly Christians.

Throughout the nation, members of Plymouth Rock's local *Christian Committees of Correspondence* join together to pray for this nation, to study and apply God's word in all of their affairs, and to obey Christ's mandate to serve Him by serving others (*Matthew 25:31-46*).

For further information on its works and materials, and what you can do to help reclaim America for Christ, please write or call us!

PLYMOUTH ROCK FOUNDATION
P.O. Box 577
Marlborough, NH 03455
(603) 876-4685